MERCHANDISE BUYING AND MANAGEMENT

SECOND EDITION

MERCHANDISE BUYING AND MANAGEMENT

SECOND EDITION

John Donnellan

HOLYOKE COMMUNITY COLLEGE

Fairchild Publications, Inc.

New York

Executive Editor: **Olga Kontzias**
Project Editor: **Joe Miranda**
Assistant Editor: **Beth Applebome**
Copy Editor: **Fran Marino**
Art Director: **Nataliya Gurshman**
Production Manager: **Priscilla Taguer**
Cover Design: **Delgado Design, Inc.**
Interior Design: **Lloyd Lemna Design**

Second Edition, Copyright © 2002
Fairchild Publications, Inc.

First Edition, Copyright © 1996
Capital Cities Media, Inc.

Second Printing, Copyright © 1999

Library of Congress Catalog Card Number: 2001087112

ISBN: 1-56367-190-5

GST R 133004424

Printed in the United States of America

BRIEF CONTENTS

EXTENDED CONTENTS

PREFACE

The second edition of *Merchandise Buying and Management* combines the successful elements of the first edition with helpful suggestions for improvement from reviewers and adopters. Written for college-level courses dealing with retail buying and the management of retail inventories, the text covers topics that are important to those aspiring to become buyers within retail organizations and to those who will become store-management personnel with responsibilities for managing retail sales and inventories. The material is presented within the context of a contemporary retail environment in which buyers often act as fiscal managers as well as product developers and store managers play important roles in sales productivity and assortment planning. Retail technology is a theme that runs throughout the book, tied to topics such as space management, electronic data interchange, and point-of-sale systems. Updated images and supporting examples ensure that the second edition of *Merchandise Buying and Management* is in step with the times, as does expanded coverage of topics such as e-commerce and international merchandising.

Sixteen chapters are organized into five parts. The five chapters that compose part one explain the structure of the retail industry. *Retail Merchandising* covers the retailer's role in bringing the consumer products from their point of production to their point of consumption and the merchandising function of a retail enterprise. *Retailing Formats* categorizes retail stores by their merchandising strategies, while *Retail Locations* covers the various settings in which retail stores operate. *Retail Growth and Expansion* is a discussion of the strategies that retailers use to grow and remain competitive in the marketplace. *Communicating with Consumers* looks at the various groups of consumers that retailers cater to and some of techniques that retailers use to attract customers to their stores.

The three chapters in part two are product oriented. *Fashion Merchandising* contrasts the merchandising of fashion goods with basic goods, while *Brands and Private Labels* contrasts the merchandising of nationally distributed products with goods developed for exclusive distribution by a single retailer. *Merchandise Resources* describes the wholesale marketplace and the various types of suppliers from which retailers buy their merchandise.

Part three includes chapters that deal with inventory performance and the fiscal aspects of retail merchandising. *Measures of*

Productivity covers the critically important concepts of turnover and sales-per-square foot. *Merchandising Accounting* interprets fundamental accounting concepts from a retail perspective, while determining the value of retail inventories as organizational assets is the topic of *Inventory Valuation.*

The three chapters in part four involve planning, purchasing, and pricing retail inventories. *Pricing* covers the concepts of markup and markdowns, as well as promotional pricing strategies. *Planning* covers several mathematical procedures for determining the amount of inventory that is needed to achieve an organization's sales goals. Price, delivery, and payment negotiations between retail buyers and their suppliers are covered in *Purchase Terms.*

Part five has two sections. *Merchandising Controls and Report Analysis* is an explanation of various reports that are used to evaluate sales and inventory performance. *Store Layout and Merchandise Presentation* deals with some fundamental store-design and merchandise-presentation concepts with which both buyers and store managers should be familiar.

Summary points, a list of key terms and concepts, and discussion questions are included in each chapter. Problems are included in chapters with computational procedures. Most chapters include sidebars and company profiles with "real-world" examples relating to material covered within the chapter. A glossary of key terms concludes the text.

The Instructor's Guide for *Merchandise Buying and Management*, 2nd edition includes chapter teaching tips; suggestions for individual and team projects; references; case studies; answers to end-of-chapter discussion questions and problems; enrichment activities; as well as chapter examination questions in the form of multiple choice, true and false, and essay questions. This edition also includes a PowerPoint presentation to aid instructors in classroom presentation.

Acknowledgments

I extend sincere thanks to members of the editorial staff at Fairchild Books for their support in preparing this second edition: to Olga Kontzias for her willingness to share her talent and expertise in all phases of this project; to Beth Applebome for her efficient work in researching the book's visual components; to Joe Miranda for his patient direction in manuscript preparation and scheduling; to Nataliya Gurshman who served as art director; to Sylvia Weber who coordinated a most enlightening review program; and to Patricia Mink Rath, for writing the Instructor's Guide and creating the PowerPoint presentation.

Reviewers selected by the publisher were also helpful in revising this edition. They included Bettie Davis, Community College of Philadelphia; Cynthia Jasper, University of Wisconsin—Madison; Teresa Robinson,

Middle Tennessee University; Celia Stall-Meadows, Northeastern State University; and Nancy Stanforth, Oklahoma State University.

I am especially grateful to the many companies who granted permission to use their organizations' proprietary materials as visuals.

This book is dedicated to Ed Herbert, with gratitude for unending support in all I do.

JOHN DONNELLAN

THE STRUCTURE OF THE RETAIL INDUSTRY

- Retail Merchandising

- Retailing Formats

- Retail Locations

- Retail Growth and Expansion

- Communicating with Consumers

RETAIL MERCHANDISING

The task of assembling an assortment of merchandise that appeals to a store's customers is a challenging proposition. Meeting this challenge requires knowledge of consumer products, consumer behavior, and the store's strategy for growth and profit. Fundamental to this knowledge is an understanding of the role that retail stores play in channeling products from producers to consumers and the ways in which retail enterprises are structured to perform this function. This chapter covers these two topics, as well as the personal qualifications necessary for individuals who wish to pursue careers in the exciting field of retail merchandising.

After you have read this chapter, you will be able to discuss:

The role of retailing in the marketing channel.

The merchandising functions within a retail organization.

The skills needed for success in merchandising careers.

THE MARKETING CHANNEL

The **marketing channel** represents the flow of goods from point of production to point of consumption. The model traces the distribution of a product from the manufacturer, or producer, to the final consumer, or ultimate user of the product. The marketing channel is sometimes referred to as the *distribution channel*, *distribution pipeline*, or *supply chain*.

The marketing channel is composed of *channel members* who are classified according to the function they perform. A **producer** converts materials (such as fabric) and/or component parts (such as zippers) into products (such as jackets). A **wholesaler** facilitates the distribution process by buying large quantities of goods from producers and reselling smaller quantities to other channel members, a process called *breaking bulk*.[1] A **retailer** sells products and/or services to final **consumers** who actually use the product, or derive personal benefit from the service.

It is important to note that retailers sell services as well as products. Hairstylists and travel agents are service retailers. A bank that offers financial services to consumers, such as home mortgages, car loans, and checking accounts, performs a *retail* banking function. The same bank may provide similar services to businesses but, in so doing, performs a *commercial* banking function. Wholesalers and retailers do not physically change the products that they buy and sell. Because they link producers and consumers, wholesalers and retailers are often called *channel intermediaries*. The channel interactions that occur between retailers of non-food products, such as apparel and home furnishings, and other channel members is the subject matter of this textbook.

Retailers perform an indispensable function in the distribution of goods to final consumers. A consumer who pays $50 for a blouse is getting far more than fabric, buttons, and workmanship for her money. Inherent in the retail price are the costs associated with assembling a selection of blouses in an assortment of fabrications, styles, colors, brands, and prices at a single location. A retail price also covers the cost of amenities, such as attractive facilities, salesperson assistance, and payment options that may include a store charge account, personal checks, or third-party charges, such as Visa and MasterCard. Without retailers as points of distribution, consumers would need to travel to production sources all over the world to purchase goods.

Retailing is an important segment of the U.S. economy. The industry accounts for 20 percent of the nation's gross national product and 18 percent of all employment. Retailing grew by two million jobs over

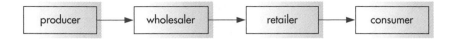

Figure 1.1

The marketing channel represents the flow of goods from producers to consumers.

the past decade. Within the next five years, the industry will expand by another three million jobs.[2, 3]

Streamlining Distribution

Channel members are sometimes bypassed in the distribution process for the sake of expediency. Because of less handling, goods purchased by a retailer directly from a producer spend less time in the distribution pipeline than goods distributed through a wholesaler. Time is a critical factor when dealing with perishable goods, such as food, or goods with short selling cycles, such as fashion apparel.

Cost is another reason why retailers bypass wholesalers. The selling price of a product increases as it passes from one marketing channel member to another in that each channel member's selling price must cover the channel member's operating costs and profit. A retailer can circumvent wholesalers' operating costs and profits by buying directly from producers. The retailer then has the option of selling the products more profitably or passing the savings on to consumers in the form of low competitive prices.

Wal-Mart, the world's largest retailer, is a model of streamlined distribution. By bypassing intermediaries, Wal-Mart profitably prices its offerings lower than many of its competitors.[4,5] Though buying directly from producers is advantageous for many retailers, wholesalers play an important role in the distribution of certain categories of merchandise to certain types of retailers, a topic covered in Chapter 8.[6]

Vertical Integration

Performing more than one channel function is called **vertical integration**. Companies vertically integrate for increased channel control and for the fiscal advantages associated with performing multiple channel functions. A producer that sells its product lines directly to consumers

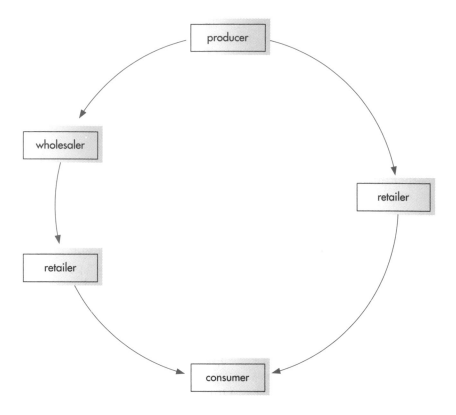

Figure 1.2

Retailers bypass wholesalers in the marketing channel to streamline the distribution process.

through **manufacturer-sponsored specialty stores**, or *signature stores*, is vertically integrated. These stores facilitate direct contact between producers and consumers and permit producers to retain control over the presentation and sale of their product lines. Some producers also use signature stores as laboratories to test new items.[7, 8, 9] Coach is a producer of a line of fine handbags and small leather goods distributed through prestige department and specialty stores. Coach also operates an international retail division of more than 100 signature stores. Laura Ashley and Liz Claiborne are other examples of vertically integrated producers that operate signature stores.

Retailers vertically integrate when they develop their own product lines for exclusive distribution in their stores, a merchandising concept called *private labeling* covered in Chapter 7. The Limited, Inc. is a vertically

Figure 1.3

Coach is a vertically integrated producer that operates its own specialty stores. *Courtesy of Fairchild Publications, Inc.*

integrated retailer. Through an operating division called Mast Industries, The Limited, Inc. develops and sources many of the products sold at stores owned by The Limited, Inc., including Express and Victoria's Secret. Gymboree is distinctive among childrenswear retailers because of its fashionable private-label lines developed by the company's own staff of designers who work directly with factories in the Far East to produce goods for more than 200 Gymboree stores.[10]

Companies that vertically integrate risk alienating other channel members. Producers that operate manufacturer-sponsored specialty stores compete directly with the retailers that sell their products through conventional distribution channels. Similarly, producers resent retailers that develop private-label goods that are often imitations of products that producers have painstakingly developed.[11, 12]

RETAIL ORGANIZATIONAL STRUCTURES

A **table of organization**, or *organizational chart*, is a diagram that depicts a company's corporate structure. An organizational chart reflects the various functions performed by an organization and the

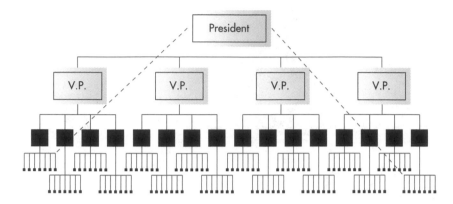

Figure 1.4

A table of organization depicts a company's corporate structure and chain of command.

way in which organizational activities are *departmentalized*, or grouped into organizational units. A table of organization defines the hierarchy, or *chain of command*, in an organization, as well as lines of communication and responsibility. Chairman of the board, president, chief executive officer (CEO), chief financial officer (CFO), chief operating officer (COO), and vice president are some of the *top management* titles that appear at the top of a table of organization. These functions have a broader scope of authority and responsibility and a higher salary than lower-level functions. Because the number of functions decreases as one proceeds from the top of a table to the bottom, tables of organization are often called *organizational pyramids*.

As organizations grow, organizational functions with a broad range of responsibility are often split into more specialized functions. An apparel retailer may split the function of *buyer of junior sportswear* into two more specialized functions, *buyer of tops* and *buyer of bottoms*, when business reaches the point that it requires and can support two distinct functions. In general, the tables of organization of large retail organizations have many specialized functions, while the tables of organization of small retail organizations have fewer functions that are more general in scope.

In 1927, Paul Mazur, an investment banker, was commissioned by the National Retail Dry Goods Association, now the National Retail Federation, to develop a model organizational structure for retail stores. Mazur proposed a table of organization with four major functions:

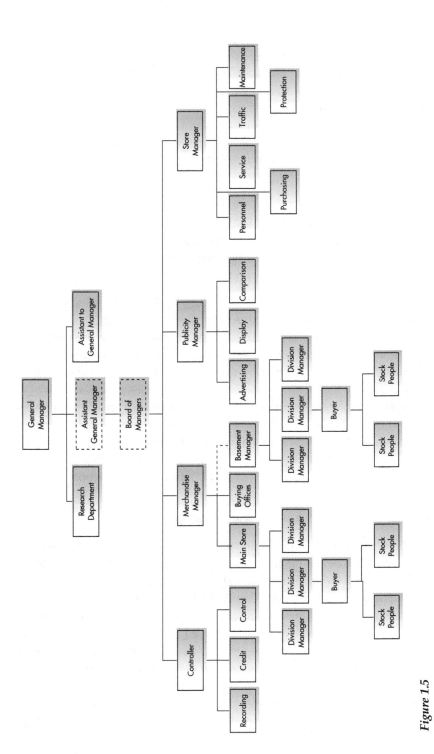

Figure 1.5

The table of organization developed for retail stores by Paul Mazur in 1927.

- *Merchandising* Responsible for procuring merchandise to be resold to customers. These duties were primarily performed by *buyers*.
- *Publicity* Responsible for stimulating sales through advertising, display, and other promotional venues.
- *Control* Responsible for the fiscal functions typical of most organizations, such as accounts payable, accounts receivable, and payroll.
- *Store management* Responsible for sales-support functions, facilities management, and the warehouse functions of receiving, checking, and marking goods.[13]

Mazur's proposed structure is still the core of most contemporary retail tables of organization. However, the organizational growth and the need for a higher degree of specialization have required several enhancements to Mazur's plan. For instance:

- The territorial expanse of multiunit retail operations spurred the creation of geographically defined pyramids of *regions* and *districts*, an organizational concept discussed later in this chapter.
- As retailers began to recognize the importance of people as an organizational resource, *personnel*, originally a store-management function, evolved into a separate organizational function called *human resources*.
- Because the first computer applications in retail stores were fiscal in nature, most retailers relegated computer operations to the finance division. As computer applications became pervasive throughout the entire organization, most retail companies began spinning off *information systems* (IS) as a freestanding organizational function.[14]

The Separation of Buying and Selling

In Mazur's day, most retail organizations were single-store operations in which buying and selling occurred under one roof. Because Mazur identified *buying* and *selling* as related activities, he proposed a merchandising function that included responsibility for both merchandise procurement and selling-floor activities such as customer service and stock keeping.

As single-unit retail operations evolved into multiunit chains, buying became a centralized corporate-level function performed independently from the operation of stores. The store-level merchandising activities once orchestrated by buyers became store-management functions. Today, the **store operations**, or *store administration*, function in a retail organization is a descendent of Mazur's store-management function, but a far cry from the facilities-management function that Mazur originally proposed. The contemporary store-operations function is likely to include considerable merchandise-related responsibilities, such as assortment planning, merchandise presentation, and inventory management.

Line and Staff Functions

Organizational functions can be grouped into two categories based on the type of activities performed. A **line function** performs mainstream activities fundamental to an organization's mission. Buying and selling merchandise are a retailer's mainstream activities, thus merchandising and store operations are a retailer's line functions. These functions are sometimes referred to as the *store line* and the *buying line*.

A **staff function** supports or advises line functions and/or other staff functions, but is not directly involved in an organization's mainstream activities. A retail organization's legal department is a staff function that supports both line and staff functions by performing activities such as negotiating leases and interpreting statutes that govern truth in advertising. However, the legal department is not directly involved in a retail organization's mainstream activities of buying and selling.

Authority is clearly defined through a chain of command in a line function. Within store operations, an assistant store manager reports to a store manager, who reports to a district manager, who reports to a regional manager, who reports to a director of stores. Staff authority is not as clearly defined. Though the managers of staff functions have authority within their departments, staff managers merely "advise" the managers of other functions without having formal decision-making authority over them. Staff managers sometimes have *functional authority* over other managers in matters that involve their areas of expertise.

Different managerial perspectives are often the source of organizational conflict between staff and line managers. Though the ultimate goal of every retail organization is to make a profit, line and staff managers sometimes adopt divergent strategies for attaining this common goal. For instance, a store manager maximizes profit by employing a competent selling staff. A corporate-level human resource department maximizes profit by establishing salary ranges for various organizational functions. Thus, a store manager's ability to hire top-notch salespeople may be constrained by the human resource department's salary structures.

This is not to say that organizational conflict between line functions in retail organizations is nonexistent. The following scenario portrays a common dispute between a store manager and buyer:

The dress department of a store within a chain of department stores fell short of its monthly sales goal. When asked to explain the shortfall, the store manager listed the following reasons:

- The styles were too dressy. The store caters to career women, yet social-occasion looks dominated the assortment.
- The prices were too high. The store serves a middle-income market where good value is the primary purchase criterion.
- Size assortments were skewed. The assortment included an overabundance of larger sizes (12s and 14s) and too few smaller sizes (4s and 6s).

Based on observations made during periodic store visits, the buyer retorted with the following reasons for the sales shortfall:

- The merchandise was poorly presented. Looks were not pulled together in any cohesive fashion by color, fabric, or vendor, and customers were likely frustrated by racks of sale goods that were not sized. Furthermore, the store's alterations department should be steaming goods wrinkled in shipment.
- Staffing was inadequate. To conserve expenses, the store manager reduced the selling staff, thereby hampering customer service. Also, newly hired sales associates were poorly trained and unmotivated.

In essence, the store manager blamed the buyer for the sales shortfall, and the buyer blamed the store manager.

Conflict between buyers and store managers has become legendary in retail organizations. Some companies promote empathy between the store line and the buying line by including training stints in both the buying office and stores in their executive-training programs.

RETAIL MERCHANDISING

The term *merchandising* has many connotations. In the apparel industry, merchandising involves the planning, development, and presentation of a product line suitable for a firm's intended customers.[14] Mazur cited a classic definition of retail merchandising: "to have the right goods, at the right time, in the right quantities, and at the right prices."[15]

In a broad context, *retail merchandising* includes all of the activities directly or indirectly associated with procuring and reselling merchandise. In a narrow context, retail merchandising embraces only the merchandise-procurement function. In this textbook, **retail merchandising** will be defined in the broader context to include all of the activities associated with buying, pricing, presenting, and promoting merchandise.

Corporate and Field Functions

Organizational functions can be classified by where the function is performed. A **corporate function** is performed within a company's central organization or corporate office. In a retail organization, buying, sales promotion, and finance are all corporate functions performed in a corporate office. A **field function** is performed in a remote or satellite operation away from the corporate office. In a retail organization, the store-operations function is a field function performed in stores. Within the broad context of retail merchandising, merchandising functions are performed both corporately and in the field.

Though some merchandising functions are common to all retailers, the job titles associated with these functions often differ from one organization to another. The titles and responsibilities described in the following sections are common to most retailers.

Corporate-Level Merchandising Functions

Buying is the main function of a corporate merchandising division. Traditionally buyers were responsible for a diverse group of activities that included inventory planning, selection, and allocation. However, the growth of large retail chains has fostered greater specialization in executing the buying function. Many retailers have split buying into four specialized functions: buying, planning, distribution, and product development.

A **buyer** buys and prices merchandise for resale. A buyer's challenge is to compose assortments that will appeal to the organization's intended customers, obtaining the best possible goods at the lowest possible prices. Buyers explore the offerings of the wholesale marketplace by visiting domestic and foreign markets and through frequent interaction with producers' sales agents. Buyers are also responsible for pricing goods low enough to be competitive with other retailers, yet high enough to meet an organization's profit objectives.

The magnitude of a buyer's responsibility is defined by annual sales volume, and, as might be expected, the buyer of a $100-million department is paid a higher salary than the buyer of a $1-million department. The importance of a buying position may also be linked to the complexity of the wholesale market or the risk associated with purchase decisions. A purchase decision for fashion goods, such as dresses, involves higher risk than a purchase decision for basic goods, such as hosiery. Buying decisions for fashion goods are based on uncertain predictions of consumer acceptance of new styles. An inaccurate prediction will result in poor sales, and the need to sell off the inventory at profit-threatening prices. Buying decisions for basics are often just reorders of historically best-selling brands, styles, colors, and sizes.

A **planner** projects sales and inventories based on an analysis of sales history, current market trends, and the organization's performance objectives. Planning is a statistical function that requires astute analytical aptitude and the ability to make multidimensional decisions. A **distributor** allocates arriving shipments of merchandise to individual stores based on each store's capacity, current sales trends, and inventory levels. Often called *allocators*, distributors correct stock imbalances in stores, and are a critical link between stores and the corporate merchandising division. A **product developer** determines which products to develop internally with the store's private label. Product developers establish specifications for the design, production, and packaging of these goods. They are also responsible for contracting producers to manufacture the goods according to the specifications.

The interdependence of the activities of buyers, planners, distributors, and product developers requires harmonious interaction among all four functions. In some retail organizations, the planning and distribution functions are combined. In small, conventionally structured organizations, the buyer is responsible for planning and distribution, as well as buying. The product-development function exists only in stores that engage in private labeling.

Many organizations use titles such as *senior* planner or *lead* analyst to indicate seniority or level of responsibility. As the title suggests, an *assistant buyer* assists a buyer with various day-to-day activities, and is often being groomed for a buying position. An *associate buyer* is one step closer to the goal of buyer, and often assumes responsibility for buying a category of goods within the buyer's total area of responsibility.

Buying, planning, allocation, and product-development responsibilities are typically assigned by merchandise department. A **department** is a

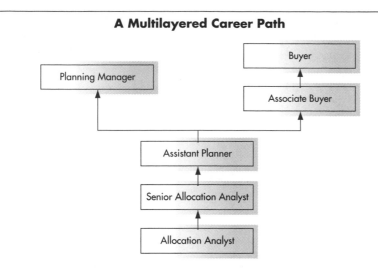

A Multilayered Career Path

Allocation Analyst: This is your first opportunity to impact our stores across the country by analyzing sales trends, making crucial distribution decisions, and acting as a liaison between our Distribution Centers and our Buyers. Every step of the way you'll apply and develop your analytical, strategic and creative problem-solving skills.

Senior Allocation Analyst: Handle a greater volume of merchandise allocation, and develop your leadership skills as you train and supervise Allocation Analysts, ensure that work flow within the department is evenly balanced, and see that timely decisions are being made.

Assistant Planner: Enhance your management skills as you work closely with the Planning Manager to create and implement seasonal merchandising plans, assess developmental needs, and train Analysts and Senior Analysts in the development of distribution strategies.

Planning Manager: As a Planning Manager, you'll enjoy full empowerment to build, in essence, your own business worth approximately $150 million. You will work with a Divisional Merchandise Manager and Buyers to determine short and long-term strategies, create seasonal merchandising plans, and partner with other Merchandising executives to ensure that objectives are being met. You will also manage a staff of five to eight Associates and participate in the development of our future Planning Managers and Buyers.

Associate Buyer: Team up with an experienced Buyer as you become increasingly involved in buying decisions. You'll get a first-hand view of our operations, identify strategies for buying trips, and after acquiring the necessary experience, travel to vendor sites and develop negotiating skills.

Buyer: Enjoy full autonomy to handle a sales volume averaging $55–75 million annually. Traveling frequently to New York City and other domestic and international centers, you'll maintain vendor relationships and purchase merchandise for T.J. Maxx and Marshalls stores nationwide.

Figure 1.6

Corporate-level merchandising responsibilities at The TJX Companies include distribution, planning, and buying functions. *Courtesy of The TJX Companies, Inc.*

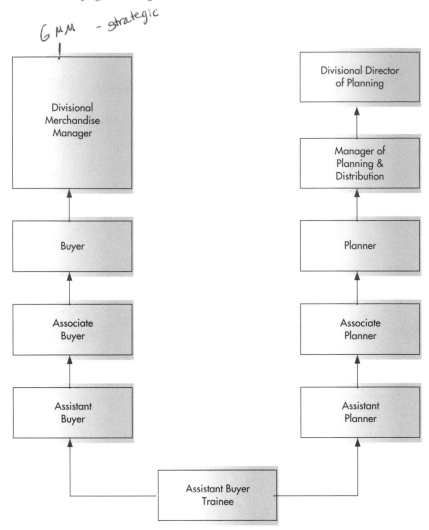

GMM - strategic

Figure 1.7

Organizational hierarchies for planning and distribution often parallel organizational hierarchies for buying.

group of related merchandise. A **division** is a group of related depart-ments. Divisions and departments are identified by product line. A *men's division* is composed of several *men's departments,* such as men's outer-wear, men's suits and sport coats, men's designer collections, and men's accessories. A **divisional merchandise manager** (DMM) is responsible for a merchandise division. The DMM monitors the sales, inventories, and assortments of the departments within the division to ensure consistency with the organization's merchandising and profit objectives. DMMs report to a **general merchandise manager** (GMM) who manages a group of related merchandise divisions. A GMM is typically at the vice-president or senior-management level. Organizational hierarchies for planning and distribution often parallel organizational hierarchies for buying.

Visual merchandising is a corporate-level merchandising function responsible for store decor, signage, display, fixturing, and standards for presenting merchandise. Visual merchandisers work with buyers to develop *planograms*, or floor layouts, and with **store planning** to design new stores or renovate existing ones. A store's **fashion director** is responsible for researching dominant color, style, and design trends in apparel, accessories, and home furnishings markets. The fashion director communicates this information to buyers, so that they can strategically select assortments consistent with current trends, and to other departments where fashion-trend information is critical, such as advertising and visual merchandising.

Store-Level Merchandising Functions

In general, store-level merchandising functions ensure that merchandise is presented on the selling floor in a manner consistent with a company's visual standards, and that inventory levels and assortments are appropriate for the store's sales objectives. Store merchandising functions sometimes include responsibility for operational activities as well. Considerable communication occurs between store and corporate merchandising functions.

A **general manager**, or *store manager*, is ultimately responsible for the merchandising and operations of a store. A general manager is sometimes assisted by an operations manager, a human resource manager, and/or a **store merchandise manager**. Large stores sometimes have more than one store merchandise manager, each responsible for specific merchandise divisions. There is little consistency among the titles for this function. Titles synonymous with store merchandise manager include *divisional sales manager* and *assistant store manager of merchandising*. A **department manager**, or *sales manager*, usually reports to a store merchandise manager, and is responsible for an area defined by department or division. This position usually includes both merchandising and operational responsibilities.

The store merchandising hierarchy just described is typical of large stores: a department store, such as Macy's, or a full-line discounter,

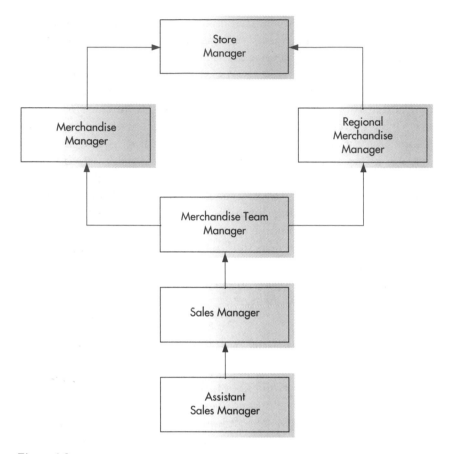

Figure 1.8

A hierarchy of store-level merchandising positions.

such as Kmart. The management structure of a specialty store, such as The Gap, is much simpler, composed of a store manager and one or more assistant managers. The responsibilities associated with these positions are very general in nature, encompassing both merchandising and operational duties.

Multistore retailers have a geographically defined organizational hierarchy that links the stores to the corporate office. A **district manager** is responsible for a group of stores located within a defined geographic area. The number of stores in a district varies from one retail organization to another, and even within the same organization depending on the distance between stores. In the densely stored areas

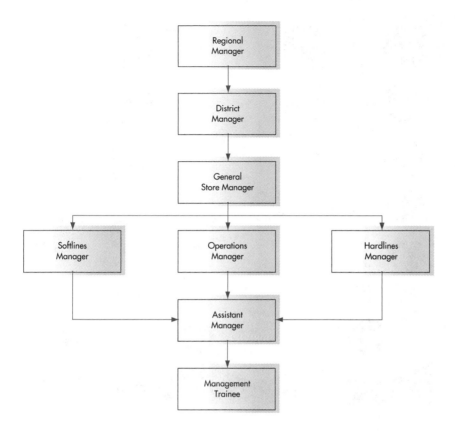

Figure 1.9

Multistore retailers have a geographically defined organizational hierarchy that links stores to the corporate office.

of the Northeast, a district may include 12 stores within a 50-mile radius. A district in the Southwest may have eight stores within a 100-mile radius. The amount of time required to travel to the stores in the Southwest is compensated for by responsibility for fewer stores. A **regional manager** supervises a group of district managers and reports to a corporate level person, such as a vice-president or director of stores. Some organizations link stores to the corporate office with only one managerial level, typically the regional level.

Since merchandising activities occur at both store and corporate levels, the topics covered in this textbook are relevant to students wishing to pursue either corporate merchandising or store administration

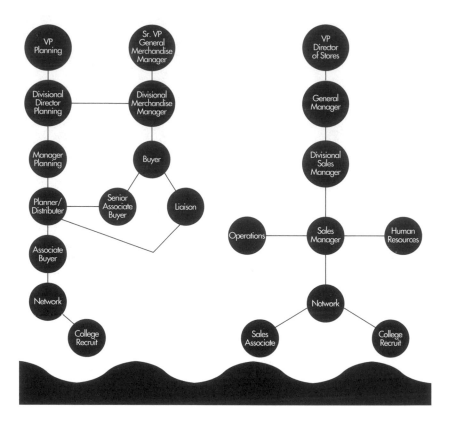

Figure 1.10

The store line and buying line at one department-store chain.

careers. Though industry restructuring has diminished the number of corporate merchandising career opportunities, considerable opportunities remain for store-management executives with merchandising savvy. Knowledge of retail merchandising is also important for students interested in retail sales promotion, shopping-center administration, or any phase of the distribution of consumer goods.

Qualifications for Merchandising Positions

There is rigorous competition for the highest paid and most gratifying retail merchandising positions. Merchandising functions at all levels of an organization require dynamic, productive individuals, challenged

Figure 1.11

What Wal Mart looks for in an aspiring buyer. © *Wal-Mart Stores, Inc.*

by aggressive goals and committed to standards of excellence. Specific qualifications for merchandising positions differ from one retail organization to another depending on factors such as a company's size, culture, merchandise mix, and operational strategy. Though there is no set of qualifications universally required by all retailers, the following summarizes a few skills that major retailers have cited as fundamental to success in their organizations.[16]

Decision-Making Skills Buyers must make decisions frequently and quickly. Retail merchandising requires the ability to evaluate information from multiple sources as a basis for making decisions with far-reaching implications. Planners determine the weighted importance and interaction of market trends, the economy, competition, and consumer behavior to project the amount of inventory that a buyer should purchase. An understated projection will yield inventories that are too low to meet the organization's sales potential. An overstated projection will result in excessive inventories, a poor investment of the company's fiscal resources.[17]

KEY COMPETENCIES FOR MERCHANDISING EXECUTIVES

The following is a list of key competencies for merchandising executives as identified by Kurt Salmon Associates, a management-consulting firm specializing in retailing and consumers products.

Is visionary: Explores inspiring possibilities; uses insight to create future successes; pursues innovations in products, services, technology, and managerial methods.

Results oriented: Develops and implements strategies consistent with the company's goals; uses all available resources to accomplish objectives; sets high performance standards.

Takes risks: Has the courage to act when faced with uncertainty or opposition; willing to move beyond the status quo.

Seeks innovative solutions: Actively collects and synthesizes information from diverse sources to maintain a broad, inclusive perspective; continually conducts market research; remains open to new ideas.

Mentors: Recruits and develops new talent; delegates responsibility and relinquishes authority to subordinates; promotes optimal training, compensation, and recognition systems; encourages frequent exchange and feedback; fosters continuous improvements.

Source:
*Staff. (May 6, 1998).
A roadmap for retail
training.* Women's
Wear Daily. *pp. 9–10.*

Communication Skills The ability to communicate effectively, both orally and in writing, with people inside and out of the organization is fundamental to the success of a merchandising executive. Conveying ideas to superiors, directives to subordinates, and negotiating price, payment arrangements, and advertising allowances with suppliers are just a few of the instances in which carefully honed communication skills are a necessity.[18]

Analytical and Problem-Solving Skills Computers have reduced the amount of computational and clerical activities associated with merchandising functions, allowing merchandising executives to devote more time to analyzing reports of sales, inventory, and profit. Physical remoteness from stores has increased reliance on these reports. A single store merchant can "eyeball" inventory and see that "mediums are low," and that it's time to reorder. In large multiunit operations, this type of stock replenishment decision is based on reports that define inventory status quantitatively.[19, 20]

Figure 1.12

Saks Incorporated's management-training program prepares individuals for both store-line and buying-line positions. *Courtesy of Saks Incorporated. Photo courtesy of JWG Associates, Inc.*

Figure 1.13

Jacobson's job description and performance appraisal for a buyer. © 2001 Jacobson Stores Inc.

JACOBSON'S
JOB DESCRIPTION
Buyer

Responsibilities:

To achieve established gross margin goals by effective inventory management and careful monitoring of sales, pricing, turnover, and markdowns.

To develop a constant awareness of current market trends and offerings.

To cultivate positive relationships with vendors.

To seek opportunities for new business.

To monitor our competitive position through careful observation of our competitors' pricing, advertising, and assortments.

To offer merchandise assortments consistent with our customers' quest for value, quality, and fashion.

To work cohesively with

Visual Merchandising in developing fashion trend statements.

Store Planning in determining fixture requirements for new or renovated stores.

Advertising in developing a multimedia marketing strategy.

To act as mentor to subordinates, helping them to grow by regular counseling and coaching.

To communicate effectively within the buying organization and with stores.

To implement practices to improve productivity and efficiency.

Organizational Relationships:

Reports to a Divisional Merchandise Manager. Works closely with Advertising, Finance, Logistics, MIS, and Stores.

Cultural Requirements:

Ability to function as a team player and to focus on the success of the total organization.

Position Requirement:

Strong merchandising skills to build balanced assortment plans and vendor programs, and be aware of current fashion trends. Must also have strong analytical skills to understand gross margin components and 12 month plans development. Must have a passion for the buying and selling of merchandise.

Job Demands:

Work environment is a typical office setting. Travel required, annual amount contingent upon area of responsibility.

JACOBSON'S

JOB PERFORMANCE APPRAISAL
Buyer

Merchandise Selection and Distribution

Selects merchandise consistent with Jacobson's standards for quality, taste level, and pricing structure.

Maintains appropriate breadth and depth of assortments.

Distributes merchandise to reflect each store's current selling trend and inventory status.

Researches and tests new vendors.

Develops new products.

Financial

Meets established sales goal.

Achieves gross margin dollars.

Achieves gross margin return on investment.

Market Relations

Represents and promotes Jacobson's effectively in the market.

Maintains relationships with vendors that are conducive to Jacobson's long-term trade advantage.

Negotiates effectively to maintain the most desirable terms and concessions.

Works effectively with U.S. and overseas buying offices.

Planning and Analysis

Effectively uses the tools of the Merchandise Information Office to identify inventory imbalances among stores.

Reacts to positive selling trends.

Monitors and updates open-to-buy.

Advertising and Sales Promotion

Selects appropriate merchandise for advertised events.
Purchases to cover advertised merchandise.
Develops creative special events, including shows of collections, personal appearances.

Communication

Visits stores regularly.

Keeps stores informed of new merchandise, fashion trends, and presentation techniques through buyer's bulletins and videotapes.

Communicates well with stores and responds quickly to their needs.

Accepts constructive criticism well.

Procedural Detail

Prioritizes work well.

Responds in a timely manner when merchandise is ready to disposition in the Distribution Center.

Accurately executes purchase orders, key recs, returns-to-vendors, markdowns, and other merchandise control documents.

Other

Assists the Divisional Merchandise Manager in training and developing assistant buyers.

Relates effectively to subordinates and peers.

Performs the duties assigned by the Divisional Merchandise Manager necessary to assure Jacobson's continued growth.

- **Computer Skills** Merchandising executives use computers to generate orders, retrieve sales and inventory information, and communicate by e-mail. Though it is impossible to be exposed to all of the available hardware and software with merchandising applications, a fundamental understanding of computer capabilities, the keyboard, and basic computer terminology is highly useful to the aspiring merchandising executive.
- **Organizational Skills** Merchandising positions require careful orchestration of the human and fiscal resources of the organization. The administrative skills used to manage time, develop procedures, and prioritize tasks are critical to the success of a merchandising executive.
- **Mobility** Mobility is a requirement for some merchandising positions. Large multistore organizations sometimes require store executives to relocate, and buyers must be willing to travel to domestic and foreign markets. Though company-paid travel adds to the attractiveness of a buying position, the travel is often not as glamorous as it seems. Buying trips allow little time for sightseeing and other recreational activities, since there is typically much to accomplish in a short time period.

Some feel that good taste is a qualification for merchandising positions, especially in the area of fashion goods. However, the ability to translate customers' tastes into merchandise assortments is more important than personal taste. Upon reviewing a fashion jewelry line, a buyer of impeccable taste once declared to the sales representative: "This is the ugliest, most ostentatious line that I've seen this season! I'll take it. My customers will love it!"

Many organizations have structured training programs to groom aspiring merchandising executives to fill projected employment needs. Trainees are promoted from entry-level positions to more advanced levels of responsibility upon successful completion of specified levels of training. Because of the desirability of these programs, competition for entrance into them is intense, and the result of an intense screening process. Large retail organizations are more likely than smaller companies to have structured training programs.

Colleges and universities have responded to students' growing interest in retailing careers. Funded in part by a grant from Sears, Indiana University developed a Center for Education and Research in Retailing. The center's goal is to forge alliances between the retail industry and the university by involving retail executives in curriculum planning and

Company Profile 1.1

Sears U—Higher Education Retail Style

Sears University is an internally operated management-development initiative that offers both classroom education and self-study programs to Sears managers at all levels. While some Sears University programs center around buying skills, merchandising, and human-resource management, other programs are designed to help participants function as change agents and strategic leaders. The programs are offered at Sears' Hoffman Estates, Illinois headquarters and at ten regional training centers nationwide. Courses are taught by seasoned line managers, training and development experts, and faculty consultants. The roster of students at Sears University includes management trainees recruited from college campuses, an elite cadre of troops who emerge from a rigorous screening process.

Sears seeks to identify 12 managerial traits when it scouts campuses for future executives. Those characteristics include integrity, an ability to facilitate change, a commitment to customer service, business knowledge and literacy, problem-solving sills, team-building skills, interpersonal-communication skills, a commitment to diversity, interpersonal skills, initiative, a sense of urgency, and the capacity to develop associates. Since its establishment in 1994, more than 20,000 managers annually participate in Sears University training programs that range from one day to one week in length.[1]

Source:
1 Seckler, V. (August 4, 1998). Sears' courtship blossoms. Women's Wear Daily. *p. 15*

development, and by sponsoring conferences on topics of interest to retailers nationwide. Retail organizations have been highly supportive of higher education's outreach endeavors. Founded in 1983, the Center for Retailing Studies at Texas A&M University is sponsored by more than 50 prominent retail organizations.[21]

SUMMARY POINTS

- The marketing channel represents the flow of goods from point of production to point of consumption.
- Marketing-channel members are sometimes bypassed in the distribution process in the interest of time or cost.
- Performing more than one function in the marketing channel is called vertical integration.

- A table of organization depicts a company's corporate structure and defines an organization's lines of communication and responsibility.
- Paul Mazur proposed a table of organization for retailers that included four major functions: merchandising, publicity, control, and store management.
- Line functions are fundamental to an organization's mission. Staff functions are support functions. Merchandising and store operations are a retailer's line functions.
- Retail merchandising includes all of the activities associated with buying, pricing, presenting, and promoting merchandise at both store and corporate level.
- Merchandise procurement responsibilities are defined by four functions: planning, buying, distribution, and product development. The responsibilities associated with these functions are typically defined by department.
- Store-level merchandising ensures that merchandise is presented in a manner consistent with a company's visual merchandising standards and that inventory levels and assortments are appropriate for the store's customers and sales objectives.
- Decision-making skills, communication skills, analytical skills, computer skills, and organizational skills are necessary for those pursuing merchandising careers.

FOR DISCUSSION

1. Discuss some of the disadvantages of separating the buying and selling functions in a retail store.
2. If you have ever held a position in a retail store, discuss the interactions that you may have observed between line and staff managers, or between store operations and corporate merchandising.
3. Which corporate merchandising position most entices you? Which store merchandising position most entices you? Why?
4. Match your aptitudes to the qualifications for success in retail merchandising. How can you cultivate yourself in the area(s) in which you have assessed yourself as weak?
5. Search the Internet for the Web sites of some major retail organizations. Link to information about executive-training programs. Which programs do you think best prepare people for the rigors of a retailing career?

KEY TERMS AND CONCEPTS

buyer

consumer

corporate function

department

department manager

distributor

district manager

division

divisional merchandise
manager

fashion director

field function

general manager

general merchandise
manager

line function

manufacturer-sponsored
specialty store

marketing channel

planner

producer

product developer

regional manager

retailer

retail merchandising

staff function

store merchandise
manager

store operations

store planning

table of organization

vertical integration

visual merchandising

wholesaler

ENDNOTES

1. Levy, M. & Weitz, B. (1995). *Retailing Management*. Chicago: Irwin. p. 8.

2. Staff. (January 1999). Following the road to different exits. Careers in Retailing, a publication of *Discount Store News*, p. 9.

3. Tillman, R. (November 1998). A retail career: The path to success. *Retailing Issues*, pp. 1–5.

4. Dentzer, S. (May 22, 1992). Death of a middleman. *U.S. News & World Report*. p. 56.

5. Stalk, G., Evans, P. & Shulman, L. (March-April 1992). Competing capabilities: The new rules of corporate strategy. *Harvard Business Review*. pp. 57–69.

6. Dolan, P. & Samek, S. (1992). *Facing the forces of change 2000: The new realities in wholesale distribution*. Distribution Research and Education Foundation, Washington, D.C. pp. 57–69.

7. Lisanti, T. (February 7, 1994). Time is right for supplier as retailer. *Discount Store News*. p. 9.

8. Halverson, R. (May 11, 1998). Bypassing the marketers in the middle. *Discount Store News*. pp. 70, 108.

9. Socha, M. (May 14, 1998). Building stores and sales. *Women's Wear Daily*. p. 14.

10. Mitchell, R. (May 23, 1994). A children's retailer that grows up fast. *Business Week*. p. 95.

11. Reda, S. (June 1995). When vendors become retailers. *Stores*. pp. 18–21.

12. Monget, K. (April 3, 1995). Sara Lee stores get retailers' OK. *Women's Wear Daily*. p. 10.

13. Mazur, P. (1927). *Principles of Organization Applied to Modern Retailing*. New York: Harper & Brothers.

14. Glock, R. & Kunz, G. (1995). *Apparel Manufacturing*. New York: Macmillan. p. 602.

15. Mazur, P. (1927). *Principles of Organization Applied to Modern Retailing*. New York: Harper & Brothers. p. 66.

16. Donnellan, J. (1996). Educational requirements for management level positions in major retail organizations. *Clothing and Textiles Research Journal*, 14 (1), 16–21.

17. Tillman, R. (November 1998). A retail career: The path to success. *Retailing Issues Letter*. pp. 1–5.

18. Ibid.

19. Moin, D. (June 28, 1995). Buried by paperwork, buyers lament loss of creative juices. *Women's Wear Daily*. pp. 1, 8–9.

20. Tillman, R. (November 1998). A retail career: The path to success. *Retailing Issues Letter*. pp. 1–5.

21. D'Innocenzio, A. (May 13, 1998). Schools tout retail careers. *Women's Wear Daily*. pp. 14, 16.

chapter two

RETAILING FORMATS

B y definition, all retailers sell goods and/or services to final consumers. However, retailers differentiate themselves from each other by factors such as the type of merchandise offered, pricing strategies, and the size and location of their facilities. Though every retail organization struggles for uniqueness in the marketplace, many adopt similar merchandising and operational strategies. This chapter classifies retailers according to those similarities.

After you have read this chapter, you will be able to discuss:

The distinctions among various retailing formats.

The current marketplace status of these formats.

Nonstore retailing.

DEPARTMENT AND SPECIALTY STORES

Some retail stores are classified by characteristics of their assortments. **Breadth** refers to the number of unique items in a selection of merchandise. An extensive selection is described as *wide* or *broad* in terms of breadth. A limited selection is described as *narrow*. **Depth** refers to the *assortment* within a selection. An extensive assortment is described as *deep*. A limited assortment is described as a *shallow*. Wal-Mart offers its customers a broad selection of merchandise that includes sporting goods, toys and hardware. However, the assortments within these categories are shallow when compared to assortments at stores dedicated exclusively to these merchandise categories, such as Sports Authority (sporting goods), Toys "R" Us (toys), and Home Depot (hardware). None of the three can match Wal-Mart in terms of overall breadth; however, within the categories in which they specialize, they carry deeper assortments than Wal-Mart.

There is often a trade-off between breadth of selection and depth of assortment for the obvious reason that having extensive breadth *and* depth would require a mammoth store. A retailer that increases a store's breadth by adding new categories of merchandise consumes space that might otherwise be dedicated to maintaining deep assortments within categories. A retailer that decreases a store's breadth by eliminating categories of merchandise frees space to deepen assortments. Such decisions have considerable profit implications. The Limited Stores, Inc. has improved its profit performance over the years by carrying deeper assortments of fewer but more profitable items in its stores.[1]

Figure 2.1

Macy's and JC Penney are familiar department store chains. *Courtesy of Fairchild Publications, Inc. (right).*

Some retail stores are identified by the breadth or depth of their offerings. A **department store** has considerable breadth in that it carries many categories of merchandise. **Softlines**, such as apparel and household-textile products, are the mainstay of department-store offerings. *Full-line* department stores also offer **hardlines**, or nontextile products, such as furniture and consumer electronics.

A department store satisfies the shopping needs of a diverse group of consumers, including men, women, and children, with goods at more than one price level. Department-store prices are based on conventional pricing strategies for the products and/or manufacturers' suggested retail prices.[2] Department stores carry well-known, nationally distributed, brand-name merchandise, such as Estée Lauder cosmetics, Haggar menswear, and Braun countertop kitchen appliances, and complement their selections of brands with privates labels. Some highly recognized department-store names include Bloomingdale's, Dillard's, and Macy's.

A **specialty store** has limited breadth in that it carries a single or limited number of merchandise categories such as casual apparel, footwear, jewelry, or gifts. Specialty stores cater to a narrowly defined group of customers often characterized by gender, income, or lifestyle segment. Career women, gourmet cooks, and trend-conscious teens are some of the customers to whom specialty stores cater.[3,4] Specialty stores can be single-unit, privately owned operations, or they can be

Figure 2.2

Ann Taylor is an apparel specialty store.

Source:

1. Hazel, D. (May 1999) Bearing fruit: Banana Republic's rebranding efforts have turned the chain into a headquarters for casual Friday. Shopping Centers Today. *pp. 145–148.*

Company Profile 2.1

Banana Republic — A Specialty Store

Founded in 1978 by Mel and Patricia Ziegler, Banana Republic was created as a high-quality, natural-fiber alternative to the disco polyester that dominated the era. Inspired by a secondhand shop in Sydney, Australia, the Zieglers created a prototype that was a cross between Australian outback and "Out of Africa." The company was perfectly positioned at a time when Indiana Jones was having a profound impact on fashion, and khaki was becoming the uniform of the decade.

In 1983, Banana Republic was acquired by San Francisco-based Gap, Inc. Gap embarked upon an aggressive expansion program, and by 1988 the chain had grown to 100 stores. But by the early 1990s the safari look had crashed, nearly taking Banana Republic with it. The company conducted some consumer research and determined that there was a huge demand for casual-workplace apparel at a time when "casual Friday" was becoming a weeklong phenomenon. Banana Republic donned a new look that was somewhere between Brooks Bros. and Gap weekend wear. The stores underwent a physical transformation as well. Adventure-oriented fixtures were abandoned for a brighter more spacious look. Light woods replaced dark floors and cleaner fixtures replaced movie-set tables and racks. It's been onward and upward for Banana Republic since. Today, there are more than 300 Banana Republic stores in the United States and Canada.[1]

part of a chain of several hundred stores, such as Ann Taylor, Sharper Image, and Banana Republic.

In general, specialty-store offerings are characterized as narrow and deep. Though their selections are limited to one or a few categories of merchandise, the assortments within these categories are usually extensive. Department stores offer greater breadth than specialty stores, but typically not as much depth. However in recent years, most department stores have de-emphasized their hardlines categories thus permitting greater depth within their softlines offerings. The depth/breadth gap that once separated department stores and specialty stores has narrowed so that many department stores rival the deep assortments of their specialty-store competitors.[5]

The Status of Department Stores

The origins of most department stores can be traced to the major cities of the nineteenth century. Most were multifloor emporiums with hundreds of categories of merchandise, including toys, sporting goods, and major appliances. Apparel was departmentalized by price, ranging from *bargain basement* and *main floor*, to the higher-priced goods on upper floors. Primary services, such as hair salons, restaurants, and travel agencies, were typical department-store offerings.[6]

Figure 2.3

Marshall Field's State Street store in Chicago is among the few remaining department store "emporiums." *Courtesy of Marshall Field's.*

The contemporary department store is a smaller version of its urban ancestor. Hardlines represent a considerably smaller percentage of its offerings. Low-end price points in apparel have also been eliminated. Today, most department stores are **anchors**, or major tenants, in enclosed suburban shopping centers. Some department-store chains have closed their urban flagships, including Rich's of Atlanta. Other urban department stores have been considerably downsized. Once independently owned, most department stores are now part of publicly owned corporations that operate many stores.[7]

There is considerable speculation relative to the viability of the department store and its likelihood of survival. The list of department stores that have failed in recent decades includes Gimbels of New York, a cornerstone of U.S. retailing, as well as Bonwit Teller and B. Altman, also of New York, Garfinkel's of Washington, D.C., Frederick & Nelson of Seattle, and Joske's of San Antonio, to name but a few.

The demise of department stores has been attributed to many factors. A complex organizational hierarchy often inhibits a department store's reaction to changes in the marketplace. Less complex organizations can respond more rapidly to changes in consumer expectations, fashion trends, and competition. By virtue of its size, a department store's operating expenses are higher than those of retailers that operate smaller facilities and more streamlined organizations. Others cite competitive factors as the source of department-store misfortunes. They feel that department stores lack uniqueness, and that consumers are bored with the sameness of selection among competing stores.[8] Increased competition from other retailing formats is another major reason for the department store's decline in popularity.[9, 10, 11]

In spite of dismal prognostications, the department store remains an important retail-industry segment. Many customers appreciate the convenience of one-stop shopping, and many producers rely on the prestige of department stores to give credibility to their brand names. As symbols of fashion leadership, department stores are often the distribution point at which producers introduce new products or innovative styles to consumers. Department stores still account for more than a quarter of all sales and traffic in the shopping centers in which they are located.[12]

Thriving department-store conglomerates, such as the May Department Stores Company and Federated Department Stores, attest to the viability of the department-store format.[13] Both organizations have enhanced profitability by investing in state-of-the-art technology, reducing operating expenses, streamlining organizational structures, improving customer service, and building strong supportive partnerships with their suppliers.[14, 15, 16, 17, 18, 19, 20]

Hard-to-Classify Stores

Some stores seem to fit neither the department-store nor the specialty-store mold, catering to too few customer needs to be a department store, or to too many customer needs to be a specialty store. These stores are crossbreeds that fall somewhere in the middle of a continuum defined at one end by department stores and the other end by specialty stores. Stores such as Saks Fifth Avenue, Neiman Marcus, and Nordstrom, are consistent with the department-store paradigm in that they are large multidepartmental units that often anchor shopping centers. However, some feel that these stores are more closely akin to specialty stores in that their offerings are almost exclusively apparel. In spite of this limitation, these stores are typically recognized as department stores though they are often referred to as *departmentalized specialty stores* or *specialty department stores* to distinguish them from larger department-store formats.

Because of a geographic expanse of several hundred stores, J.C. Penney and Sears are sometimes referred to as *general-merchandise*

Figure 2.4

Saks Fifth Avenue and Lord & Taylor are among those "hard-to-classify" stores.
Courtesy of Fairchild Publications, Inc. (left)

chains or *national department stores*. However, these terms are dated and seldom used today. Though lacking the panache of many of its competitors, J.C. Penney is a generally considered a department store. Likewise, Sears is a department store with broader selections than other department stores.[21]

DISCOUNTING

A **discounter** is a retailer that sells goods at prices that are lower than the conventional prices of other retailers. Low wholesale prices and low operating costs are fundamental to a discounter's low-price strategy. Discounters procure goods at favorable prices by buying large quantities of first-quality goods, or by buying manufacturers' closeouts, end-of-season merchandise, and overruns. Discounters maintain low operating expenses with "no-frills" operationally efficient facilities. Self-service is another concept that contributes to operational efficiency at discount stores. Customer purchases are processed at a centralized checkout area, or *front end*. This approach to customer service is more economical than the decentralized type of customer service at conventional stores. Labor-intensive supplementary services, such as gift-wrap and alterations, are also absent at discounters.

The emergence of discounting as a significant sector of the U.S. retail industry did not occur until after World War II. However, discounters can be traced back to the turn of the century when "undersellers," such as S. Klein of Manhattan and J.W. May of Brooklyn, sold apparel at prices that undercut department stores.[22]

Types of Discounters

Discounting is a highly diverse retail-industry segment. There are several types of discounters, each unique in terms of merchandising strategy:

Full-Line Discounter A **full-line**, or *general-merchandise*, **discounter** offers a wide selection of merchandise that often includes apparel, home accessories, consumer electronics, housewares, health-and-beauty-care products, and toys. Offerings sometimes include automotive and hardware. Full-line discounters feature lower-priced brands not offered by department stores, such as Fruit of the Loom underwear, Wrangler jeans, and Maybelline cosmetics. Like department stores, full-line discounters

Figure 2.5

Target is one of the "Big Three" full-line discounters. However, Target distinguishes itself from Wal-Mart and Kmart by being more upscale than its two major competitors. *Courtesy of Fairchild Publications, Inc.*

complement their branded offerings with private-label merchandise, especially in the apparel categories. Many full-line discounters have upscaled their image by offering higher-priced brands and emulating the decor, fixturing, and merchandise-presentation strategies of department and specialty stores.[23, 24]

The *Big Three* discounters are Wal-Mart, Kmart, and Target. Collectively, the three operate nearly 5000 stores spanning every state. A *regional discounter* operates approximately 100–200 stores in a specific region of the country. Based in Rocky Hill, Conn., Ames is the nation's largest regional discounter with several hundred stores in the Northeast and the Midwest. Regional discounters face strong competition from the Big Three and for some, survival is a struggle.[25, 26]

Category Killer A **category killer**, or *specialty discounter*, offers a deep assortment of branded merchandise in a single merchandise category. Category killers "kill" the category of business for more generalized retail formats, such as department stores and full-line discounters, whose assortments are shallow by comparison.[27] Toys "R" Us is one of the largest and best-known category killers, capturing well over 20 percent of all retail toy sales in the United States.[28] Other category killers

Sources:

1. *Sicard, A. (May 1998). Diamond retailer sparkles.* Shopping Center World. *p. 186.*

2. *Sicard, A. (May 1988). We're Entertainment sells fun.* Shopping Center World. *p. 188.*

3. *Brookman, F. (March 1997). Ultra3 prototype puts new face on cosmetics retailing.* Stores. *pp. 40–41.*

EMERGING CATEGORY KILLERS

Based in Akron, Ohio, Only Diamonds is a 5000-square foot diamond superstore with five times the diamond selection of a conventional jewelry store. Stones at Only Diamonds range in size from one-fifth of a carat to five carats in all shapes and colors. Professionally trained diamond consultants help customers with their selections. Customers can also watch a film on diamond mining and buying, and peruse a library of books on diamonds. Each Only Diamonds purchase comes with a certification of authentication from an independent gem lab.

Based in Flemington, New Jersey, We're Entertainment is a 30-unit superstore chain of entertainment-theme apparel, accessories and gift items that sport the images of the most popular icons from cartoons, comics, movies, television shows, and musical groups. Appealing to customers of all ages, We're Entertainment puts the fun back into shopping with 4500-square-foot stores that feature carnival-type mirrors, big-screen televisions, and theater-quality sound systems.

Based in Romeoville, Illinois, Ultra3 is a chain of more than 60 beauty superstores in eight states. Each 10,000-square-foot store sells mass-market and prestige fragrances, cosmetics, and hair-care products as well as vitamins, jewelry, and accessories. A hallmark of each store is a salon whose professional services include haircuts, manicures, waxing, coloring, and perms.

include Circuit City (consumer electronics) and Sports Authority, the nation's largest sporting-goods retailer.

A category killer's success is often rooted in identifying an unsatisfied need in the marketplace.[29] The founders of Home Depot determined that consumers bought do-it-yourself (DIY) merchandise at either full-line discount stores, where prices were low but service was poor, or at small, privately owned "mom and pop" hardware stores, where service was good but prices were high. They developed a 100,000-square-foot home improvement store serviced by professional carpenters, electricians, and plumbers, to satisfy consumer demand for extensive selections, low prices, and good service.[30]

Most of the well-known category killers are hardlines specialists. However, many category killers specialize in softlines. The Men's Wearhouse is a Fremont, California-based category killer of men's tai-

charrette
Art & Design Supply Superstore

Visit the largest art supply store in suburban Boston.
Our 16,000 square foot store offers fine art supplies,
studio furniture, drafting and design supplies and much more.
Call for product demonstration schedules.

31 Olympia Avenue • Woburn, MA
781-935-9657
At the intersection of Rte. 93 & 95 (Exit 36 off 95)

Figure 2.6

A category killer offers unbeatable selections within a single product line. *Courtesy of Charrette.*

lored clothing offering department-store brands that are 20 to 30 percent less than department-store prices.[31]

Off-Price Discounter An **off-price discounter**, or *off-pricer*, buys manufacturers' irregulars, seconds, overruns, closeouts, canceled orders, and returns from other retailers. Off-pricers also buy end-of-season and closeout merchandise from other retail stores.[32] Though off-pricers have the reputation of carrying damaged goods and last year's styles, many now offer first-quality in-season merchandise. Some manufacturers make goods especially for off-price stores making productive

Figure 2.7

Off-pricers are positioned as department store competitors.

use of extra reams of fabric and slack production time.[33] Positioned as department-store competitors, off-pricers sell department-store brands at prices 20 to 60 percent less than regular-price retails. Leading off-pricers include Marshalls, T.J. Maxx, Burlington Coat Factory, and Kids "R" Us.[34, 35, 36]

Closeout Store A **closeout store** is a clearance operation through which a retailer eliminates slow-selling or end-of-season merchandise from its regular-price stores. Closeout stores are sometimes criticized for salting their offerings with manufacturers' closeouts that were never part of their regular-price stores' offerings.[37] Department store-sponsored closeout stores, such as Nordstrom Rack and Off 5th-Saks Fifth Avenue, are popular examples of closeout stores.

Manufacturer's Outlet A **manufacturer's outlet** was originally conceived as a "no-frills" break-even operation for unloading a producer's overruns and irregulars. Today, most manufacturers' outlets are profitable operations in attractive settings with first-quality merchandise. Producers that were operating at less than full production capacity found that they could increase their production capacity to 100 percent and profitably sell the additional merchandise in their outlet stores.[38] Some manufacturers produce lines specifically for distribution in their outlet stores.[39] As in the case of manufacturer-sponsored specialty stores, producers that operate outlet stores run the risk of channel conflict by competing with the conventional retail channel members that they supply. The National Shoe Retailers' Association, a trade group of independent shoe retailers, once adopted a resolution that criticized shoe manufacturers that channel first-run merchandise to factory-outlet stores in direct competition with their retail accounts, giving the impression that independent shoe retailers are overpriced.[40, 41]

Warehouse Club A **warehouse club**, or *membership club*, is a wholesale/retail hybrid that offers deep discounts on a limited number of food and general-merchandise items. About two-thirds of a warehouse club's business is from small businesses; the other third is from consumers.[42] Customers pay a membership fee to shop in a warehouse club. Thus, a warehouse club generates income before customers make a single purchase. Operating at the lowest profit margin of any retailer, warehouse clubs epitomize the "no frills" concept with cement floors and steel-rack fixtures. Supermarkets are

---

FROM THE ANNALS OF DISCOUNTING HISTORY

The origins of many discounting formats can be traced to entrepreneurial founders:

- In 1908, Edward Filene opened the Automatic Bargain Basement as a clearance operation to rid the upper floors of his family's namesake department store of markdowns and closeouts. Today, Filene's Basement is an off-price retailer operated independently of the "upstairs" Filene's, now a division of May Department Stores.
- Frieda Loehmann gave birth to off-price discounting in the 1920s when she stalked the designer showrooms on New York's Seventh Avenue in search of samples and canceled shipments to sell at bargain prices in her namesake store in Brooklyn.
- Though its origins are obscure, retail-history pundits often identify the Ann and Hope Mill Outlet as the first general-merchandise discounter. The Rhode Island-based manufacturer of tinsel and corsage ribbons began selling discounted greeting cards and housedresses in a retail store in 1953.
- The warehouse club was pioneered by Sol Price who opened the first Price Club in San Diego in 1978.

most vulnerable to the competition from warehouse clubs; however, warehouse clubs also compete with general-merchandise discounters and category killers.[43,44] Though a relatively new concept, the format has already matured leaving little growth opportunity for existing clubs or new entrants. The two largest warehouse-club retailers are Costco and Sam's Club, a division of Wal-Mart.

Supercenter A **supercenter**, or *combination store*, is a combined supermarket and full-line discount store. The concept was inspired by *les hypers*, an enormous 200,000-square-foot format introduced in France in 1960. With assortments ranging from food to fashion. *Hypermarkets* were France's response to a lack of American-style supermarkets, discount stores, and enclosed shopping centers. The supercenter is actually a scaled-down version of the *hypermarket*. The supercenter links the frequency of visit of the food shopper with the higher profit margins of the full-line discounter. Though a relatively new concept in many areas, Meijer of Grand Rapids has been operating in this format for many years, as has Fred Meyer of Portland, Oregon.[45] Epitomizing the concept of one-stop shopping, supercenters are the fastest growing discount-store format. Both Kmart and Wal-Mart are planning to open a considerable number of Super Kmart Centers and Wal-Mart Supercenters over the next several years.[46, 47, 48, 49, 50]

Figure 2.8

A warehouse club epitomizes the "no frills" concept.

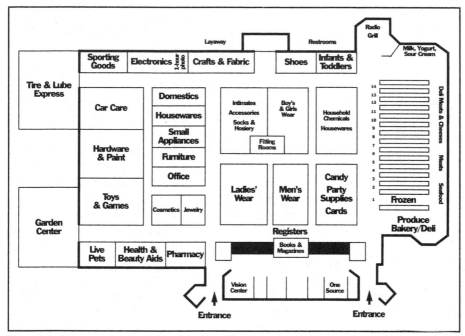

The layout of the supercenter prototype in Fayetteville, Ark.

Figure 2.9

A supercenter combines the offerings of a full-line discounter and a supermarket under one roof. *Courtesy of Wal-Mart.*

OTHER RETAILING FORMATS

The retailing formats defined in the previous section typify most of the retail stores currently operating in the United States. However, the list is in no way exhaustive. There are other retailing formats that are not as prominent as those just mentioned. Some are peculiar to a specific category of merchandise:

Weekend warrior The *weekend warrior* is a no-frills retailing concept that curbs operational costs by only opening to the public during times that they are most likely to shop. Men's Wearhouse operates a weekend warrior called K&G Mens Center. Filene's Basement has a Friday-Saturday-Sunday operation called Aisle 3.[51] Dallas-based Tuesday Morning operates in a similar fashion. The chain of home accessories closeout stores opens for six- to ten-week periods four times a year.[52]

Sources:
1. *Faircloth, A. (March 16, 1998). The best retailer you've ever heard of.* Fortune. *pp. 110–112.*
2. *Seckler, V. (August 4, 1999). Kohl's growth engine seen producing $10b in five years.* Women's Wear Daily. *pp. 1, 8–9.*

Company Profile 2.2

Kohl's — A Retailing Hybrid

Kohl's is a Milwaukee-based retailer that straddles the fence between being a department store and a full-line discount store. A centralized checkout at the store's entrance conveys an image of Wal-Mart, however, the store's strong emphasis on brand-name apparel, such as Lee jeans, Fieldcrest linens, and Reebok footwear, makes it seem more like a department store.

Conventional wisdom scoffs at the notion of positioning a company as neither one thing nor another. However, Kohl's has disproved that logic and has capitalized on the fact that it's like nothing else in the retail world. As a hybrid department store/full-line discounter, it is uniquely positioned to please the vast masses who represent a broad cross section of middle America.

Kohl's typical shopper is a women in her 30s or 40s who juggles a family and a job and has an annual household income of $20,000–$70,000. Kohl's busy customers are attracted to clean bright stores where everything is easy to find. Stores are laid out in human scale—an average of 85,000 square feet, about half the size of a typical department store. Unlike the merchandise groupings of department stores, Kohl's presentation is by classification so that women's blouses are all in one location and not spread throughout the store. The strategy has worked for Kohl's. The company has been a Wall Street sweetheart for the past several years, and its recent penetration into the Northeast has been met with great consumer acceptance. The company is expected to grow to 800 units by 2007.[1,2]

Warehouse showroom Pioneered by Levitz Furniture, the nation's largest furniture retailer, the *warehouse showroom* is a selling-floor display of accessorized room settings attached to a warehouse of inventory from which customers can drive away with their purchases instead of waiting six to eight weeks for special orders to arrive from manufacturers.

Megastore/Superstore The terms *megastore* and *superstore* are often used to refer to an especially large category killer or specialty store. The 100,000-title book emporiums popularized by Barnes & Noble and Borders are called megastores. With expanded assortments of home accessories, Mega Marshalls and T.J. Maxx 'n More are megastore versions of Marshalls and T.J. Maxx. Located in upscale, high-traffic metropolitan areas, such as New York's Fifth Avenue and Chicago's

Michigan Avenue, Niketown is a superstore that features Nike's entire line of athletic footwear in a high-tech multimedia setting with sports memorabilia displays.[53, 54]

Destination store A *destination store* is a retailer that has considerable customer drawing power because of a unique or extensive merchandise assortment. Destination stores are attractive as shopping-center tenants because of their ability to lure customers. Category killers, such as The Home Depot, are considered destination stores. The pharmacies, banks, florists, and quick-processing photo labs in superstores are often called *destination services*.[55]

Extreme Value Store An *extreme value store* is a general-merchandise discounter that sells basic household, food, and health-and-beauty-care items. Smaller than other full-line discount stores, extreme-value stores cater to low- and fixed-income consumers in locations not often served by larger formats. Family Dollar and Dollar General are the two largest extreme-value chains.[56, 57]

Airport Shop As the name implies, an *airport shop* is located in an airport terminal. These specialty-store retailers cater to the many high-income leisure and business travelers who spend considerable

Figure 2.10

Barnes & Noble is an example of a megastore.

time in airports because of flight delays and slack time between check in and departure times. Once home to souvenir shops and hot dog stands, airports are now attracting more upscale retailers such as Gap and Victoria's Secret. Airport-shop offerings are sometimes indigenous to the locale. The retail mix at Washington National Airport includes the National Zoo Store and a Smithsonian Museum Store.[58, 59, 60]

Franchises and Lease Departments

Some retail operations are special types of partnerships between two or more parties. A **franchise** is a contractual agreement between a *franchisor* and *franchisee* that gives the franchisee the right to sell a franchisor's product line or service. The franchisor often provides a source of supply, a set of operating procedures, and a national advertising program. The franchise is purchased by the franchisee for a price based on the franchise's success record and growth potential. The terms of the franchise agreement are often very rigid, specifying hours of operation, facility design, and so on. This insures consistency among all franchised operations, a goal fundamental to maintaining the integrity of the franchise. Profits generated from operating the franchise are shared by the franchisor and the franchisee.

The most commonly known franchises are in the fast-food industry. Consumer-goods franchises include RadioShack, Athlete's Foot, and Hallmark Cards. Sweets From Heaven is a Pittsburgh-based retailer of bulk and wrapped candy that operates both company-owned stores and franchises.[61] Though a franchisee is most often an independent operator, the franchisee may be another retailer. Kmart is the nation's largest franchisee of Little Caesar's restaurants.[62]

Sometimes franchises are limited to a specific product line. Best known in the retailing of automobiles and gasoline, *product* or *trade franchises* are strategic partnerships between a producer and a retailer to sell a product. The producer provides the retailer with product training and marketing incentives. The retailer, in turn, agrees to maintain specified levels of inventory, sales staffing, and promotional activity. *Authorized dealership* is a term often used to refer to a product or trade franchise. This type of arrangement occurs between many major appliance producers, such as RCA and Whirlpool, and consumer-electronics retailers, such as Circuit City.

A **lease department** is a retailer that leases space from another retailer to operate as a department within the latter's store. Rent is

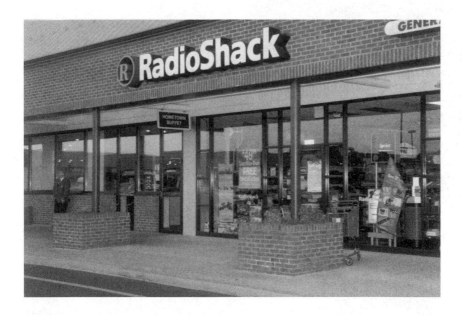

Figure 2.11

Some RadioShack stores are franchised operations.

based on the lease department's sales and the amount of space occupied. The most common type of lease departments include:

- Traffic-generating services, such as restaurants and photography studios.
- Departments with large, difficult to manage inventories, such as shoes.
- Departments that require specialized selling, such as fine jewelry.

Some lease departments retain their identity operating as a store within a store. Other lease departments operate anonymously, blending in like any other department adhering to the store's policies, operating procedures, and promotional calendar. Lease departments operate within many different types of retailing formats. Revillon Furs operates fur salons at 30 Saks Fifth Avenue locations. Finlay Enterprises operates fine-jewelry departments in Marshall Field's stores. Cole National Corporation operates more than 800 Sears Optical Centers.[63]

Figure 2.12

Cole National Corporation operates Sears Optical Center as a lease department. *Photo reprinted by arrangement with Sears, Roebuck and Co. and is protected by copyright. No duplication is permitted.*

Dying Breeds

Retailing is a dynamic industry within which new formats are constantly evolving. However, constant changes in consumer buying habits have made casualties as frequent as births in the retail industry. The *catalog showroom* and the *variety store* are two long-enduring retailing formats currently on the brink of extinction.

The catalog showroom is a discount retailer of jewelry, consumer electronics, home accessories, sporting goods, and juvenile products. Catalog showrooms flourished during the post–World War II decades by selling department-store brands at discounted prices at a time when other discounters sold only lower quality *off-brands*. Catalog showrooms had difficulty withstanding competition from category killers and full-line discounters as they began to offer major brands at competitive prices. Service Merchandise is the only major catalog-showroom operator still functioning, though in recent years the company has become more of a hardlines specialty store than a true catalog showroom.[64, 65, 66]

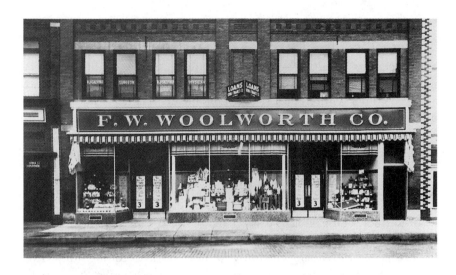

Figure 2.13

Variety stores once dotted virtually every downtown shopping area. *Bettman/Corbis.*

The *variety store*, or *5&10* or *dime store*, dates back to the nine-teenth century when merchants such as Sebastian S. Kresge and Frank W. Woolworth opened stores that sold goods at five- and ten-cent retails. Inflation and expanded assortments that included housewares, linens, fashion jewelry, and cosmetics, eventually made "5&10" a misnomer. Variety stores remained a dominant retailing format for many decades dotting virtually every downtown shop-ping area and the earliest suburban shopping centers. Variety stores had difficulty competing with a growing number of full-line dis-counters that offered many of the same merchandise categories in greater depth. Recognizing the dismal future of this format, some of the major variety-store chains diversified into areas with greater growth potential. In 1962, the S.S. Kresge Company opened the first Kmart in a Detroit suburb, and eventually abandoned its variety-store format. Likewise, F.W. Woolworth became a diversified con-glomerate of specialty stores operating under banners that include Foot Locker, Champs Sports, and Northern Reflections.[67,68] The five-and-dime era came to an end in 1997 when F.W. Woolworth, then owned by the Venator Group, announced the closing of its remaining Woolworth stores.[69]

NONSTORE RETAILERS

Some retailers conduct business without storefront facilities. **Direct marketing** is a term that defines a direct relationship between a retailer and a customer without the use of a retail facility. There are two forms of direct marketing. **Direct selling** uses personal explanation or demonstration to sell a product. **Direct-response marketing** uses a nonpersonal print or electronic medium to communicate with consumers.

Direct Selling

Door-to-door selling and the party plan are two commonly known forms of direct selling. An age-old form of direct selling, **door-to-door selling** is the practice of canvassing customers at home. The declining number of women at home during the day and a reluctance to open the door to strangers have all but eradicated door-to-door sales.[70] Avon, remembered for its famous "Avon calling" door-to-door campaign has virtually abandoned door-to-door selling. The company now targets women in the workplace as both sales representatives and customers.[71]

The *party plan* is a form of direct selling in which a demonstrator presents a product line to a group of customers in the home of a host/hostess. Tupperware, a producer of high-quality plastic storage containers, is among the best-known party-plan marketers. In response to the changes in the lifestyle of today's homemaker, Tupperware has taken the party out of the home and into the workplace with the "rush-hour party" held at the end of the workday. Tupperware also targets an increasing number of single households by including men in their market.[72, 73, 74]

Network marketing, or *multilevel marketing*, is a strategy used by some direct-selling organizations to reward sales representatives for recruiting other sales representatives. Commissions are based on personal sales as well as the sales of a "downline" of recruits. Among the largest network marketers are Amway household products and Nu Skin skin-care products.

Catalog Retailing

Catalog, or *mail-order*, **retailing** is a form of direct-response marketing. Catalogs were originally intended for customers who lacked convenient access to retail stores. However, the focus of catalogs changed as shopping centers and automobiles made stores accessible to virtually all customers. Today's catalogs are intended for time-pressed consumers who want the convenience of shopping at home. The Direct Marketing Association reports the existence of more than 10,000 catalogs of consumer goods.[75] Some of the largest catalog merchants include Lands' End, Spiegel, J. Crew, and L.L. Bean.[76]

Full-line general-merchandise catalogs were once the hallmark of catalog retailing. However, catalog retailing has evolved into a specialty business within recent years. In 1993, Sears abandoned the publication of its 1500-page *Big Book* of general merchandise in favor of several smaller catalogs, including *Great Kitchens* and *Leather Connections*. To offset declining sales from its 650-page general-merchandise catalog, Spiegel created several specialty catalogs including *Spiegel Now*, a catalog of contemporary apparel and home furnishings, and *Details*, a shoes and accessories catalog.[77]

Some catalog companies are diversified retailers that publish multiple catalogs. The Williams-Sonoma family of catalogs includes, *Williams-Sonoma* (food and housewares), *Gardener's Eden* (gardening supplies), *The Pottery Barn* (home accessories), *Hold Everything* (storage containers), and *Chambers* (bed and bath linens and accessories).[78]

Some retailers operate as both storefront retailers and catalogers. Though essentially a catalog retailer of high-end gift items, The Sharper Image also operates nearly 100 stores. Though essentially a department-store operator, Macy's created *Macy's by Mail* to reach customers who do not live near a Macy's store but are familiar with the famous name.[79] Some retailers intertwine their storefront and catalog businesses. Talbots, a retailer of classic clothing for women and children, uses catalog sales as an indicator of potential store sites. Talbots begins to explore an area as a possible store location when catalog sales from the area reach $150,000.[80]

Rising paper and postage costs pose constant threats to the viability of catalog retailers. To combat inflation, many catalog retailers have reduced catalog dimensions, number of pages, and circulation. Neiman Marcus streamlined its catalog operation by publishing fewer catalogs with more general appeal.[81, 82, 83]

Electronic Retailing

Electronic retailing is the most contemporary form of direct-response retailing. Often referred to as *home shopping*, electronic retailing has three formats that use television as the direct-response medium:

Figure 2.14

Linensource and Lands'
End are nonstore retailers
that conduct business
through catalogs. *Courtesy
of Linensource;* © *Lands' End,
Inc. Used with permission.*

- An *infomercial* is a program-length product demonstration sometimes hosted by a celebrity. Infomercials have become a popular format for selling cookware, exercise equipment, and various types of services.
- A *television shopping channel* is a cable channel dedicated to talk-show-style programming in which merchandise is presented to viewers who can then order by phone. Analysts once predicted that television shopping would quickly evolve into a $150 billion retail segment that would threaten the viability of conventional retailing. However, the predictions never came true. In fact, shopping channels have had problems with a tawdry image and the fact that time-pressed customers are unwilling to adjust their schedules to view merchandise. QVC and HSN are the two major shopping channels.[84]
- *Interactive television* is a form of electronic shopping in which consumers take electronic "shopping trips" on their TV screens, and then place an order, charge it to a credit card, and choose a delivery option by using a remote and a modem. The availability of interactive television is limited because of the high cost involved in replacing existing cable wire with fiber-optic cable needed for interactive television. As a result, interactive shopping is growing slowly.[85, 86, 87, 88]

E-commerce

E-commerce, or *online shopping*, is an increasingly popular form of electronic retailing in which a retailer operates a Web site that allows customers to shop over the Internet. A retailer can operate its own Web site independently or become a "tenant" in a "cybermall." J. Crew, Nordstrom, and OfficeMax all operate their own Web sites. Williams-Sonoma, The Sharper Image, Burdines, and Caswell Massey are tenants in Dream Shop, an electronic shopping mall owned by AOL Time Warner.[89]

A few retailers, such as Amazon.com, use the Internet as their only selling venue. However, most retailers use e-commerce to supplement sales from other formats such as stores and catalogs. Some retailers sell only a small representation of their total offerings online. Best Buy, a consumer-electronics chain, only sells CDs on the Internet.[90,91] Macys.com primarily offers gift-oriented items, such as cashmere sweaters and watches, and basic re-orderable items, such as women's

Source:

1. Coast to Coast
*(Sping 1998) A corpo-
rate publication of
Federated Department
Stores.*

Company Profile 2.3

Macy's — A Marriage of Tradition and Progress

Though steeped in more than a century of tradition, Macy's has become the department-store leader in e-commerce. The development of macys.com began when consumer interest in the Internet was in its infancy. Since then its growth has been exponential. The site is worth visiting. Almost all items include color photos and detailed descriptions. Assortments within an ever-growing number of merchandise categories are constantly changing.

Engaged couples can even set up their wedding-gift registry online. Their wedding guests can then purchase gifts on-line with specifications to have them wrapped and sent to the couple with personalized notes.

Macys.com is especially popular for holiday gift-giving occasions such as Chanukah, Christmas, Mothers' Day, and Fathers' Day. The site generates a lot of plus business for Macy's in states where the department-store chain does not have a major presence. The average order from states such as Iowa, Alabama, and Rhode Island, is much higher than from states in which Macy's stores are heavily penetrated. Customers can also find a list of Macy's store locations and phone numbers on the site, as well as information about Macy's special events including its annual spring Flower Show. The fact that more than a half million people access information about Macy's renown Thanksgiving Day Parade is testimony of the popularity of the Macy's Web site.[1]

hosiery.[92] Other retailers offer their complete product line on the Internet. Approximately 95 percent of the Eddie Bauer product line is available at eddiebauer.com. The retailer offers promotional incentives to its online customers, such as "weekly specials" and "great buys," and profiles them for promotional e-mailings based on their online purchase histories. Some retailers offer more than merchandise on their Web sites. Foot Locker's Web site features articles by top sports writers, on-line games and contests, and a chat room.[93]

Catalog retailers have been quickest to develop Web sites. The Lands' End Web site features a 3D virtual model that bears a likeness to the customer based on information that is input on a customer's hair color, height, and waist and shoulder measurements. The model then "tries on" items that the customer has selected from the pages of the Web site to giving the customer an idea of how the selected items will look on her.[94]

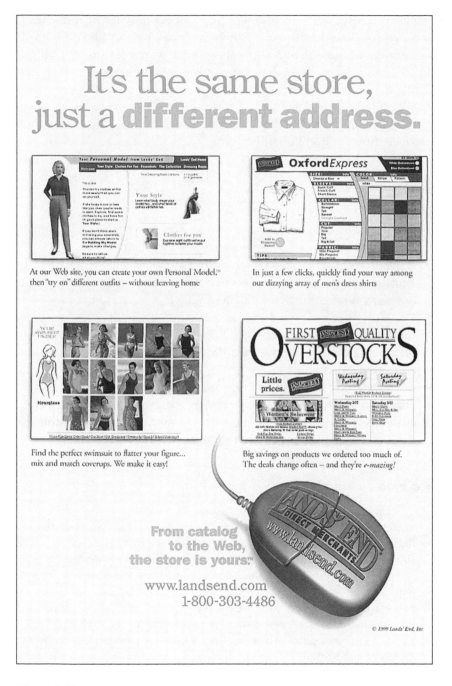

Figure 2.15

Lands' End is a leader in e-commerce. © *Lands' End, Inc. Used with permission.*

E-commerce is a vertical-integration opportunity for manufacturers who wish to sell directly to consumers. Timex has a Web site with an assortment of more than 300 watches and a search feature to facilitate purchase decisions. Though e-commerce is generating just a small percentage of general-merchandise sales at this point, the format is expected to grow exponentially within the next few years. The concept is especially appealing to time-pressed, desk-bound workers who don't have the time for traditional shopping.[95]

SUMMARY POINTS

- Breadth refers to the number of unique items in an assortment. Depth refers to the selection within an assortment.
- A department store satisfies multiple customer needs with many categories of merchandise. A specialty store caters to the specific needs of a narrowly defined group of customers.
- Discounters offer low prices in a "no-frills" setting. There are several distinct types of discounters: full-line discounters, category killers, off-pricers, closeout stores, manufacturers' outlets, warehouse clubs, and supercenters.
- Other retailing formats include franchises and lease departments.
- Direct marketing is nonstore retailing; direct-response marketing employs a nonpersonal medium to communicate with customers; direct selling involves personal selling.

FOR DISCUSSION

1. Make a list of retailers that operate within the same retailing format and sell the same categories of merchandise. Search the Internet for each store's Web site and obtain clues that identify the type of customer to which each retailer caters. Do the retailers on your list compete for the same customers? Explain.
2. Make a list of stores in your area. Classify each by retailing format and explain your classification. Are some stores difficult to classify? Why?
3. Identify some categories of merchandise not sold by category killers. Do any represent opportunities for an entrepreneurial retailer? Explain.
4. Discuss the future of e-commerce. Do you feel the concept will continue to grow? What types of merchandise do you think sell best on the Internet?

KEY TERMS AND CONCEPTS

anchor	direct selling	off-price discounter
breadth	discounter	softlines
catalog retailing	door-to-door selling	specialty store
category killer	e-commerce	supercenter
closeout store	electronic retailing	warehouse club
depth	franchise	
department store	full-line discounter	
direct marketing	hardlines	
direct-response	lease department	
marketing	manufacturer's outlet	

ENDNOTES

1. Cunningham, T. (May 18, 1999). Express makes a turn, but Limited Stores, Structure, take hits. *Women's Wear Daily*. pp. 1, 13.
2. This description of a department store is consistent with the National Retail Federation's definition of a department store as a multidepartmental soft-lines store with a fashion orientation, full markup policy, carrying national branded merchandise and operating stores large enough to be shopping center anchors. By contrast, the U.S. Department of Commerce defines a department store as an establishment normally employing 25 people or more, having sales of apparel and softlines that amount to 20 percent or more of total sales, and selling each of the following lines of merchandise: furniture, appliances, radios, and TV sets; a general line of apparel for the family; household lines and dry goods. To qualify as a department store, sales of each of these lines must be less than 80 percent of total store sales. An establishment with total sales of $10 million or more is classified as a department store even if sales in one of the merchandise lines exceed the maximum percent of total sales, provided that the combined sales of the other two groups are $1 million or more. The U.S. Department of Commerce is a dated definition that was composed when "radios and television sets" were standard department store offerings, and when $10 million was a considerable amount of business.
3. Adler, S. (September 12, 1994). Specialty stores do the right thing. *Home Furnishings Daily*. pp. 20A–21A.
4. Staff. (November 1994). Rating the stores. *Consumer Reports*. pp. 712–722.
5. Schultz, D. (August 1991). Expansion: Specialty retailers tinker with revamped formats and larger stores to lure customers back. *Stores*. pp. 43–45.

6. Cohen, D. (March 1993). Grand emporiums peddle their wares in a new market. *Smithsonian*. pp. 122–133.

7. Sternlieb, G. & Hughes, J. (August 1987). The demise of the department store. *American Demographics*. pp. 31–33, 59.

8. Levy, W. (1987). Department stores. The next generation: Form and rationale. *Retailing Issues Newsletter*, 1(1). pp. 1–4.

9. Barnett, T. Nelson, M.; King, P. & McCormick, J. (December 11, 1989). Shop till they drop. *Newsweek*. pp. 76–78.

10. Strom, S. (January 11, 1994). Retailers' drive to consolidate. *New York Times*. pp. D1, D2.

11. Barmash, I. (August 1998). Department stores battle discounters. *Shopping Centers Today*. p. 36.

12. Strom, S. (February 3, 1992). Department stores remain a strong franchise. *New York Times*. pp. D1, D4.

13. Chandler, S. (November 27, 1995). An endangered species makes a comeback. *Business Week*. p. 96.

14. Sinderman, M. (January 1998). Department stores ride the wave. *Shopping Center World*. pp. 28–30.

15. McCloud, J. (January 1997). Department stores get new lease on life. *Shopping Center World*. pp. 16–19.

16. Department stores ride the wave. (January 1988). *Shopping Center World*. pp. 28–29.

17. Berry, K. (April 22, 1994). Are department stores up to the task? *Investor's Business Daily*. p. A3.

18. Crites, J. (August 1992). The next chapter in department store retailing. *Chain Store Age Executive*. pp. 24A–26A.

19. Forsyth, J. (August 1993). Department store industry restructures for the 90s. *Chain Store Age*. pp. 29A–30A.

20. Lagnado, I. (April 10, 1994). The department store, revitalized. *New York Times*. p. C17.

21. Gill, P. (February 1990). What's a department store? *Stores*. p. 8.

22. Staff. (September 21, 1992). Discounting: Chronicles of its evolution. *Discount Store News*. pp. 49, 104.

23. Pogoda, D. (October 6, 1994). Jousting with Wal-Mart. Better clothes, better trappings. *Women's Wear Daily*. p. 24.

24. Swisher, K. (August 11, 1991). Attention, shoppers! Here come the big, flashy discount stores. *Washington Post*. pp. H1, H6.

25. Young, V. (April 28, 1998). Venture to shut rest of units. *Women's Wear Daily*. p. 19.

26. M. Hartnett, (May 1997). Results reveal surprising strength for some regional discount chains. *Stores*. pp. 58–60.

27. Staff. (November 27, 1995). Reinventing the store. *Business Week*. pp. 84–96.

28. Strom, S. (December 19, 1994). Toys "R" Us still titan of toyland. (Springfield, Mass.) *Union News*. pp. G1, G2.

29. Staff. (December 11, 1989). Staples, Inc. *The Wall Street Transcript*. p. 95685.

30. Thompson, R. (February 1992). There's no place like Home Depot. *Nation's Business*. pp. 30–32.
31. Retail Scoreboard: DNR's listing of the top executives at nineteen of the country's leading store groups. (May 1995). A supplement to *Daily News Record*. p. 14.
32. The term *off-price* is sometimes used to refer to any retailer that sells goods at discounted prices.
33. Steinhauer, J. (December 23, 1996). Off-price retailers lead upswing. (Springfield, Mass.) *Union-News*.
34. Barmash, I. (March 1981). How they're selling name brands off-price. *Stores*. pp. 9–14, 55.
35. Staff. (December 7, 1986). Racking up competition. *Los Angeles Business Journal*.
36. Reidy, C. (June 27, 1999). Remaking an original. *The Boston Globe*. pp. G1–G7.
37. Pogoda, D. (May 12, 1993). Closeout stores: Retailing's last stop. *Women's Wear Daily*. pp. 8–9.
38. Yazigi, M. (July 5, 1998). Bye bye bargains. *The New York Times*. pp. 9–12.
39. Staff. (August 1998). Outlet malls: Do they deliver the goods? *Consumer Reports*. pp. 20–25.
40. Edelson, S. (April 4, 1995). Once a poor relation, outlets go legit—and trouble looms. *Women's Wear Daily*. pp. 1, 8, 9.
41. Orgel, D. (December 14, 1992). The outlet game: New players face new rules. *Women's Wear Daily*, p. 13.
42. Staff. (March 1, 1993). Warehouse club closeup. Evolution key to continued club success. *Discount Store News*. pp. 17–24.
43. D'Innocenzio, A. (April 14, 1993). Warehouse clubs: Is the novelty wearing off? *Women's Wear Daily*. p. 14.
44. Troy, M. (March 17, 1997). Supercenters, clubs reshaping U.S. grocery store business. *Discount Store News*. pp. 4, 53.
45. Fred Meyer is now owned by Kroger, the nation's largest food retailer.
46. Lieback, L. & Longo, D. (May 3, 1993). Discounters spearhead supercenters' decade. *Discount Store News*. pp. 1, 18.
47. Staff. (August 1, 1994). Supercenters: Anatomy of a hybrid. A supplement of *Women's Wear Daily*, Fairchild Publications.
48. Tosh, M. (June 7, 1995). Supercenters: The race is on. *Women's Wear Daily*. p. 14.
49. Edelson, S. (October 11, 1995). Supercenters get nod in Wal-Mart expansion plans for next year. *Women's Wear Daily*. pp. 1, 13.
50. Staff. (August 1, 1994). Supercenters. A supplement of *Women's Wear Daily*. Fairchild Publications.
51. Duff, M. (May 5, 1999). Aisle 3 joins the weekend pioneers. *Discount Store News*. pp. 1, 44.
52. Baily, S. & Syre, S. (September 19, 1998). Basement planning new chain. *The Boston Globe*. pp. C1, C7.
53. Feeney, M. (December 11, 1997). Pumping up the volumes. *The Boston Globe*. pp. C1, C8.

54. Staff. (January 22, 1997). Gap plans to build Fifth Ave. Megastore. *The New York Times.*

55. Seckler, V. (February 12, 1997). Supercenters: A long shadow. *Women's Wear Daily.* pp. 1, 16, 35.

56. Faircloth, A. (July 6, 1998). Value retailers go dollar for dollar. *Fortune.* pp. 164–166.

57. Barmash, I. (June 1998). "Dollar" discount store cash in on growth. *SCT Retailing Today.* p. 27.

58. Steinhauer, J. (June 29, 1998). Airports look more and more like regular shopping malls. *The* (Springield, Mass.) *Union-News.* p. C5.

59. Dunlap, D. (August 2, 1998). Grand Central reborn as a beaux-arts mall. *The New York Times.* pp. 33, 34.

60. Edelson, S. (July 14, 1997). Trains, planes and chains. *Women's Wear Daily.* pp. 8–9.

61. Staff. (May 1999). Can store offers pieces of heaven. *Shopping Center World.* pp. 50–52.

62. Feder, B. (August 16, 1993). Dining out at the discount store. *The New York Times.* pp. D1, D2.

63. Staff. Finlay to buy Zale's leased jewelry departments. *Women's Wear Daily.*

64. Staff. (December 7, 1992). Retailing for the new millennium. *Discount Store News.* pp. 53–63.

65. Gilligan, G. (June 1997). Demise of Best Products ends an era. *Shopping Centers Today.* pp. 21, 22.

66. Cienski, J. (November 9, 1996). Catalog showrooms fading fast. (Springfield, Mass.) *Union-News.* p. A7.

67. Miller, A. (January 4, 1993). A dinosaur no more. *Time.* pp. 54–55.

68. Pogoda, D.. (October 20, 1993). Woolworth's closings: What went wrong? *Women's Wear Daily.* p. 16.

69. Beck, R. (July 18, 1997). Woolworth to close all its stores. (Springfield, Mass.) *Union-News.* pp. B7, B10.

70. Underwood, E. (September 9, 1991). The modern trials of the Fuller Brush Man. *Adweek's Marketing Week.* pp. 16–17.

71. Reynolds, P. (August 21, 1996). Avon: Still calling. *The Boston Globe.* pp. C1, C5.

72. Klebnikov, P. (December 9, 1991). The power of positive inspiration. *Forbes.* pp. 245–249

73. Roha, R. (November 1991). The ups and downs of downlines. *Kiplinger's Personal Finance Magazine.* pp. 63–70.

74. Staff. (December 1992). Door-to-door selling grows up. *Black Enterprise.* pp. 76–90.

75. D'Innocenzio, A. (December 9, 1998). Coping with a catalog crunch. *Women's Wear Daily.* pp. 8–9.

76. Gill, P. (July 1990). Targeting direct mail. *Stores.* pp. 42–47.

77. Edelson, S. (February 21, 1997). Spiegel's new consistency. *Women's Wear Daily*. p. 17.

78. Weingarten, T. (June 9, 1997). The tastemaker. *Newsweek*. pp. 60–61.

79. Socha, M. (Decmeber 9, 1998). Coping with a catalog crunch. *Women's Wear Daily*. pp. 8–9.

80. Reda, S. (July 1995). Talbots thrives with innovative synergies, consumer research. *Stores*. pp. 34–35.

81. Haran, L. (November 6, 1995). More fear than cheer for catalogers. *Advertising Age*. p. 4.

82. Whalen, J.(November 13, 1995). Less is more for Neiman Marcus catalogs. *Advertising Age*. p. 52.

83. D'Innocenzio, A. (November 1, 1995). Catalog's new survival tactics. *Women's Wear Daily*. pp. 12, 14.

84. Edelson, S. (November 8, 1995). Fashion reevaluates flickering fortunes of TV home shopping. pp. 1, 8–9.

85. Marx, W. (October 1995). Interactive TV put on pause. *Catalog Age*. pp. 5, 54.

86. Carlin, P. (February 28, 1993). The jackpot in television's future? *The New York Times Magazine*. pp. 36–41.

87. Morgenson, G. (May 24, 1993). The fall of the mall. *Forbes*. pp. 106–112.

88. Zinn, Laura. (July 26, 1993). Retailing will never be the same. *Business Week*. pp. 54–60.

89. Mander, E. (December 1996). 'Hit' or miss. *SCT/Retailing Today*. p 13.

90. Heller, L. (March 9, 1998). Jury's still out on best sales strategy. *Discount Store News*. p. 18.

91. Silverman, D. (April 7, 1998). The Internet beckons but fashion continues to be wary of the Web. *Women's Wear Daily*. pp. 1, 6–7.

92. Moin, D. (November 19, 1998). Macy's Web site gets a major apparel upload. *Women's Wear Daily*. p. 14.

93. Scally, R. (May 11, 1998). Woolworth ups Foot Lockers' Web presence. *Discount Store News*. p. 23.

94. Zimmermann, K. A 'model' site for Lands' end. *Women's Wear Daily*.

95. Mitchell, R. (December 7, 1998). Why AOL really clicks. *U.S. News & World Report*. pp. 52–53.

chapter three

RETAIL LOCATIONS

An age-old axiom asserts that the three factors that contribute most to a retailer's success are *location, location,* and *location*. Proponents of nonstore retailing might disagree with this posture. However, in spite of the success of many nonstore formats, most retail industry pundits concur that location can make or break a storefront retailer. Chapter 3 considers the synergy between retailing format and retail location along with the various location options available for retail stores.

After you have read this chapter, you will be able to discuss:

The various shopping environments in which retailers operate stores.

The important role that location plays in a retailer's success.

65

UNPLANNED SHOPPING DISTRICTS

The earliest retail shopping districts were unplanned clusters of stores that evolved in the centers of cities. Known to many as *downtown*, a **central business district** *(CBD)*, or *urban core*, is a vital hub of commerce and transportation. The great department-store emporiums were founded in CBDs. Many cities had two or more department stores that rivaled each other for market dominance by distinguishing themselves in terms of size or prestige.

Specialty stores were also an important part of the CBD's retail mix. Though many CBD specialty stores were single-unit independent operations, CBDs were also the original home of national specialty chains, including Kay Jewelers and Lerner Shops.[1] In spite of the fact that there was no strategic master plan for locating stores within a CBD, districts defined by categories of goods, such as jewelry, menswear, women's apparel, or furniture, often evolved in large CBDs.

CBDs are no longer major retail shopping districts, except in the case of some large urban metropolises. Several factors have contributed to the decline of the popularity of CBDs as retail locations. The proliferation of the automobile meant that public transportation was no longer an important factor in drawing shoppers downtown. In fact, traffic congestion and the expense and inconvenience of parking a car diminished the city's attractiveness as a shopping destination. The urban decay that has plagued many cities has caused many shoppers to perceive cities as unattractive and unsafe places to shop.

The migration of customers to the suburbs is perhaps the factor that has contributed most to the demise of downtown retail districts.[2] However, as suburbs become saturated with retail stores, some retailers have shown renewed interest in metropolitan locations including Kmart, Barnes & Noble, Bed Bath & Beyond, and Toys "R" Us. TJX Companies, the parent company of Marshalls and T.J. Maxx, has developed an off-price prototype called A.J. Wright designed especially for urban areas underserved by other retailers.

Secondary business districts *(SBDs)*, or *subshopping districts*, often sprouted in outlying areas of cities as populations migrated to urban perimeters. Likewise, **town centers** evolved in towns and suburbs peripheral to cities. SBDs and town centers have historically been important as locations for independently owned specialty stores and service retailers. Some towns have been aggressive in

Figure 3.1

Secondary business districts and town centers are home to many independently owned specialty stores and service retailers.

their attempts to retain a strong retail character within their communities. The town of Schaumburg, Illinois, acquired 29 acres of underutilized property and then parceled it to developers who built retail and professional buildings under strict zoning and development guidelines.[3]

In recent years, chain-store retailers that typically locate in shopping malls have shown interest in town centers. About one-third of Gap's stores are in "neighborhood" locations.[4] In the Old Town section of Pasadena, California, local merchants operate alongside Crate & Barrel, J. Crew, Banana Republic, and other national chains.[5]

Unplanned commercial districts often evolve on busy thoroughfares in cities and towns. These districts are popular locations for many **free-standing stores**, stand-alone facilities with their own parking areas. Free-standing stores are typically destination stores, such as car dealerships, furniture stores, supermarkets, movie theaters, fast-food restaurants, or big-box discounters. Traffic congestion is a frequent problem along these thoroughfares.[6]

Figure 3.2

A free-standing store is a stand-alone destination store with its own parking facilities. *Courtesy of Fairchild Publications, Inc.*

PLANNED SHOPPING CENTERS

A **shopping center** is a commercial complex with onsite parking that is developed, owned, and managed as a unit. Shopping centers blossomed on the retail landscape during the years following World War II as real-estate developers responded to the needs of rapidly growing numbers of consuming suburbanites.[7] The International Council of Shopping Centers (ICSC) has identified several distinct types of shopping centers.

Neighborhood Center A **neighborhood center** includes approximately 30,000–150,000 square feet of retail space. Supermarkets or large drugstores are often major tenants in a neighborhood center. Service retailers, such as dry-cleaning establishments and shoe-repair shops, characterize the remaining tenant mix.

Community Center A **community center** includes approximately 100,000–350,000 square feet of retail space. A supermarket and a full-

Figure 3.3

Snowden Square in Columbia, Maryland, is an example of a community center.
Courtesy of The Rouse Company.

line discounter are often the major tenants in a community center. Specialty and service retailers are typical of the remaining tenant mix. Category killers and off-pricers are sometimes major tenants in community centers.

Regional Center A **regional** shopping **center** has approximately 400,000–800,000 square feet of retail space with two or more department stores as major tenants. Specialty stores of apparel, gifts, and home furnishings and accessories complement the assortments of the department stores.

Superregional Center A **superregional center** has more than 800,000 square feet of retail space with three or more department stores as major tenants. The department stores are complemented by general-merchandise and specialty retailers that collectively offer broad selections and deep assortments of apparel and home furnishings. Food courts are a common feature of superregional centers, as are various forms of entertainment, such as movie theaters and miniature golf.[8]

Table 3.1 ICSC SHOPPING CENTER DEFINITIONS

Type	Concept	Sq. Ft. (Inc. Anchors)	Acreage	Number	Typical Anchor(s) Type	Anchor Ratio*	Primary Trade Area**
Neighborhood Center	Convenience	30,000–150,000	3–15	1 or more	Supermarket	30–50%	3 miles
Community Center	General Merchandise; Convenience	100,000–350,000	10–40	2 or more	Discount dept. store; supermarket; drug; home improve.; large specialty/disc. apparel	40–60%	3–6 miles
Regional Center	General Merchandise; Fashion (Mall, typically enclosed)	400,000–800,000	40–100	2 or more	Full-line dept. store; jr. dept. store; mass merchant; disc. dept. store; fashion apparel	50–70%	5–15 miles
Superregional Center	Similar to Regional Center but has more variety and assortment	800,000+	60–120	3 or more	Full-line dept. store; jr. dept. store; mass merchant; fashion apparel	50–70%	5–25 miles
Fashion/Specialty Center	Higher end, fashion oriented	80,000–250,000	5–25	N/A	Fashion	N/A	5–15 miles
Power Center	Category-dominant anchors; few small tenants	250,000–600,000	25–80	3 or more	Category killer; home improve.; disc. dept. store; warehouse club; off-price	75–90%	5–10 miles
Theme/Festival Center	Leisure; tourist-oriented; retail and service	80,000–250,000	5–20	N/A	Restaurants; entertainment	N/A	N/A
Outlet Center	Manufacturers' outlet stores	50,000–400,000	10–50	N/A	Manufacturers' outlet stores	N/A	25–75 miles

* The share of a center's total square footage that is attributable to its anchors.
**The area from which 60–80% of the center's sales originate.

Reprinted with permission of the International Council of Shopping Centers Research Quarterly, Volume 1, Number 1, May 1994. © 1994 by the International Council of Shopping Centers, Inc., New York, New York.

Strips and Malls

Most neighborhood and community centers are **strip centers**, linear arrangements of stores with an open-air canopy and off-street parking in front of the stores. J.C. Nichols built the first strip center, Country Club Plaza in Kansas City, Missouri, in 1922.

Commonly referred to as malls,[9] most regional and superregional centers are roofed and climate-controlled with an inward orientation of stores connected by a pedestrian walkway. Open-air and/or decked parking surround most regional and superregional centers. The first enclosed shopping center, Southdale, opened in a Minneapolis suburb in 1956. The development of the Interstate Highway system spurred the growth of regional and superregional centers. Sites at highway interchanges became desirable mall locations because of their high visibility and easy accessibility.

The trading area from which a shopping center draws its customers is a function of its size. Large shopping centers draw from a

Figure 3.4

Strip centers are attractive to retailers because of their heavily trafficked locations and relatively low rent structures. *Courtesy of Weingarten Properties.*

wider trading area than small centers, in that consumers will travel a greater distance for an extensive selection of stores. The value of space in a shopping center is a function of the number of shoppers that the center attracts. Thus, rent in large, heavily trafficked centers is higher than rent in small centers. For this reason, many regional centers have aspired to become superregional centers by adding new anchors and additional space for more specialty stores.[10, 11]

Other Types of Shopping Centers

Other types of shopping centers incorporate the characteristics of both strips and malls, but are distinct in terms of location and retail composition.

Mixed-Use Center A **mixed-use center**, or *MXD*, is a retail, office, parking, and hotel complex that sometimes includes a convention center, and/or a high-rise condominium or apartment complex in one sprawling development. MXDs were often part of revitalization projects to salvage decaying cities. The MXD's retail component was an

Figure 3.5

Perimeter Mall is a superregional center in Atlanta, Georgia, with four anchors and more than 100 other shops, services, and restaurants. *Courtesy of The Rouse Company.*

effort to maintain the CBD as a viable shopping district. Airwalks often connected the MXD to local department stores and other retail complexes. Though many urban MXDs have been successful as office and hotel facilities, most never realized their developers' expectations as retail centers.

MXDs have been catalysts for development in suburban areas as integral parts of planned suburban communities in high-growth, densely populated areas. *Washington Post* reporter, Joel Garreau, has dubbed these areas *edge cities*, mini-metropolises that have sprung up along interstate highways within the shadows of major urban cores.[12, 13]

Pedestrian Mall A **pedestrian mall** is an open-air shopping district created by closing off the streets within a group of blocks to create a park-like ambiance of trees and benches. Pedestrian malls were an attempt by urban planners to recapture the business that downtown shopping districts were losing to suburban centers by emulating the freedom and safety that customers enjoy walking from store to store in enclosed shopping centers. The first pedestrian mall was built in Kalamazoo, Michigan, in 1959. Other examples include Fresno's Fulton Mall, the Mid-America Mall in Memphis, and Miami Beach's Lincoln Road Mall.

Unfortunately, pedestrian malls were not the answer to the declining retail business of the CBD. Critics of the concept claim that pedestrian malls hamper retail business because of the confusing traffic patterns created by rerouting vehicular traffic. Some pedestrian malls have been converted back to conventional paved roadways with sidewalks.[14]

A close kin of the pedestrian mall is the *transit mall*, which is a pedestrian mall closed to traffic except public transportation. Minneapolis' Nicollet Mall and Chicago's State Street Mall are examples of this concept.[15, 16]

Festival Marketplace A **festival marketplace**, or *urban specialty center*, is a shopping center composed of specialty stores, pushcart peddlers, and walkaway food merchants that is often a tourist attraction within a city's cultural and entertainment center. Festival centers are sometimes a creative reuse of abandoned warehouses or factories, such San Francisco's Ghirardelli Square, a converted chocolate factory with a view of Golden Gate Bridge. Other urban specialty centers include Boston's Quincy Market and Faneuil Hall Marketplace, New York's South Street Seaport, Baltimore's Harborplace, and Miami's Bayside. The Rouse Company of Columbia, Maryland, is the reputed innovator and leading developer of festival marketplaces.

Figure 3.6

The Rouse Company is the leading developer of festival marketplaces. Their properties include Boston's Faneuil Hall and New Orleans' Riverwalk. *Courtesy of The Rouse Company.*

Outlet Center An **outlet center** is a strip or enclosed center with a tenant mix composed of factory outlet stores. Originally attracting retailers of moderately priced goods, such as Van Heusen shirts and Hanes underwear, an increasing number of producers of upscale merchandise now operate outlet stores. The tenants of Woodbury Common in Central Valley, New York, include Dansk, Charles Jourdan, Donna Karan, Mark Cross, Waterford, and Gucci.

Outlet centers are experiencing significant growth as manufacturers recognize the advantages of vertical integration. To avoid conflict between manufacturers and their conventional retail channels, outlet centers are often located in excess of 50 miles from traditional distribution channels, though some recently developed centers fall within this geographic boundary.[17]

Outlet centers are destination centers to which customers drive an average of 125 miles and where tour buses are the mainstay of marketing programs. The Lake Erie Outlet Center is located 50 miles from Cleveland and Toledo, and 100 miles from Columbus. The center benefits from its proximity to the Lake Erie vacation area, which annually attracts 7.5 million tourists.[18, 19, 20, 21, 22] Though manufacturers' outlets represent the majority in an outlet center's tenant mix, off-pricers are

Figure 3.7

Woodbury Common in Central Valley, New York, is an outlet center with an upscale mix of stores. *Courtesy of Fairchild Publications, Inc.*

also becoming more common in these centers, leading some to refer to an outlet center as an *off-price center* or a *value-oriented center*.

Power Center A **power center** is typically an open-air center with a tenant mix of big-box discounters, such as category killers, warehouse clubs, off-pricers, full-line discounters, and supercenters. The mix is sometimes supplemented by a strip of smaller stores with a food supermarket and/or full-line discounter. Becoming popular in the mid-1980s, the genre grew quickly through the 1990s. Power centers, like strip centers, operate on a low-cost of occupancy structure. The centers are often located near a superregional center in an effort to feed off its traffic.[23]

Power centers rely on the consumer's interest in value shopping versus recreational or fashion shopping. Because each store in a power center is a destination store, there is less browsing, cross shopping, and comparison shopping from store to store than there is in a mall. As destination centers, power centers claim that 85 percent of power-center shoppers buy something upon each visit, versus only 50 percent of mall shoppers.[24, 25, 26, 27]

Survival of the Fittest

The growth of the shopping-center industry in the United States has been explosive. In 1960, there were 4500 shopping centers in the United States. By 1990, the number had increased to 36,650, a growth rate

Figure 3.8

A power center is typically an open-air center with a tenant mix of big-box discounters.

higher than the growth rate of the population, retail sales, or any other economic indicator.[28] Most observers concur that the marketplace is saturated with shopping centers. Atlanta-based Equitable Real Estate Investment Management, Inc. predicts that several hundred regional malls will close during the early years of the twenty-first century.[29] Most experts concur that future shopping-center development will be the renovation, expansion, and new use of existing centers, and not ground-up construction of new centers.[30]

Over the years, many shopping centers have had to reinvent themselves to remain viable in the light of new competition and changing customer needs. Strip centers are a good example of the type of resiliency needed to remain competitive in a saturated marketplace. Before the era of enclosed centers, strip centers were often anchored by department-store *branches* that offered the same breadth of selection as their urban counterparts but considerably less depth.[31] In the 1960s, most department stores abandoned strip centers for larger units at regional or super-regional centers. More recently, industry consolidation among full-line discount stores caused additional strip-center vacancies.

As times changed, many strip centers aggressively replaced department stores with emerging discount-store formats, such as off-pricers and category killers. Strip-center owners touted their heavily trafficked locations and low-cost rent structures, as well as a claim that strip centers attract time-pressed destination shoppers more likely to purchase than the browsers who shop regional or superregional centers.[32, 33] Some strip centers strengthened their market position as destination centers by adding office space for physicians and dentists. Others enhanced their image as value-oriented centers by building out-parcel units for big-box tenants such as warehouse clubs.[34]

Landscaping, better signage, and improved ingress and egress have made many strip centers pleasant shopping destinations.[35,36] Today, strip centers are the preferred location of many retailers, including some that have abandoned malls in favor of strip centers. Lechters, the nation's largest housewares specialist, has replaced more than 60 mall-based stores with 25 larger strip-center stores.[37]

Many regional centers have had to reinvent themselves in the light of growing competition from superregional centers.[38] Like strip centers, some regional centers have repositioned themselves as value-oriented centers by replacing shuttered department stores with category killers, off-pricers, and full-line discounters.[39, 40, 41] Having lost Sears to an abutting superregional center, South Hills Mall in Poughkeepsie,

Source:

1 *Sonnenfeld, S. (May 1999). Deep South's defining center.* Shopping Center World. *pp. 222–223.*

C o m p a n y   P r o f i l e   3 . 1

Lenox Square — The Evolution of a Shopping Emporium

Lenox Square is as much a part of Atlanta's history as Coca-Cola, Delta Air Lines, and *Gone with the Wind*. Located in Atlanta's upscale Buckhead neighborhood, Lenox Square has become both a major tourist attraction, and a catalyst for development. But Lenox Square wasn't always so perceived. When scouting for tenants in 1959, the center's developers had a hard time convincing Atlanta's retail community that the wave of its future was in a 665,000-square-foot open-air shopping center in a relatively undeveloped part of town.

As Buckhead grew, Lenox Square enjoyed a retail monopoly until 1969 when Phipps Plaza opened diagonally across the street. The opening of the two-level enclosed center marked the beginning of a rivalry that would brew between the two centers and would last until 1998 when they were both acquired by Indianapolis-based Simon Property Group. But until its marriage to Phipps Plaza, Lenox Square fought hard to retain its position as Buckhead's premier shopping destination. In 1972, it underwent its first major expansion. The center was enclosed and Neiman Marcus was added as an anchor along with 50 new specialty stores. In 1980, a 90,000-square-foot food court was created, and in 1987 approximately 40,000 square feet of new retail space was added. The last major expansion occurred in 1993 when the center underwent a $60 million makeover that included the addition of a 187,000-square-foot upper level.

Now that both Lenox Square and Phipps Plaza have common ownership, they are marketed collaboratively making Buckhead one of the nation's most renowned shopping areas.[1]

New York, leased its anchor locations to Burlington Coat Factory and a supermarket.[42] Some regional centers have created a community-center ambiance with libraries, dry cleaners, post offices, veterinary clinics, and health clubs.[43, 44] The Bergen Mall in Paramus, New Jersey has a chapel that draws as many as 400 worshipers to daily services.[45]

The Mix of Stores in a Shopping Center

A shopping center's tenant mix is often the result of a carefully executed marketing strategy. Leasing agents maximize the number of customers drawn to a center with a synergistic mix of stores that offer a broad selection of merchandise categories, brands, and services.

The strategy for composing a tenant mix is based on the nature of the competition between tenants. Stores that are **directly competing** offer the same merchandise. **Indirectly competing** stores offer the same type of merchandise, but different selections of prices and brands. **Complementary stores** stimulate each other's sales. An apparel store and a shoe store are complementary in that the sale of a new outfit in the apparel store might stimulate the sale of a pair of shoes in the shoe store.

The ideal tenant mix includes indirectly competing and complementary stores. As indirect competitors, J.C. Penney and Lord & Taylor contribute to a center's breadth of selection and attractiveness to a diverse group of customers. Complementary stores enhance customer convenience and one-stop shopping. Direct competition fails to enhance business in a shopping center in that the directly competing stores cannibalize each other's sales.

A tenant mix must be consistent with a center's desired image and the type of customer that the center hopes to attract. A *value-oriented center* is well represented by off-pricers and manufacturers' outlets. The term *fashion center* implies the presence of upscale apparel stores, such as Victoria's Secret and Banana Republic. Anchors strongly influence a shopping center's image. A center anchored by J.C. Penney and Sears conveys a moderate-price image. A center anchored by Nordstrom and Bloomingdale's conveys an upscale image.[46]

To ensure compatibility with other stores in a center, some retailers have **cotenancy requirements**. As an upscale retailer of home furnishings and accessories, Crate and Barrel's cotenancy requirements include the presence of other prestigious stores, such as Ann Taylor, Banana Republic, and Coach, and at least one fashion-oriented department store, such as Lord & Taylor.[47]

SUMMARY POINTS

- Unplanned shopping areas include central business districts, secondary business districts, and town centers.
- Planned shopping centers include open-air neighborhood and community centers, called strips, and enclosed regional and superregional centers called malls.
- Other types of planned centers include mixed-use centers, pedestrian malls, outlet centers, and power centers.

- Some shopping centers struggle for survival in the light of keen competition and an over-stored marketplace.
- An ideal mix of stores in a shopping center includes indirectly competing and complementary stores.

FOR DISCUSSION

1. Identify the following types of shopping districts/centers in your local area and the stores that are in each:

   town center   community center
   neighborhood center   power center

2. Identify a regional and superregional center in your area. How do they compare in terms of the number of anchors and the types of stores? The number of stores? At which center do you prefer to shop? Why?

3. Identify an MXD in a familiar city. Assess its retail component. Assess the retail environment of the CBD in which the MXD is located.

KEY TERMS AND CONCEPTS

central business district   indirect competition   secondary business
community center   mixed-use center   district
complementary stores   neighborhood center   shopping center
cotenancy requirement   outlet center   strip center
direct competition   pedestrian mall   superregional center
festival marketplace   power center   town center
free-standing store   regional center

ENDNOTES

1. The predecessor of Lerner New York, now a division of The Limited.
2. Ghosh, A. & McLafferty, S. (Fall 1991). The shopping center: A restructuring of post-war retailing. *Journal of Retailing*, 67, 3. pp. 253–267.
3. Lockwood, C. (February 1998). Suburban Main Street gaining favor. *Shopping Centers Today*. pp. 23–24.
4. Reda, S. (June 1997). Back to Main Street. *Stores*. pp. 24–28.
5. Reidy, C. (May 28, 1998). Finding the city a pretty good buy. *The Boston Globe*. pp. D1, D5.
6. Howe, P. (January 31, 1999). After the sprawl. *The Boston Globe*. pp. C1, C3.
7. Staff. (1987). The evolution of regional shopping centers. Equitable Real Estate Investment Management.

8. Reynolds, M. (August 1990). Food courts: Tasty! *Stores*. pp. 52–54.

9. Webster defines a mall as a "shaded walk or public promenade" and a "shop-lined street for pedestrians only." Thus, a mall is not necessarily enclosed. Bal Harbour Shops is an upscale, open-air shopping center located north of Miami Beach, Florida. The open-air pedestrian walkways that connect the stores at Bal Harbor Shops are closed to vehicular traffic.

10. Doocey, P. (February 1992). Northeast rally. *Stores*. pp. 67–69.

11. Pearson, B. (August 1993). The times, they are a changing. *Stores*. p. 73.

12. Garreau, J. (1991). *Edge City: Life on the New Frontier*. New York: Doubleday.

13. Peterson, E. (January 1986). MXD-mall excitement. *Stores*. pp. 144–146, 151–152, 187.

14. Steinhauer, J. (November 5, 1996). When shoppers walk away from pedestrian malls. *The New York Times*. pp. D1, D4.

15. Houstoun, L. (June 1990). From street to mall and back again. *Planning*. pp. 4–10.

16. Robertson, K. (December 1990). The status of the pedestrian mall in American downtowns. *Urban Affairs Quarterly*, 26, 2. pp. 250–273.

17. Staff. (August 1998). Outlet malls: Do they deliver the goods? *Consumer Reports*. pp. 20–25.

18. Apfel, I. (July 1996). What is an outlet center. *American Demographics*. pp. 14–15.

19. Hogan, B. (September 1996). Outlet evolution. A special supplement to *Shopping Centers Today*. pp. S3–S4.

20. Bredin, A. (March 1992). Outlet centers prosper. *Stores*. pp. 63–65.

21. Morgenson, G. (May 27, 1991). Cheapie Gucci. *Forbes*. pp. 43–44.

22. Staff. (April 1990) Factory outlet centers keep their distance. *Chain Store Age Executive*. pp. 39–42.

23. Robaton, A. (May 1996). Power centers may be losing momentum, experts caution. *Shopping Centers Today*. pp. 1, 16, 188.

24. McCloud, J. (August 1994). Power center development explodes across U.S. *Shopping Center World*. pp. 34–41.

25. Staff. (September 1986). Power centers: Everybody wins. *Chain Store Age Executive*. pp. 35–40.

26. Staff. (November 18, 1992). Power centers fast and focused. *Women's Wear Daily*. pp. 14, 18.

27. International Council of Shopping Centers. (May 1994). *Research Quarterly*. Vol. 1, No. 1.

28. Ghosh, A. & McLafferty, S. (Fall 1991). The shopping center: A restructuring of post-war retailing. *Journal of Retailing*, 67, 3. pp. 253–267.

29. Mander, E. (May 1997). Regional malls: Aging or ageless? *Shopping Centers Today*. pp. 107, 110, 220.

30. Moin, D. (October 31, 1995). The great mall sprawl. *Women's Wear Daily*. pp. 10–11.

31. Many branches were in fact *twigs*, stores that offered only a limited number of merchandise categories available in the flagship.

32. Walker, C. (October 1991). Strip malls: plain but powerful. *American Demographics*. pp. 48–51.

33. Edelson, S. (August 9, 1995). Strip centers: The chain reaction. *Women's Wear Daily*.

34. Robaton, A. (October 1995). Strip center execs seeks service tenants. *Shopping Centers Today*. p. 57.

35. Staff. (December 1995). Community Centers thrive despite retail turmoil. *Stores*. pp. 46–47.

36. Peterson, E. (March 1990). Strip centers: Changing? *Stores*. pp. 53–54.

37. Duff, M. (March 23, 1998). Lechters to exit mall locations in favor of strip centers. *Discount Store News*.

38. Edelson, S. (January 22, 1997). Shopping-mall mania: cannibalizing a market that's already glutted. *Women's Wear Daily*. pp. 1, 8–9.

39. Mander, E. (February 1997). Malls and big-box tenants are finding common ground. *Shopping Centers Today*. pp. 1, 7.

40. Peterson, E. (February 1990). The 1990s: What's ahead. *Stores*. pp. 73–76.

41. Edelson, S. (August 9, 1995). A new hybrid: The category killer moves in. *Women's Wear Daily*. p. 8.

42. Rudnitsky, H. (March 30, 1992). Battle of the malls. *Forbes*. pp. 46–47.

43. Schneiderman, I. (November 25, 1997). Changes urged for regionals. *Women's Wear Daily*. p. 13.

44. Muhlebach, R. (May 1998). Retail cycle through the decades. *Shopping Center World*. pp. 70–80.

45. Edelson, S. (May 8, 1996). Regional malls borrow town square concept as apparel sales fall. *Women's Wear Daily*. pp. 1, 8–9.

46. Campbell, J. (Summer 1996). Time to shop. *Regional Review*, a publication of the Federal Reserve Bank of Boston. p. 12.

47. Staff. (May 1996). Refurnishing the mall. *Shopping Centers Today*. pp. 29–48.

chapter four

RETAIL GROWTH AND EXPANSION

Bigger is often better in today's retail environment. Large retail organizations have distinct competitive advantages over smaller retailers because of their dominance of the marketplace and the clout that they exert with suppliers.[1] To remain competitive, aggressive retail organizations continually pursue growth opportunities by opening stores in new markets, buying existing retail enterprises, and developing new formats or merchandising concepts. Chapter 4 covers some of the strategies used by retailers to position themselves for continued growth.

After you have read this chapter, you will be able to discuss:

The impact of centralization on operational and fiscal efficiency.

Retail expansion strategies.

The importance of international retailing.

Opportunities for independent retailers.

CENTRALIZATION

Centralization is an organizational strategy used by companies to enhance fiscal and operational efficiency. **Centralization** involves performing functions affecting an organization's remote operations from a central location, usually a corporate office. In a retail organization, *centralized buying* means that the process of buying merchandise to resell in stores within a multistore organization is orchestrated from a corporate office. **Decentralization** is the opposite of centralization. *Decentralized buying* means that individual stores within a multistore organization are responsible for buying their own merchandise.

Centralization is a concept fundamental to the success of many retailers. To understand the impact of centralization, consider the following scenario:

Sydney Todd is the owner of five children's specialty stores in Florida called Monkeys and Pumpkins. Sydney opened her first store on Fort Lauderdale's Los Olas Boulevard in 1995. The store's immediate success spurred the opening of a second store in Palm Beach, and subsequent stores in South Miami Beach, Key West, and St. Augustine. Sydney's expansion plans are aggressive. She hopes to open stores in Savannah, Naples, and Charleston within the next year. Within five years, Sydney hopes to increase the Monkeys and Pumpkins' portfolio of stores to 20.

Figure 4.1

Existing Monkeys and Pumpkins locations.

Syndey has a constant eye open for talented people to run new stores. Monkeys and Pumpkins' store managers have considerable responsibility. Though the stores have a common identity, they function autonomously. The manager at each store is fully responsible for merchandising and operating his/her store with the assistance of an office and selling staff.

The organizational strategy that Sydney has adopted to operate her stores is rare. In multistore retail organizations, functions not requiring customer proximity are often centralized in a corporate office. Individual stores perform only those activities directly related to selling, and the operational activities of maintaining the store and inventory. Functions, such as buying, accounting, and sales promotion, are executed centrally.

The Advantages of Centralization

To understand the advantages of centralization, consider the positive results of Sydney Todd's decision to centralize Monkeys and Pumpkins' buying functions at an office facility in Orlando.

- Redundancies are reduced. Prior to centralization five buyer/managers shopped the wholesale childrenswear markets and processed five sets of orders. By centralizing, one buyer can cover the same markets and process a single set of orders for all stores.
- Specialization is fostered. Prior to centralization, five buyer/managers performed a diverse range of merchandising and operational functions. In a centralized organization, buyers devote their undivided attention to buying. As centralized organizations grow, job functions are often split into more specialized functions. Syndey may find that her expansion plans will require hiring additional buyers. At this point, the single childrenswear buying function might be split into more specialized functions by defining buying responsibilities according to childrenswear market segments, such as boys, girls, and infants.
- Expenses are reduced. Though operating a central organization is costly, Sydney has more than offset the cost of operating a corporate office by eliminating the merchandising functions in each of the stores.
- Quantity discounts are realized. The buyer/managers wrote orders for *hundreds* of items. The central buyer now writes orders for *thousands* of items, thus qualifying for the price incentives that suppliers offer to companies that place large orders.

Figure 4.2

Centralization has laid the groundwork for future expansion at Monkeys and Pumpkins.

- Consistency among stores is enhanced. The selections at Monkeys and Pumpkins were inconsistent from one location to another when each store's assortments were chosen by different buyer/managers. With one buyer maintaining assortments for all stores, Monkeys and Pumpkins' image is more consistent from one location to another.
- Groundwork for expansion is laid. The inventory needs of the new stores that Sydney is planning can be served by the existing central buying structure without having to add additional staff.

Advancements in transportation and communication have facilitated centralization. The Interstate Highway Act of 1955 enabled the construction of an infrastructure to receive goods at national and regional distribution centers and then to expediently transport them to a network of stores. Computer systems that track sales and inventory activity at hundreds of retail locations, triggering orders for the immediate replenishment of goods as they are sold, have made it possible to orchestrate the buying function for a vast complex of stores from a single location.

In spite of the many positive outcomes that result from centralization, there are some that decry it, claiming that centralization strips stores of their ability to respond to local market conditions.[2] In response to this dilemma, some retailers adopt a decentralized or regional merchandising approach. Dillard's is a highly successful department-store chain that groups stores by geographic regions defined by climate and customer profile. Each region has a buying organization to serve that region. The company feels that regional differences require different merchandise assortments and that customers' needs are best met when buyers are close to the point of sale.

J.C. Penney reaps the efficiencies of centralized buying and the advantages of local control through a system in which corporate-level buyers show product lines to store-level merchandisers using an electronic-satellite system before placing orders with their vendors. The store-level merchandisers determine their individual store's assortments by style, size and color based on local tastes, demographics and climate, as well as on information provided by the corporate buyer that includes a ranking of items by sales potential. The corporate buyers make purchase commitments to their vendors based on the stores' assortment decisions. Though an interesting hybrid of both centralized and decentralized buying concepts, the system has its flaws. In 1998, J.C. Penney centralized buying for about a third of its merchandise so that buyers could make earlier commitments to suppliers, and to speed up the time that it takes to get merchandise onto the selling floor.[3, 4]

Centralization is not a new concept nor is it peculiar to retailing. The early variety-store chains were centralized operations. The strategy is applied in every industry with multiunit operations, including financial services, manufacturing, and service franchising.

RETAIL OWNERSHIP

Knowledge of a retail organization's ownership structure is fundamental to understanding its competitive position and potential for growth. Type of ownership is often tied to the manner in which a retail organization carries out its merchandising function and the way in which the organization is managed.

Ownership of a retail organization can be either public or private. A **public**, or *publicly held*, retail organization has many owners, or shareholders. A public company's stock is available to the general public and is sold, or traded, on a public stock exchange, such as the New York Stock Exchange (NYSE) or the American Stock Exchange (AMEX). The stock of a **private**, or *privately held*, retail organization is not traded on a public exchange. A private company has fewer owners than a public company, sometimes only one. The owners are sometimes a family, or they can be a group of investors within or outside the organization. When a publicly held organization is bought by private investors, the organization is said to be *taken private*.

Public companies often evolve from private companies. Private companies go *public* with an **initial public offering** (IPO) of stock on a public exchange. The money obtained from the sale of stock is used as capital to expand the organization. From its 1998 IPO, the T. Eton Co. raised nearly $200 million in capital to finance refurbishing its stores. The Toronto-based department-store chain had been family-owned since 1869.[5]

By going public, the original owners relinquish some of their control over the organization in that, as owners, the new shareholders acquire voting power that can be exercised in the organization's decision making. The original owners of a public company can retain voting control in the organization by retaining ownership of more than 50 percent of the company's stock. The Dillard family owns a majority of the stock of Dillard Department Stores.

The term *independent* is often used to refer to a single, privately owned store. However, privately held multistore retailers are also "independent." Though small retail organizations are likely to be private, and large organizations are likely to be public, size is not an absolute indication of public or private ownership.

Chains and Coglomerates

A retail organization is often dubbed relative to the number of stores that it operates. A **chain** of retail stores is two or more stores with the same ownership and identity. The word chain is often used to refer to a

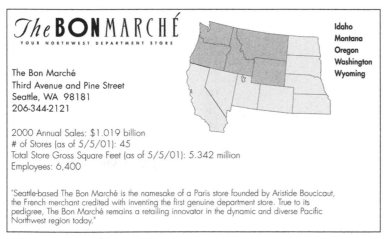

Figure 4.3

A regional chain operates stores within a specific region of the country. *Courtesy of Federated Department Stores, Inc.*

large group of value-oriented stores, such as Sears or Kmart. However, a chain can be as few as two stores and the use of the term is irrelevant to type of retail format. Chains are classified as local, regional, or national, relative to their geographic span of stores:

- A local chain operates stores within a narrow geographic area, usually defined by a city and its outlying areas.
- A regional chain operates stores within a region or regions of the country, such as the Southwest, or Northeast.
- A national chain operates stores in virtually every region of the country.

As retail companies grow, they often become part of organizational structures that further enhance their growth. A **conglomerate** is an organization that unites the ownership of independently operated **subsidiaries**, or *operating divisions*. A conglomerate is often referred to as a *parent company*, or *parent organization*. Federated Department Stores is one of the oldest retail conglomerates in the United States. Founded in 1929, Federated united the ownership of New York's Abraham & Strauss and Bloomingdale's, Cincinnati's Lazarus Department Stores, and Boston's Filene's. Today, Federated's portfolio of stores includes more than 400 department stores in six operating divisions that still includes Bloomingdale's, as well as New York-

Figure 4.4

Founded in 1929, Federated Department Stores is one of the oldest existing retail conglomerates. *Courtesy of Federated Department Stores, Inc.*

based Macy's, Miami-based Burdines, Atlanta-based Rich's, and Seattle-based The Bon Marche.

The operating divisions in a conglomerate remain autonomous though a conglomerate is often organized to perform centralized functions for its operating divisions. Federated Merchandising (FM) is the division of Federated Department Stores responsible for developing merchandising programs for the Federated operating divisions. FM provides leadership in the areas of merchandise systems, visual presentation, inventory-management, and merchandise distribution. FM is also responsible for coordinating private-label programs for all Federated divisions.

Though operating divisions within a conglomerate are essentially autonomous, the level of centralized authority exercised by the conglomerate over the operating divisions varies from one organization to another. May Department Stores is a highly centralized conglomerate. Though May's operating divisions have different banners, including Foley's of Houston, Filene's of Boston, and Hecht's of Washington, D.C., functions such including store design, operating systems, and television advertising are coordinated centrally at May's St. Louis headquarters.[6, 7]

A retail organization can be decentralized at conglomerate level but centralized at division level. The operating divisions of The Limited, Inc. have complete merchandising and operational autonomy.[8] Though financial controls are administered centrally, each division develops its own merchandising strategy independent of the parent company. Though The Limited is a decentralized conglomerate, its operating divisions are highly centralized. Store operations are rigidly orchestrated through operating manuals, floor plans, and other forms of communication disseminated from each division's Columbus, Ohio headquarters

In general, a high degree of centralization is often associated with a conglomerate's success. Federated Department Stores was once a highly decentralized conglomerate. Each division operated as a distinct retail entity with little control by Federated's Cincinnati headquarters. However, Federated's failure to eliminate organizational redundancies with a higher degree of centralization led to a decline in profitability during the early 1980s. Federated's depressed stock value made it ripe for a takeover by the bargain-hunting Campeau Corporation, a Toronto-based real-estate company.[9, 10]

RETAIL GROWTH AND EXPANSION

A basic tenet of organizational development is that companies need to grow in order to survive. Retailers grow through mergers and acquisitions. A **merger** occurs when two or more companies are combined to form a new organization. When two organizations are merged, or *consolidated*, the corporate structure of one company, typically the weaker or smaller, is dissolved leaving a single corporate structure to support both companies. In 1969, The Dayton Company of Minneapolis merged with J.L. Hudson's of Detroit to form the Dayton Hudson Corporation.[11] In 2000, the conglomerate was renamed the Target Corporation to reflect the identity of its stellar-performing full-line discount-store operation.[12]

Not every merger is a perfect union. In 1988, Ames Department Stores acquired Zayre, another full-line discounter. The intent was to gradually infuse the Zayre stores with Ames' corporate culture while allowing them to retain their identity. However, the incompatibility between Ames and Zayre became evident quickly. Ames' nonpromotional pricing strategy alienated Zayre customers who were accustomed to a barrage of sale events. The results were disastrous. Ames filed bankruptcy in 1990, and closed most of the Zayre stores before emerging from bankruptcy in 1993. In 1999, Ames acquired the 155-unit Hills Department Stores becoming the nation's fourth largest full-line discounter. Instead of operating two distinct formats, Ames converted the Hills to Ames prototypes making for a much happier marriage.[13, 14]

Operating divisions within a conglomerate are sometimes merged for the sake of operational efficiency.[15] The 1998 merger of Saks Fifth Avenue and Proffitt's resulted in a $75 million annual savings achieved through leveraging the costs of advertising media, insurance, packing and wrapping supplies, logistics, product sourcing and several back-office operations including the credit, real-estate, and legal departments,[16, 17]

Acquisitions

Some retail organizations grow by buying other organizations. An **acquisition**, or *takeover* or *buyout*, is the purchase of one organization by another. Toys "R" Us acquired Baby Superstore, a 70-unit category killer of infant apparel, toys and furniture, to extend the market presence of its Babies "R" Us operation to an additional 20 states.[18]

Acquisitions are typical of a department store's growth strategy in that department stores have reached a saturation point in most markets with few opportunities for building new stores. Porffitt's is an Alcoa, Tennessee-based department-store chain that has grown considerably in recent years through the acquisition of regional department-store chains including Younkers (DesMoines), Parisian (Birmingham), Carson Pirie Scott (Chicago), and Hernberger's (St. Cloud). Dillard Department Stores has pursued a similar growth strategy. By its 1998 acquisition of Mercantile Stores, Dillard's simultaneously entered the Cincinnati market and strengthened its market position in Denver.[19]

Figure 4.5

Toys "R" Us is a diversified retail conglomerate that operates Toy "R" Us, Kids "R" Us, and Babies "R" Us.

Sometimes the organization being acquired is happy about being bought, recognizing organizational or merchandising compatibility or that the acquiring organization is in a position to provide financing to an otherwise poorly capitalized or fiscally troubled company. In this case, the acquisition is called a **friendly takeover**, and the acquiring company a **friendly suitor**. However, the organization being acquired may be unhappy about being bought out fearing organizational or merchandising incompatibility, or the loss of jobs due to organizational streamlining. An acquisition resisted by the organization being acquired is called a **hostile takeover**.

A **bidding war** sometimes ensues between two or more parties interested in acquiring the same organization. The parties attempt to outbid each other by a series of counteroffers often resulting in the sale of an organization's stock for a price greater than its worth. In 1988, the Campeau Corporation offered the shareholders of Federated Department Stores $4.2 billion for the company. As a result of a two-month bidding war with Macy's, Campeau paid $6.6 billion for Federated, a price far greater than the value of the company.

Acquisitions are sometimes defined by who the buyers are, or by the terms of financing. An **internal buyout** is the acquisition of an

Sources:

1 Barmash, I. (August 5, 1995). *Restructurings create retail niches.* Shopping Centers Today. *pp. 4, 27.*

2 Logan, S. (January 1995). *The small store—a struggle to survive.* Retail Issues Letter.

3 Frantz, J. (December 1997). *Surviving and thriving in big box's shadow.* SCT Retailing Today. *p. 43.*

4 Staff. (June 21, 1995). *A 12-step program to revive fashion.* Women's Wear Daily. *pp. 1, 6–9.*

5 D'innocenzio, A. (June 25, 1997). *Small stores discover niche marketing can be gateway to survival.* Women's Wear Daily. *pp. 1, 6–7.*

OPPORTUNITIES FOR SMALL STORES

The dominance of the marketplace by large retail corporations is obvious even to the casual observer. These *power retailers* have definite competitive advantages over small independently owned retailers. A power retailer's broad selections, deep assortments, and low prices are certainly difficult to match. However, in spite of the formidable presence of large-scale retailers, the marketplace abounds with many opportunities for independent retailers. Independent retailers can differentiate themselves by offering unique items not available in large stores. Many vendors too small to conduct business with large retailers are anxious to have independent retailers as customers.[1, 2, 3] Independents can respond to local events, regional tastes, and weather conditions in a way that power retailers cannot.[4] Vivienne Tam is an upscale female-apparel resource that likes working with its specialty-store customers finding them more spontaneous and less bureaucratic than department stores.[5]

organization by its employees. In 1986, 348 Macy's executives acquired Macy's from its shareholders in the largest internal buyout of any retail organization in history. An acquisition financed through debt is called a **leveraged buyout** (LBO). The Campeau Corporation paid over $11 billion for the acquisitions of Allied Stores and Federated Department Stores in 1986 and 1988 respectively. The acquisitions were financed primarily through debt, a problem that caught up with Campeau and its creditors shortly thereafter.

Divestiture is the sale of an organization's assets. Retail organizations divest themselves of stores or entire operating divisions to generate capital or to concentrate on other areas of business. Federated Department Stores sold two specialty-store divisions, Aeropostale and Charter Club, to concentrate on its core department-store business.[20] Unprofitable units or divisions are also likely candidates for divestiture.

The Federal Trade Commission (FTC) is a regulatory agency that reviews all proposals for acquisitions and mergers. The FTC monitors unfair competition and determines if the resulting organization will restrict competition by its dominance in the marketplace. In 1998, the FTC blocked the merger of Office Depot and Staples claiming that the synergies created by merging the two office-supply superstores would be an unfair competitive advantage to smaller competitors.[21]

Diversification

Diversification is an organizational growth strategy that involves entering a line of business that differs from present businesses. Organizations diversify when they perceive limited growth within their existing businesses or when they endeavor to serve the needs of new groups of customers. Target Corporation is a diversified conglomerate with a portfolio of stores that includes four formats:

- A fashion-oriented full-line discount-store division called Target
- An upscale department-store division called Marshall Field's
- A value-oriented specialty department-store division called Mervyn's
- A direct-marketing division called Rivertown Trading Company that produces catalogs such as Wireless and Signals.

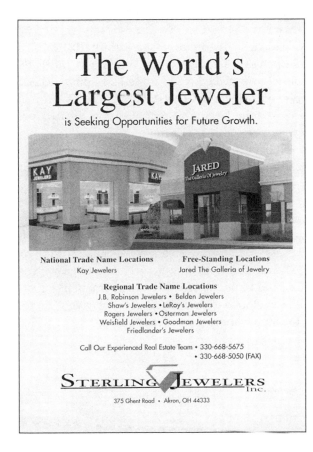

Figure 4.6

Sterling Jewelers is a diversified retailer that operates a free-standing format, a national mall-based format, and a host of regional mall-based formats. *Courtesy of Sterling Jewelers, Inc.*

Diversified companies insulate themselves against environmental changes that may affect their existing businesses. Recognizing the potential of direct marketing and e-commerce, Federated Department Stores acquired Fingerhut, a direct-marketing retailer, to take advantage of Fingerhut's expertise in catalog and Internet retailing with the intent of growing Federated's existing direct-marketing enterprises such as Macy's by Mail and Macys.com.[22, 23]

Some retail organizations diversify by developing new merchandising concepts. The Venator Group, Inc., formerly the Woolworth Corporation, is a retail conglomerate that has grown by developing a diversified portfolio of more than 20 merchandising concepts including Northern Reflections, Champs Sports, and various Foot Locker formats. Experimenting with new concepts is a chancy business. Though some Venator concepts, such as Foot Locker, have been instant success stories, other merchandising experiments have fizzled. Face Fantasies, a value-priced cosmetics outlet; Frame Scenes, a retailer of prints and frames; and J. Brannam, a discount apparel chain, are among Venator's fatalities.[24]

Developing new merchandising concepts too closely related to existing concepts may lead to a dilemma called **cannibalization**. In 1988, The Limited Inc. opened Cacique, a French-inspired intimate-apparel store that too closely mimicked The Limited's highly successful Victoria's Secret. Cacique never realized The Limited's growth expectations and was closed in 1998.[25] Cannibalization also occurs when a chain opens new stores too close to existing stores.

Some large-format retailers diversify by spinning off scaled-down formats. For areas not large enough to support a full-line store, Saks Fifth Avenue created smaller versions of its prestigious specialty department-store concept: Saks "main street" stores for the town centers of affluent communities, and Saks "resort stores" for prestigious vacation spots, including Southampton, New York; Palm Beach; and Carmel-by-the-Sea.[26, 27] Staples Express is a modified version of Staples' big-box format that caters to the needs of offices in large urban settings such as Washington, D.C.; Boston; and Philadelphia.[28] To complement its superstore format, Circuit City developed a mall-based concept called Circuit City Express featuring the store's more gift-oriented items.[29]

BANKRUPTCY

Unfortunately, a discussion of the growth and expansion of retail organizations is incomplete without a discussion of bankruptcy. **Bankruptcy** occurs when an organization becomes insolvent or incapable of paying its debts. In essence, an organization is bankrupt when its liabilities exceed its assets. The Federal Bankruptcy Act was enacted in 1898 to establish guidelines for insolvent debtors to pay their creditors. The act was written in sections or chapters; the most often cited is Chapter 11.[30]

In 1978, Federal Bankruptcy Laws were rewritten to "protect" companies from their creditors by prohibiting their petitioning a court for liquidation of a debtor's assets to pay its debts. Chapter 11 freezes a debtor's indebtedness to lending institutions, suppliers, and bond holders. The debtor organization retains its assets for use in a **plan of reorganization** (POR) designed to help the debtor regain profitability.[31] Some of the actions typical of a POR include:

- Terminating the organization's leadership, and hiring a "turn-around" leader with a track record of rescuing ailing retailers.
- Closing unprofitable stores.
- Implementing expense-saving measures.
- Selling unprofitable units or divisions. The sell-off infuses the company with cash to reduce debt, and generally results in a smaller but better-focused organization.[32]

Because its pre-Chapter 11 debts are frozen, a bankrupt retailer starts with a clean slate and can obtain a new line of credit from lending institutions to continue shipments from suppliers. Creditors are willing to extend credit to the retailer since Chapter 11 guarantees that indebtedness incurred after the Chapter 11 filing will receive priority payment, taking precedence over the payment of any old debt. Emergence from bankruptcy occurs when the company becomes profitable. Pre-Chapter 11 debts are settled by offering creditors equity in the company as partial debt payment. Thus, the creditors become the owners of the company. When Barneys New York came out of bankruptcy, its creditors ended up owning 93.5 percent of the equity in a reorganized company.[33]

Many retail bankruptcies are rooted in leveraged buyouts. The financing for these acquisitions is often obtained by using the assets of the organization as collateral to borrow from lending institutions and the issue of high-yield, high-risk **junk bonds**[34] The interest payments on these large debts puts an added expense burden on the retailers. When business goes sour for any period of time, sales can no longer support the interest payments. Much of the funding for the Campeau Corporation's purchase of Allied Stores and Federated Department Stores was through junk bonds that carried an annual interest debt of

$600 million. Eventually, the merged Allied/Federated was unable to meet its interest payments. The company filed bankruptcy owing more than $8 billion to more than 40,000 creditors.[35]

Critics of the Federal Bankruptcy Laws claim that the 1978 revisions to Chapter 11 encourage reckless management, knowing that the government shields bankrupt companies from their creditors. Some feel that retailers often file Chapter 11 to rectify poor management decisions.[36, 37] Shopping-center landlords are especially critical of Chapter 11 claiming that many retailers who file Chapter 11 do so to get out of bad leases.[38]

Why does the federal government "protect" organizations that have been haphazard in their fiscal management at the expense of creditors who, in good faith, financed and supplied the debtor? Consider the tragic alternative to Chapter 11: lost jobs, vacant storefronts, fewer points of distribution for suppliers, and fewer shopping alternatives for consumers.[39]

INTERNATIONAL RETAILING

Within a 25-year period, retail space in the United States grew exponentially, rising from 8 square feet per capita to a staggering 20 square feet per capita.[40] As the United States marketplace becomes saturated with retail stores, expansion in less competitive foreign markets has become a viable alternative to domestic growth.[41, 42] Assortment, convenience, and value make U.S. retailing very exportable to countries where limited selection, short shopping hours, and high prices are the norm.[43, 44] About 60 percent of the largest U.S. retailers operate internationally.[45]

Foreign Growth Opportunities

Several factors have made the global marketplace ripe for retail expansion. The North American Free Trade Agreement (NAFTA) created the world's largest free-trade zone between the United States, Canada, and Mexico, while the European Union (EU) has consolidated the European marketplace paving the way for expansion there.[46] Revisions of the General Agreement on Tariffs and Trade (GATT) have lowered tariffs worldwide and have opened doors to other foreign markets. A growing demand for Western goods has presented opportunities for retailers in

Company Profile 4.1

Zale — Making a Comeback

Irving, Texas-based Zale Corp. is the nation's largest specialty retailer of fine jewelry operating more than 700 stores in four divisions called Zales, Gordon's Jewelers, Bailey Banks & Biddle Fine, and Zales Outlet.

Within the next few years, the Zales division will itself grow to about 1000 stores. But the jeweler's success has not always been so clear cut. In 1992, Zale Corp. became overextended in debt and filed for Chapter 11 bankruptcy. As part of its plan of reorganization, the company closed approximately 700 unprofitable stores within its four divisions. The POR included the hiring of a new management team that would give the company a new direction. The team immediately embarked upon a merchandising strategy involving improving selection, quality, service, and merchandise presentation. The team introduced marketing strategies such a "Brilliant Buys" in which key items are value priced and promoted through advertising and in-store signage. The results were dazzling.

In 1993 Zale Corp. emerged from Chapter 11 bankruptcy a stronger and more competitive company. Today its objective is to become "The Gap of retail jewelers" a reachable goal if recent history is any indicator of future success.[1]

Source:
1 Staff. (November 1998). Zales Jewelers makes dazzling recovery. Shopping Centers Today. *p. 36.*

Asian countries, while emerging middle classes in Thailand, Indonesia, Maylasia, Hong Kong, and Singapore have attracted many U.S. retailers.[47] With a population of 950 million, India holds huge promise as a developing market.[48] China, with a quarter of the world's population, is yet another growth opportunity.[49, 50]

Foreign expansion is not as simple as domestic expansion. Often retailers must adapt their merchandising strategies to local consumer culture. Wal-Mart learned the hard way that Brazilian men do not wear white underwear, and that ice makers are slow-sellers in countries where cocktails are served straight up. In Chile, J.C. Penney misread local taste, which favors understated clothing, and offered expensive lines in the flashy colors popular in more tropical markets such as Miami and Mexico.[51] Gap found that French customers are smaller than U.S. customers, that Germans like dark colors, and that Europeans in general found greeters at the door intimidating.

Restrictive and inefficient governments add to the perils of foreign expansion. Some countries enact laws to restrict competition. Japan protects small, family-owned business with its Large-Scale Retail Stores Law that

Figure 4.7

As the United States marketplace becomes saturated with retail stores, expansion to foreign markets has become a viable alternative to domestic growth. *Sergio Dorantes/Corbis.*

makes it difficult for companies with large-store formats to enter the country. In France, retailers are banned from advertising on television on the theory that only hypermarkets can afford to buy TV time, putting small shops at a disadvantage.[52] Germany has laws that restrict evening, Saturday afternoon, and Sunday hours.[53] In some countries, approval of construction plans by governmental authorities can take as long as five years.[54]

Unstable economic conditions make foreign expansion risky. Between 1971 and 1973, Pier 1 opened stores in Australia, England, France, West Germany, and the Netherlands. The company closed the stores by the mid-1970s because of worldwide inflation and a deregulated exchange rate on the dollar.[55] Home Depot once scrapped plans to expand into Mexico because of the devaluation of the peso.[56]

Expansion to English-speaking countries is often the safest route for U.S. retailers. Zale's first foray into foreign expansion was the acquisition of Peoples Jewellers, Canada's leading fine jeweler.[57] For both language and cultural reasons, U.S. companies seeking to enter Europe typically open shop in Great Britain first.[58] Gap's first store was

Company Profile 4.2

Wal-Mart—At Home and Abroad

When Wal-Mart announced that it would try to sell donuts in a Wal-Mart store in China, experts warned them that Chinese customers would be turned off by the sweetness. As it turned out, Wal-Mart sold 10 million donuts in China during its first year of operation in that country. The outcome of that one experiment is typical of the surprising results of global experimentation by the world's largest retailer.

Acquisition is Wal-Mart's typical vehicle of entry into foreign markets especially when barriers to foreign entry prevail. Typically, the company likes to partner with a foreign retailer to learn the local customs before the actual acquisition takes place. The results can be disastrous otherwise.

In Brazil, Wal-Mart found that local customers like to string three shopping carts together while shopping, a practice that severely slows the checkout process. In Mexico, Wal-Mart buyers were perplexed by the fact that electric-stove accessories weren't selling. They then discovered that the vast majority of Mexican consumers cook with gas. However, Mexican consumers weren't entirely unwilling to adapt to U.S. purchase patterns. Bagels became a food sensation upon their introduction into Mexico by Wal-Mart. The company sold 1.6 million of them during their first year of operation in that country.[1]

Source:
1 *Staff. (September 1998) Adaptation, experimentation guide Wal-Mart global venture. Stores. pp. 22–24.*

in Great Britain. The company now has more than 100 stores in several European countries. Still the process is a slow one. In the United States, Gap opened 59 Old Navy stores in a year. It took Gap ten years to open that number in Great Britain.[59]

Foreign Expansion Strategies

Retailers wary of direct investments in foreign countries sometimes opt for less risky forms of foreign expansion including joint ventures, licensing agreements, and franchising. In a **joint venture**, a foreign partner makes an uncharted course more navigable by sharing knowledge of local laws, customs, and industry alliances. Nine West, the nation's leading retailer of women's shoes, operates stores in Hong Kong as joint ventures with Toppy International, an apparel company that also owns Episode, an upscale women's-apparel chain. Pier 1 has forged joint-venture partnerships in which Pier 1 supplies the merchandise and operational expertise and its joint-venture partners develop and operate the stores.

Licensing is a contractual arrangement whereby a retailer allows another company to conduct business under the retailer's name in exchange for a percentage of profit. Hong Kong-based Dickson Concepts operates licensed Brooks Bros. stores in Southeast Asia. Dickson Concepts portfolio of franchises include Kenneth Cole, Polo Ralph Lauren, and Joan & David. The company's retail network includes more than 270 department stores and in-store shops in 22 countries.[60]

Franchising is another foreign-expansion option. The Southampton, England-based Body Shop has franchised more than 90 percent of its stores. Seventy percent of the company's sales are generated outside the United Kingdom.[61, 62] Sometimes foreign-expansion strategies vary by country. Pier 1 makes direct investments in English-speaking countries, but favors joint ventures in non-English-speaking countries.[63] Though most Brooks Bros. stores in Southeast Asia are Dickson Concepts franchises, in Japan, Brooks Bros. stores are joint ventures with Daidoh, a Japanese manufacturer.

Shopping centers are another exportable concept. The Mills Corporation, a shopping-center developer, is joining forces with Tishman Speyer, a real-estate developer, to build value-oriented shopping centers in Brazil, Germany, Japan, and the United Kingdom. Most of the tenants will be U.S. retailers looking to expand overseas.

SUMMARY POINTS

- In a centralized retail organization, functions that do not require proximity to customers are performed collectively for all stores in a central location for efficiency and cost effectiveness.
- Retail ownership can be public or private. Retail organizations can be structured as conglomerates, chains, or single-unit operations.
- Retail organizations expand by developing new merchandising concepts and through, acquisitions, and mergers. They downsize through divestiture.
- Bankruptcy occurs when an organization's liabilities exceed its assets. Chapter 11 protects a bankrupt retailer from its creditors while it reorganizes to become a profitable organization.
- As the U.S. marketplace becomes saturated with retail stores, retailers are extending their boundaries beyond domestic borders into locations in Asia, Europe, and South America.

FOR DISCUSSION

1. A high degree of centralization ensures consistency among stores in a retail organization. What are the positive aspects of this "consistency"? What are the negative aspects?
2. Search the Internet for the annual reports of some of the retail conglomerates mentioned in this chapter. Evaluate each in terms of the diversity of its operating divisions.
3. Explore the Web sites of a few department-store conglomerates, such as May Department Stores and Federated Department Stores, and a few specialty-store conglomerates, such as The Limited, Inc and Gap, Inc. Find information on the history of each organization. Compare the growth strategy of the department-store conglomerates to the specialty-store conglomerates.
4. Search the Internet for recent news stories on a retail organization currently in Chapter 11. What factors contributed to its bankruptcy? Discuss elements of its POR. When is emergence from Chapter 11 expected?
5. Choose a retail organization that you feel is ripe for foreign expansion. Randomly select a foreign nation as a possible location for a store. Research information pertaining to the country's culture and economy. Would the retailer be a good fit?

KEY TERMS AND CONCEPTS

acquisition	divestiture	junk bond
bankruptcy	franchising	leveraged buyout
bidding war	friendly suitor	licensing
cannibalization	friendly takeover	merger
centralization	hostile takeover	plan of reorganization
chain	initial public	private company
conglomerate	offering	public company
decentralization	internal buyout	subsidiary
diversification	joint venture	

ENDNOTES

1. Schiller, Z., Zellner, W. & Stodghill, R. (December 21, 1992). Clout! More and more, retail giants rule the marketplace. *Business Week*. pp. 66-73.
2. Loeb, W. (May 1992). Unbundle or centralize. *Retailing Issues Newsletter*. pp. 1-4.
3. Forest, S. (March 23, 1998). One more face-lift for Penney. *Business Week*. pp. 86-88.

4. Reda, S. (May 1998). J.C. Penney puts product flow on FAST track. *Stores*. pp.49-51.

5. Staff. (June 4, 1998). Eton hoping to reap $176 million from IPO. *Women's Wear Daily*. p. 26.

6. Stone, D. (May 1990). Mergers and acquisitions—Good and bad news. *Retailing Issues Letter*. pp. 1–4.

7. Cuneo, A. (August 3, 1998). May seeks single agency to boost branding efforts. *Advertising Age*.

8. Loeb, W. (May 1992). Unbundle or centralize: What is the answer? *Retailing Issues Letter*. pp. 1–4.

9. Gilman, A. (May 1990). Who was minding the store? *Retailing Issues Letter*. p. 5.

10. Bivins, J. (September 1998). Ten years after: A look back. *Shopping Centers Today*. pp. 64–65.

11. Ryan, T. (July 15, 1998). Proffitt's details its plans for big savings with Saks. *Women's Wear Daily*. p. 11.

12. Moin, D. (January 14, 2000). Dayton Hudson Corp. renaming itself Target. *Women's Wear Daily*. p. 2.

13. Liebeck, L. (January 25, 1999). With offer completed, Ames readies for Hills transition. *Discount Store News*. p. 3.

14. Liebeck, L. (November 23, 1998). Ames bolsters regional presence with Hills takeover. *Discount Store News*. pp. 1, 42.

15. Moin, D. (January 23, 1995). Federated merges Rich's, Lazarus into $2.2B unit. *Women's Wear Daily*. pp. 2, 4.

16. Edelson, S. & Curan, C. (July 7, 1998). Proffitt's stock takes a hit on Saks deal; Outlook is for stability. *Women's Wear Daily*. p. 4.

17. Moin, D. (December 1, 1998). R. Brad martin: Safeguarding the Saks image. *Women's Wear Daily*. pp. 1, 8–9.

18. Staff. (October 21, 1996). Babies "R" Us now No. 1. *Discount Store News*. pp. 1, 94.

19. Moin, D. (May 19, 1998). Dillard's will acquire Mercantile Store; Deal pegged at $2.9B. *Women's Wear Daily*. pp. 1, 4.

20. Palmieri, J. Federated approaches sale of specialty unit to its management. *Women's Wear Daily*. pp. 1, 15.

21. Hirsh, M. (June 2, 1997). But nary a trust to bust. *Newsweek*. pp. 44–45.

22. Staff. (March 15, 1999). Retailer buys Fingerhut marketing company. *Marketing News*. p. 15.

23. Moin, D. (February 12, 1999). In unexpected move, Federated to acquire Fingerhut for $1.7B.

24. Rickard, L. (May 15, 1995). Woolworth walking down a new path. *Advertising Age*. p. 4.

25. Moin, D. (January 27, 1998). Limited seen ready to ax Cacique chain while growing others. *Women's Wear Daily*. pp. 1, 16.

26. Barmash, I. (June 1997). Diversity helps preserve Saks' appeal. *Shopping Centers Today*. p. 36.

27. Moin, D. (December 1, 1997). Main Street's productivity is outpacing Saks' plan. *Women's Wear Daily*. pp. 1, 2.

28. Duff, M. (May 11, 1998). Downsizing for upside potential. *Discount Store News*. pp. 2, 83–84.

29. Barmash, I. (March 1998). Circuit City growth defies industry slump. *SCT Retailing Today*. pp. 24, 26.

30. Chapters 7 and 13 are other commonly cited chapters. Chapter 7 involves liquidation of an organization's assets to pay its debts. Chapter 13 is much like Chapter 11, but more commonly used for individuals or sole proprietorships versus large organizations.

31. Rutberg, S. (January 27, 1992). The Macy Watch. *Women's Wear Daily*. pp. 4, 5.

32. Fields, G. (February 2, 1992). Back from the brink. *Miami Herald*. pp. 1K, 4k.

33. Moin, D. & Young, V. (May 21, 1998) End of Ch. 11? Barneys, Isetan reach accord. pp. 1, 14, 15.

34. Stone, D. (May 1990). Mergers and acquisitions—Good and bad news. *Retailing Issues Letter*. pp. 1–4.

35. Byczkowski, J. (February 2, 1992). Bouncing back from bankruptcy. *Cincinnati Enquirer*. pp. I1, I2.

36. Wilner, R. (November 20, 1995). Lawyers: Need new uses for Ch. 11. *Women's Wear Daily*. p. 12.

37. Passell, P. (April 12, 1993). Critics of bankruptcy law see inefficiency and waste. *New York Times*. pp. A1, A6.

38. Robaton, A. (April 1996). Landlords call for bankruptcy reform. *Shopping Centers Today*. pp. 1, 34–35.

39. Piccin, N. (March 18, 1996). Bankruptcy: Do or die? (Springfield, Mass.) *Union-News*. pp. C1–2.

40. Silverman, D. (October 30, 1997). Has expansion boom finally brought retail to saturation point? *Women's Wear Daily*. pp. 1, 10–11.

41. Shern, S. (February 1994). Going global. *Chain Store Age Executive*. pp. 38–39.

42. Kahn, J. (June 7, 1999). Wal-Mart goes shopping in Europe. *Fortune*. pp. 105–112

43. Dwyer, P. (Novembr 29, 1993). Shop till you drop hits Europe. *Business Week*. pp. 58–59.

44. Edelson, S. (June 25, 1997). Mills plans to export malls. *Women's Wear Daily*. p. 12.

45. Staff. (January 1998). Global 2000 highlights. A special supplement to Stores. p. S4.

46. Thorne, S. (September, 1998). Retailer looking ahead to advent of Euro currency. *Shopping Centers Today*. pp. 1, 69.

47. Knight-Reidder, N. (September 20, 1996). Wal-Mart's pink Barbies touch ground in Indonesia. *The Boston Globe*. p. A12.

48. Secker, V. (January 21, 1998). Store seeking growth urged to pay attention to developing nations. *Women's Wear Daily*. pp. 1, 23.

49. Staff. (August 1995). Asia is the hottest market, report says. *Shopping Centers Today*. p. 1.

50. Feinberg, P. (July 1998). Local partners key for overseas growth. *Shopping Centers Today*. p. 51.

51. Krauss, C. (September 6, 1998). Despite uncertain world markets, a big U.S. retailer bulls into Latin America. *The New York Times*. pp. 1, 11.

52. Dwyer, P. (November 29, 1993). Shop till you drop hits Europe. *Business Week*. pp. 58–59.

53. Kahn, J. (June 7, 1999). Wal-Mart goes shopping in Europe. *Fortune*. pp. 105–112.

54. Mander, E. (March 1998). For outlets, Europe a boon and a bear. *Shopping Centers Today*. p. 32.

55. Staff. (May 1998). Pier 1 looks abroad with a cautious eye. *SCT Retailing Today*. p. 58.

56. Krauss, C. (September 6, 1998). Despite uncertain world markets, a big U.S. retail bulls into Latin America. *The New York Times*. pp. 1, 11.

57. Seckler, V. (March 18, 1999). Ales inks deal for Peoples. *Women's Wear Daily*. p. 5.

58. Kahn, J. (June 7, 1999).Wal-Mart goes shopping in Europe. *Fortune*. pp. 105–112.

59. Tagliabue, J. (April 24, 1996). Enticing Europe's shoppers. *The New York Times*. pp. D1, D20.

60. Moin, D. (August 7, 1997). Dickson on the move: Signs deal to operate Brooks Bros. in Asia. *Women's Wear Daly*. pp. 1, 22.

61. Wentz, L. (September 18, 1995). Global retailers get ready for new shopping empires. *Advertising Age International*. pp. I–35, 42.

62. Ibid.

63. Feinberg, P. (July 1998). Local partners key for overseas growth. *Shopping Centers Today*. p. 51.

chapter five

COMMUNICATING WITH CONSUMERS

Customers' needs, tastes, and spending power differ relative to factors such as gender, age, income, and lifestyle. To develop a strategy for selecting specific merchandise categories, brands, sizes, styles, items, and colors, buyers need a clear profile of a store's intended customers. Chapter 5 deals with some of the ways in which a retailer defines its customer base, and some of the strategies used by retailers to draw customers into their stores.

After you have read this chapter, you will be able to discuss:

The consumer segments to whom retailers cater.

The concept of store image.

The sales-promotion function in retail stores.

RETAILERS AND THEIR CUSTOMERS

A **market** is a group of customers with the potential to buy. Claiming that there is "a market" for something implies that there is a group of customers with the desire or need for it, and the financial resources to purchase it. A **mass market** is a large group of customers with similar characteristics and wants. Mass-market characteristics are often described as "typical" or "mainstream." Thus, people who are average height, middle income, or light readers are mass-market customers. Wal-Mart is a mass-market retailer that caters to mainstream America. More than 90,000,000 customers pass through Wal-Mart's doors each week.

A **niche market** is a small group of customers with characteristics and wants that differ from the mass market. Niche-market members are not typical or mainstream. People who are very tall, very wealthy, or who read a book a week are niche-market customers. By virtue of their height, spending power, or favorite pastime, the wants and needs of these niche-market members differ from the wants and needs of the members of the mass market. Niche markets are typically undersatisfied or dissatisfied with mass-market offerings.

Though niche markets are smaller than the mass market, niche-market customers tend to be loyal to the retailers who respond to their needs. A man who wears a size 48-extra-long suit becomes dedicated to the big-and-tall men's store that consistently carries a deep assortment of goods in his hard-to-find size. A man of average proportion is not likely to be as dedicated to a specific apparel retailer in that his needs are satisfied by any number of department stores, full-line discount stores, and off-pricers.

Market Segmentation

Market segmentation is the process of identifying niche markets. **Target marketing** is responding to the wants and needs of a niche market with a marketing strategy that may include a mix of products, services, or advertising. Markets can be segmented, or defined, based on several types of characteristics. Demographic and psychographic characteristics are the most common bases for segmenting markets.

Demographic segmentation involves identifying markets by objectively measured and quantifiable characteristics, such as gender, age, education, and income. For the past 50 years, baby boomers have attracted considerable attention as a demographic group. Born between

Figure 5.1

A niche market is a small group of customers with characteristics that differ from the mass market. *Courtesy of J. Baker, Inc.*

Sources:

*1 Duff, M. (October
5, 1998). Organized
Living's catalog
business extends to
sixth location.*
Discount Store
News. *pp. 18, 21.*
*2 Duff, M. (July 12,
1999). Home Depot
debuts new format.*
Discount Store
News. *pp. 1, 80.*

TARGET MARKETING

Organized Living is a catalog retailer that sells practical solutions to organization problems in the kitchens, bathrooms, garages, workrooms, and laundries of space-starved consumers.[1] The company, whose slogan is "Simplify busy lives, one room at a time," based its market positioning on the fact that most U.S. consumers live in a dwelling with fewer than 5.5 rooms, and that the number-one reason for moving in the United States was for more space.

Home Depot created its Villager's Hardware concept, a scaled-down, service-oriented version of its superstore format with 40 percent of its mix devoted to home décor and housewares. Villager's Hardware's positioning was based on research that showed that women initiate 80 percent of home-improvement projects.[2]

1946 and 1964, baby boomers comprise one-third of the U.S. population. They control more than 50 percent of the nation's disposable income, and 75 percent of the nation's personal assets.[1] Because of their size as a market, marketing organizations have catered to the whims of baby boomers at every stage of life through which they've passed. Disposable diapers, junior-size apparel, sugary cereals, minivans, bottled water, and designer jeans are but of few of the products popularized by baby boomers.[2] For many marketers, baby boomers become increasingly attractive as they age.[3] Greeting-card companies, such as Hallmark and American Greeting, have found that people between the ages of 55 and 64 purchase more greeting cards than members of any other age group.[4,5]

Demographic characteristics are important to retailers. Off-price retailers seek markets with well-educated, discerning consumers who recognize the value of brand-name offerings at prices lower-than-conventional prices.[6] Though high income is a desirable demographic characteristic for many retailers, some retailers target low-income markets. Dollar General and Family Dollar target households with annual earnings of less than $25,000 in areas not served by other general-merchandise retailers.[7] TJX Companies targets lower-middle-income urban blue-collar customers with family earnings under $40,000 a year with its newest off-price concept called A.J. Wright.[8,9]

Because of constant shifts, demographic characteristics warrant continuous monitoring. A historically low birth rate in the 1970s caused the teenage population to drop off considerably through the end of the 1980s. In response to this demographic trend, many department stores significantly downsized their junior departments. Some of the stores that catered to the teen market, including Susie's, Ups 'N Downs, and Merry-Go-Round, went out of business. However, in 1992 the teenage market started growing twice as fast as the rest of the population. By 2010, the nation's teen market is expected to max out at 35 million. Several retailers of teen-oriented product lines, such as Gadzooks, Pacific Sunwear, and Hot Topic, have strategically positioned them-selves to meet the needs of the exploding teen market with aggressive expansion plans.[10,11]

Some retailers age right along with their customers. Pier 1, the nation's largest retailer of home accessories, once sold incense, beads, and candles to the flower children of the 1960s. In time, Pier 1's flower children became

Figure 5.2

Pacific Sunwear meets the needs of the exploding teen market.

Pier 1 Imports—Changing with Its Customers

Pier 1 Imports made its debut in 1962 in San Mateo, California, as a single store catering to the lifestyle of the baby boomers. However, as the "flower children" of the 1960s grew into the "yuppies" of the 1980s, Pier 1 replaced its assortments of bean bags, love beads, incense, and sea nymphs with selections of high-quality home furnishings and accessories that include leather chairs and pinewood armoires. All of this came about by keeping an eye on customers.

Pier 1 knows that today its typical customer is a well-educated female between 18 and 49 with an annual household income of $55,000. Most customers are homeowners, with about half owning homes val-ued at more than $100,000. Pier 1 is in tune with its customers' psychographic profile. The company knows that its shoppers will pay extra for quality and style but that they don't want to spend frivolously. Pier 1 knows that its customers are trend-setters who look for unusual combinations of color and shape and like owning things that no one else has. It knows that its customers are cultured with interest in products inspired by art and architecture from different countries.

With this customer profile in mind, Pier 1 buyers scout the wholesale markets of more than 50 countries looking for distinctive assortments that will appeal to customers at nearly 1000 Pier 1 stores.[1]

Source:

1 Howell, D. (July 12, 1999). Pier 1 reflects on record year improvement still a priority. Discount Store News. p. 4.

---

affluent nesters. Over a ten-year period, the median annual household income of Pier 1's customers rose from $26,500 to $53,000. Pier 1 responded to this transition with more upscale assortments.[12]

Psychographic segmentation involves identifying markets according to their values, attitudes, and lifestyles. Psychographic characteristics are important to retailers. For instance, the values, attitudes, and lifestyle of mothers who work out of the home affect how and where they shop. Because they're time-pressed, they spend less time browsing. They place a high value on convenience and service. They espouse one-stop-shopping and become dedicated to retailers that satisfy multiple needs.[13,14,15] In response to the needs of this lifestyle market segment, Kmart developed an advertising campaign that centered around its reputation as a value-oriented, full-line discounter catering to the "busy budget-conscious mom."[16]

Lifestyles have a profound effect on customer profiles. Fast food, cable TV, and an increasingly sedentary lifestyle have produced a growing population of overweight consumers. Sears and J.C. Penney have responded to the needs of the one in five children under the age of 16 who are obese with[17] husky sizes for boys and plus-sizes for girls.[18] Saks has devoted an entire floor of its Beverly Hills location to Salon Z, a shop that caters to plus-size women[19] who now represent more than 40 percent of the female population.[20] Psychographic characteristics are often associated with certain demographic groups. Aging baby boomers are said to be more independent, active, and healthier than previous generations of older Americans. They fear aging and will spend freely on products to help them look young and retain their youth.[21,22,23,24,25]

Many stores define their customers in both demographic and psychographic terms. Banana Republic's customers are "clothing enthusiasts," a third of whom have an annual household income of more than $100,000.[26] Talbots defines its typical customer as over 30, well educated, socially and culturally aware, and having a median household income of $80,000.[27] Retail conglomerates often target multiple markets. The Gap operates three casual-apparel specialty-store divisions: Banana Republic, The Gap, and Old Navy. Each division is targeted to a different market segment based on price. Banana Republic is positioned at the high end of the market, The Gap in the middle, and Old Navy at the low end.[28] The Zale Corp., the nation's largest fine-jewelry retailer, operates three divisions, each distinct in terms of price. The average price at Zale's Jewelers is $250; at Gordon's Jewelers it's $300; and at Bailey Banks & Biddle it's $500.[29]

Retailers with large-store formats also cater to different types of customers. At Nordstrom, *Savvy* is a shop that houses cutting-edge lines such as Vivienne Tam, Vertigo, and Theory. *Town Square* is for better career and casual looks such as Jones New York and Liz Claiborne. European and U.S. designers, including Calvin Klein, Marni and Missoni, are housed in *Collectors*.[30,31] However, even the largest retailer lacks the physical capacity to satisfy every market. Attempting to be "everything to everyone" can result in shallow, disjointed assortments.

Micromerchandising

Micromerchandising involves tailoring an individual store's product mix to the local market based on the store's database of customer-purchase history and knowledge of local tastes and demographics.[32] Sears sells fringed suede vests and skirts during rodeo season in a handful of Texas

Source:
1 Holstein, W.
(December 21, 1988).
Data-crunching
Santa: Wal-Mart
knows what you
bought last
Christmas. U.S.
News & World
Report. pp. 44–46.

Company Profile 5.2

Wal-Mart—The Master of Micromerchandising

Each Christmas, the Wal-Mart store in Decatur, Georgia, features a Christmas-decoration display of African-American angels and ethnic Santas. The music section promotes seasonal selections by popular rappers. There's a selection of brown-skinned dolls, including Aria, a doll outfitted in traditional African-American garb. Twenty miles away in Dunwoody, a mostly white suburb, the local Wal-Mart's music selection showcases holiday tunes by country superstar Garth Brooks. Out of the hundreds of dolls in the Toy department, only a few are dark skinned.

Structuring assortments consistent with the demographics and buying habits of local customers used to be a balancing act performed by Wal-Mart's store-level merchandisers. But for the past several years, Wal-Mart has come to rely on computers to perform this awesome task. Every bit of information about who buys what at a Wal-Mart store is fed back to the company's Bentonville, Arkansas, headquarters where it is stored in a data warehouse that is larger than any other commercial data warehouse in the nation, and perhaps second in size only to the Pentagon's. Each Wal-Mart store's data is interfaced with information about the demographics of the communities from which the store draws its customers. Besides ethnicity, geographic location, local sports affiliations, many other traits are factored into the profile. Powerful number-crunching systems look for sales trends by product line within each store. Demographic factors are then factored into the analysis to predict which products will sell best. The end result is a distinct personality for each Wal-Mart store tailored to the wants and needs of local customers.[1]

stores in January. In New Orleans, Saks Fifth Avenue offers an extensive assortment of long dresses for Mardi Gras.[33] The Kmart in New York's Greenwich Village has a dorm shop to cater to the large number of college students in the area.[34]

Wal-Mart is an industry leader in micromerchandising. Wal-Mart's Tom's River, New Jersey, store responds to the needs of a large senior market with inexpensive canes, large-size women's apparel, golf equipment, and greeting cards designed for retirees. About 80 percent of the goods carried at the Wal-Mart store in Mountain View, California, and the store in Union City are the same. But the Mountain View store caters to the Silicon Valley crowd with eye-catching displays of mountain bikes and health supplements like echinacea. For the more blue-collar crowd in Union City, there is stronger emphasis on home entertainment, especially televisions.[35]

Other Types of Segmentation

Markets can be segmented other than by demographic and psychographic characteristics. **Geographic segmentation** involves profiling customers by geographic region of the country. Climate is an obvious reason for this segmentation. Ski parkas are an important apparel category in Minnesota, but not in Louisiana. Consumer tastes are also geographically linked. Observers note that the Dallas unit of Barneys New York failed because it featured black minimalist fashions and low-heeled shoes at a time when Dallas was still into bright hues, high heels, glitz, and big hair.[36] Type of geographic area, such as urban, suburban, or rural, is another segmentation factor that affects assortments. When Kmart opened a store Manhattan, the company strategically edited categories such as lawn-and-garden and automotive.

Family-life-cycle segmentation is based on marital status and the presence or absence of dependent children in a family. Murphy and Staples have identified 13 life-cycle stages in the *Modernized Family Life Cycle* shown in Figure 5.3.[37] Purchasing power and spending habits differ at each stage of the family life cycle relative to the number of dependent children. A *middle-aged married without dependent children* has more spending potential than a *young married with children;* however the latter is a more lucrative target for retailers of juvenile furniture. The Murphy and Staples family life cycle reflects a more contemporary perspective than previous versions of the family life cycle that did not consider the effect of divorce on families. Divorce is an important economic consideration, since divorce breaks families into smaller, less affluent units. Recognizing that furniture purchases are tied to the family life cycle, Ikea developed an ad campaign targeted to customers experiencing significant life changes, such as marriage, the birth of a child, and divorce. One ad in the series portrayed a newly divorced woman who wanted new furniture so "that I can have guys over maybe in, like, ten years."

Ethnic segmentation has become an important marketing strategy because of the rapid growth of populations of consumers of African, Asian, and Latino descent. Some retailers have responded to the transition of the United States from a homogeneous "melting pot" to an ethnically diverse "salad bowl." Sears offers a line designed by Alvin Bell

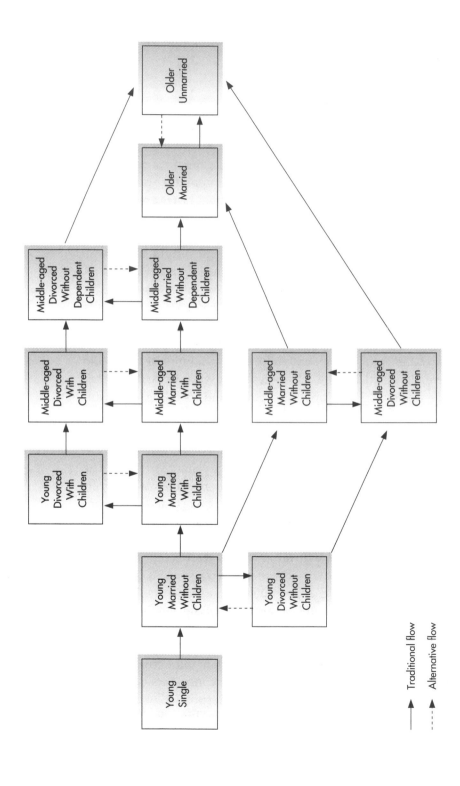

Figure 5.3

The Modernized Family Life Cycle.

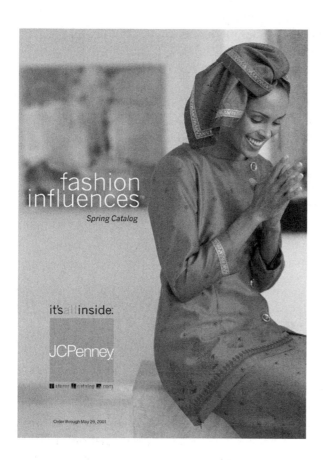

Figure 5.4

J.C. Penney recog-
nizes the importance
of targeting ethnic
markets. *J.C. Penney
Company, Inc.*

for African-American women called Mosaic.[38] To reach Latino customers, Sears created a Spanish-language advertising campaign called
"Todo Para Ti (Everything For You) to air on the Telemundo and
Univision networks. J.C. Penney features the creations of Anthony
Mark Hankins, a dramatic line with rich vibrant colors and ethnic
prints in lush fabrics designed for the contemporary African-American
woman.[39] Even shopping centers have gotten on the ethnic-segmenta-
tion bandwagon. Milpitas Square is an Asian-themed shopping center
just outside San Jose, California. The mall has Asian restaurants, bak-
eries, specialty food stores, and an Asian-owned bank.[40] Ethnic distinctions within consumer populations are important to retailers. For
instance, men in general spend an average of $71 a month on apparel.
However white men spend only $66 compared to $99 for black men,
and $94 for Latino men.[41]

Geodemographic segmentation involves segmenting markets by neighborhoods typified by lifestyle. This microcosmic segmentation is based on information from various synthesized sources, including the U.S. census, mailing lists, and marketing surveys. PRIZM is the original and most widely used neighborhood target marketing system. PRIZM defines every neighborhood in the United States based on 60 demographically and psychographically distinct neighborhood types called clusters.[42,43]

Retailers use geodemographic information to determine new store sites, plan product assortments, and target customer mailings. The Bon Marche uses PRIZM clusters to typify the shopper most likely to shop its monthly *Day-O-Sale*. By targeting only the clusters with inhabitants likely to shop *Day-O-Sale*, The Bon Marche edited its mailing list of 750,000 customers to 500,000, and saved $1.5 millions in direct-advertising costs over time.

COMMUNICATING WITH CUSTOMERS

Positioning refers to the marketplace position that a product occupies relative to other products within the same category. To be successful, products must be uniquely positioned and clearly differentiated from their competitors.[44] Product positioning is often defined by the product's characteristics and/or target market. Estee Lauder is the nation's leading producer of prestige cosmetics lines. The company has four uniquely positioned lines. Estee Lauder is a fragrance-oriented line for older customers. Clinique is a hypoallergenic line for younger suburban-types. Prescriptives is a high-fashion line for urban customers. Origins is a "green" line featuring New Age products such as aromatherapy oils.[45]

Retail stores, like consumer products, are positioned. Image is a term used in retailing that is closely allied to positioning. A store's **image** is the way it is perceived by the public. References to a store's image include *value-oriented*, *fashion-forward*, and *prestigious*. Though negative images are never intended, some stores are perceived as *stodgy*, *over-priced*, or *boring*.

A store's image is the result of a carefully honed marketing strategy involving multiple factors. Location and physical facilities are store-image components. Though the lines of demarcation are blurring, mall and strip-center tenants are distinct in terms of service, price, and fashion. A store's architecture, interior decor, fixturing, signage, and merchandise presentation can deliver messages of prestige, service, or price. Marble floors and scenic elevators convey an image distinctly different from vinyl tile and shopping carts. Talbots is an upscale specialty retailer of classic female and children's apparel that uses architectural elements, such as entry foyers, maple flooring, and wainscoting, as well as antiques and equestrian-theme prints to convey a gracious, residential ambiance in its stores.

The merchandise division of a retail organization plays a critical role in creating and maintaining a store's image. Buyers' choices of brands, styles, fabrics, and colors reflect a store's image. To reinforce an image of fashion, a buyer searches the market for the latest styles and trends. To maintain an image of value, a buyer seeks opportunistic buys of goods that can be retailed at prices lower than competitors'. Buyers are arduous in their efforts to convey a consistent image throughout an entire store or department. Casual Corner, a chain of female-apparel stores, has suffered in recent years from an inconsistent fashion image that seesaws between career and casual looks.[46]

STORE NAME AND IMAGE

A store's name can reflect its image. Long-established retail enterprises often bear the family name(s) of their founder(s). However, more contemporary names often identify a store's offerings or target market. The word *mart* in Wal-Mart and Kmart conveys a discount image. The word *club* in Charter Club conveys an image of exclusivity. Store names such as *Petite Sophisticate*, *Kids "R" Us*, and *Casual Male*, convey clear images of product line and target markets.

Old Navy was originally known as *Gap Warehouse*. When Gap, Inc., Old Navy's parent company, decided to expand its value-oriented concept nationally, it hired a marketing company to come up with a name with a little more imagination. *Forklift* and *Monorail* were the two top choices. *Old Navy* came from the side of a building. The name was chosen because it was seen as being "euphonious, unpretentious, suggestive of canvas and discipline."[1] Even departments within stores undergo name changes occasionally. To create an image of being a cool place to shop for image-conscious youth, Bon-Ton, a York, Pennsylvania-based department-store chain dubbed its junior departments *Club X*, and its young men's *Ziga-T'z*.[2]

Sources:

1 *Caminiti, S. (March 18, 1996). Will Old Navy fill the gap?* Fortune. *pp. 59–62.*

2 *Bernier, R. (December 9, 1998). Department stores try hard to fit in with cool crowd.* Wall Street Journal.

Figure 5.5

To attract younger contemporary customers, Ethan Allen repositioned itself with new colorful, eclectic, and casual furniture lines.

Sometimes stores are repositioned with a new image. Ethan Allen Interiors was long known for its stodgy collections of colonial reproductions. The conservative styles were an anathema to the 20- and 30-year-olds at the heart of the home-buying market. To attract younger contemporary customers, Ethan Allen repositioned itself with new colorful, eclectic, and casual lines including Shaker, Farmhouse, and Country French. The company even replaced many of its white-column storefronts with art-deco facades.[47,48,49]

Sears used its famed *Come See the Softer Side of Sears* advertising campaign to shift its position from a hardlines retailer to a fashion-oriented store.[50] J.Crew attracted a younger customer changing its styling from the preppy button-down looks that originally brought the cataloger fame to trendy retro looks.[51]

Sales Promotion

In a retail organization, the **sales promotion** function is responsible for inducing customer traffic and sales by communicating information to customers pertaining to assortments, prices, services, and other sales incentives. An effective sales promotion strategy positions a store in the minds of consumers and is thus an important factor in defining a store's image. Sales promotion encourages repeat business and customer loyalty.

Sales promotion functions include advertising, publicity, and special events. **Advertising** conveys a message to a large group of people through a mass medium, such as newspapers, magazines, radio, and television. The cost of delivering the message is paid for by an advertiser or sponsor. Newspapers are a local advertising medium appropriate for retailers with trading areas that parallel a newspaper's circulation. Regional and national retailers reach their customers by advertising in many newspapers. Because newspapers attract a diversely demographic readership, retailers that target a diverse group of customers are appropriate newspaper advertisers. An age-old alliance between department stores and newspapers dates back to their historical growth alongside each other in cities populous enough to support both. Department stores and full-line discounters continue to be major newspaper advertisers, though newspapers now share retail advertising budgets with newer forms of advertising, such as television.[52]

The preprinted insert has become a popular newspaper-advertising vehicle. Often called *circulars,* the most common type of insert is the multipage 10-by-15-inch tabloid. The piece is prepared by the retailer's

Figure 5.6

The preprinted insert has become a popular newspaper-advertising vehicle. © *Sears, Roebuck and Co. 2000.*

advertising department, printed, and then sent to various newspapers for insertion into the folds of a specific edition, often a Sunday paper. Newspapers charge retailers an insertion fee of approximately 25 cents per insert for inserting the piece and for using the newspaper to carry the advertising message.

Preprinted inserts are an alternative to the conventional practice of placing ads within the paper. Retailers prefer preprinted inserts for two major reasons:

- Preprinted inserts can be printed on paper that reproduces color with greater clarity than newsprint.
- The cost of producing and inserting an insert is less than buying the same amount of space within the paper.

Magazines are a national advertising medium whose major advertisers are producers of nationally distributed consumer products and services. As a national medium, magazines are a popular advertising vehicle among national retailers, but not common for local or regional retailers. Unlike newspapers, magazines are targeted to readers with clearly defined interests, such as sports, fashion, and health. The products and services advertised in magazines reflect their readership. Priscilla of Boston, the prestigious wedding gown design house, advertises in *Modern Bride, Weddings and Brides,* and *Bride's* magazine. Producer-sponsored magazine advertising sometimes includes the names of retailers at which the product line is available.

Like newspapers, radio is a local advertising medium. Radio's inability to convey a visual message limits its desirability as an advertising medium for retailers who need to convey the physical attributes of their assortments. However, radio is an effective advertising medium for events, such as a *One Day Sale.*

As a national advertising medium, television is most appealing to national retailers. J.C. Penney, Sears, and Kmart conduct extensive prime-time advertising on major television networks and cable stations. Small independent retailers, and the regional divisions of department store conglomerates, buy television time though local network affiliates and cable companies. The high cost of producing quality television advertising makes it a prohibitive advertising vehicle for many independent retailers.

Direct-response advertising, such as catalogs, bill enclosures, and flyers, is another form of retail advertising. Commonly called direct mail, a store's charge customers are the likely recipients of direct-response advertising. Retailers occasionally use **out-of-home advertising,** such as

Figure 5.7

A store's charge customers are the likely recipients of direct-mail pieces. *Courtesy of Nordstrom and Bloomingdale's.*

billboards and transit advertising that appears on various forms of public transportation.

Publicity is "free advertising" through a mass medium in the form of news coverage. A retailer's newsworthy events include the announcement of plans for new stores, the appointment of new executives, or the latest quarterly report of earnings. The news media often rely on buyers as news sources for timely comments on fashion, hot items, and consumer purchasing.

Special events are promotional attractions, such as informal modeling, "how-to" seminars, and appearances of television and sports celebrities that create an exciting shopping atmosphere in stores. Though special

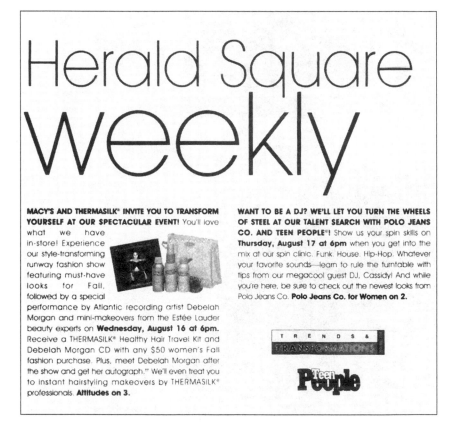

Figure 5.8

Special events are a traffic-generating promotional strategy often used by department stores. *Macy's East.*

events are often considered the domain of department stores, other types of retailers, including discounters, include special events in their promotional strategy. The concept of the "store as theater" was popularized at Bloomingdale's flagship at Lexington and 59th in New York where "spritzing" by fragrance company models, book signings by famous authors, and cooking demonstrations are everyday occurrences.

The merchandise division is often the source of special events. Suppliers frequently offer retailers special-event opportunities, such as product demonstrators, appearances by designers, or the use of vintage collections of their product line. Cole of California, a division of Authentic Fitness Corporation, offers a collection of swimsuits that documents swimwear styles from the Roman "bathing suit" worn around 395 A.D. to Cole's 1964 *Scandal Suit* collection. The collection is loaned to retail stores for displays or runway shows and has been displayed at Nordstrom, Bloomingdale's, and Macy's.

Types of Retail Advertising

Retail advertising is classified according to the type of goods advertised and/or the message conveyed.

Regular-price advertising **Regular-price advertising** features premier assortments at conventional prices. Brand, quality, styling, and assortment are emphasized in regular-price advertising; price is typically downplayed. Regular-price advertising reinforces an image of fashion or prestige and is common among department and specialty stores.

Promotional Advertising Commonly called "sale" advertising, **promotional advertising** features a retailer's regular offerings at discounted prices. Value is emphasized in promotional advertising with comparisons of the promotional price to the regular price. The discounted price is typically offered for a specified period stated in the ad.

Clearance Advertising Like promotional advertising, **clearance advertising** features goods at discounted prices. However, clearance goods are residual assortments of end-of-season, slow-selling, or discontinued merchandise.

Institutional Advertising Often called image advertising, **institutional advertising** reinforces a store's position as a leader in value, service,

Figure 5.9

Regular-price advertising reinforces an image of fashion or prestige. *Lord & Taylor*.

Figure 5.10

Clearance advertising features residual assortments of end-of-season, slow-selling, or discontinued merchandise at discounted prices. *Courtesy of The Bon-Ton.*

fashion, or prestige. Institutional advertising often characterizes the lifestyle of the store's targeted customers, without reference to specific merchandise or prices.

Retail advertising is often tied to a promotional theme or event, such as a *Men's Wardrobe Sale,* an *After Inventory Clearance,* or a *Fall Fashion* catalog. Events are categorized by their scope.

- A storewide event includes virtually all categories of merchandise in a store, such as an *Anniversary Sale* or *Summer Clearance.*
- A divisional event includes a single merchandise division, such as *Great Gift Ideas for Dad* ad, or a *Back-to-School* sale.
- A departmental event includes a single department or category of merchandise, such as a *Fragrance Festival* or a *Dress Bonanza.*
- A vendor event includes a single vendor, such as *Vanity Fair Week.* The advertising expense for vendor events is usually shared with the supplier, a topic to be discussed in Chapter 14.

Though events typically encompass multiple items, some retailers choose to advertise single items. Regular-price ads for single items are often semi-institutional in nature, symbolizing a store's image or prestige. The products featured in single-item promotional ads are usually exceptional values and powerful traffic inducers.

The sales promotion and merchandising functions are closely allied in a retail organization, sometimes falling within the same organizational pyramid. The two work in tandem to develop promotional strategies, budgets, and event schedules. Advertising is responsible for the creative development and production of advertising pieces and for coordinating the purchase of media space and time. The merchandising division is responsible for choosing the merchandise that appears in ads and ascertaining that the goods are consistent with the theme or event. Buyers often obtain photographs or art from their suppliers for ads, or they provide samples to be photographed or sketched. Buyers furnish product information for the copy or wording of ads. They then proofread the copy to ensure that product descriptions and prices are correct. Buyers are also responsible for obtaining support from suppliers to share the cost of advertising their goods, a topic to be discussed in Chapter 14. A merchandising division is responsible for insuring the arrival of goods in stores by the time an ad breaks and for ascertaining adequate levels of inventory. There is hardly a more frustrating shopping experience than to travel to a store in response to an ad and find a paltry selection of advertised goods or, worse yet, none at all.

Personal Selling

Personal selling is one-to-one communication between a salesperson and a customer. In manufacturing organizations personal selling is a marketing function. However, in a retail organization, the human resource division is typically responsible for personal-selling programs and personal-selling training. As a store-level function, the supervision of personal-selling falls within the realm of store administration. Though the merchandising division is not directly responsible for personal selling, buyers are often the source of the product information that is used to train salespeople on the features and benefits of the goods that they are selling in stores.

Retailers have historically attached more importance to procuring goods than to selling goods, a distinction that is obvious when salaries for the two functions are compared. Low wages coupled with the erratic work schedules contribute to a high turnover rate among retail salespeople, who are often not committed to selling as a profession. Customer service in retail stores is often inhibited by sales force reductions to cut operating expenses.[53]

Many retailers recognize that good customer service is a competitive advantage and that good service can influence a consumer's choice of retail outlet. RadioShack favorably positioned itself in the highly competitive consumer-electronics market with its *"If you've got questions, we've got answers"* campaign that ensured easy-to-understand product-use instructions for non-technically oriented customers[54,55,56]

Most retailers have some type of customer-service program to foster good customer relations and to reward star sellers. Some retailers use a "canned" sales approach, a step-by-step selling technique. The following steps are typical of many canned approaches:

- *Greet the customer.* Avoid closed ended questions or cliches that will yield a reflexive "no" such as, "May I help you?" "Hi! A little muggy out there today!" is a better ice breaker.
- *Determine the customer's wants and needs.* "Looking for a Mother's Day gift?" or "What's her favorite color?"
- *Explain product features and benefits.* "This blend of polyester and cotton is perfect for a busy person with little time for ironing."
- *Suggest additional merchandise.* "How about a moisturizer to go with the cleanser?"
- *Close the sale.* "Thanks so much, Ms. Jones. No problem with returning the scarf if the match isn't perfect."

The pitch is typical of those used in department and specialty stores. Though discount stores are essentially self-service, discounters convey an image of service through "greeters" at the store entrances, efficient front-end operations, liberal return policies, and various customer services. Ikea provides customers with free tape measures, pencils, and paper. Strollers, free diapers, and childcare are offered to shopping parents.

Loyalty Programs

A loyalty program is an individualized mass-marketing strategy of tracking customer purchases to anticipate their future needs. The concept involves identifying customers at point-of-sale by their credit cards or other identification vehicles, such as frequent-shopper cards,

Bloomingdale's Rewards Program

makes shopping with your Bloomingdale's card
the smartest thing you can do. The more you use it,
the more benefits you receive.

What could be sweeter?

	BLOOMINGDALE'S CARD $0-499*	PREMIER $500-2499*	PREMIER PLUS VISA* $1000-2499*	ULTIMATE PREMIER $2500 or more*	ULTIMATE PREMIER VISA* $2500 or more*
No annual fee	■	■	■	■	■
Advance notice of sales	■	■	■	■	■
Bloomingdale's catalogs	■	■	■	■	■
Complimentary personal shopping services	■	■	■	■	■
Easy return privileges	■	■	■	■	■
Flexible payment programs†	■	■	■	■	■
Preview Days with additional savings		■	■	■	■
Seasonal special offers		■	■	■	■
Mailings for premieres, fashion shows and special events		■	■	■	■
Invitations to private events			■	■	■
Free shipping & handling with your Bloomingdale's By Mail, Ltd. order			■	■	■
Free deluxe gift wrap			■	■	■
Earn 3% Rewards on all Bloomingdale's purchases			■	■	■
Earn 1% Rewards on VISA® purchases			■		■
Earn periodic double Rewards of 6% on all Bloomingdale's purchases			■	■	■
Triple Rewards event			■	■	■
Free local delivery				■	■
Periodic newsletter				■	■
Exclusive offers and events				■	■

*Annual spending on Bloomingdale's credit card. All cards subject to credit approval. Premier Plus VISA® and Ultimate Premier VISA® by invitation only.
† Subject to credit approval. See sales associates for details.

Figure 5.11

Loyalty programs reward shoppers for dedicated patronage with perks. *Courtesy of Bloomingdale's.*

gift registries, or sign-ups for drawings, and maintaining a database of their brand and style preferences using their purchase histories. Loyalty programs reward shoppers for dedicated patronage with perks, such as advance notice of promotional events, free gift wrapping, and discounts.

The criterion for determining preferred customers is spending over a period of time, typically a year. At Saks, customers earn one point for every dollar they spend. At the end of the year, the points are converted to bonus certificates that can be used for future purchases. The value of the bonus certificate is 2 percent of sales for spending between $2000 and $4999, 4 percent for spending between $5000 and $9999, and 6 percent for spending more than $10,000.[57] Loyalty programs have been successful for many retailers. Charming Shoppes, the Bensalem, Pennsylvania-based company that operates more than 1000 Fashion Bug and Fashion Bug Plus stores, saw average purchases increase by as much as 8 percent upon implementation of its loyalty program.[58]

Loyalty programs recognize that not all customers are equal and that shoppers with the same demographic characteristics, such as family size, age or household income, do not purchase similar quantities and types of merchandise. By tracking customer purchases, loyalty programs can identify consumers who are sensitive to price or prefer particular brands. Loyalty programs are used to identify cross-selling opportunities. A customer who purchases an expensive brass bed may be sent information on luxurious satin sheets or a designer bed-linen ensemble. Marketing to customers on a one-to-one basis costs less than traditional mass marketing.

Loyalty programs have been facilitated by sophisticated database systems such as the STS Customer Profile System that tracks the department, category of merchandise, style number, and brand of a purchase, as well as customer characteristics such as size, occupation, hobbies, and birthday. Targeted mailing lists can be derived from the database on any combination of criteria. STS can also evaluate the effectiveness of promotional mailings by tracking customer purchases of the goods featured in the mailing. A store can take notice when a consumer's purchases decline and can decide how to entice her back to the store.[59]

Using databases to reinforce relationships with consumers is widely used in direct marketing. The concept is gaining greater acceptance among storefront retailers in an effort to personalize their customer transactions, enhance service, foster long-term customer loyalty, and tap more revenue from core customers.[60]

SUMMARY POINTS

- A market is a group of customers with the desire and ability to buy. Retailers develop merchandising strategies to satisfy the wants and needs of markets that are undersatisfied or dissatisfied with current retail offerings.
- Large markets are segmented into smaller markets on the basis of similar geographic, demographic, ethnic, psychographic, family life cycle, or geodemographic characteristics.
- A store's image is the way that it is perceived by the public. Retailers develop an image to position themselves in the marketplace and to distinguish themselves from their competitors.
- Sales promotion is an organizational function responsible for advertising, special events, and publicity.
- Personal selling involves one-to-one communication with customers.
- Loyalty programs use historical customer purchase data to anticipate future purchases.

FOR DISCUSSION

1. Visit several stores in a regional shopping center that sell the same category of merchandise. Based on your observations of the physical characteristics of the store, profile the target market(s) of each store by demographic, psychographic, and other segmentation characteristics.
2. Refer to the previous question. Characterize each store's image. What cues led you to these conclusions?
3. Collect various forms of print advertising from newspapers, magazines, and direct-mail pieces representing a variety of retail stores. Classify each ad as regular-price, promotional, clearance, or institutional. Can any be classified in two categories?

KEY TERMS AND CONCEPTS

advertising	ethnic segmentation	image
clearance advertising	family-life-cycle	institutional advertising
demographic	segmentation	loyalty program
segmentation	geodemographic	market
direct-response	segmentation	market segmentation
advertising	geographic segmentation	mass market

niche market

out-of-home advertising

personal selling

positioning

promotional advertising

psychographic

segmentation

publicity

regular-price advertising

sales promotion

special events

target marketing

ENDNOTES

1. Brookman, F. (October 2, 1998). Retailer predicts beauty migration. *Women's Wear Daily*. pp. 12, 14.
2. Hartnett, M. (February 23, 1998). The "gold" in Oldies is yet to come. *Discount Store News*. p. 17.
3. Cook S. (September 1989). Riding the silver streak. *Retailing Issues Newsletter*. pp. 1–3.
4. Elliott, S. (January 2, 1996). Middle age catches up with the me generation. *The New York Times*. p. C4.
5. Dortch, S. (February, 1997). Greetings, America. *American Demographics*. pp 4–9.
6. Mander, E. (May 1998). Pier 1's boat comes in with $1 billion sales. *SCT Retailing Today*. pp. 55–56, 58.
7. Faircloth, A. (July 6, 1998). Dollar for dollar. *Fortune*. pp 164–166.
8. Reidy, C. (January 10, 1998). New Stores to serve urban areas. *The (Springfield, Mass.) Union-News*.
9. Reidy, C. (September 18, 1998). A.J. Wright aims to break old habits. *The Boston Globe*.
10. Reda, S. (January 1997). Wet Seal leads revival of teen apparel market. *Stores*. pp. 42–44.
11. Ellis, K. (May 1998). Strtegies at retail. A supplement to *Women's Wear Daily*. pp. 16, 18.
12. Mander, E. (May 1998). Pier 1's boat comes in with $1 billion sales. *SCT Retailing Today*. pp. 55–56, 58.
13. Staff. (May 1997). Recognizing retail excellence. *Shopping Center World*. pp. 112–124.
14. Kenyon, K. (March 1997). Survey: Shoppers are often too busy to shop. *SCT Retailing Today*. p. 17.
15. Edelson, S. (January 14, 1999). Retailing's race against time. *Women's Wear Daily*. pp. 8–9.
16. Ibid.
17. Staff. (November 17, 1997). Special sizes in girls', boys' are a real "plus" for retailers. *Discount Store News*. pp. 41–42.
18. Panzner, M. (June 22, 1998). Retailers: beware of "bigfoot" (or keep larger sizes in stock). *Marketing News*.
19. Women sizes 14 and over.
20. Steinhauer, J. (September 20, 1995). In stores, big is beautiful. *The New York Times*. pp. C1, C8.

21. Yohalem, K. (January 1997). Millenium marketing, Part I. *Specialty Stores/The Business Newsletter.* p. 7.
22. Schleuter, S. (August 31, 1998). Maturing market offers an opportunity niche. *Marketing News.* pp. 12, 14.
23. Hartnett, M. (February 23, 1998). The "gold" in Oldies is yet to come. *Discount Store News.* p. 17.
24. Kerr, D. (May 25, 1998). Where there's gray, there's green. *Marketing News.* p. 2
25. Reibstein, L. (September 16, 1996). Rippling abs in 30 days or your money back. *Newsweek.* p. 77.
26. Hammond, T. (April 21, 1997). Banana republic head eyes new formats and revived catalog. *Women's Wear Daily.* pp.1, 12–13.
27. Fact Sheet. (1997). Talbots, Hingham, Mass.
28. Kaufman, L. (July 29, 1998). Downscale moves up. *Newsweek.* pp. 32–33.
29. Moin, D. (June 15, 1998). Once in bankruptcy, Zale outlines program to restore the luster. *Women's Wear Daily.* pp. 1, 8–9.
30. Greenwald, J. (March 24, 1997). Losing its luster. *Time.* pp.64–65.
31. Lee, G. (February 23, 1998). Service and selection mark Nordstrom's invasion of southeast. *Women's Wear Daily.* pp. 1, 4–5.
32. Troy, M. (June 7, 1999). Five stores, five states, five variations. *Discount Store News.* p. 96.
33. Edelson, S. (May 1, 1997). Micromerchandising: When retailers grow by thinking smaller. *Women's Wear Daily.* pp. 1, 12–13.
34. Seckler, V. (March 26, 1997). Kmart's mixed bag in Manhattan. *Women's Wear Daily.* p. 16.
35. Holstein, W. (December 21, 1998). Data-crunching Santa. *U.S. News & World Report.* pp. 44–45.
36. Moin, D. (January 16, 1996). Industry says Barney's lost touch. *Women's Wear Daily.* p. 24.
37. Murphy, P. & Staples, W. (June 1979). A modernized family life cycle. *Journal of Consumer Research.* pp. 16–17.
38. Cuneo, A. (May 5, 1997). New Sears label woos black women. *Advertising Age.* p. 6.
39. Reynolds, P. (September 19, 1995). Designed with black women in mind. *The Boston Globe.* pp. 51, 56.
40. Deck, C. (November 1996). Asian malls serve California's ethnic market. *Shopping Centers Today.* pp. 24, 28.
41. Wynter, L. (June 15, 1994). Business and Race. *The Wall Street Journal.*
42. Mitchell, Susan. (February 1995). Birds of a feather. *American Demographics.* pp. 40–48.
43. Cohen, E. (June 21, 1999). Demos alone don't sell products. *Marketing News.* p. 16.
44. Moin, D. (June 8, 1998). Differentiate or die retail. *Women's Wear Daily.* pp. 10–11, 15.
45. Rutberg, S. (September 22, 1995). Lauder going public. *Women's Wear Daily.* pp. 1, 6–7.

46. DiInnocenzio, A. (July 1, 1998). Casual corner: More relaxed. *Women's Wear Daily.* p. 9.

47. Roush, C. (July 11, 1994). Rearranging the furniture at Ethan Allen. *Business Week.* p. 102.

48. Miller, M. (December 11, 1997). The old new. *The Boston Globe.* pp. E1, E2.

49. Neuborne, E. (October 20, 1994). Furniture stores carve out new niche. *USA Today.*

50. Greenwald, J. (December 23, 1996). Reinventing Sears. *Time.* pp. 53–55.

51. Bongiorno, L. (May 5, 1997). J. Crew plays dress-up. *Business Week.* pp. 127–28.

52. Hurley, M. (June 19, 1996). Hills stores hand hope on upgrading technology. *Women's Wear Daily.* p. 12. S

53. Glen, P. (1990). *It's Not My Department.* New York: William Morrow.

54. Gaboda, G. (Nvember 10, 1997). Sprint retail stores aim to demystify phone technology for consumers. *Marketing News.* p. 2.

55. Anderson, S. (May 13, 1996). RadioShack looks like a palace now. *Business Week.* pp. 153–4.

56. Heller, L. (January 4, 1999). RadioShack provides foundations for Tandy turnaround. *Discount Store News.* pp. 32–34.

57. Zimmermann, K. (August 20, 1997). Nordstrom tests loyalty. *Women's Wear Daily.* p. 20.

58. Murphy, P. (January 1999). Charming Shoppes scores sales gains with card-based loyatlty program. Stores. pp. 52–54.

59. Raider, A. (June 21, 1999). Programs make results out of reach. *Marketing News.* p. 14.

60. Staff. (May 15, 1995). Talbots' database pampers customers. *Discount Store News.*

THE DEVELOPMENT AND DISTRIBUTION OF CONSUMER PRODUCTS

- Fashion Merchandising

- Brands and Private Labels

- Merchandise Resources

chapter six

FASHION MERCHANDISING

The world of fashion is a dynamic and highly competitive arena that provides challenging and rewarding careers to millions. Though the word *fashion* is often associated with women's apparel and accessories, the concept is far more pervasive. Fashion is inherent in men's, women's and children's apparel, home furnishings, food, entertainment, and virtually every facet of culture. Fashion is an integral part of our economic system that embraces a host of industries including manufacturing, advertising, and retailing. Entire textbooks and courses are dedicated to a comprehensive study of fashion. The following is an abbreviated discussion of some fashion concepts and their relevance to retail merchandising.

After you have read this chapter, you will be able to discuss:

The pervasiveness of fashion.

Basic fashion terms.

The relevance of fashion to retail merchandising.

FASHIONS AND TRENDS

Fashion is an expression widely accepted by a group of people over time.[1] The group that accepts a fashion is usually defined by demographic and/or psychographic characteristics. Young marrieds, senior citizens, and urbanites are among the groups associated with certain fashions. The time period that defines the duration of a fashion varies. Something may be fashionable for a short time, such as a month, or remain fashionable for decades.

The acceptance of a fashion by one group is independent of its acceptance by another. Apparel fashionable among young adults may not be fashionable to teens. Levi Strauss found that young people didn't think their internationally famous brand was "cool." Though survey respondents expressed confidence in the quality of Levi's jeans, they felt them more suitable for their parents or older siblings. They themselves preferred Tommy Hilfiger and Ralph Lauren. To increase acceptance among fashion-conscious teens, Levi Strauss embarked upon an aggressive promotional campaign to attract young consumers.[2,3]

Trends

A **trend** implies the direction or movement of a fashion. The word *trend* is often used synonymously with fashion.[4] Thus, something that is

---

STYLE VS. FASHION

Style refers to an item's distinctive characteristics or design features. *Turtleneck*, *mock turtleneck*, and *crew neck* are collar treatments that define the style of a garment, just as *cocktail-*, *ballerina-*, and *tea-length* indicate skirt lengths. The word *style* is not synonymous with fashion, though popular use of the word sometimes implies that it is. Something that is dated is said to be *out-of-style* when, in fact, it is *out-of-fashion*. Something said to be stylish, is really in *fashion*. Only when a style is popular, is it a fashion. All fashions have at least one style, but not all styles are fashions. Fashions change, styles do not. Safari jackets may be fashionable one season and not the next, however a safari jacket is always a style whether or not it is fashionable.

Figure 6.1

Fashion acceptance by one group is independent of its acceptance by another group. *Courtesy of Lord & Taylor and Bob's Stores.*

trendy is also *fashionable*. Trends are described in ways that imply degree of acceptance (a *strong* or *key* trend), direction (an *emerging* or *dying* trend), duration (a *seasonal* trend), or relationship to other trends (a *secondary* or *background* trend). Trends are identified in a multitude of areas, including apparel, home furnishings, and lifestyles.

Manufacturers of consumer products follow trends because of their impact on customer purchases. The "Casual Friday" trend has blossomed into a week with more than 60 percent of the nation's workforce now having the option of dressing casually every day.[5] Apparel manufacturers have capitalized on the "dressdown" trend. Levi Strauss created Dockers, a line of relaxed-fit cotton trousers that has become a casual-workplace staple. Levi Strauss also conducts corporate-casual fashion shows and has given guidance to more than 20,000 companies concerning the revision of their dress-code policies.[6]

Retailers have also reacted to the corporate-casual trend. In 1997, Gap launched a Gap@Work campaign which was kicked off publicly at

Figure 6.2

In response to the casual-dressing trend in the workplace, Brooks Brothers has adopted a more casual merchandising approach. © *Elliott Kaufman Photography*.

the New York Stock Exchange as 3000 traders donned Gap khaki trousers and open-neck shirts for the first Casual Friday in the Exchange's 205-year history.[7] Brooks Brothers, a long-established retailer of traditional menswear, introduced Soft Classics, a line of relaxed sport coats, trousers, shirts, and ties for young men between the ages of 25 and 40. To promote the sale of its casual-workplace looks, Saks Fifth Avenue conducts casual-office-dressing seminars at the New York's prestigious Park Avenue Club.[8]

Cocooning, or *nesting*, is a lifestyle trend associated with the increasing amount of time that people spend at home engaged in activities such as entertaining, exercising, or working.[9] Cocooning has stimulated the sale of furniture, exercise equipment, and consumer electronics for leisure spaces, such as dens and playrooms, as well as products for home entertaining, such as gourmet cookware and casual glassware and dinnerware. Crate & Barrel, Ikea, Pier 1, and Pottery

Figure 6.3

Cocooning has stimulated the sale of home-entertaining products.

Barn are among the many retailers that are major benefactors of the cocooning trend.[10, 11]

The wellness trend reflects a heightened interest in health and longevity. The trend has spurred sales of health-related products such as vitamins, therapeutic furniture, and exercise equipment. Once relegated to off-the-beaten-track locations in shopping centers,

Source:

*1 Nelson, E.
(December 9, 1998).
The hunt for the hip:
A trend scout's trail.*
The Wall Street
Journal. *pp. B1, B4*

Company Profile 6.1

Wet Seal—Looking for Trends in All the Right Places

Wet Seal is a Foothill Ranch, California-based company that caters to the teen market under both the Wet Seal and Contempo Casuals monikers. The company's success is predicated on an ability to identify fast-flying teen fashion trends in time to sell them in its several hundred stores.

The company searches high and low for inspiration. It looks at The Gap and Old Navy, but most of the time it looks for something edgier. Striving to be contemporary, the company maintains links to teenage lifestyles by reading *Seventeen* magazine, watching popular TV shows, and attending concerts by popular rock bands.

Wet Seal trend searchers stop kids on the street in Manhattan, London, and Tokyo, and visit fashion shows in Milan and Paris. Then at weekly corporate meetings, buyers caucus with the company's top executives to review sales and regional trends. They then decide what the next bestsellers might be. Past hits have included slinky black skirts, fake leathers and furs, and baby barrettes.

Sometimes Wet Seal fashions become the inspiration for its major competitors. Once Wet Seal developed a sweater styled like a sweatshirt with a hood and zipper. It wasn't long before it appeared at Banana Republic. However, not all fashion experiments are a success at Wet Seal. A v-neck sweater vest brought in for back-to-school one year bombed. However, Wet Seal prides itself on its ability to move quickly and by marking down merchandising errors, and the company makes a practice of not investing heavily in any one item.[1]

nutritional stores like GNC are now prominently located in most shopping centers.[12]

Aggressive retailers translate trends into opportunities for new business. A school-uniform trend has been gaining momentum in some areas as a way of combating violence and poor academics in schools. J.C. Penney and Sears have capitalized on this trend by working with school districts to develop uniform colors and styles. Macy's developed its own navy-and-white uniform under its Charter Club label.[13]

Trends can be associated with certain "looks," colors, or brands:

- *Backwoods chic* is an apparel trend that includes flannel shirts, vests, and hiking boots. Eddie Bauer and L.L. Bean, Abercrombie & Fitch, and Northern Reflections are major purveyors of this trend.[14]

- Sizzling orange, electric blue, and acid green are *techno-bright* colors that have had stints of popularity in junior-apparel lines.[15] The colors have new names each time they reappear on the fashion scene.
- According to Teenage Research Unlimited, a Northbrook, Illinois, marketing-research group, the coolest teenage brands are Nike, Tommy Hilfiger, and Sony.[16]

Trends are as numerous as the products associated with them. *Downaging* is a trend defined by the popularity of products of the past among aging baby boomers. *Egonomics* refers to consumers' desire for personal expression.[17] Not all trends bolster business. A victim of Casual Friday, the women's sheer hosiery business declined considerably in the final years of the last millenium.

THE FASHION LIFE CYCLE

The **fashion life cycle** represents the evolution, culmination, and decline of fashion acceptance. The fashion life cycle has four phases: introduction, growth, peak, and decline.[18]

- *Introduction* A fashion is *avant garde* during the introductory stage of the fashion lifecycle. During this stage, fashion apparel is called **high fashion** and is only available through designers or very exclusive stores. Prices during the introductory phase are high, but **fashion leaders**, or trendsetters, are willing to pay the price for the sake of exclusivity and novelty.
- *Growth* A fashion's introductory phase is followed by a period of rapid growth. **Knockoffs**, less-expensive copies of popular high fashions, are typical of the growth phase. A.B.S. is a New York-based company that "reinterprets" high fashion with mass-produced knockoffs in less expensive fabrications. Within a week after a runway debut, a $200 version of a $12,000 Versace creation can appear on the selling floor of Macy's.[19] Growth-phase fashions are adopted by **fashion followers**. Fashion leaders abandon a fashion at this point. Their commitment to exclusivity motivates them to explore the latest fashions.
- *Peak* At this point, a fashion has reached its sales potential. A plateau where sales neither increase or decrease is sometimes characteristic of a fashion's culmination.

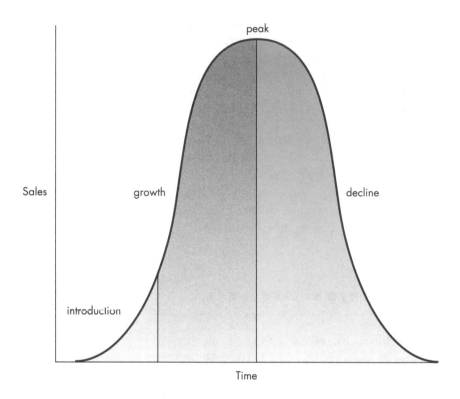

Figure 6.4

The fashion life cycle.

- *Decline* Diminishing sales are characteristic of a fashion's decline. During this phase, most retailers have marked the fashion down for clearance to make room for fashions in earlier cycle phases. **Fashion laggards** purchase the fashion during this stage, as well as nonfashion customers who have no interest in fashion.

Though all fashions pass through the various phases of the fashion life cycle phases, the duration of the cycle or any of its phases varies from one fashion to another. Something may be fashionable for a single season or for many years. Durability and replacement rates often determine the length of a fashion life cycle. Goods with limited durability, such as apparel, have shorter fashion life cycles than durable goods, such as home furnishings. Fashions targeted for the young evolve and die so quickly that they are often referred to as *disposable*. A function of

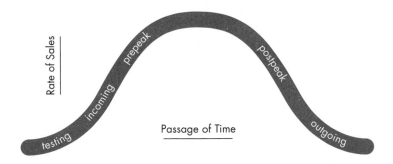

Figure 6.5

One store's interpretation of the fashion life cycle.

sales and time,[20] the fashion life cycle reinforces the notion that consumer purchases define fashion and that many of the "fashions" that
appear on fashion show runways are styles that never really become
fashion.

Fads and Classics

Fads and classics are fashion life-cycle extremes. A **fad** has a short fashion
life cycle. Fads rise and fall in popularity quickly, enduring for as little
time as a few weeks. Some call fads *miniature* or *minor* fashions, hesitant
to classify fads as true fashions because of their brief acceptance. Fads are
especially popular among the young. Fads that have attained historical
significance in the annals of American pop culture include hula-hoops
(c.1958), mood rings (c.1975), and hot pants (c.1971).[21]

Fads generate generous revenues for retailers who identify their
emergence early. Fads represent a high risk, however. When they die,
they die quickly. Fads purchased late in the fashion life cycle must be
sold off at drastic price reductions.

A **classic** has a long fashion life cycle. Some are reluctant to classify
a classic as a fashion since the term *fashion* implies change and classics
seldom change. When classics do change, the changes are very subtle.
Classics remain popular indefinitely, which is why the word *timeless* is
frequently associated with classics. Often referred to as *traditional*, classics appeal to customers with conservative taste. Classics include navy
blue wool blazers, strings of pearls, and the color black. Unlike fads,
classics are low risk with stable rates of sale season after season. Classic

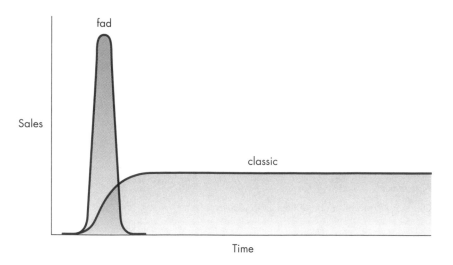

Figure 6.6

The fashion life cycle of fads and classics.

apparel is often promoted as *investment dressing*, accentuating the enduring acceptance of classics season after season.

Talbots is a retailer of classic looks for women. Though Talbots' merchandise is continuously updated through color, fabric, and silhouette, it is designed to remain stylish year after year and to work with what the customer already owns.[22] Some customers are dedicated to classic looks. Eddie Bauer, the casual-apparel specialty division of Spiegel, offended its loyal customer base of 25- to 45-year-old suburbanites when they abandoned hunter green and navy for kiwi and electric blue by emulating the color palettes of brands such as Nautica and Tommy Hilfiger. They quickly reverted back to more traditional color palettes after several seasons of high markdowns.[23]

THE TRICKLE THEORIES

The trickle theories explain the transmission of fashion acceptance from one socioeconomic group to another. There are three trickle theories:

There is no rule that says play dates are just for children.

Talbots

IT'S A CLASSIC

APPAREL • ACCESSORIES • SHOES
STORES 1-800-TALBOTS TALBOTS.COM

Figure 6.7

Classics are enduring fashions that remain popular season after season.

- the trickle-down theory
- the trickle-across theory
- the trickle-up theory

The **trickle-down theory** traces the origins of fashion to upper socioeconomic classes. The theory proposes that lower socioeconomic groups imitate the fashions of the upper socioeconomic classes, and that the wealthy abandon a fashion when it is mimicked by the lower classes. The emulation of fashion worn by famous entertainers is an example of the trickle-down theory. When Madonna burst onto the pop-culture scene in the early 1980s wearing a lacy bustier and chunky crucifix, she started a fashion phenomenon of "lingerie looks" and religious-inspired jewelry.[24] The trickle-down theory supports the long-held notion that a year or more passes before the high fashions that appear on the runways of the fashion centers of Milan, Paris, and New York are reinterpreted as mass fashion.[25]

The **trickle-across**, or *diffusion*, **theory** suggests that fashion is simultaneously adopted across all socioeconomic groups. Proponents of the trickle-across theory claim that the trickle-down theory is dated in that it does not consider the impact of mass communication and computerized design and production capabilities on accelerating the availability of high-fashion knockoffs in mass markets. The trickle-across theory accounts for the fact that similar fashions appear concurrently at stores that cater to diverse socioeconomic groups. A knockoff of a Neiman Marcus fashion may appear concurrently at Wal-Mart. The Neiman Marcus fashion may be 100 percent wool with finished seams and a folded hem. The Wal-Mart fashion may be a polyester blend with unfinished seams and a taped hem. Though fabric and construction are different, the same fashion is available simultaneously at both stores.[26]

Still other fashion theorists find evidence of a **trickle-up theory**, or *status float phenomenon*. The theory proposes that fashions float up from lower socioeconomic groups to higher socioeconomic groups. Consistent with the trickle-up theory, Bloomingdale's created a *Rent* boutique inspired by the popular musical that revolves around a group

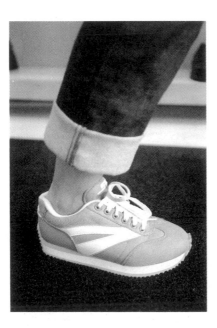

Figure 6.8

The status-float phenomenon proposes that nonfashion items can evolve into high-priced fashions. *Republished with permission of Globe Newspaper Company, Inc., from the September 13, 2000 issue of* The Boston Globe, © 2000.

of artsy East Village New Yorkers struggling in a world of AIDS and drugs. Bloomingdale's collaborated with Necessary Objects, a junior-sportswear manufacturer, to create the line of retro-wear tops and bottoms of thrift-shop vintage-chic fashions worn by the *Rent* cast. [27]

One trickle theory may be more prevalent at one time than another. Some fashions travel in multiple directions. Looks popularized by The Gap have simultaneously appeared on the runways of Girogio Armani, and the aisles of Kmart.[28]

THE FASHION/BASIC CONTINUUM

Merchandise is often classified as being either "basic" or "fashion." **Basic goods** are functional goods that change infrequently and are generally considered necessities.[29] **Fashion goods** are aesthetically appealing goods that change frequently and are generally considered nonnecessities.

Basic goods and fashion goods can be represented at the opposite ends of a continuum. Goods at the far left of the continuum are purely basic. Men's white cotton T-shirts are at this end. Their fabrication, styling, and color do not change from one season to another. A T-shirt is a functional garment worn for warmth and to protect outer garments from body oils and perspiration.

Goods at the far right of the continuum are purely fashion. Fashion jewelry[30] is at this end. The coloration, composition, and styling of fashion jewelry changes each season. Fashion jewelry is not a necessity. It is used for adornment and purchased for its aesthetic value.

Basic Merchandise → **Fashion Merchandise**

- no change
- functional
- necessity

- occasional change
- functional and aesthetic characteristics

- frequent change
- aesthetic
- nonnecessity

Figure 6.9

Fashion/Basic continuum.

Basics are purchased on a replacement basis and out of necessity. A mattress pad is purchased when an old one wears out. Customers do not typically walk by a display of mattress pads and expound: "What a great looking mattress pad! I think I'll buy one!" Price coupled with need is more likely to be the purchase incentive.

Fashion purchases are based on consumer desire for novelty and change. Uniqueness of styling, color, or texture entice consumers to buy fashion goods, as does the way in which the goods are packaged or displayed. A consumer purchases a $350 Coogi sweater because of its interesting coloration and texture. A less expensive sweater could fulfill a functional need for warm clothing.

Goods that fall between these extremes on the continuum have both basic and fashion characteristics. A coat is an apparel necessity in many climates in that it insulates the body from the cold. The functional characteristics of a coat do not change from season to season. However, fashion elements, such as color, styling, and fabrication, change seasonally.

Merchandise on the left half of the continuum is primarily basic with limited fashion qualities. This includes goods, such as pastel-colored bath towel ensembles, flannel pajamas, and pumps in basic colors, such as black, brown, and beige. These goods are most often purchased as replacements, but uniqueness of color or some minute variation in style will sometimes induce the consumer to buy more frequently than necessary or to buy multiple quantities.

Merchandise on the right half of the continuum is primarily fashion with some basic characteristics. These goods have functional uses, however their purchase is based primarily on characteristics of styling, prestige, or color.

Transforming Basics into Fashion

Producers entice consumers to buy other than on a replacement basis by transforming basic goods into fashion goods with new product features or interesting styles, colors, or fabrications. Victoria's Secret spurred the transition of women's innerwear from a basic business to a fashion business. White and beige bras, slips, and panties in cotton, nylon, and rayon have been transformed into fashion assortments of coordinated slips, bras, and panties in an array of colors and prints in luxury fabrications such as silk and satin.

Men's underwear has not been overlooked by the fashion industry. The introduction of color and sexy styles, such as the bikini, have added a fashion dimension to men's underwear, a merchandise category that was once dominated by white cotton and cotton-blend T-shirts and athletic shorts. Men's underwear sales have been further augmented by the transformation of the boxer short, long considered a vestige of the past worn only by older men, into a fashion item available in assortments of solid and patterned silks.

Producers of consumer products retain customer interest in their goods with a continuous flow of product changes. Color is the simplest and least costly change to implement in that changing color does not require new designs, fabrics or materials, production patterns, or manufacturing setups. In a survey of catalog retailers conducted by *Consumer Reports*, respondents claimed that only one out of five items in a new edition of a catalog had not appeared in previous editions. The other four out of five items were new colors or textures

Figure 6.10

Customers buy more frequently than on a replacement basis when basic goods are transformed into fashion goods. *Macy's East.*

Company Profile 6.2

Joe Boxer and the Basic Fashion Continuum

Turning basic into fashion is just what Nick Graham did when he parlayed a pair of yellow smiley-face underpants into a multi-million dollar novelty phenomenon known as Joe Boxer.

Graham began his career as a 27-year old member of a rock band looking for a way to make money. He taught himself how to sew and began designing and making ties that he sold to department and specialty stores. As a joke, he created a pair of X-rated boxer shorts for a store buyer as a wedding gift. He then developed his first item for retail stores: a pair of red-plaid boxers with a raccoon tail that sold out at Saks Fifth Avenue. Hence Joe Boxer was born.

Since then the Joe Boxer empire has expanded to sleepwear and childrenswear. The line is sold in more than 4000 stores in the United States and abroad. Appealing to a young nontraditional customer, the line's image is based on fun and a little bit of blasphemy. Outrageous publicity stunts have helped to build Joe Boxer's brand identity. By dressing up as a flight attendant for Virgin Atlantic Airways, Graham got 400 travelers to change their underwear in mid-flight.

His 14,000 square-foot New York showroom is as whimsical as his product. The décor includes an 8-foot-tall revolving banana, funhouse mirrors, and talking walls. Graham's ability to take a product and revolutionize it was a quick way of becoming recognized in the fashion industry. He considers Joe boxer not just an underwear company but a graphics design company.[1]

Source:

1 Lee, J. (January 31, 1999). *Having fun, right down to his... oh, never mind.* The (Springfield, Mass.) Union News.

of previously appearing styles.[31] Periodic color changes are also important to the home furnishings industry. Major appliances appeared in pastel colors in the 1950s; *harvest gold* and *avocado green* in the 1970s; and *almond* in subsequent decades. The periodic change of color dates appliances that otherwise don't change very much, and encourages consumers to buy a complete set of coordinated appliances when one wears out.

Fashion changes are often reinterpretations of successful fashions of the past. The simple black sleeveless shift dress popularized by actress Audrey Hepburn in the 1950s was brought back in the 1990s through the collections of Michael Kors and Dolce & Gabbana.[32] In the same decade, Volkswagen reinvented its ever-popular Beetle with modern conveniences, such as multispeaker stereo, power windows, and cruise control.[33]

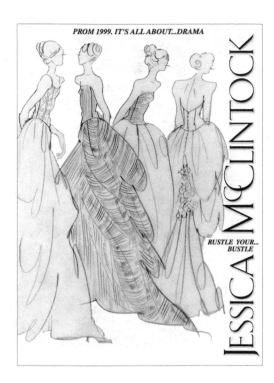

Figure 6.11

New fashions are sometimes reinterpretations of fashion of the past. *Courtesy of Jessica McClintock.*

Not every attempt to transform a basic business into a fashion business is successful. In the mid-1960s, the menswear industry launched a casual, lapel-less suit with a mandarin collar called the Nehru, confident that the style would be a success as traditional dress standards began to ease. However, men were not ready to replace their traditional dark wool suits with this revolutionary new fashion. The Nehru was an abysmal failure and became the laughingstock of the menswear industry. Today, men's apparel undergoes far more fashion change than three decades ago. Occasionally vests appear, lapel and pant widths change, as do the treatment of vents, pleating, and cuffs. However, the Nehru taught the menswear industry a lesson that fashion change in suits should be gradual.

Though consumers reject drastic change, they will not buy unless they perceive an appreciable difference between current and previous offerings. The fashion change that draws the line between consumer acceptance and consumer rejection is a fine one contingent upon many factors such as the target market, economic conditions, and the

Figure 6.12

The Nehru-inspired suit was an unsuccessful attempt to transform a basic business into a fashion business. *Bettman/Corbis.*

type of merchandise. There is no universal answer to the question of how much change is too little and when is it too much. Perhaps the best response is "to make something familiar look new."

FASHION INFLUENCE

Fashion change is rooted in the changes that occur in technology, the economy, and society. Producers react to these environmental changes by designing or developing products consistent with these changes.

The technological advances that have contributed to the growth of the fashion industry date back to the Industrial Revolution and the invention of the sewing machine (c. 1850) that enabled the production of mass-produced *ready-to-wear* garments that could be purchased from racks in stores. Technological development remains a fashion catalyst today. Zenga, the most popular menswear brand at Neiman Marcus, became popular because of its use of innovative fabrics, such as cashmere corduroy and Microtene, a lightweight, water-resistant cloth.[34]

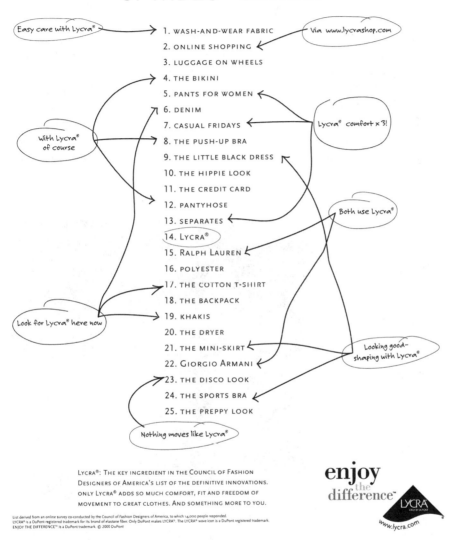

TOP FASHION INNOVATIONS
OF THE 20TH CENTURY

Easy care with Lycra®

1. WASH-AND-WEAR FABRIC
2. ONLINE SHOPPING — Via www.lycrashop.com
3. LUGGAGE ON WHEELS
4. THE BIKINI
5. PANTS FOR WOMEN
6. DENIM
7. CASUAL FRIDAYS — Lycra® comfort x 3!
8. THE PUSH-UP BRA
9. THE LITTLE BLACK DRESS
10. THE HIPPIE LOOK
11. THE CREDIT CARD
12. PANTYHOSE
13. SEPARATES — Both use Lycra®
14. LYCRA®
15. RALPH LAUREN
16. POLYESTER
17. THE COTTON T-SHIRT
18. THE BACKPACK
19. KHAKIS
20. THE DRYER
21. THE MINI-SKIRT
22. GIORGIO ARMANI — Looking good-shaping with Lycra®
23. THE DISCO LOOK
24. THE SPORTS BRA
25. THE PREPPY LOOK

With Lycra® of course

Look for Lycra® here now

Nothing moves like Lycra®

LYCRA®: THE KEY INGREDIENT IN THE COUNCIL OF FASHION DESIGNERS OF AMERICA'S LIST OF THE DEFINITIVE INNOVATIONS. ONLY LYCRA® ADDS SO MUCH COMFORT, FIT AND FREEDOM OF MOVEMENT TO GREAT CLOTHES. AND SOMETHING MORE TO YOU.

enjoy the difference™ LYCRA® www.lycra.com

List derived from an online survey co-conducted by the Council of Fashion Designers of America, to which 14,000 people responded.
LYCRA® is a DuPont registered trademark for its brand of elastane fiber. Only DuPont makes LYCRA®. The LYCRA® wave icon is a DuPont registered trademark.
ENJOY THE DIFFERENCE™ is a DuPont trademark. © 2000 DuPont

Figure 6.13

Manufacturers communicate information about fashion to their retailers through advertising. *Courtesy of DuPont.*

Fashion is linked to economic conditions. A mill that produces velvet claims that black is the preferred color of apparel manufacturers during trying economic times. Because black is a classic color, consumers feel that they will get more wear out of a black-velvet garment than a garment in a frivolous fashion color that will be worn only once or twice. Fashion reflects societal trends. Back in the 1930s, Buxton, a small-leathergoods company, created the two-toned Lady Buxton billfold in response to the needs of a greater number of women who were entering the workforce.[35]

The sources of fashion influence are too numerous to mention. However, popular entertainment as a fashion catalyst is worth noting. Since the advent of motion pictures, actors, actresses, and entertainers have had profound fashion influence.[36] The film *Saturday Night Fever*

Figure 6.14

The film *Saturday Night Fever* gave birth to discomania and the disco shirt worn by John Travolta. *Paramount/MPTV*

gave birth to *discomania* and the *disco shirt*, a polyester, pointed-open-collar shirt worn by John Travolta in the leading role. Jewelry by Carolee produced a line of spray pins and grand-style bold pieces chock full of pearl and colored stones that emulated the jewelry worn by Madonna in the screen production of *Evita* in which the "material girl" had 85 wardrobe changes. Estee Lauder created a cosmetic line called The Face of Evita, while Nicole Miller included tango dress and top-handle handbags in her collections that season.[37]

The fashion influence of movies is not limited to apparel and accessories. Classic Leather, a Hickory, North Carolina-based furniture manufacturer created a line of dressing vanities, gaming tables, beds, desks and leather-upholstered settees called the RMS Titanic Artifact Collection. The pieces were copied from the first-class staterooms, dining rooms and smoking lounges depicted in the 1998 blockbuster *Titanic*.[38]

Television is also an important fashion medium. Dana Kellin jewelry has been popularized by the cast of *Friends, ER,* and *Beverly Hills 90210*.[39] In 1999, American Eagle, the Warrendale, Pennsylvania-based retailer of casual apparel, entered a product tie-in deal to outfit the cast of WB's highly rated television drama *Dawson's Creek*. In addition to outfitting Dawson's angst-filled characters each week, American Eagle also got to use the actors as models for its catalog, in-store advertising, and Web page.[40]

THE FASHION INDUSTRY

The U.S. fashion industry grew rapidly after World War II when Seventh Avenue apparel manufacturers began to visit European fashion centers to copy and mass produce European couture. The *rag* business became the *fashion* business paralleling the country's rapid growth.[41] Today, fashion is an integral part of our economic system and so much a part of our culture that it is difficult to find a product that does not have some inherent element of fashion.

Retailers communicate fashion to their customers through advertising, sales promotion, product presentation, and direct selling. Though fashion stimulates sales, fashion adds to the complexity of a retailer's job. When bed linens were white, buying decisions were often just reorders of the most popular selling sizes and fabrications. Today, a household-textile buying decision involves a vast number of purchase

Sources:
1 *Gibney, F. (August
30, 1999). The allure
of commodity chic.*
Time. *p. 41.*
2 *Givhan, R.
(August 29, 1999).
On target at Target.*
(Springfield, Mass.)
Sunday Republican.
pp. E5, E7.
3 *Herbers, J. (July
18, 1999). A design
for everyone.*
(Springfield, Mass.)
Sunday Republican,
pp. E1, E4.
4 *Branch, S. (May
24, 1999). How
Target got hot.*
Fortune.
pp. 169–174.

Company Profile 6.3

Target—A Lesson in Affordable Fashion

Retailers such as Banana Republic and The Limited make their living by translating runway fashions into affordable and wearable garments for the wardrobe of the average U.S. consumer. But the democratization of fashion is not limited to apparel or to upscale retailers.

Minneapolis-based Target, the nation's third-largest full-line discounter, has differentiated itself from its competitors with a flare for fashion that transcends all of its product lines including home furnishings. Its commitment to home fashion was evident when the company hired Michael Graves, a renowned architect and founder of the Postmodernist movement in architecture, to design a collection for the home that included a product assortment ranging from spatulas to patio furniture. The cross-fertilization between industrial design and home accessories was unprecedented. However, Graves noted that he was never one to see a dichotomy between designing the outside of a building and what goes into it, noting that architects from Michelangelo to Frank Lloyd Wright were responsible for designing cathedrals as well as the candlesticks within them. Graves works in close association with a 22-member trend merchandising team that scours cities from Boston to Bilbao looking for the latest trends, be it a color or a new high-tech fabric.

The fashion-forward strategy has worked for the upscale discounter. Target customers spend an average of $40 per shopping visit compared to Kmart's $24 and Wal-Mart's $30. The Target shopper is younger than the Kmart or Wal-Mart shopper, and has a higher family income. At a time when consumers often voice criticism of the sameness of merchandise from one retailer outlet to another, Target has found its niche in the marketplace by catering to the customers who refuse to sacrifice style for value.[1,2,3,4]

options that includes many merchandise resources, each offering myriad colors, patterns, and styles. A sheet department is as fashionable as an apparel department, boasting of designer names that include Calvin Klein and Ralph Lauren. Fashion adds risk to retail buying decisions. Large retailers commit to hundreds of thousands of dollars for a single fashion item or a group of related fashion items. Faulty fashion predictions impact sales and profit.

SUMMARY POINTS

- Fashion is an expression that is widely accepted by a group of people over time.
- A trend implies the direction or movement of a fashion. The word *trend* is often used synonymously with fashion.
- The fashion life cycle depicts the growth, culmination, and demise of a fashion.
- Fads are short-lived fashions. Classics are long enduring fashions.
- Fashion goods have aesthetic qualities, change frequently, and are generally considered nonnecessities. Basic goods have functional qualities, change infrequently, and are generally considered necessities.
- Fashion acceptance can be explained by the trickle-down, the trickle-across, and the trickle-up theories.
- Sales are stimulated by the transformation of basic goods into fashion goods.
- Fashion is influenced by technological, economic, and societal change. Famous people and popular entertainment also influence fashion.

FOR DISCUSSION

1. Trace the transformation of several products from a basic business to a fashion business.
2. Identify some emerging trends. What impact will these trends have on fashion and the products that consumers will buy?
3. Identify some fashions of the past that have recently reappeared. How do the recent fashions differ from their predecessors? Have the recent fashions been as successful?

KEY TERMS AND CONCEPTS

basic goods	fashion goods	trend
classic	fashion laggard	trickle-across theory
cocooning	fashion leader	trickle-down theory
fad	fashion lifecycle	trickle-up theory
fashion	high fashion	
fashion follower	knockoff	

ENDNOTES

1. Definitions of fashion vary because of the theoretical or occupational biases of the originators that include fashion theorists, designers, and merchants.

2. Himelstein, L. (December 1, 1997). Levi's is hiking its pants up. *Business Week*. pp. 70, 75.

3. Socha, M. (November 17, 1998). Levi's new campaign is youth driven. *Women's Wear Daily*. p. 17.

4. Fraser, K. (1981). *The Fashionable Mind: Reflections on Fashions, 1970–1981*. New York: Knopf. p. 145.

5. Marler, S. (August 1999). Casual catches on. In *WW California*, a special supplement to *Women's Wear Daily*. p. 46.

6. Kate, N. (April 1998). Lose the suit. *American Demographics*. pp. 31–32

7. Marler, S. (August 1999). Casual catches on. *WWD California*, a special supplement to *Women's Wear Daily*. p. 46.

8. Solomon, J. (September 30, 1996). Why worry about pleat pull and sloppy socks. *Newsweek*. p. 51.

9. Faith Popcorn, a futurist, coined the word *cocooning*.

10. Edelson, S. (August 30, 1995). At the malls: The home Stretch. *Women's Wear Daily*. p.14.

11. Reda, S. (August 1994). Home and hearth motivate shoppers. *Stores*. pp. 46–49.

12. Liebeck, L. (May 11, 1998). Welcoming the wellness generation. *Discount Store News*. pp. 77, 100–103.

13. Staff. (April 1996). Popularity of uniforms spurs back-to-school jitters. *Stores*. pp. 79–80.

14. Saporito, B. (March 30, 1998). Can Nike get unstuck? *Time*. pp. 48–53.o

15. Large, E. (January 12, 1997). Time to get bold. *The (Springfield, Mass.) Union-News*. pp. E1, E2.

16. Silverman, D. (May 1998). Tracking Teens. A supplement to *Women's Wear Daily*. pp. 6, 8.

17. Staff. (June 8, 1998). Tormorrow's trends. *Discount Store News*. pp. 64, 69.

18. Nystrom, P. (1928). *Economics of Fashion*. New York: Ronald Press. p. 18.

19. Steinahuer, J. (November 7, 1997). The sincerest form of flattery: Mass marketing. *The New York Times*.

20. An indication of fashion acceptance

21. Staff. (June 14, 1999). The loose abuse of the word "fashion." *Footwear News*. p. 16.

22. Much, M. (April 1, 1996). The new America. *Investor's Business Daily*.

23. Cuneo, A. (September 14, 1998). Brands in trouble—in demand. *Advertising Age*. p. 30.

24. Chandler, S. Desperately seeking a fad. *Business Week*. p. 78.

25. Meadus, A. (October 24, 1994). From runways to mass: A slow trickle. *Women's Wear Daily*. p. 8.

26. King, C. (1963). Fashion adoption: A rebuttal to the "trickle down" theory. Proceedings of the Winter Conference of the American Marketing Association. December 27, 28. Boston. edited by Stephen Greyser.

27. Ryan, S. (November 21, 1996). Watch-and-wear fashions. *The Boston Globe.* pp. E1, E7.

28. Caminiti, S. (March 18, 1996). Will Old Navy fill the gap? *Fortune.* pp. 59-62.

29. The term *staple* is often used synonymously with basic. Technically, staples are goods with year-round demand, as opposed to seasonal goods that are only in demand at certain times of the year. The term *basic* is not associated with seasonal or year-round demand.

30. The preferred trade term for costume jewelry.

31. Staff. (October 1994). Mail-order shopping: Which catalogs are best? *Consumer Reports.* pp. 621–626.

32. Reynolds, P. (September 28, 1995). Coming down a runway near you: Audrey Hepburn. *The Boston Globe.* pp. 53, 57.

33. Naughton, K. & Vlasic, B. (March 23, 1998). The nostalgia boom. *Business Week.* pp. 58–63.

34. Rossant, J. (March 4, 1996). Is that Zenga you're wearing? *Newseek.* P. 84–85.

35. Parr, K. (July 20, 1998). Buxton at 100: Building on history. *Women's Wear Daily.* p. 17.

36. Ellis, K. (August 1999). L.A. apparel's yellow brick road. In *WWD California*, a special supplement to *Women's Wear Daily.* p. 36

37. Robin, D. (December 19, 1996). Eyes on Evita. *The (Springfield, Mass.) Union-News.* pp. B11, B12.

38. Nowell, P. May 3, 1998). Company cashes in on Titanic-type furniture. *The (Springfield, Mass.) Sunday Republican.* pp. G1, G22.

39. Meadus, A. (March 4, 1996). TV trendsetters worth watching. *Women's. Wear Daily.* pp. 10, 12.

40. Quick, R. (June 12, 1999). Fashion coup at "Dawson's Creek." *The Wall Street Journal.*

41. Staff. (December 15, 1970) Man of the year. *Clothes.* pp. 26–32.

chapter seven

BRANDS AND PRIVATE LABELS

Most consumer products are identified in one of two ways: by a name associated with the product producer, such as Sony; or a name associated with the store in which the product is sold, such as Macy's Charter Club. Consumers link certain characteristics, such as price, quality, styling, and reliability, to product names. Retailers make other associations, including profit and sales potential, with product identities. Chapter 7 deals with two types of products: national brands that bear an identity associated with their producer, and private labels that bear a name exclusive to the store in which they are sold.

After you have read this chapter, you will be able to discuss:

The concept of branding.

Licensing.

Private labeling.

BRANDED MERCHANDISE

Branded, or *brand-name,* **merchandise,** is identified by a name and/or symbol associated with certain product characteristics, such as price, quality, fit, styling, and prestige. These characteristics position a product in the marketplace by distinguishing it from its competitors. Packaging and/or labeling are often important elements of brand identification.[1] Recognizable brand names include Lee jeans, Giorgio fragrances, and Fruit of the Loom underwear. Coca Cola is the planet's most ubiquitous brand. Its worth is estimated at $39 billion.[2]

A **designer,** or *signature,* **brand** bears the name of a designer, such as Christian Dior or Tommy Hilfiger. A *power brand* is a term used to refer to a highly recognizable, high-volume-generating brand. A *niche brand* is less recognizable than a power brand, but has a dedicated customer following.[3] Wilson sporting goods, Black & Decker countertop appliances, Maybelline cosmetics, and Mattel toys are power brands at full-line discount stores.

A brand is sometimes referred to as a *manufacturer's brand* or a *national brand.* Many "national brands" are in fact "international brands." Levi Strauss, the largest apparel manufacturer in the world, has production facilities in more 40 countries, and has sold more than 2.5 billion pairs of jeans worldwide since its founding in 1853. Other brands have existed for many years. Jantzen (swimwear) was founded in 1910, Bulova (watches) in 1875. Some brands have gained worldwide prominence in a relatively short time. DKNY was established in 1984, Reebok in 1981.[4]

Intense competition for market dominance leads to a continuous emergence of innovative branded products.[5] In 1951, Hanes developed the seamless stocking.[6] Later Hanes product developments included Underalls, the all-in-one pantyhose, and an opaque microfiber for Hanes Soft Touch hosiery. Totes was the innovator of the pop-up umbrella. Small Wonder, a full-size umbrella that folds to a compact eight inches, is a more recent Totes development.[7] Product innovation is not limited to apparel and accessories. Timex developed Indiglo, a patented night-light technology that more than doubled the watchmaker's sales in two years.[8]

Brands and Advertising

Producers of branded products use advertising and sales promotion to position their products in the marketplace and to generate consumer demand for them. By advertising directly to consumers, manufacturers

Figure 7.1

A brand is distinctive with characteristics that differentiate it from its competitors.
Courtesy of Zena/W.E. Stephens.

pull products through the marketing channel in that retailers are inclined to carry products that they know consumers will ask for upon seeing them advertised.[9] Advertising is an expensive proposition. Nike advertising expenditures exceed $200 million a year. Levi Strauss spends more than $100 million annually.[10] Moreover, advertising expenditures are often linked to a brand's success. The advertising budget for L'eggs

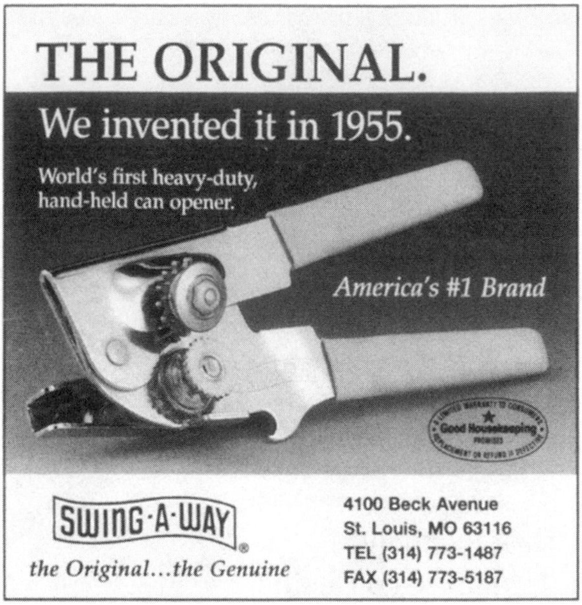

Figure 7.2

Intense competition for market dominance leads to a continuous emergence of innovative branded products. *Courtesy of Swing-A-Way.*

hosiery exceeds the advertising expenditures for competitive brands. As a result, L'eggs accounts for over half of the hosiery sales in the food, drug, and mass-market retail channels in which the brand is distributed.[11]

Various forms of advertising and sales promotion are used to promote brands.[12] Calvin Klein's marketing strategy includes a mix of television and out-of-home advertising, as well as countless fashion-oriented consumer magazines. Chic jeans increases its brand-name recognition with TV ads, product hang tags, and in-store displays. Other brands concentrate on a single advertising medium. Vanity Fair (innerwear) advertises almost exclusively in fashion and lifestyle magazines.[13]

Advertising for brands is often image-oriented, portraying the lifestyle of the targeted consumer. The advertising for Polo/Ralph Lauren has a "weekend-in-the-country" appeal. Calvin Klein advertising has an "urban-sensuous" appeal. Tommy Hilfiger ads have a youthful American spirit appeal. According to one observer, Ralph is wealth, Calvin is hedonism, and Tommy is happiness.[14]

Brands and Retail Stores

The retail channels through which brands are distributed play an important role in establishing a brand's image relative to price, fashion, and intended customer. As a bridge-sportswear line, Ellen Tracy is distributed through upscale specialty department stores, such as Nordstrom and Bergdorf Goodman. Gitano value-oriented apparel and accessories are distributed through full-line discount stores. Lancome, Elizabeth Arden, and Clarins are *prestige* cosmetics lines sold in department stores. Maybelline, Max Factor, and Cover Girl are *mass-market* cosmetics lines packaged for self-selection and sold in discount stores and drug stores.[15]

Producers protect their brand image by ensuring that their products are not sold to unintended retail channels by third-party wholesalers called **diverters.**[16] In the aftermath of natural disasters such as hurricanes and tornadoes, Estée Lauder buys back its own product from the insurance companies that acquire damaged stock from department stores, fearing that the product will otherwise be bought by diverters and then sold to discount stores.

Many brands owe their initial success to an introduction by a reputed retailer. Estee Lauder cosmetics were introduced at Saks Fifth Avenue in 1950. The men's designer-label movement began in December 1965 when Lord & Taylor opened the first John Weitz shop at its Fifth Avenue store.[17] Bloomingdale's was the first to open its doors to Liz Claiborne, destined to become one of the fastest growing women's apparel lines in Seventh Avenue history.[18]

Just as brands use retailers as a market-positioning tool, retailers use brands to define their image.[19] Wal-Mart enhanced its low fashion profile by adding labels such as White Stag sportswear and Puritan menswear to its assortments.[20] The Bon-Ton upgraded its fashion image with a stronger presence of brands such as Liz Claiborne, Tommy Hilfiger, and Nautica.[21]

Brand Positioning

The apparel industry uses a price/quality hierarchy to position lines:

Designer lines are exclusive creations of a reputed designer. Their distribution is limited, sometimes restricted to the designer's boutiques.

Bridge, or *diffusion,* **lines** are the lower-priced designer creations with limited distribution through prestigious stores, such as Saks Fifth Avenue and Bloomingdale's.

Better lines and **moderate lines** are broadly distributed lines that appear at less prestigious department store conglomerates, such as May and Dillard's. Moderate lines have broader distribution than better lines, and may also appear at stores such as J.C. Penney or Sears.

Budget, or *mass-market,* **lines** are carried in value-oriented stores such as full-line discounters.

Figure 7.3

Retailers use brands to define their image and position themselves in the marketplace. *Courtesy of Mary Jane Denzer.*

The following breakdown of designer, bridge, better, moderate, and budget lines in the misses sportswear industry best exemplifies the system:

- Designer—Donna Karan, Calvin Klein
- Bridge—DKNY, Adrienne Vittadini, Anne Klein II, Ellen Tracy
- Better—Liz Claiborne, Jones New York, JH Collectibles, Carole Little, Susan Bristol
- Moderate—Alfred Dunner, Chaus, Koret, Norton McNaughton, Cricket Lane
- Budget—Russ, Cherokee, Chic, Wrangler, Gitano, Brittania

The classification system is often adapted to other product categories. In a department-store handbag department, Louis Vuitton and Fendi are the designer lines. Bridge lines include Coach and Dooney & Bourke. Better lines include Liz Claiborne. Moderate handbags include the store's opening-price-point brands that are often the store's private labels.

Producers sometimes alter their distribution strategies when they see opportunities for larger market share. Evan Picone was a better misses sportswear line that was repositioned by new owners as a moderate line. Originally a department-store hosiery line, Underalls was eventually repositioned as a **mass-market line**. Recognizing the need for a moderately priced jeanswear brand for department and specialty

Figure 7.4

Producers of branded products often support the sale of their product line at the retail level with inventory-management services and cooperative advertising incentives.
Couristan, Inc , creative elegance in fine area rugs and broadloom, Fort Lee, NJ.

stores, the VF Corporation rechanneled its Lee brand from full-line discounters to department and specialty stores. Unwilling to give up its healthy discount store business, VF created a line called Riders as a replacement for Lee at discount stores.

Sometimes producers attempt to increase market share by distributing their brands through multiple retail channels. Multiple-channel distribution is upsetting to upscale retailers who feel that a brand's image is sullied when distributed through value-oriented retailers. OshKosh B'Gosh, a producer of trendy childrenswear, irked many of its upscale department-store accounts, such as Bloomingdale's and Macy's, when it began to distribute through J.C. Penney and Sears.[22,23] Upscale stores often discontinue brands when their producers begin distributing them through less prestigious stores. Both May Department Stores and Federated Department Stores discontinued Revlon's Ultima II line because of broadened distribution through J.C. Penney.[24,25] Being snubbed by an upscale retailer is not necessarily devastating to a brand. Macy's discontinued Levi's jeans when Levi Strauss began to distribute the line through J.C. Penney and Sears. J.C. Penney eventually became one of Levi Strauss' largest accounts. Several years later, Macy's resumed carrying the line.

Producers of branded products often support the sale of their products at the retail level by providing product training, promotional aids, and funds for store-sponsored advertising. Producers sometimes provide fixtures and signage especially designed for their product to enhance consistent and prominent presentation in all stores. Branded product producers sometimes share the risk of carrying a line by allowing retailers to return slow-selling goods for credit after an agreed-upon selling period.[26]

Brand Extension

Brand extension involves adding related products to an existing line of branded products, or developing a new product line with the same brand identity. By extending a brand, a producer capitalizes on a brand's reputation, as well as the company's production expertise, and the channel relationships established with existing products.[27] Jockey International's reputation for quality men's underwear prompted the development of Jockey For Her, a line that now generates sales nearly equivalent to the sales of Jockey's long-established men's line. Dockers is a Levi Strauss brand that began as a line of casual cotton menswear.

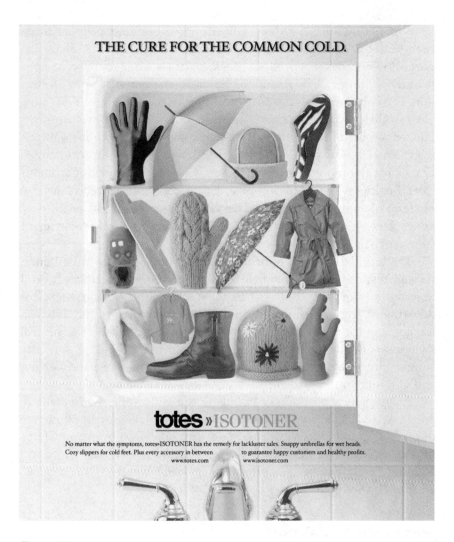

Figure 7.5

Totes, well-known for its umbrellas, expanded their brand to include products such as coats and hats. *Courtesy of Totes Isotoner Corporation.*

Dockers now includes licensed lines of outerwear, shoes, socks, belts, and small leather goods, a line of cotton women's wear, and a boy's line. Multiple extensions result in a *megabrand,* a brand that encompasses several related merchandise categories, such as dresses, accessories, shoes, and sportswear.

Some companies produce a portfolio of branded product lines, each targeted to different markets. Jessica McClintock's dress-line portfolio includes Scott McClintock, a dress and sportswear line; Jessica McClintock Bridal; and the Jessica McClintock designer collection. The company also produces Gunne Sax, a junior line; and Gunne Sax for Girls, a dressy apparel line for infant through preteen girls. Jantzen's portfolio of women's swimwear lines includes Jantzen Sport, an active-inspired line; Electric Beach a junior line; and Jantzen Classic for the more mature customer. When its upscale department-store business began to stabilize, Liz Claiborne, acquired several moderate labels, among them The Villager, a megabrand of dresses, accessories, and shoes, distributed through low-end department stores such as Sears.

The brands within a portfolio are often intended for distribution through a specific retail channel. The Warnaco Group produces several innerwear brands, including Warner's, Olga, and Calvin Klein for department stores; Fruit of the Loom for discounters; and the Van Raalte label for Sears. The Authentic Fitness Corporation has several swimwear brands, including Speedo, a performance line for specialty stores; White Stag, a mass-market line for discount stores; and Jantzen and Catalina for department stores.

A company's portfolio of brands is sometimes highly diversified. Along with its signature food products, the Sara Lee Corporation produces L'eggs and Hanes hosiery, Playtex and Bali innerwear, and Totes umbrellas. The VF Corporation's portfolio of branded products includes Vanity Fair and Vassarette innerwear, Wrangler and Lee jeans, and Jantzen swimwear.

Brand-Driven Purchases

A consumer choice based primarily on brand preference is called a **brand-driven purchase.** Purchases are brand-driven when clear distinctions differentiate brands.[28] When clear distinctions do not differentiate brands, consumers adopt a "one brand is as good as the next" attitude basing their purchases on factors such as price or color, with minimal consideration of brand. Fragrances purchases are brand driven because of each brand's distinctive scent. Purchases of denim blue jeans are brand-driven because of each brand's unique fit.[29] The purchases of designer-label apparel, cosmetics, and toys are also brand-driven. Consumers are reluctant to accept substitutes for purchases that are

Figure 7.6

Each of VF Corporation's casual-apparel brands is targeted to a different group of customers. *Courtesy of VF Corporation.*

brand-driven. Customers who consistently purchase the same brand are called *brand loyal*.

To understand the concept of brand-driven purchases, consider the male customer who consistently purchases Levi's 501 blue jeans. Three product characteristics are important to him: a consistent fit, easy care, and durability. The customer is not enticed by lower-priced competitive brands that he has found are not as comfortable, nor as durable. The same customer may make a necktie purchase irrelevant to brand. His selection of a tie is based solely on color, pattern, and the feel of the fabric. The product features relevant to fit, care, and durability that influenced his jeans purchase are irrelevant to his necktie purchase in that neckties are a standard size, they typically require dry cleaning, and they do not have points of stress to cause concern for durability. The jeans purchase is brand-driven. The necktie purchase is not. When approached by a salesperson in a retail store, the customer states his needs as "a pair of Levi's 501" and a "tie to go with a navy-blue suit."

LICENSING

Licensing involves the use of a merchandising property in the design of a product or a product line. Merchandising properties have many forms, including brand names (Totes), designer names (Calvin Klein), trademarks (Coca-Cola), designs (a polo player on a horse), characters (the Rug Rats), celebrity names (Celine Dion), sports teams (the Dallas Cowboys), and various forms of entertainment, such as movies (*Titanic*), television shows (*Beverly Hills 90210*), and special events (the Olympics). In a licensing agreement, the owner of the merchandising property (the licensor) permits (licenses) a producer (the licensee) to use the property for a fee, or royalty, of about 5 to 6 percent of sales.[30] The licensee is responsible for the design, production, and distribution of the product. *Cross licensing* involves the use of two licensed properties, such as a necktie depicting Bugs Bunny wearing a New York Giants sweatshirt.

Licensing provides the licensor with an opportunity to extend a brand without having to develop, produce, or market a new product. A property becomes licensable after a reputation for prestige, quality, style, or popularity has been established in the marketplace.[31] The licensee reaps the marketing advantage of the established reputation or popularity of the merchandising property.[32] To protect the reputation of the merchandising property, licensors most often reserve the right to approve the material, color, quality, and design of the licensed product.[33]

Licensed products are often related to product lines from which they are descended.[34] The names of apparel designers appear on lines of accessories. Dinnerware companies license designs to producers of table linens and glassware. The London Fog moniker appears on licensed hats, umbrellas, and children's outerwear. General Mills licenses the Betty Crocker name for a line of cookware and countertop appliances.

Licensing can be very lucrative brand-extension ventures. Polo Ralph Lauren's 26 licenses generate more than $4 billion in sales for products that include everything from tableware to towels.[35] However, extensive licensing can diminish the exclusivity of a designer's cachet. Halston's high-fashion image was severely tainted in 1983 when the company licensed a line of female apparel called Halston III for distribution at J.C. Penney.[36] The name eventually disappeared from the marketplace until an investment firm reintroduced the brand in 1998 as a moderate line of men's, women's, and home lines for department-store distribution.[37,38]

Figure 7.7

Steve Madden, best known for its shoes, licenses some of its other product lines.
Courtesy of Steve Madden, Ltd.

Licensees often have considerable expertise in the design, production, and distribution of licensed products.[39,40] Hanes produces licensed hosiery lines for Donna Karan and Liz Claiborne. Timex makes Guess and Monet watches. Oneida produces silver flatware for the Guess Home Collection. Extending a brand by licensing to experts who understand the

Table 7.1a	SHARES OF ALL LICENSED PRODUCT RETAIL SALES BY PRODUCT CATEGORY

Product Category	Retail Sales
Accessories	$ 6.20
Apparel	11.60
Domestics	4.20
Electronics	1.06
Food/Beverage	5.24
Footwear	2.03
Furniture/Home Furnishings	0.75
Gifts/Novelties	6.00
Health and Beauty	3.70
Housewares	2.18
Infant Products	2.16
Music/Video	1.18
Publishing	4.23
Sporting Goods	2.25
Stationery/Paper	3.10
Toys/Games	7.26
Video games/Software	3.26
Other—small size category	0.20
TOTAL	$66.60

Dollar Figures in Billions;
United States and Canada only

Table 7.1b	SHARES OF ALL LICENSED PRODUCT RETAIL SALES BY PROPERTY TYPE

Property Category	Retail Sales
Art	$ 4.74
Celebrities/Estates	2.55
Entertainment/Character	15.80
Fashion	11.80
Music	0.97
Nonprofit	0.65
Publishing	1.50
Sports	13.14
Trademarks/Brands	12.64
Toys/Games	2.55
Other—small size category	0.26
TOTAL	$66.60

Dollar Figures in Billions;
United States and Canada only

design, production, and distribution of a product is often a more prudent marketing strategy than developing brand extensions internally. Donna Karan is often criticized for keeping brand extensions in-house by industry observers who see greater growth opportunities in licensing.[41]

Licensor and licensee relationships are sometimes intricately woven. London Fog produces a Sperry Topsiders outerwear line for Stride Rite, a shoe company that has licenses for producing footwear for Levi Strauss and Tommy Hilfiger.[42] Liz Claiborne is the licensee for DKNY Active and DKNY Jeans.[43,44] Liz Claiborne Intimates is produced by Jockey International.[45]

Some companies are essentially licensing organizations. Calvin Klein produces its image-setting women's sportswear collection. However,

Calvin Klein jeans are produced by Designer Holdings; Calvin Klein underwear by The Warnaco Group; Calvin Klein shoes and handbags by the Nine West Group.[46] Calvin Klein fragrances are produced by Unilever, the producer of Elizabeth Arden cosmetics and other fragrances, such as White Diamonds and Passion. Calvin Klein hosiery is produced by Kayser-Roth, the producer of No-Nonsense pantyhose.[47]

Licensing is a $70 billion industry in the United States. Apparel and accessories represent the largest category of licensed products. Popular licensed apparel items include T-shirts, sweatshirts, and sleepwear.[48] Other commonly licensed categories include novelties, toys, and stationery. Licensed products represent a significant amount of sales volume for many retailers. Some have assigned a buyer to be solely responsible for identifying hot properties and for merchandising shops and coordinating promotions tied to the licensed properties.

The licensing of designer names began in 1924 when the famous French designer Coco Chanel permitted the use of her name on a newly developed fragrance. The association was a controversial one at a time when designer names appeared only on high fashion couture. Chanel No. 5 was an immediate success and remains so today. However, not every licensing effort is as successful. Some licensing debacles include Bill Blass chocolates, Ralph Lauren westernwear, and Yves Saint Laurent jeans. In general, licensing efforts fail when the brand extension strays too far from the core product line conceptually and/or when the core product line and the extension appeal to different groups of customers.[49]

PRIVATE LABELS

Private-label merchandise bears the name of the retail store in which it is sold, or a name used exclusively by the retailer. Products with a Brooks Brothers or Gap label are private-label goods, as are products with the Erika Taylor or Claybrooke labels used exclusively by May Department Stores. Unlike branded goods that are "presold" by producer-sponsored advertising and sales promotion, the retailer relies on its own reputation to validate the quality, style, or value of private-label merchandise. A Nordstrom label conveys an image of fashion to a consumer, while a Kmart label conveys an image of value. Private-label goods are produced according to retailers' specifications for color,

Figure 7.8

Federated Department Store has popular private labels. *Courtesy of Federated Department Stores, Inc.*

styling, and fabrication. The goods are then packaged and labeled with a retailer's name or logo, or name unique to the retailer.

Some stores, such as Ann Taylor and The Gap, offer only private labels. Other retailers, such as department stores and full-line discounters, balance a mix of both branded and private-label merchandise, hoping to draw brand-conscious customers, and also to reap the generous profit margins of private labels. These retailers offer consumers brand and price alternatives by strategically locating private label goods adjacent to branded goods.

Some producers specialize in the design and production of private-label goods. Cygne Designs is a New York-based private-label resource of male and female sportswear. Cygne's customers include Ann Taylor, The Limited, Dillard's, Federated, Dayton Hudson, and J.C. Penney. Some companies are both private-label contractors and licensees of branded lines. El Paso-based Sun Apparel is the private-label jeans contractor for Wal-Mart's Faded Glory label, The Limited's Express label, J.C. Penney's Arizona Jeans Co. label, and Federated Department Stores' Badge label. Sun Apparel is also the licensee for the Polo Ralph Lauren jeans line.[50]

Retailers that conduct considerable private-label business often have product-development functions within their merchandising organizations responsible for designing private-label goods and contracting their production. MAST Industries is a division of The Limited that designs products for the various Limited divisions according to buyers' specifications. MAST then sources fabric and production. Within an eight-week period, the item is distributed throughout hundreds of Limited stores.

Private labeling is not a new concept. Since the 1940s, Macy's has had one of the most successful private-label programs in the department-store industry. Private labeling was the cornerstone of the merchandising strategies at J.C. Penney and Sears. There are countless satisfied customers who can attest to the quality and value of their Kenmore washing machines, Toughskins jeans, DieHard automotive batteries, and Craftsman tools that they purchased at Sears.

Positioning Private Labels

Private labels are frequently positioned as the opening, or lowest, price-point in a basic category of merchandise.[51] However, some private labels are upscale fashions targeted to customer segments not satisfied by branded offerings. Saks Fifth Avenue's private-label collections include:

- The Works—a career line in the lower bridge price points
- Real Clothes—a casual line of silks and linens
- SFA Collections—knitwear and sportswear in the higher bridge price points

Private-label goods are often knockoffs of successful branded products or product lines. The best-selling department-store brands of robes and sleepwear appear as private labels at full-line discounters,

Figure 7.9

Macy's promotes its *Charter Club* private label as a brand. *Macy's East.*

including Honors at Target, Upstart at Wal-Mart, and Ashley Taylor at Kmart. Macy's Charter Club and J.C. Penney's Hunt Club apparel lines bear a striking resemblance to Polo/Ralph Lauren.[52] Tastefully designed in-store shops for private-label collections further contribute to the designer illusion.

Sometimes the illusion is too close for comfort. Salvatore Ferragamo Italia sued May Department Stores for violating Ferragamo's "Gancini" trademark by selling handbags with clasps that bore a design identical to the Gancini insignia, a design resembling *omega* in the Greek alphabet.[53] Though the producers of branded goods are frustrated by the value-oriented imitations of their lines, consumers benefit from the rivalry. The competition between the innovators and the imitators ensures a continual flow of distinctive merchandise to the marketplace.

The Pros and Cons of Private Labels

Advantages Private labels are advantageous to retailers for several reasons:

- Wholesale costs for private-label goods are less than the wholesale cost of branded goods of comparable quality. Product-development and marketing costs are inherent in the price of branded goods. Product development and marketing costs for private-label goods are minimal.[54]
- Because of lower costs, a retailer can price private-label goods more competitively and more profitably than branded goods. Retailers often rely on private labels to boost their profits.[55] The comeback of many departments stores has been attributed to closer attention to their private labels, especially in women's apparel.[56]
- Private-label goods are exclusive to a store. This exclusivity allows the retailer considerable pricing latitude since consumers have no basis for price comparison.
- Retailers can develop private-label goods targeted specifically to their customers without being restricted to the offerings of the marketplace.[57] Kmart's Everyday coordinating bed and bath ensembles by Martha Stewart are made for "style-challenged" customers who want simple solutions to home decorating.[58]

Disadvantages In spite of their advantages, several disadvantages are associated with private-label merchandise:

- There is no national advertising or any type of vendor support to promote the sale of private-label goods.
- Consumers shun private labels as substitutes for brand-driven purchases. They sometimes associate a private label's low price with low quality.
- Private labeling is often a capital-intensive proposition. Goods contracted overseas are paid for months in advance of their arrival. This precludes many small or undercapitalized retailers.

Exclusive Lines

Lines created exclusively for a retailer with a brand or designer name should not be confused with private labeling. Benetton produces an apparel line called Benetton USA for exclusive distribution at Sears. The line is less expensive than the Benetton line sold at Benetton stores in the

Source:
1 *Gross, E. (January
1998). Crazy Horse:
J.C. Penney's private
label brands.* American
Sportswear &
Knitting Times.
pp. 21–24.

Company Profile 7.1

J.C. Penney—When a Private Label Becomes a National Brand

In a study conducted by Kurt Salmon Associates for Fairchild Publications, J.C. Penney's private-label Arizona jeans line was ranked among the best-known names in denim in the United States. J.C. Penney has proven that a department store's private labels are not just a way of reaping greater margins, but a mechanism for carving out a unique niche in a marketplace. Though Arizona is J.C. Penney's best-selling private label, the company boasts of several other private-label success stories. Among them are Hunt Club, classic American sportswear for men, women, and children; St. John's Bay weekend casualwear for men and women; and the J.C. Penney Home Collection, primarily a textile-product line that also includes home furnishings and lamps. The company's oldest surviving but lesser-known brand, is Big Mac workwear sold only through J.C. Penney catalogs.

Many of J.C. Penney's private labels are displayed as collections in boutiques that mimic the Ralph Lauren and Tommy Hilfiger shops in more upscale department stores. J.C. Penney's private labels account for more than 40 percent of the company's total retail sales.[1]

United States and throughout the world.[59] Only Bloomingdale's is a collection of apparel and home furnishings with noted designer names such as Calvin Klein, created exclusively for Bloomingdale's. Bloomingdale's is also involved with a co-branding experiment with Tahiri, an upscale women's apparel line, in which both the designer's name and the store's name appear on the label of a collection designed by Tahiri for exclusive distribution at Bloomingdale's.[60]

Private Labels as Brands

The word *brand* or *branded* is used to refer to goods marketed by their producer. However, Kurt Salmon Associates, an international management consulting organization, defines a *brand* as any recognizable name that adds value to a product because of consumers' perceptions of the name. A name that is meaningful to consumers is a brand. A name that is meaningless, is not a brand. Some retailers promote their private labels with extensive advertising. J.C. Penney supports its private-label programs with television advertising, newspaper inserts, and direct mail. Macy's advertises private labels alongside its branded goods.

Some retailers extend their private label as one would extend a brand. Eddie Bauer stores now feature home-accessories items such as frames, clocks, and decorative accessories. Banana Republic offers bed and bath ensembles made of the same fabric as its apparel.[61]

According to the Kurt Salmon interpretation, these stores "brand" their private-label merchandise.[62] Therefore, *The Gap* is a brand, since consumers associate The Gap's name with quality and value.[63] This explanation justifies the seemingly paradoxical reference to private labels as *store brands* or *private brands*.[64]

SUMMARY POINTS

- Branded merchandise is identified by a name and/or symbol that consumers associate with certain product characteristics such as price, quality, value, fit, styling, and prestige.
- Consumer purchases are brand-driven when clear distinctions exist among competing brands and when the distinctive characteristics are important to the consumer.
- Brands are extended by the addition of related products or product lines. Licensing is a form of brand extension requiring no capital investment on the part of the licensor.
- Private-label merchandise is exclusive to a retailer's product mix and affords a retailer an opportunity for higher profit margins.

FOR DISCUSSION

1. Search the Internet to obtain the histories of several branded products. Compare the brands' growth relative to innovative product development, brand extension, creative advertising and promotion, and licensing agreements.
2. Determine which products within a category of merchandise at a local department store or full-line discounter are private labels and which are brands. Compare the private labels to the brands in terms of quality, price, fashion level, and percentage of total product mix in the store. What distinctions, if any, do you observe?
3. Visit the Web sites of several brands and determine if they are part of a portfolio of brands. What distinctions do you see among the brands within the proftolio in terms of target customer and channel of distribution?

KEY TERMS AND CONCEPTS

better line	budget line	mass-market line
brand-driven purchase	designer brand	moderate line
brand extension	designer line	private label
branded merchandise	diverter	
bridge line	licensing	

ENDNOTES

1. Lewis, R. (November 8, 1995). What's a brand worth? *Women's Wear Daily*. pp. 10–11, 20.
2. Ibid.
3. Ibid.
4. Much of the information on branded products in this chapter was obtained from the October 1998 edition of *The Fairchild 100*, a supplement to *Women's Wear Daily*, edited by Edward Nardoza.
5. Lewis, R. (November 8, 1995). What's a brand worth? *Women's Wear Daily*. pp. 10–11, 20.
6. Staff. (August 1952). The seamless stocking. *Department Store Economist*. pp. 68–70.
7. Meadus, A. (February 1996). Umbrellas on the rise. A supplement to Women's Wear Daily. p. 10.
8. Underwood, E. (April 25, 1994). Indiglo watch lights up better times for Timex. *Brandweek*. pp. 30–32.
9. A *push* strategy involves business-to-business advertising by one channel member to the next.
10. Staff. (May 15, 1998). The Big Spenders. *Women's Wear Daily*. pp. 8–10.
11. Staff. (November 1997). The top 100. In *Fairchild 100*, a supplement to *Women's Wear Daily*. p. 9.
12. Ozzard, J. (October 1995). How to build a brand. Denim Network. A supplement to *Women's Wear Daily*. p. 10, 22.
13. Friedman, A. (November 8, 1995). Vendors build brand loyalty. *Women's Wear Daily*. p. 12.
14. Parr, K. (October 31, 1996). The image makers. *Women's Wear Daily*. p. 16.
15. Staff. (May 16, 1997). The hit parade. *Women's Wear Daily*. p. 16.
16. Tode, C. (March 13, 1998). Diverters win battle, but the war rages on. *Women's Wear Daily*. p. 10.
17. Parola, R. (May 22, 1992). The designer decades. *Daily News Record*. pp. 81–82.
18. Darnton, N. (August 1992). The joy of polyester. *Newsweek*. p. 61.
19. D'Innoncenzio, A. (November 1997). Retailers and makers share glory. A supplement to *Women's Wear Daily*. p. 34.

20. Lee, G. (November 15, 1995). Wal-Mart says private brands have built its apparel image. *Women's Wear Daily*. p. 15.

21. Seckler, V. (November 5, 1997). The Bon-Ton bets on better brands. *Women's Wear Daily*. pp. 22–23.

22. Ozzard, J. (June 22, 1994). Lee stakes a new claim. *Women's Wear Daily*. pp. 8–9.

23. Siler, J. (July 15, 1991). OshKosh B'Gosh may be risking its upscale image. *Business Week*. p. 140.

24. Born, P. (March 4, 1994). May dropping Ultima, cites "diluted cachet." *Women's Wear Daily*. pp. 1, 11.

25. Born, P. (April 8, 1994). Federated to drop Revlon's Ultima II. *Women's Wear Daily*. p. 4.

26. Ozzard, J. (October 1995). How to build a brand. Denim Network. A supplement to *Women's Wear Daily*. p. 10, 22.

27. Socha, M. (November 1997). Brand extension catapults awareness. A supplement to *Women's Wear Daily*. p. 30.

28. Staff. (April 1996). Brand loyalty rules sporting goods market. *Stores*. p. 85.

29. Purchases of denim blue jeans are generally considered brand-driven. However, according to a March 10, 1995 article in *Women's Wear Daily* (pp. 1, 6–8), private labels have been gaining considerable market share.

30. V.M.Y. (February 16, 1999). Licensing fees not always a five-percent solution. *Women's Wear Daily*. p. 38.

31. Pogoda, D. The extension dilemma. *Women's Wear Daily*. pp. 13, 17.

32. Wilensky, D. (June 17, 1996). *Discount Store News*. p. 33.

33. Lazar, B. (February 16, 1998). Licensing gives known brands new life. *Marketing News*. p. 8.

34. Pogoda, D. (May 27, 1998). To license or not. *Women's Wear Daily*. p. 34.

35. Greenfeld, K. Ralph's rough ride. *Time*. pp. 68–70.

36. Pogoda, D. & Ozzard, J. (October 23, 1995). Image: Is it everything? *Women's Wear Daily*. pp. 22–23.

37. Krol, C. (September 23, 1996). Halston uses $5 mil in ads to help resuscitate image. *Advertising Age*. p. 24.

38. Luscombe, B. (May 4, 1998). Boggie nights are back. *Time*. pp. 70–71.

39. Friedman, A. (December 6, 1995). A blueprint for brand licensing. *Women's Wear Daily*. p. 14.

40. Young, V. (February 16, 1999). Licensing: Dollars and sensitivity. *Women's Wear Daily*. pp. 34–36.

41. Staff. (October 31, 1996). Donna Karen. In *Fashion Revolution: The Mega Niche*, a supplement to *Women's Wear Daily*. p. 8.

42. Staff. (June 2, 1997). Stride Rite's best foot forward. *Business Week*. p. 130.

43. Lockwood, L. (December 16, 1997). Karne, Claiborne set mega-licensing deal for jeans, acivewear. *Women's World Daily*. pp. 1, 13–13.

44. Lee, G. (May 21, 1998). The home advantage. *Women's Wear Daily*. pp. 8–9.

45. Monget, K. (April 5, 1999). As megabrands grow, retailers give big push to private label. *Women's Wear Daily*. pp. 1, 8.

46. Ryan, T. June 18, 1997). Next IPO from Calvin? He says no, but get a load of the numbers. *Women's Wear Daily*. pp. 1,10–11.

47. Feitelberg, R. (March 4, 1996). Makers look to pump upmarket with value-added products. *Women's Wear Daily*. pp. 18–19.

48. Friedman, A. (December 6, 1995). A blueprint for brand licensing. *Women's Wear Daily*. p. 14.

49. Pogoda, D. The extension dilemma. *Women's Wear Daily*. pp. 13, 17.

50. Lockwood, L. (September 12, 1998). Two Lauren licenses, Jones and Sun, said to be talking marriage. *Women's Wear Daily*. pp. 1, 13.

51. Edelson, S. (March 1, 1999). Fueled by designers, private label moves to a higher plateau. *Women's Wear Daily*. pp. 1, 8.

52. Staff. (November 1998). Sorting out the stores. *Consumer Reports*. pp. 12–17.

53. Staff. (June 25, 1996). Italian designer sues May Department Stores. *The Boston Globe*. p. 43.

54. Harvey, M. & Kasulis, J. (January 1998). Retailer brands—The business of distinction. *Retailing Issues Letter*. pp. 1–5.

55. Troy, M. (June 22, 1998). Dollar General sees PL apparel as key to increasing bottom line. *Discount Store News*. pp. 1, 60.

56. Chandler, S. (November 27, 1995). An endangered species makes a come-back. *Business Week*. p. 96.

57. Ozzard, J., Lockwood, L. & D'Innocenzio, A. (March 30, 1995). Private label powers up. *Women's Wear Daily*. pp. 6–8.

58. Liebeck, L. (March 9, 1998). The mileage of Martha Stewart keeps extending every day. *Discount Store News*. p. 39.

59. Seckler, V. (June 19, 1999). Sears "megabrand" move: Benetton USA. *Women's Wear Daily*. pp. 6–7.

60. Edelson, S. (March 1, 1999). Fueled by designers, private label moves to a higher plateau. *Women's Wear Daily*. pp. 1 8–9.

61. Lee, G. (May 21, 1998). The home connection. *Women's Wear Daily*. pp. 8–9.

62. Cuneo, A. (July 27, 1998). Private-label lessons. *Advertising Age*. pp. 1, 31.

63. Mander, E. (December 1996). Gap aspires to be seen as a "global brand." *SCT/Retailing Today*. p.18

64. DeNitto, E. (September 13, 1993). They aren't private labels anymore—They're brands. *Advertising Age*.

chapter eight

MERCHANDISE RESOURCES

As marketing-channel intermediaries, retailers play a critical role in linking producers and consumers. Understanding the role of retailers as channel intermediaries requires knowledge of the interactions that occur between retailers and their customers, as well as knowledge of the interactions that occur between retailers and their suppliers. The terms *vendor, supplier,* and *resource* are commonly used to refer to the sources from which retail buyers obtain merchandise to sell in their stores. Chapter 8 covers the various types of merchandise resources and the ways in which retailers interface with them.

After you have read this chapter, you will be able to discuss:

The resources from which retail buyers obtain merchandise.

The places at which retail buyers and their suppliers transact business.

Imports as part of a merchandise mix.

The functions of a resident buying office.

MANUFACTURERS

A **manufacturer** uses labor and machinery to convert raw materials into finished products. The traditional concept of manufacturing encompasses a comprehensive range of functions, such as product design, materials procurement, and the complete production process. Today, the role of the manufacturer is often less inclusive.[1] Many manufacturing organizations *assemble* finished products with component parts produced by other manufacturers. Some manufacturing organizations are actually design companies that develop product concepts and then contract other manufacturers to make the product according to clearly defined specifications. Many contract foreign producers because of the low labor costs in some countries. Manufacturers sometimes operate their own production facilities in foreign countries to reap this economic advantage.

Figure 8.1

Some manufacturers employ a direct sales force to sell their product lines. *Cole Haan is a trademark of Cole Haan and is used with permission.*

COLE HAAN

Cole Haan, an international leader in fashion footwear and accessories, has exceptional opportunities for a professional in our New York City office.

Junior Account Executive
Women's Accessories

Cole Haan has an immediate opportunity for a Junior Account Executive supporting our growing Women's Accessories business. The Junior AE will be responsible for short and long term development of business relationships with select Northeast accounts toward achievement of sales goals. In addition, the position will assist in compiling and analyzing retail sales information and will provide general administrative support for the Women's Accessories Sales department. The qualified candidate will have a minimum of 2 years in wholesale sales or sales assistant experience, the ability to establish and maintain effective working relationships, strong organizational and communication skills, and proven skills with MicroSoft Word and Excel.

Please send or fax your resume to:
**Human Resources Dept., Cole Haan,
One Cole Haan Drive, Yarmouth, ME 04096.
Fax: (207) 846-3477.
Email: colehaan.HR@colehaan.com**

Cole Haan is an Equal Opportunity Employer.

Direct Sales Forces

Some manufacturers employ an internal staff of salespeople to sell their products to retailers. A **direct sales force** is responsible for meeting with prospective retail buyers, explaining the features of the organization's product line, and processing orders. As the liaison between the manufacturing organization and its retail accounts, a direct sales force often troubleshoots problems with delivery, damaged goods, and credits for returned merchandise. The members of a direct sales force are regular, permanent employees of the manufacturing organization. Their sales responsibilities are often assigned by geographic territory. They are often paid a commission based on what they sell. Members of a direct sales force are often called *account representatives* or *account executives*.

Manufacturers' Sales Representatives

Some manufacturers contract the services of manufacturers' representatives as an alternative to employing a direct sales force. A **manufacturer's sales representative**, or *manufacturer's rep*, is an independent sales agent whose income is based on commissions earned by selling manufacturers' products within a defined geographic territory. Reps perform a brokerage function in that they bring buyers and sellers together without themselves assuming title, or ownership, of the goods that they sell. Manufacturers provide reps with product training, samples, and leads, as well as marketing-communication tools, such as sales literature, catalogs, and other collateral material. Reps often maintain their own offices and showrooms, and absorb their own expenses for travel, support staff, and employee benefits. A rep firm may employ several reps, or a rep can work alone.

Many manufacturers' reps are multiline reps, selling *compatible* but *noncompetitive* lines for more than one manufacturer or principal. Lines of belts, umbrellas, and cold weather accessories (such as gloves, scarves, and hats) are noncompetitive in that a retail buyer's decision to purchase one line is independent of his or her decision to purchase another. The lines are compatible in that the responsibility for buying these lines is typically designated to the same buyer in most retail organizations. Showing multiple lines on a single sales call spreads the cost of sales over several lines.

Some companies employ both a direct sales force and manufacturers' reps, assigning reps to low-volume territories not large enough to warrant the expense of a direct salesperson. Though companies with a

Pepe Jeans

LONDON

Seeking an aggressive and experienced sales representative with denim experience for our men's and junior's division. The following territories are available:
A) Phila., Baltimore, Washington, PA
B) Illinois, Wisconsin, Indiana, Missouri, Michigan and Ohio.
Qualified applicants, please fax resume to:

**212-719-5353
Jean Design Ltd.**

Figure 8.2

Some manufacturers contract for the services of manufacturers' sales representatives as an alternative to a direct sales force. *Courtesy of Pepe Jeans.*

direct sales force exercise greater control over their sales function, there are several advantages to hiring manufacturers' reps:

- A rep has a developed sales territory with established retail accounts and can often penetrate a territory more efficiently than a direct salesperson.
- The compatibility of a rep's lines is often the basis for *synergistic sales,* where the sale of one line stimulates the sale of another.
- Unlike a direct sales force, a rep is paid only on what is sold with no additional employment expenses for travel or benefits.

Manufacturers and manufacturers' reps seek each other through the *reps wanted* and *lines wanted* classified sections of trade publications. The Atlanta-based Bureau of Wholesale Sales Representatives is a trade association that offers a search service called *BureauMatch* that matches reps seeking lines with manufacturers seeking reps.

The direct-buying policies of many large retailers has threatened the livelihood of manufacturers' reps. Power retailers, such as Wal-Mart, circumvent third-party interactions with reps by dealing directly with producers. By averting manufacturers' reps' commissions, retailers can negotiate lower prices with producers.

Figure 8.3

Manufacturers'
sales representatives
are often multiline
reps who sell compatible but non-competing lines.
*Courtesy of Patti and
David Murphy.*

MERCHANT WHOLESALERS-DISTRIBUTORS

Some manufacturers sell indirectly to retailers through an intermediary
called a **merchant wholesaler-distributor**. Unlike manufacturers' reps
who do not assume title of the goods that they sell, merchant wholesaler-distributors buy manufacturers' products, and then resell them to
retailers. These wholesalers facilitate the distribution of goods from
producer to retailer. A producer minimizes its sales transactions by selling to a limited number of wholesalers, instead of directly selling to

many retailers. A retailer minimizes its purchase transactions by buying products from a few wholesalers, instead of directly from many producers. Wholesalers also sell products for industrial, commercial, and institutional use. *Distributor* and *jobber* are names commonly used to refer to wholesalers.

A wholesaler's selling price is most often higher than a producer's selling price in that the wholesaler's price must cover the wholesaler's operating costs and profit, though the volume discounts that wholesalers obtain from manufacturers cover a portion of these operating costs. In spite of higher prices, retailers sometimes elect to buy from wholesalers because of shorter lead time, the time lapse between the point at which an order is placed and the point at which an order is delivered. Small, independent retailers buy from wholesalers because wholesalers accept smaller orders than producers who often have minimum-order requirements that exceed the inventory needs of many small retailers. Small, frequently delivered orders minimize a retailer's inventory investment, resulting in lower inventory carrying costs.

Many wholesalers offer financial, logistical, and marketing support to their customers. A *rack jobber* performs virtually all of a retailer's inventory-management and promotional functions for a product line. Based in LaVergne, Tennessee, Ingram Merchandising Services is the nation's largest rack jobber for home entertainment products, serving full-line discounters, supermarkets, and video, music, book, and computer software stores. IMS's product assortment includes more than 6000 audio titles, 6000 video titles, 1000 book titles, and 16,000 computer-software products. An IMS merchandising specialist attractively displays an assortment of titles tailored to each store's market on fixturing provided by IMS. A computerized inventory-management system replenishes stock as it is sold to ensure the constant availability of even the most popular titles. Selections are periodically adjusted based on rate of sale to maximize sales, and minimize inventory and space investments. Ingram also provides an advertising program for key titles and new releases.

With the exception of imports, the typical channel of distribution for the retailers and the product categories discussed in this text does not include wholesalers. However, wholesalers are used extensively in food distribution and by small, independent retailers for certain categories of merchandise, such as toys, sporting goods, consumer electronics, hardware, prerecorded music, books, and office supplies. As in the case of other industries, there has been much consolidation within the wholesaling sector. The number of consumer-magazine distributors has decreased from more than 300 to fewer than 20 within recent years.[2]

Clearly there are economic advantages to buying directly from a source of production instead of a wholesaler. Braun's Fashions, a Plymouth, Minnesota-based chain of value-priced female apparel stores, attributes its emergence from Chapter 11 bankruptcy to a change in buying strategy from buying Asian imports through wholesalers to buying directly from manufacturers.[3]

IMPORTS

Imports add variety and distinction to merchandise assortments with fabrications, designs, and workmanship unique to their country of origin, and unavailable in the United States. Italian leathers, hand-loomed Indian rugs, and Belgian lace are all examples of distinctive imports. Wedgwood china from England, Louis Vuitton luggage and accessories from France, and Bally shoes from Switzerland, have enhanced the exclusivity of the offerings of many U.S. retailers for decades.

Imports are often less expensive than goods of comparable quality made in the United States because of the lower wages paid to workers in less-industrialized countries. Lower prices are especially true of labor-intensive products such as shoes, gloves, and men's shirts. Labor unions are often critical of retailers that sell imports, claiming that importing erodes the U.S. manufacturing base, and exploits the underclasses of underdeveloped countries. However, price-conscious consumers are unfazed by organized labor's position, and are more likely to make a purchase decision based on product appeal and value than on country of origin.

Manufacturers, wholesalers, and retailers import. As noted earlier in this chapter, many manufacturing organizations import domestically designed products produced by foreign contractors. Both domestic and foreign wholesalers import goods to the United States to sell directly to retailers or through manufacturers' reps. Large retailers bypass importers as channel intermediaries by directly importing goods. To avoid wholesalers' markups, Crate & Barrel directly imports its assortments from more than 300 overseas factories. Some retailers operate foreign buying offices that work in tandem with their domestic

Figure 8.4

Imports can add variety and distinction to merchandise assortments. *Courtesy of the Italian Trade Commission.*

Nippers Slippers

Quality Infants' Slippers for ages 3 to 24 months.

NOVELTY DESIGNS

COMFORTABLE

UNIQUE & PLAYFUL

Made in Australia of 80% wool and 20% viscose upper. Trims made of 100% pure Australian lambswool.

Imported and Distributed by:
STERLING IMPORTS
Four Copley Place ▪ P.O. Box 78 ▪ Boston, MA 02116-6504
TEL: (617) 267-1176 ▪ FAX: (617) 421-9530
Contact: Liane Crawford

Figure 8.5

Some domestic wholesalers import goods to sell directly to retailers.

buying organization to source goods, place orders, and arrange shipment. May Department Stores owns and operates eight such offices in Hong Kong, Taipei, Seoul, Bangkok, Singapore, Manila, New Delhi, and Colombo, Sri Lanka. Retailers that do not maintain foreign buying offices often contract the services of *commissionaires* familiar with a foreign market. A **commissionaire** is paid a commission to act as a retailer's agent in the market by screening resources, facilitating order placement, ensuring quality control, and making payment and shipping arrangements.

Imports are subject to **tariffs**, or *duties*, levied by the U.S. government to restrict foreign competition. Tariffs are based on import penetrations and the competitive price of domestic goods. Imports are restricted by **quotas**, quantitative limitations placed on the amount of merchandise that may be imported from a country within a time period. Quotas are established by country and by category of merchandise. The Generalized System of Preferences (GSP) allows certain products to be imported from developing countries without quotas. Importers often employ the services

HONG KONG AGENT

OVER 10 yrs — Existing business exp & connections with Chinese National I/E Corp., looking for U.S. Importers of ladies apparel to manufactured in proc. For further info please contact Ms. Suiko Mabel Lee at fax (254).236. 85522 or G.P.O. Box 8750 Hong Kong

SOURCING

By Israeli experienced agent in Israel and other countries. No duty or quota from Israel. Top quality. Contact NY office 212. 326.1120.

Figure 8.6

A commissionaire is paid a commission to act as a retailer's agent in a foreign market.

of **customs brokers**, agents licensed by the U.S. Treasury to represent importers in customs matters. Customs brokers expedite goods through customs by preparing the necessary customs forms, processing the payment of tariffs, and arranging for inland transportation.

The Downside of Imports

Though imports have many advantages, there are several factors that a retailer must consider when making a decision to buy imported goods:

- High procurement costs, involving overseas buying trips, packing, shipping, insurance, storage, tariffs, and commissionaires' and customs agents' fees, inflate the final actual, or **landed cost** of imports.
- Landed costs are sometimes uncertain because of fluctuations in currency rates of exchange.
- Imports require a longer lead time than domestic goods, sometimes as long as a year. Shipping delays can result in costly markdowns when merchandise arrives at the end of, or even after, the selling season for which it was purchased.
- Imports tie up a retailer's capital for considerable time in that imports are paid for prior to being shipped, long before the point at which they will generate sales.
- Retailers that import directly are responsible for compliance with the laws that govern tariffs and quotas, as well as those that govern product safety standards and labeling for textile fiber identification and care requirements.
- It is often difficult to collect on damaged or unacceptable goods, and it is costly to return them.

MARKETS

Retail buyers transact business with suppliers in several types of settings. Large retail organizations have *sample rooms* in which traveling vendors show their lines by appointment. Today, buyers are more likely to view lines in nonretail locations remote from their stores. The current offerings of manufacturers, manufacturers' reps, wholesalers, and importers are often displayed in **showrooms** staffed by a sales force which presents the product line to prospective buyers. Showrooms for a particular merchandise category or group of related categories are often located in a **major showroom building**. In New York, 1411 and 1407 Broadway are major showroom buildings for moderate-to-better dresses and sportswear; 500

Figure 8.7

A major showroom building facilitates one-stop buying for retail buyers. *Courtesy of Abramson Brothers, Inc.*

and 512 Seventh Avenue are moderate-to-bridge women's outerwear buildings.[4] Forty-One Madison Avenue, 225 Fifth Avenue, and 230 Fifth Avenue are New York's major showroom buildings for giftware.

A **market** is a place where buyers and sellers come together to transact business. A market is often identified as a city, or a section of a city, in which a number of showrooms of related product categories are located. New York's Toy Center, or toy market, is bound by Madison and Sixth Avenues and 21st and 27th Streets. New York's fashion-accessories market is composed of approximately 20 buildings between Fifth and Eighth Avenues and 35th and 39th Streets. New York's legendary Garment District (now called the Fashion Center) is bordered by Fifth and Ninth Avenues and 35th and 41st Streets. Some markets are also major manufacturing centers. Providence, Rhode Island, is the manufacturing center and major market for fashion jewelry. The offerings of more than 2100 home furnishing manufacturers are permanently displayed in 150 showroom buildings in High Point and Thomasville, North Carolina, the production source of most of the furniture manufactured in the United States.

Though New York is still the nation's leading market for high-fashion apparel, its importance as an apparel market has diminished in recent years because of the growth of Atlanta, Chicago, Dallas, and Los Angeles as major markets.[5] These regional markets sometimes specialize in specific categories of merchandise. Dallas is the ultimate roundup for westernwear including tack lines, western boots, hats, outerwear, and accessories. Smaller secondary markets are located in Boston, Charlotte, Denver, Kansas City, Miami, Minneapolis, Pittsburgh, San Francisco, and Seattle. Their draw is limited to the geographic areas in which they are located. A decline in the number of manufacturers' sales representatives and retail buyers has threatened the viability of many of these small markets.

Designed for "one-stop shopping" for buyers, a **merchandise mart** houses an entire market under one roof. Chicago's Merchandise Mart is the oldest mart in the United States, built by the preeminent merchant Marshall Field in 1930. The Atlanta Apparel Mart, the Denver Merchandise Mart, and The Fashion Center in San Francisco are other examples of merchandise marts.

A **market center** is a cluster of marts. An example is the Dallas Market Center, a six-building complex of 6.9 million square feet housing more than 2400 showrooms including:

- The International Menswear Mart, housing more than 3000 lines of men's and boys' apparel and accessories.

10 TiPS FOR SHOPPING
THE FASHION CENTER

1. Plan early. Not all showrooms require appointments but a 1 - 2 month lead time will ensure that you see all the resources on your list. Advance scheduling also helps when booking hotels and airlines. Call Carol Sommers at The Travel Services Program office at 800-776-1116 or 212-532-3400 for help with your travel plans.

2. Establish parameters. Determine your goals in terms of price points, sizes, delivery deadlines, quantities and fabrics.

3. Develop a resource target list. Contact The Fashion Center BID office a few weeks in advance of your trip and ask for category lists of manufacturers [Ph: 212-764-9600; Fx: 212-764-9697]. Read Women's Wear Daily to stay on top of trends, store merchandising concepts and merchandise range.

4. Try new vendors. New firms are constantly opening in The Fashion Center. Make sure you include a few of them on your agenda. You never know when you will discover a fashion diamond.

5. Reconfirm addresses. Firms often move location and addresses may have changed since your last visit. Be sure to double check addresses.

6. Ask questions in advance. Call manufacturers to determine if they will be able to meet your basic requirements in terms of delivery, payment schedules, etc. An hour of advance homework can save a half day of buying time!

7. Check trade show calendars. Consider tieing in your buying trip with a specific New York trade show. You'll enjoy an expanded market overview and see more resources.

8. Map out your schedule. Refer to The Fashion Center map on pages 18 - 19 when planning your appointments. A well-planned itinerary will make the most efficient use of your travel time.

9. Allow at least one hour per showroom visit. Your buying trip is critical to the success of your retail operation. Make sure you have ample time to devote to selection and negotiation.

10. Plan some play time. In addition to the world's best fashion, New York City offers world-class dining, theater, arts and entertainment. Make sure they're a part of your schedule, **too!**

Figure 8.8

The Fashion Center gives tips to buyers for shopping in New York City. *Reprinted courtesy of Fashion Center Business Improvement District.*

- The International Apparel Mart, housing more than 12,000 lines of women's and children's apparel and accessories.
- Market Hall for temporary exhibits.
- The Trade Mart and the World Trade Center, housing more than 17,000 lines of toys, stationery, residential furnishings, and decorative accessories.

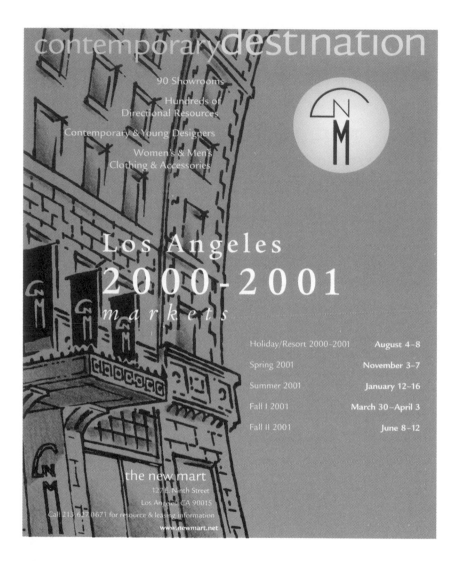

Figure 8.9

A trade show is a group of temporary exhibits for a single category of merchandise. *Courtesy of The New Mart.*

TRADE SHOWS

A **trade show** is a group of temporary exhibits in a convention center, merchandise mart, or hotel, at which vendors of a single category of merchandise, or group of related categories, present goods to retail buyers. Trade-show exhibitors are often grouped together by product category or price level. Exhibits at the National Association of Men's Sportswear Buyers (NAMSB) show are grouped as contemporary, jean-swear, leather/outerwear, young men's and activewear, accessories, and footwear. Some trade shows cater to niche markets. Atlanta's Celebration is a prom, pageant, social-occasion dress show held every August.[6] Some trade shows have an international flavor. The Blenheim Group of London produces large international shows that attract buyers worldwide, including *Salon International de la Mode Enfantine*, a semi-annual show held in Paris.

The duration of a trade show ranges from a few days to a week. A trade show and its related events are often referred to as a *market* or *market week*. Some markets are annual events, others occur more frequently. Apparel markets are held as often as five times a year to coincide with the seasonal release of lines. The annual schedules for most apparel markets include:

- Fall I or Transition—April
- Fall II—June

Figure 8.10

Merchandise marts, such as California Mart, house an entire market under one roof.
Courtesy of Fairchild Publications, Inc.

High Point—the Epicenter of Home Furnishings

Source:

1 Vigue, D. (October 26, 2000). Taking license with furniture at High Point. The Boston Globe. pp. H1, H9.

Twice a year, thousands of interior designers, decorators, and architects from around the world flock to High Point, North Carolina, for the International Home Furnishings Market, the coffee-table equivalent of New York's Fashion Week. Retail-store furniture buyers descend upon the furniture capital of the world to shop their way through a mind-boggling one million square feet of showroom space in 17 buildings, while catching up on the latest trends in furniture, decorative accessories, and drapery and upholstery fabrics. It takes a week, a comfortable pair of shoes, and a game plan to cover the market. Even the most seasoned buyers are sometimes overwhelmed by the amount of market that needs to be covered in such a short span of time.

Licensed lines have been the rage at High Point in recent years. Fashion designer Jessica McClintock joined forces with Lexington Furniture to produce a line called *Sophie's Attic*. The line includes reproductions reminiscent of bygone eras and people. *Uncle Martin's secretary* is a Victorian-style piece with pivoting mirror, glass handles, and carved-wood doors.

Model Kathy Ireland fulfilled a lifelong dream of having her own furniture line by working with Vanguard to develop a furniture line for families with children. Mix-and-match pieces in cozy cottage styles have kid-friendly slipcover patterns. Kid-sized armchairs in checkered patterns make children feel welcome in the living room. Ireland's pieces also take a nod at nostalgia with Nana's rocker, rocking chairs in distressed wood and English-country inspired antique pieces that look as if they have been passed down through the generations.[1]

- Resort/Holiday—August
- Spring—October/November
- Summer—January

At markets, buyers get the opportunity to meet with major design and manufacturing executives and to network with buyers of the same merchandise category from other retail organizations. Trade shows offer educational opportunities in the form of seminars by industry experts. Topics at Atlanta's AmericasMart have included cross-merchandising apparel with giftware, visual merchandising, and technology.[7] The Dallas Market Center publishes the "New Buyer's Kit." The primer on retail buying is a 65-page book that contains a glossary of terms for buying, shipping and delivery, and credit, as well as suggestions for working the market and planning open-to-buy.[8]

A market's lure is enhanced by fashion shows, cocktail parties, and big-name entertainment.[9] The WWDMagic show in Las Vegas has hosted such headline performers as Rod Stewart, Hootie and the Blowfish, and Gloria Gaynor.[10] With 2800 exhibitors and more than 100,000 attendees, the Super Show is the world's largest sporting goods, sports apparel, and athletic footwear trade show. Sponsored by the Sporting Goods Manufacturers Association, the annual event also held in Las Vegas attracts more than 100,000 buyers. Sports celebrities, bungee jumping, and dirigible-like inflated sports products are typical of the show.[11]

Trade Show Sponsors

A trade show is coordinated by a sponsor who secures the trade-show facility and then rents space to exhibitors for a fee based on the size of the exhibit booth. The fee covers:

- *Drayage* or the movement of goods from the facility's loading dock to the booth
- Booth furniture such as tables, chairs, and risers
- A listing in the trade-show directory of exhibitors by product category compiled for the convenience of the buyers
- Publicity efforts designed to draw attendees to the event, such as advertisements in trade publications subscribed to by buyers

Trade shows can be sponsored by trade associations, market centers, and/or management firms that specialize in trade-show production. George Little Management is the largest producer of trade shows for consumer goods. Some trade-show producers specialize in certain types of shows. ENK International is a New York-based company that produces high-fashion apparel and accessories shows such as Accessorie Circuit, Intermenzo Collections, and Fashion Coterie.[12] Some shows that are sponsored by trade associations are:

- The International Toy Fair sponsored annually in New York by the Toy Manufactures of America featuring the products of nearly 2000 toy manufacturers from around the world.
- The All Candy Expo sponsored annually in Chicago's McCormick Place by the National Confectioners Association featuring nearly 400 exhibitors.[13]
- The Fashion Footwear Association of New York (FFANY), and the School and Home Office Products Association (SHOPA) also sponsor trade shows.[14]

Figure 8.11

Sometimes trade shows are sponsored by trade associations. *Provided by Fashion Footwear Association of New York (FFANY) .*

Some trade shows are co-sponsored. The International Western Market and Western Lifestyle Show is sponsored by the American Equestrian Marketing Trade Association and the International Menswear Mart in Dallas. WWDMagic is cosponsored by *Women's Wear Daily*, a trade publisher, and MAGIC International, a trade-show producer.[15]

RESIDENT BUYING OFFICES

A **resident buying office**, or *buying office,* is a marketing and research consulting firm that serves as an adviser to a group of member, or client, stores. Located in major market centers, buying offices provide market information, merchandising guidance, and other services to their membership. New York City is home to the largest number of buying offices. Some have branches in other cities in the United States and around the world. Many buying offices specialize in certain categories of merchandise and/or types of stores, limiting their services to areas such as bridal, furs, or large sizes. The members of a buying office are often similar in terms of merchandise mix, size, and retailing format.[16]

The original buying offices were buying services for the owners of apparel stores too distant to make frequent trips to New York, the major fashion market. For a fee, an office assumed the responsibility of selecting and ordering all or part of a client store's inventory. This allowed member stores to devote full-time attention to the task of operating their stores without the interruption of time-consuming and costly market trips.

The primary role of the present-day buying office is that of adviser, product developer, and importer for member stores. Buying offices forecast future market conditions by studying consumer behavior, demographics, and emerging trends. The information is channeled to client stores through a communication network of bulletins, surveys, and reports. Buying offices facilitate buyers' market trips by arranging travel and hotel accommodations, compiling lists of recommended resources to visit, and providing office space. Offices host buyers' meetings during major markets as a forum for exchanging ideas. Some offices respond to the needs of individual members by store visits and by researching solutions to problems peculiar to a store.

Market coverage responsibility in a buying office is assigned by merchandise category to *market specialists* sometimes called *market reps* or *resident buyers.* Market specialists communicate market conditions to client stores, such as fashion trends, new resources, hot items, opportunistic buys, and promotional opportunities. Their market expertise is based on daily market contact and information from various sources, such as vendors, member stores, mills, research firms, designers, and the trade media.

The wholesaling of private-label merchandise has become an important buying-office function. Buying offices source large quantities of goods for the collective needs of many member stores, and then

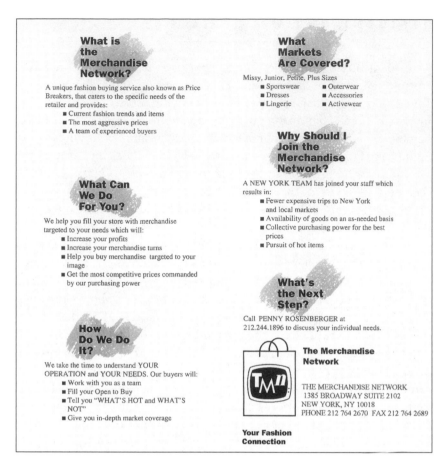

Figure 8.12

Buying offices provide their members with market information and merchandising guidance. *Courtesy of The Merchandise Network.*

resell the goods to their clients enabling even the smallest independent store to participate in private-label programs. Another buying office function is **group buying**, the pooling of orders for merchandise, store fixtures, and services from many members to meet minimum order requirements or to negotiate quantity discounts.

The development of catalogs as regular-price or promotional direct-mail pieces is another important function of the buying office. The office produces a single catalog featuring goods common to the assortments of member stores at a fraction of the cost of each store producing its own piece. Production costs are minimized by negotiating cooperative advertising from the vendors whose merchandise is featured in the catalogs.

Types of Buying Offices

There are three major types of buying offices:

Salaried Office   A **salaried**, or *fee*, **office** is the most common type of buying office. A salaried office is owned and operated independently of its member stores, most of which are privately owned specialty stores that pay the buying office an annual fee for services. Collectively, salaried offices have more members than other types of buying offices. The Doneger Group has grown to be the largest independent office through the acquisition of several other offices, such as The Certified Fashion Guild, Burns Winkler, Jack Braustein, and Young Innovators. Though small retailers are more likely to rely on the services of buying offices than large retailers, large retailers sometimes rely on buying offices for services such as importing or off-price sourcing.

Syndicated Office   A **syndicated office** is owned and operated by a retail conglomerate. May Merchandising is responsible for product development, imports, and domestic market coverage for the eight

Figure 8.13

May Merchandising is a syndicated buying office responsible for developing private-label programs for the operating divisions of May Department Stores. *Courtesy of The May Department Store Company.*

Figure 8.14

A private buying office is owned and operated by a single retail organization as an extension of its corporate merchandising function. *Courtesy of Hit or Miss, Inc.*

operating divisions of the May Department Stores Company. Federated Merchandising (FM) is a division of Federated Department Stores that is responsible for developing merchandising strategies for more than 400 Federated stores. FM coordinates Federated's innovative buying-team process whereby groups of buyers representing Federated's six department store divisions collectively determine the mix of suppliers for Federated stores. The buyers at division level then make assortment decisions on the offerings of each vendor. Federated's commitment to each of these key vendors is used as leverage to negotiate price, promotional support, delivery, and other concessions. FM was responsible for developing Federated Accelerated Sales & Stock Turnover (FASST), an inventory-management system designed to increase sales and inventory turnover by expediting the movement of goods from suppliers to the selling floor. Within recent years, several syndicated buying offices have moved from New York to their corporate-office location. The buying office for May Department Stores is now located in St. Louis.

Private Office A **private office** is owned and operated by a single retail organization as an extension of its corporate merchandising function. Through a private office, a retailer maintains market presence even when its merchandising function is executed at a corporate office remote from a major market. Stein Mart, a Jacksonville, Florida-based chain of off-price better female apparel stores, and Hit or Miss, a Stoughton, Massachusetts-based female apparel specialty store, have private offices in New York. As in the case of syndicated offices, some retailers have moved their private offices out of New York in recent years. J.C. Penney transplanted its private buying offices from New York to Dallas feeling it more important for the buying office to be close to the buyers than close to the market.[17] The trend is not significant however. Ross Stores, a California-based off-pricer recently doubled the size of its New York office.[18]

SUMMARY POINTS

- A manufacturer uses labor and machinery to convert raw materials into finished products. Manufacturers use either a direct sales force or manufacturers' reps to sell their products to retailers.
- Merchant wholesaler-distributors buy manufacturers' products and then resell them to retailers. Wholesale-distributors facilitate the distribution of goods between a producer and a retailer.
- Imports add variety and distinction to a retailer's product mix and often afford a retailer an opportunity for higher profit margins.
- Showrooms, marts, markets, and trade shows are nonretail settings in which sellers and retail buyers come together to transact business.
- A buying office is a marketing and research consultant that serves as an adviser to its member or client stores by providing market information, merchandising guidance, and other services.

KEY TERMS AND CONCEPTS

commissionaire

custom broker

direct sales force

group buying

landed cost

major showroom building

manufacturer

manufacturer's sales
   representative

market

market center

merchandise mart

merchant wholesaler-
   distributor

private office

quota

resident buying office

salaried office

showroom

syndicated office

tariff

trade show

FOR DISCUSSION

1. Search the Internet for information on some of the trade shows mentioned in this chapter. Compare the shows in terms of size, attendees, and entertainment fanfare.
2. Compare several imported and domestic items at a local retailer. Do you think that price or distinctiveness motivated the buyer's purchase? Explain.
3. Obtain information from a salaried buying office concerning its fee schedule and the services that it provides. Do you feel that the membership fee is a worthwhile investment for a retailer, relative to the benefits of membership? Explain.

ENDNOTES

1. Ellis, K. (December 13, 1995). J. Crew fights California over definition of a maker. *Women's Wear Daily.* p. 26.
2. Cockerham, P. (March 1996). Wholesale changes roil magazine business. *Stores.* pp. 20–22.
3. McCartney, J. (October 1998). Direct buying helps buoy Braun's rebound. *SCT/Retailing Today.* pp. 1, 54.
4. Staff. (September 1997). A look at 1411 Broadway. A supplement to *Women's Wear Daily.* p. 20
5. Lee, G. (December 18, 1996). Retailers speak out: Where they place the orders. *Women's Wear Daily.* pp. 28–29.
6. Lee, G. (July 14, 1999). Regional update: Getting in shape. *Women's Wear Daily.* p. 21–22.
7. Lee, G. (December 16, 1998). Atlanta's cross-marketing game. *Women's Wear Daily.* p. 29.

8. Harber, H. (July 16, 1997). The Dallas decision: Five markets per year. *Women's Wear Daily.* p. 20.

9. Freitelberg, R. (July 15, 1998). Love affair: Buyers, trade shows. *Women's Wear Daily.* p. 17.

10. Ellis, K. (August 18, 1997). Joe Loggia: MAGIC Strategist. *Women's Wear Daily.* p. 26.

11. Feitelberg, R. (February 11, 1999) Gearing up for the Super Show. *Women's Wear Daily.* p. 12.

12. D'Innocenzio, A. (December 16, 1998). N.Y. shows lure Europe. *Women's Wear Daily.* pp. 14–16.

13. Howell, D. (July 12, 1999). Out-of-this-world offerings steal show at Candy Expo. *Discount Store News.* p. 4.

14. Troy, M. (October 26, 1999). SHOPA continues to grow despite industry consolidation. *Discount Store News.* p. 35.

15. Ellis, K. (July 15, 1998). Expansion ahead for WWDMagic. *Women's Wear Daily.* p. 19.

16. Barmash, I. (May 1997). Buying offices: Once a staple, now few exist. *SCT/Retailing Today.* pp. 76, 86, 90.

17. Staff. (April 3, 1997). Belk closing its N.Y. office, moving operations to N.C. *Women's Wear Daily.* p. 14.

18. Barmash, I. (February 1998). Ross Stores' focus: a winning strategy. *Shopping Centers Today.* p. 33.

The Financial Aspects of Merchandising

- Measures of Productivity

- Merchandising Accounting

- Inventory Valuation

chapter nine

MEASURES OF PRODUCTIVITY

Maximizing returns on an organization's assets is a universal business objective. Retailers maximize their return on inventory and selling space as organizational assets by using them in such a way that sales are optimal. In general, retailers want to maximize sales while minimizing investments of inventory and space. Chapter 9 deals with some of the measures that are used to monitor the performance of inventory and selling space as organizational assets.

After you have read this chapter, you will be able to discuss:

Productivity as a measure of performance.

The relationship between turnover and stock-to-sales ratios.

Sales per square foot as a measure of productivity.

PRODUCTIVITY

Productivity is a measure of the number of units of output produced per unit of input. Stated in mathematical terms:

$$productivity = \frac{output}{input}$$

Productivity measures performance. *High* productivity is a positive indicator that output has been maximized with a minimum investment of input. *Low* productivity is an unsatisfactory indicator of an ineffective use of input. Low productivity can be corrected by increasing output, decreasing input, or both increasing output and decreasing input.

Measures of productivity are common in the manufacturing sector where input and output are often quantitatively defined. In an apparel-manufacturing operation, the productivity of a pressing function can be measured by dividing the number of garments pressed by the amount of time it takes to press them.

$$productivity = \frac{units\ pressed\ (output)}{number\ of\ hours\ worked\ by\ presser\ (input)}$$

$$productivity = \frac{2400\ garments}{8\ hours}$$

$$productivity = 300\ garments\ per\ hour$$

The concept of productivity is not as easily applied within service industries because of the difficulty in quantitatively defining output and input. Though sales are a numerically measured retail output, intangible outputs, such as customer satisfaction, are difficult to quantify. In spite of these limitations, retailers apply productivity measures whenever a relationship between input and output can be defined numerically.

TURNOVER

Turnover, or *stockturn*, is the number of times that an average inventory is sold within a time period. Turnover describes the movement of merchandise, or the velocity at which goods come in and out of a business unit, such as a department or store. Turnover reflects the amount of sales generated per dollar of inventory invested. Turnover is computed by dividing sales for a period by the average amount of inventory carried for the same period:

$$turnover = \frac{sales}{average\ inventory}$$

Turnover is generally stated as a whole number carried to one decimal place.

An **average inventory** is the average amount of inventory on hand within a time period. Average inventory can be computed by dividing the sum of the beginning and ending inventories of a period by two. The average inventory for a month is computed by dividing the sum of the inventory on hand at the beginning of the month, called the **beginning-of-month,** or *BOM,* **inventory**, and the inventory on hand at the end of the month, called the **end-of-month,** or *EOM,* **inventory**, by two.

$$average\ inventory = \frac{BOM + EOM}{2}$$

Note that the EOM inventory of one month is equal to the BOM inventory of the succeeding month. It is logical to assume that if a store closes with a $2 million inventory on hand on the last day of a month, it will open the next day with a $2 million inventory on hand. Maintaining recorded values of BOM and EOM inventories is a common inventory-control practice in retail organizations.

An average inventory for a period longer than a month is based on the average inventories of the months within the period.[1] The average inventory for a year is computed by dividing the sum of the average inventories of each month in the year by 12.

$$average\ inventory =$$
$$\frac{\dfrac{(BOM + EOM)_1}{2} + \dfrac{(BOM + EOM)_2}{2} \cdots + \dfrac{(BOM + EOM)_{12}}{2}}{12}$$

The formula can be simplified. Since each EOM is equal to the BOM of the succeeding month, the EOMs can be eliminated from the formula without affecting the value of the average. However, the EOM of the last month must be retained in the computation, since it is not repeated as a succeeding BOM.

average inventory =

$$\frac{BOM_1 + BOM_2 + BOM_3 \ldots + BOM_{12} + EOM_{12}}{13}$$

The number *13* is used as the denominator since 13 figures are used in the computation of the numerator: 12 BOMs and 1 EOM.

The formula can be adapted for other periods. The average inventory for a six-month season beginning in February and ending in July is computed as follows:

average inventory =

$$\frac{BOM_{FEB} + BOM_{MAR} + BOM_{APR} + BOM_{MAY} + BOM_{JUN} + BOM_{JUL} + EOM_{JUL}}{7}$$

Computing Turnover

Table 9.1 demonstrates the computation of turnover. The men's sweater department at Dolan's Department Store generated sales of

Table 9.1   **BOM AND EOM INVENTORIES FOR MEN'S SWEATER DEPARTMENT, DOLAN'S DEPARTMENT STORE**

Month	BOM	EOM
1	$ 2,500	$ 2,500
2	$ 2,500	$ 2,500
3	$ 2,500	$ 5,000
4	$ 5,000	$ 2,500
5	$ 2,500	$ 7,500
6	$ 7,500	$ 2,500
7	$ 2,500	$ 5,000
8	$ 5,000	$ 5,000
9	$ 5,000	$ 5,000
10	$ 5,000	$ 7,500
11	$ 7,500	$12,500
12	$12,500	$ 5,000

Each BOM is equal to the EOM of the preceding month.

$30,000 last year. The BOMs and EOMs for each month are listed in Table 9.1. Average inventory is computed as follows:

$$average\ inventory = \frac{BOM_1 + BOM_2 \ldots + BOM_{12} + EOM_{12}}{13}$$

$$average\ inventory = \frac{\begin{array}{c} \$2,500 + \$2,500 + \$2,500 + 5,000 + 2,500 + 7,500 \\ + 2,500 + 5,000 + 5,000 + 5,000 + 7,500 + 12,500 + 5,000 \end{array}}{13}$$

$$average\ inventory = \frac{\$65,000}{13} = \$5,000$$

Turnover is computed as follows:

$$turnover = \frac{sales}{average\ inventory}$$

$$turnover = \frac{\$30,000}{\$5,000} = 6.0$$

The turnover of the men's sweater department at Dolan's Department Store for last year was 6.0. In other words, an average inventory of $5000 was sold six times.

The components of the turnover formula must agree in terms of time. To compute turnover for a *year*, sales for the *year* are divided by the average inventory for the same *year*. To compute turnover for a *month*, sales for the *month* are divided by the average inventory for the same *month*. Turnover can be computed for any period; however, annual turnover is the most commonly used. (See Table 9.2.) The remaining discussion of turnover presumes the period of a year unless otherwise specified.

Though turnover is typically calculated using the retail value of sales and inventory, turnover can also be calculated using units of sales and/or inventory, or the wholesale-cost values of sales and/or inventory.

High versus Low Turnover

High turnover is generally more desirable than low turnover. The mathematical relationship between sales and average inventory in the turnover formula suggests that turnover can be increased by increasing sales, decreasing average inventory, or both increasing sales and decreasing average inventory. The latter strategy is an important merchandising objective for retailers: to generate *more sales* on *less inventory*.

Table 9.2   TURNOVER REPORT FOR FIVE CLASSIFICATIONS OF MERCHANDISE IN A TEN-UNIT CHAIN

CL.	TOTAL	SPFLD	PLAZA	LONG	WEST	EAST	BERK	ENFLD	HAMP	INGLE	MANCH
1 AV IN	35,267	4,382	1,724	2,962	2,655	5,271	3,118	4,853	2,753	3,306	4,265
SALES	44,603	3,475	1,527	2,390	2,979	7,332	4,766	5,416	3,339	7,908	5,467
TRNOVR	1.3	.8	.9	.8	1.1	1.4	1.5	1.1	1.2	2.4	1.3
2 AV IN	4,851	413	71	55	229	896	214	581	198	929	1,038
SALES	4,587	918	103	45	302	1,345	323	376	328	589	252
TRNOVR	.9	2.2	1.5	.8	1.3	1.5	1.5	.6	1.7	.6	.2
3 AV IN	16,015	1,964	52	1,010	—	2,738	3,276	1,338	64	2,888	2,588
SALES	10,309	1,232	22	890	—	1,607	1,194	539	10	3,150	1,661
TRNOVR	.6	.6	.4	.9	—	.6	.4	.4	.2	1.1	.6
4 AV IN	63,151	4,623	3,626	4,005	5,248	8,312	5,880	6,239	7,460	9,702	5,600
SALES	84,458	5,436	5,071	2,904	6,057	12,938	8,121	8,470	10,162	20,675	4,618
TRNOVR	1.3	1.2	1.4	.7	1.2	1.6	1.4	1.4	1.4	2.1	.8
5 AV IN	45,861	4,363	3,432	2,652	3,306	7,601	3,478	5,096	2,798	7,698	5,535
SALES	23,979	1,632	1,315	1,002	2,014	3,917	2,326	2,656	2,597	5,216	1,298
TRNOVR	.5	.4	.4	.4	.6	.5	.7	.5	.9	.7	.2

Period Ending 07/31/01

To demonstrate the impact of average inventory on turnover, consider the following: A jeweler consistently sells 600 gold chains each year. Sales are highly predictable in that the jeweler sells exactly 50 chains each month. To prepare for the 2002 selling period, the jeweler wrote orders for 600 chains and arranged for their delivery just prior to the beginning of the year. As anticipated, the jeweler sold 50 chains during each month of 2002. The turnover (based on units) of the gold chains is calculated as follows:

$$average\ inventory = \frac{BOM_1 + BOM_2 \ldots + BOM_{12} + EOM_{12}}{13}$$

$$average\ inventory\ 2002 =$$

$$\frac{\$600 + 550 + 500 + 450 + 400 + 350 + 300 + 250 + 200 + 150 + 100 + 50 + 0}{13}$$

$$average\ inventory\ 2002 = \frac{3900}{13} = 300$$

$$turnover = \frac{sales}{average\ inventory}$$

$$turnover = \frac{600}{300} = 2.0$$

Prior to the beginning of 2003, the jeweler sought inventory-management advice from a retail consultant. The consultant suggested that the jeweler turn the gold chains faster by carrying less inventory throughout the year. The jeweler accomplished this objective by ordering 50 chains each month instead of 600 chains at the beginning of the year thereby carrying an inventory of no more than a month's supply of chains at any point during the year. The turnover of the gold chains for 2003 is computed as follows:

$$average\ inventory = \frac{BOM_1 + BOM_2 \ldots + BOM_{12} + EOM_{12}}{13}$$

$$average\ inventory\ 2003 =$$

$$\frac{50 + 50 + 50 + 50 + 50 + 50 + 50 + 50 + 50 + 50 + 50 + 50 + 0}{13}$$

$$average\ inventory\ 2003 = \frac{600}{13} = 46$$

TURNOVER

When two components of the turnover formula are known, the third can be computed by cross multiplying. Sales can be computed by multiplying the equation by average inventory when turnover and average inventory are known:

$$turnover = \frac{x}{average\ inventory}$$

$$x = turnover \times average\ inventory$$

When sales and turnover are known, average inventory can be computed by multiplying the equation by x and dividing by turnover:

$$turnover = \frac{sales}{x}$$

$$x = \frac{sales}{turnover}$$

$$turnover = \frac{sales}{average\ inventory}$$

$$turnover = \frac{600}{46} = 13.0$$

Note that the sales for 2002 and 2003 are equal, but that the 2003 average inventory turned more than six times faster than the inventory of 2002. The consultant's suggestion to maintain smaller inventories was prudent advice that resulted in improved turnover.[2]

Why High Turnover Is More Desirable Than Low Turnover

There are several reasons why high turnover is more desirable than low turnover.

- When inventories turn slowly, customers see the "same old thing" upon each return store visit. Customers who faithfully shopped the jeweler each month in 2002 saw the same selection of chains for an entire year. In 2003, customers saw a new selection each month.

- Slow-moving goods often become *shopworn*, that is soiled or damaged because of exposure or customer handling.
- Finally, the money and space tied up in stagnant, slow-turning inventories inhibits investments in fresh new goods. Studies have shown that the annual additional cost of holding excess inventory can be 25 to 32 percent of the value of the inventory.[3]

Though high turnover is generally a desirable goal, there are disadvantages associated with excessively high turnover.

- Just as *low* turnover can be indicative of *too much inventory, high* turnover can be indicative of *too little inventory.* Again consider the jeweler's scenario: Customers who shopped at the beginning of 2002 saw an extensive selection of 600 chains. The same customers who shopped at the beginning of 2003 saw a meager selection of only 50 chains. Imagine how disappointed customers were on their 2003 visit recalling the previous extensive assortment of the previous year. Thus, high turnover may be indicative of limited assortments of styles, colors, or sizes, an inventory condition that will result in lost sales.
- There are also disadvantages with placing many small orders instead of fewer large orders. Again consider the jeweler: A single order was processed in 2002. Twelve orders were processed in 2003. This increased by twelvefold the cost of processing orders, tracking them, paying invoices, and so on.
- Buyers who purchase small quantities often forgo quantity discounts which are price incentives based on quantities purchased. A buyer must decide whether these price concessions are worth the cost of carrying higher inventories.

A buyer's job involves making critical decisions relative to how much inventory to carry. These decisions are driven by multiple factors, including desired turnover, the availability of goods, the availability of cash to pay for them, and the amount of inventory needed to maintain adequate selections. Increasing turnover is an objective to which buyers dedicate considerable attention. In its college-recruitment material, Parisian, a specialty-department-store group based in Birmingham, Alabama, boasts of turning its inventory every 3.5 months.

Turnover by Category of Merchandise

There is no universally *good* turnover rate. Acceptable turnover rates vary by category of merchandise relative to the characteristics of the goods. (See Table 9.3.) To illustrate this point, assume that the following

Table 9.3 TURNOVER FOR SELECT RETAIL STORES

Department Stores

Dillards	2.8
Federated Department Stores	2.9
Kohl's	4.5
Nordstrom	4.3

Full-line Discounters

Ames	4.0
Kmart	3.9
Wal-Mart	5.8

Category Killers

Barnes & Noble	2.6
Best Buy	6.4
Circuit City	4.7

Furniture Stores

Ethan Allen	3.0
Levitz	3.6

Home Accessories Stores

Bed Bath & Beyond	2.7
Pier 1 Imports	2.8

Off-pricers

Burlington Coat Factory	3.1
T.J. Maxx	5.0

Specialty Stores

American Eagle	2.0
Ann Taylor	4.3
The Gap	6.1
The Limited	6.3
Nine West Group	2.0

three items in a department store sell and turned at the same rate as the gold chains in 2002:

Housewares Department: Toasters—Purchasing an inventory of 600 toasters for an entire year is an acceptable (though not ideal) buying decision. Changes in toaster styles are minimal over time, and toasters do

SPECIAL ORDERS

Retailers sell goods by "special order" when style, color, size, or fabric specifications are unique to each customer. Custom draperies and monogrammed stationery are examples of special order goods. Goods for which there is infrequent demand, such as extra-long men's suits, are often special ordered, as are big ticket items, such as furniture. Special orders minimize a retailer's inventory investment, since samples are often the only inventory carried in stock. Special order goods turn quickly, since special order sales are transacted as soon as the goods are received.

In spite of these inventory management advantages, special order sales are labor intensive in that each customer's purchase requires processing an order and arranging for subsequent pick-up or delivery. Problems occur when special order specifications are incorrect or incorrectly followed. The retailer must absorb the cost of errors attributable to the store. Perhaps the greatest difficulty with special orders is that customers have become accustomed to the immediate gratification of taking their purchases home with them, an opportunity that special orders do not afford them.

not deteriorate by sitting on a stockroom shelf. The last 50 toasters on hand at the end of the year are as salable as the first 50 toasters sold at the beginning of the year.

Intimate Apparel Department: Robes—Purchasing an inventory of 600 robes for an entire year is not an acceptable buying decision. Seasonal changes in styles and fabrications require frequent inventory changes throughout the year. The lightweight spring robes in stock at the beginning of the year are not salable at the end of the year when longer styles in flannels and velours are in demand.

Coffee House: Muffins—Purchasing an inventory of 600 muffins for an entire year is an unquestionably unacceptable buying decision. A muffin's limited shelf life render it unsalable the day after delivery, not to mention 12 months later.

The examples serve to demonstrate a fundamental principle related to turnover: that **perishable goods** need to turn more quickly than nonperishable goods. Perishable merchandise has a limited shelf life or selling period. In a broad interpretation, fashion goods are *perishable*. Fashion goods are less salable over time because of seasonal changes in color, style, and fabrication. The turnover of nonperishable goods should also be monitored. Nonperishables that remain on racks or shelves for extended periods can become shopworn while tying up valuable space and inventory dollars.

STOCK-TO-SALES RATIOS

A **stock-to-sales ratio** is the proportionate relationship between a BOM and sales for the corresponding month. The formula for the stock-to-sales ratio is:

$$stock\text{-}to\text{-}sales\ ratio = \frac{BOM}{sales}$$

When sales are $10,000 and BOM is $30,000, the stock-to-sales ratio is computed as follows:

$$stock\text{-}to\text{-}sales\ ratio = \frac{\$30,000}{\$10,000}$$

$$stock\text{-}to\text{-}sales\ ratio = 3.0$$

A 3.0 stock-to-sales ratio indicates that the BOM is three times sales. Stock-to-sales ratios are most often expressed as whole numbers carried to one decimal place.

The breadth of an assortment is a determinant of its stock-to-sales ratio: the broader the assortment, the higher the stock-to-sales ratio. Consider the stock-to-sales ratios of men's dress shirts and men's sport shirts: Because dress shirts are buttoned at the neck, collar sizing must be rather precise. To accommodate this close fit, dress shirts are manufactured in collar sizes that usually range from $14\frac{1}{2}$ inches to 17 inches with half-inch increments between sizes.

Because the sleeve length of a dress shirt must correspond to the sleeve length of a jacket, the sleeve-length sizing of a dress shirt must also be precise. Therefore, dress shirts are manufactured with sleeves that vary in lengths from 32 inches to 35 inches with one-inch increments between sizes. A complete size assortment of one dress-shirt style in one color is 24 shirts, six neck sizes times four sleeve lengths.

Men's sport shirts, on the other hand, are worn unbuttoned at the neck, and their fit is unrelated to any other garment. Thus, neither the collar nor the sleeve of a sport shirt must be as exact a fit as the collar or sleeve of a dress shirt. Consequently, sport shirts are cut in four general sizes: small, medium, large, and extra-large, each size with average collar and sleeve-length combinations. A complete size assortment of one sport shirt style in one color is four shirts.

Therefore, a retailer who plans to sell an equal number of dress shirts and sport shirts will need more dress shirts than sport shirts. The amount of stock needed to sell a *single* style and color of dress shirt is 24 shirts, while the amount of stock needed to sell a *single* style and color of sport shirt is only four shirts. Thus, dress shirts will require a higher stock-to-sales ratio than sport shirts.[4]

In general, assortments with a broad range of sizes or styles require high stock-to-sales ratios. Women's shoes have a high stock-to-sales ratio because of an extensive assortment of numeric sizes and corresponding widths. Many department stores and full-line discounters have abandoned ready-made curtains and draperies as businesses because of high inventory requirements. Each style and color requires an assortment of lengths and several pairs of each to accommodate multipair purchases.

In essence, a stock-to-sales ratio is an inverse expression of turnover. A stock-to-sales ratio is computed by dividing an inventory figure (BOM) by sales. Turnover is computed by dividing sales by an inventory figure (average inventory). Thus, turnover and stock-to-sales ratios have an inverse relationship; that is, as one increases the other decreases. Consequently, a *high* turnover is indicative of a *low* stock-to-sales ratio, and *low* turnover is indicative of a *high* stock-to-sales ratio.

As merchandising concepts, turnover and stock-to-sales ratios are often uttered in the same breath. Industry observers blame Gap's commitment to maintaining an in-stock position on waist sizes ranging from 28 inches to 46 inches and nine inseam lengths for the company's constant struggle to turn inventory quickly.[5]

Buyers predicate buying decisions on turnover and stock-to-sales-ratios. Consider a slow-turning women's-hosiery department. The buyer determines that the low turnover is a result of the high stock-to-sales ratios needed to ensure complete color and size assortments within each brand. To increase turnover, the buyer

Figure 9.1

Goods with an extensive assortment of sizes have a high stock-to-sales ratio. *Courtesy of Nordstrom.*

must choose between two strategies: carrying the same number of brands with reduced assortments of size and color, or carrying fewer brands with full assortments of size and color.

The latter is the preferable alternative. Carrying the same number of brands with reduced assortments of sizes and colors will frustrate customers looking for a particular size or color within a brand. It is less frustrating to a customer to find a brand unavailable than to find many brands represented by poor assortments. A shrewd buyer would edit the number of brands carried, eliminating those that closely duplicate each other in terms of price, quality, color, and style assortment.

In theory, a stock-to-sales ratio cannot be less than 1.0. A stock-to-sales ratio is 1.0 when BOM and sales are equal, implying that all of the merchandise on hand at the beginning of the month is sold during the month. This is an infrequent circumstance except in the case of very fast-turning goods continuously replenished throughout the month, or seasonal merchandise, such as Christmas decorations where it is hoped that all of December's BOM will be sold by the end the month.

Stock-to-Sales Ratio Variations

Busy selling periods require lower stock-to-sales ratios than slower periods. To demonstrate this principle, consider an assortment of cotton sweaters available in five colors and four sizes (S/M/L/XL). Assume that the buyer plans to sell only one sweater during the first month of the season. A BOM of 20 sweaters is required, representing a complete assortment of five colors and four sizes. Assume that the buyer increases the sales plan to two sweaters. Since planned sales have doubled, should the buyer double the BOM to include two of each size and color? Hardly. A BOM of 20 sweaters is still an adequate assortment to support the sale of two sweaters since the chance of a second customer wanting the same size and color as the first customer is only 1 in 20, assuming that one size and color combination is as desirable as another. Nineteen sweaters represents a 95 percent in-stock rate ($19/20 = 0.95 = 95\%$), a very acceptable inventory position for most categories of merchandise.

When planned sales are one sweater, the stock-to-sales ratio is 20.0 (20:1). When planned sales are two sweaters, the stock-to-sales ratio is only 10.0 (20:2), substantiating the claim (though rather simplistically) that "peak" selling months require lower stock-to-sales ratios than "slow" months. At some point during the season, planned sweater sales will reach a point that will necessitate increasing the inventory of each size and color as the chance of two customers wanting the same size and color increases. However, at no point will a full assortment of sweaters be required for each customer.

Table 9.4 lists monthly stock-to-sales ratios for a department. Note that the range of ratios falls between 1.7 and 5.0. The months with the highest sales have the lowest stock-to-sales ratios, while the months with the lowest sales have the highest stock-to-sales ratios. Since periods of high sales require lower stock-to-sales ratios than periods of low sales, it is reasonable to conclude that merchandise turns faster during periods of high sales than periods of low sales. During peak selling periods, merchandise flows in and out of stores rapidly, while during slow selling periods, goods turn at much slower rates. (See Table 9.5.)

SALES PER SQUARE FOOT

Sales per square foot is a measure of productivity that reflects the amount of sales generated relative to the amount of space dedicated to selling the goods. As a productivity input, square footage represents the

Table 9.4   **MONTHLY STOCK-TO-SALES RATIOS FOR A DEPARTMENT**

Month	Sales	BOM	Stock-to-Sales Ratio
1	$ 20,000	$ 40,000	2.0
2	$ 20,000	$ 40,000	2.0
3	$ 25,000	$ 45,000	1.8
4	$ 10,000	$ 30,000	3.0
5	$ 10,000	$ 30,000	3.0
6	$ 5,000	$ 25,000	5.0
7	$ 5,000	$ 25,000	5.0
8	$ 5,000	$ 25,000	5.0
9	$ 40,000	$ 60,000	1.5
10	$ 30,000	$ 50,000	1.7
11	$ 40,000	$ 60,000	1.5
12	$ 30,000	$ 50,000	1.7
TOTAL	$240,000	$480,000	2.0

The aggregate stock-to-sales ratio for the year is 2.0 based on total BOMs divided by total sales.

capital outlay for constructing the retail space, and the operational expenses associated with renting, heating, lighting, cleaning, and staffing the space. Square footage is based on the physical dimensions of a selling area, and often includes stockrooms, fitting rooms, service areas, and adjacent aisles. The formula for computing sales per square foot is:

$$sales\ per\ square\ foot = \frac{sales}{square\ footage}$$

Sales per square foot can be calculated for any time period, however, an annual computation is the most common. Though sales per square foot productivity is most often computed for spaces occupied by entire categories of merchandise, it may also be computed for a spatial entity as small as a fixture. In advertising to retailers, Kodak claims that Picture Maker, a touch-screen digital-imaging system, can generate $4000 per square foot annually based on sales projections of $70 a day.[6]

The following demonstrates the calculation of sales per square foot: Assume that a department store allocates 1000 square feet within

Table 9.5   **BOM STOCK-TO-SALES RATIO FOR
MEN'S SPECIALTY STORES**

Category	Median
February	8.6
March	8.3
April	8.3
May	8.4
June	7.3
July	8.5
August	8.8
September	8.8
October	8.7
November	8.5
December	4.4
January	7.9

its misses sportswear area to an Alfred Dunner shop. Last year the shop generated sales of $400,000. Sales per square foot for the shop are computed as follows:

$$sales\ per\ square\ foot = \frac{sales}{square\ footage}$$

$$sales\ per\ square\ foot = \frac{\$400{,}000}{1000\ square\ feet}$$

$$sales\ per\ square\ foot = \$400$$

For each square foot of space dedicated to the Alfred Dunner line, $400 in sales were generated.

As a measure of productivity, high sales-per-square-foot values are generally more desirable than low values. The mathematical relationship between sales and square footage suggests that sales-per-square-foot productivity can be increased by increasing sales, decreasing square footage, or both increasing sales and decreasing square footage. Generating more sales in less space is a universal objective for every retailer.

Though high sales per square foot is desirable, excessively high sales per square foot can be an indication that a selling area is too crowded, and generating too much sales volume from a limited amount of space. A crowded shopping environment can inhibit sales and the effective presentation of goods while creating an uncomfortable shopping environment.

Space productivity expectations differ by category of merchandise. The physical size of merchandise is a factor. If a department store's fashion-jewelry counter and furniture department generate the same annual volume, the sales per square foot of the fashion jewelry department will be higher than the sales per square foot of the furniture department because of the lesser amount of space required to present the jewelry. Sales-per-square-foot expectations vary by type of store. (See Table 9.6.) A department store's wide aisles and comfortable shopping environment yield lower sales per square foot than space-challenged off-pricers.[7]

Turnover is another factor relevant to sales-per-square-foot expectations. If men's sport shirts and men's dress shirts generate the same annual volume, but sport shirts turn twice as fast as dress shirts, then the average inventory of dress shirts is twice the average inventory of sport shirts. Since sport shirts require only half the space of dress shirts, sport shirts are more productive in terms of sales per square foot. Gap reduced its inventory from $73 per square foot one year to $51 four years later, a move that made Wall Street happy in that lower inventory is indicative of higher turnover.[8]

Though sales per square foot is the most commonly used measure of space productivity, productivity can be measured for any unit of space. Cubic feet can be used when height or vertical dimension is a factor in presenting goods for sale, as in the case of stacked goods. Linear inches can be used to measure the space productivity of linear configurations of space, such as shelving. In the catalog industry, space is defined as pages, and sales per page are the industry's standard measure of productivity.[9] Numerators other than sales can be used as an output relative to spatial input. Some stores compute gross margin per square foot. Gross margin is a gross-profit figure from which net profit is derived and a topic that will be discussed in Chapter 10.

Retail-industry pundits play close attention to sales-per-square-foot productivity. The retail-expansion binge that has spanned the last two decades has caused considerable concern among those who follow the industry closely. During that time, retailers opened five times as many stores as they closed, an expansion rate unwarranted by commensurate growth in consumer spending. The disproportionate increase in retail space caused sales per square foot to plummet from a high of $197 in the 1970s, to $181 in the 1980s, and to $160 in the 1990s.[10]

Table 9.6 **SALES PER SQUARE FOOT FOR SELECT RETAIL STORES**

Department Stores

Dillards	$230
Federated Department Stores	$204
Kohl's	$271
Nordstrom	$384

Category Killers

Barnes & Noble	$283
Best Buy	$211
Toys "R" Us	$548

Furniture Stores

Ethan Allen	$130
Levitz	$317

Home Accessories Stores

Bed Bath & Beyond	$326
Pier 1 Imports	$203

Off-pricers

Burlington Coat Factory	$111
T.J. Maxx	$202

Specialty Stores

American Eagle	$392
Ann Taylor	$445
The Gap	$207
The Limited	$324
Nine West Group	$136

Space Allocation

Retail selling space is strategically allocated to various merchandise categories to maximize sales per square foot. Consider the following: A 10,000-square-foot specialty store generates annual sales of $3 million. The space is divided among four categories of merchandise. The square footage, annual sales, and sales per square foot for each category appear in Table 9.7. The figures in the *Industry Standard* column are hypothetical sales-per-square-foot industry standards. Standards such as these are often provided by retail trade organizations as benchmarks to which retailers can compare their performance.

Note that the store's sales per square foot of $300 is behind the industry standard of $339. In other words, the store is not generating enough sales relative to its size. Further analysis reveals the problem areas: Dresses at $100 per square foot, and outerwear at $200 per square foot are performing behind the industry standards of $250 per square foot and $320 per square foot, respectively. Sportswear and accessories are not problems. The sales per square foot of the sportswear area matches the industry standard. At $700 per foot, the sales per square foot of the accessories area far exceeds the industry standard of $400 per foot.

The problem has frustrated the owner who has tried to build dress and outerwear sales with direct-mail advertising, new merchandise resources, and promotional pricing. However, none of the tactics have been successful. It is apparent that both businesses have plateaued with little promise of future growth.

The owner decides that the best strategy for bringing the store's sales per square foot closer to industry standards is to reallocate space. The retailer determines that:

- The ideal amount of space for a $300,000 dress area is 1200 square feet ($300,000 divided by the industry standard of $250 = 1200).
- The ideal amount of space for a $400,000 outerwear area is 1250 square feet ($400,000 divided by the industry standard of $320 = 1250).
- Reducing the dress area by 1800 square feet (the present 3000 square feet less 1200 square feet), and the outerwear area by 750 square feet (the present 2000 square feet less 1250 square feet), will permit the expansion of the accessories area by 2550 square feet (1800 square feet plus 750 square feet). This will more than double the size of the accessories area (2550 square feet plus 1000 square feet is 3550 square feet).

Table 9.7   **SALES PER SQUARE FOOT FOR WOMEN'S SPECIALTY STORE**

Category	Square Footage	Annual Sales	Sales/Square Foot	Industry Standard
Sportswear	4,000	$1,600,000	$400	$400
Dresses	3,000	$ 300,000	$100	$250
Outerwear	2,000	$ 400,000	$200	$320
Accessories	1,000	$ 700,000	$700	$400
TOTAL	10,000	$3,000,000	$300	$339

The wisdom of expanding the accessories area so dramatically may be questioned. At the current annual volume of $700,000, the addition of 2550 square feet will drop the area's productivity from $700 per square foot to $197 per square foot ($700,000 divided by 3550 square feet), $203 below the industry standard. However, at $700 per square foot, the area's productivity was nearly twice the industry standard, an indication of overcrowding and unrealized sales potential. Expanding the area will create a more comfortable shopping environment, facilitate more attractive presentations of goods, and allow for expanding selections of the popular items and resources. The retailer can expect to generate considerably higher sales that will bring the resulting sales-per-square-foot productivity for the store closer to industry standards.

SPACE MANAGEMENT

Space management is the strategic arrangement of products to maximize sales with a minimum investment of space and fixtures. Space management involves the development of visual models of product arrangements called **planograms**. Planograms incorporate an organization's standards for merchandise presentation, product adjacencies, and customer convenience. Planograms ensure the consistent arrangement of goods within stores in multiunit organizations. A planogram can represent an entire store, a store section, or a single fixture or wall section. Planograms can be general, indicating the approximate location of merchandise categories, or specific, indicating the precise location of individual items on fixtures. Planograms are periodically reset to reflect seasonal changes in product assortments. Planograms of fashion goods are reset more often than planograms of basic goods.

Electronic space-management software builds predictive models of optimum inventory levels and assortments based on the wholesale cost, retail price, and turnover of each product in an assortment. "What if" capabilities allow the software user to observe the fiscal impact of adding or deleting items from an assortment. Most space-management software produces color planograms with product images in scaled dimensions that can be electronically transmitted to stores. The planograms are automatically adjusted by store based on sales data

Figure 9.2

A planogram is an optimum product arrangement. *SMSB Consulting Group, Inc., Farmingdale, NY.*

scanned at point of sale. Quantities of slow-turning items are reduced (or deleted) from the assortment, while quantities of fast-turning items are increased. One retailer added three dozen new high-ticket, high-margin items to a 200-item assortment in existing space by freeing space occupied by overstocked items, and dropping slow-moving items.[11] Movement information is also shared with suppliers to ensure timely replenishment of stock. (See Table 9.8.)

Electronic space management is closely allied to **category management**, a micromerchandising concept of managing individual brands or categories of merchandise as units of business.[12] Electronic space management was first used in the food industry. However, applications to durable goods and apparel are becoming common.[13] Sears uses electronic space management for home softlines, such as bed and bath linens and ready-made draperies, and for basic apparel, such as jeans, underwear, and hosiery.

Table 9.8 **SPACE PRODUCTIVITY REPORT COMPARING PERCENT OF TURNOVER TO PERCENT OF SPACE OCCUPIED**

Style #	% Movemt	% Space	Style #	% Movemt	% Space
3305	0.8	1.5	4147	3.4	1.8
3113	0.7	1.6	3853	1.6	1.5
6616	0.7	1.7	4918	3.5	1.6
1808	0.5	1.6	6921	2.5	1.5
2000	1.9	1.7	2426	2.4	1.7
4343	1.7	1.6	5783	2.1	1.4
9015	0.8	1.6	9687	3.7	1.8
3864	2.0	1.6	4688	3.4	1.6
7401	3.9	1.7	2498	3.0	1.5
3673	1.7	1.9	6957	3.6	1.6
8848	1.2	1.8	0289	1.9	1.6
7074	1.4	1.6	3278	3.0	1.6
3066	0.7	1.6	4489	1.1	1.4
0089	1.3	1.8	6895	0.6	1.2
7085	0.2	1.7	8980	0.9	1.5
2242	1.0	1.5	4880	1.3	1.6
2757	2.1	1.6	0890	1.2	1.8
7004	0.5	1.7	2134	0.7	3.1
5309	1.6	1.6	2778	0.7	1.4
1016	2.1	1.7	3095	1.4	1.4
1226	0.7	1.5	9800	0.5	1.4
0704	1.3	1.6	7783	0.3	1.4
1004	1.1	1.7	4348	1.8	1.8
3997	1.4	1.5	2390	2.5	1.9
5937	1.2	1.5	0063	1.5	2.8
2618	1.5	1.6	3373	0.7	1.6
9972	1.4	1.7	5218	2.6	1.8
5740	1.1	1.6	1001	2.1	1.7
5611	0.7	1.9	4979	2.5	1.5
1089	3.9	2.2		100.0	100.0
6668	2.4	1.6			

SUMMARY POINTS

- Productivity is a measure of the number of units of output produced per unit of input.
- Turnover is the number of times that an average inventory is sold over a time period. Turnover can be increased by increasing sales,

decreasing average inventory, or both. Turnover expectations differ by category of merchandise.

- A stock-to-sales ratio indicates the proportionate relationship between a BOM inventory and the sales for a month. Goods requiring extensive assortments have high stock-to-sales ratios. Goods requiring limited assortments have low stock-to-sales ratios.
- Peak selling periods require lower stock-to-sales ratios than slower selling periods.
- Sales per square foot is a measure of productivity that reflects the amount of sales generated relative to the amount of retail space dedicated to sale of the goods.

KEY TERMS AND CONCEPTS

average inventory	end-of-month inventory	sales per square foot
beginning-of-month inventory	perishable goods	space management
	planogram	stock-to-sales ratio
category management	productivity	turnover

FOR DISCUSSION

1. Compare various categories of merchandise relative to the turnover assumed for each. What characteristics of the goods influence their turnover?
2. Consider several categories or brands of merchandise relative to stock-to-sales ratios assumed for each. What assortment characteristics influence their stock-to-sales ratios?
3. Review a store's assortment of a product line with multiple styles, sizes, or colors. Are there styles, sizes, or colors that have sold out? Are there full assortments, styles, sizes, or colors that have apparently not sold at all? Are there some that are sold out? What inferences can you make about the turnover of the product line? What advice can you give to the person who places replenishment orders?
4. A shoe retailer carries a large assortment of casual, dress, and athletic shoes for men, women, and children in 4000-square-foot locations. The retailer plans to expand to open several new stores, most of which are considerably smaller than existing locations. Based on your knowledge of turnover and stock-to-sales ratios, what advice can you give the retailer relative to determining a merchandise mix for the new stores?
5. Look for a very crowded store. How do the crowded conditions affect shopping ambiance? Your ability to shop?

PROBLEMS

1. Refer to the figures in Table 9.1 to compute the following:

   - average inventory for the last quarter of the year
   - average inventory for the first six months of the year
   - turnover for the last six months of the year assuming sales of $20,000 for the period

   Assume annual sales of $30,000 and that 60 percent of the sales are generated during the last six months of the year.

2. The following list refers to the number of stock-keeping units that need to be carried to maintain a full assortment of sizes, styles, and colors for each of five lines. Assume that the average unit price is $2.50 and that average monthly sales for each line is $100. Compute the stock-to-sales ratio for each.

Line A	100 units
Line B	120 units
Line C	80 units
Line D	200 units
Line E	140 units

   What inferences can you make relative to the turnover of each item?

3. The following is a list of sales-per-square-foot figures for the merchandise division of a department store slated for expansion. Corporate sales-per-square-foot standards for each division are also included.

division	sq feet	sales/sq feet	standard
Men's	20,000	600	300
Kids'	10,000	400	250
Ready-to-Wear	50,000	350	300
Accessories	20,000	300	350
Home	30,000	300	250

   How many additional square feet are required to match corporate productivity standards? Which divisions need additional space? How much space does each need?

ENDNOTES

1. If the average inventory for a year were computed by dividing the sum of the year's beginning and ending inventories by two, the resulting figure would not be a representative average. Using the average inventories for each month accounts for the dramatic inventory fluctuations that occur in a year. Ideally, an annual average inventory should be computed by summing each day's inventory and dividing by 365, just as an average daily balance is computed on a savings account or a charge account. However, most retailers

do not maintain daily inventory balances, and the cost of generating this information would negate the value of it.

2. The data in this scenario has been manipulated to demonstrate dramatically the effect of average inventory on turnover. In real life, sales are never quite as predictable.

3. Outcalt, R. & Johnson, P. (Januray 1997). The diamond of doom. *Specialty Stores/The Business Newsletter.* p. 4.

4. For pedagogical reasons, assortment considerations other than size were ignored. Sport shirts require a broader range of styles and colors than dress shirts, a selection factor that increases their stock-to-sales ratio.

5. Munk, N. (August 3, 1998). Gap gets it. *Fortune.* pp. 68–82.

6. The machine takes up about six-square-feet.

7. Barmash, I. (July 1998). Stein Mart growth paces off-price retailers. *SCT/Retailing Today.* p. 38.

8. Munk, N. (August 3, 1998). Gap gets it. *Fortune.* pp. 68–82.

9. Chandler, S. (July 8, 1996). Lands' End looks for terra firma. *Business Week.* pp. 129–131.

10. Silverman, D. (October 30, 1997). Has expansion boon finally brought retail to saluration point? *Women's Wear Daily.* pp. 1, 10-11.

11. Robbins, G. (April 1993). Softlines, the new frontier for space management systems. *Stores.* pp. 24–26.

12. Hartnett, M. (April 1998). Category management program yields major gains for Ace Hardware members. *Stores.* pp. 56–58.

13. Friedman, A. (March 6, 1996). KSA's guide to managing a category. *Women's Wear Daily.* p. 12.

chapter ten

MERCHANDISING ACCOUNTING

Because merchandising outcomes have considerable impact on a retail organization's fiscal objectives, an understanding of financial statements is important to the organization's merchants. Chapter 10 covers the analysis and interpretation of some of the financial statements studied in accounting courses with an emphasis on merchandising applications and retail inventories.

After you have read this chapter, you will be able to discuss:

Fundamental accounting concepts from a merchandising perspective.

The interpretation of retail financial statements.

Gross margin return on investment as a measure of inventory performance.

CASH FLOW

Cash flow is the balance of cash coming into and going out of an organization. A positive cash flow means that more cash is coming into the organization than going out. A negative cash flow means that more cash is going out of the organization than coming in. A positive cash flow is preferable to a negative cash flow; however, even the most successful retailers experience negative cash flow periodically.

Consider the following: A men's shop conducts approximately 20 percent of its annual business between Thanksgiving and Christmas. The owner arranges for the delivery of goods bought for the holiday season by October 31. The retailer pays most invoices within 10 days to take advantage of early-payment discounts, and the remaining balances within 30 days. Thus, most holiday merchandise is paid for by mid-November, even though the goods will not begin to yield an appreciable amount of cash from sales until late November. About half of the retailer's customers charge their purchases to store-sponsored charge accounts. These sales do not begin to generate cash until about 30 days after the purchases are made. Full payment for holiday purchases averages 90 days.

Figure 10.1 depicts the retailer's cash flow from October through March. A negative cash flow is any point on the graph where the *cash-out* line is higher than the *cash-in* line. Periods of negative cash flow occur from mid-October through the beginning of December, and

Cash flow curve.

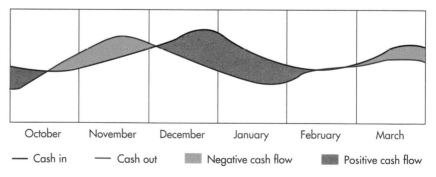

Figure 10.1

A cash flow curve.

again from the end of February through March. The latter negative cash flow is a result of the arrival and payment of spring merchandise in a period of limited cash generation due to low sales volume.

A positive cash flow is any point on the graph where the *cash-in* line is higher than the *cash-out* line, such as the period between the end of November and early February. A balanced cash flow is represented by points where the *cash-in* and *cash-out* lines coincide, for example throughout much of the latter part of February.

Retailers resolve negative cash flow with short-term borrowing from lending institutions. The borrowed funds enable retailers to meet their financial obligations to suppliers to ensure the continued shipment of orders. Short-term borrowing allows retailers to take advantage of prompt-payment discounts that help to offset the interest expense incurred by borrowing. Many retailers have an open line of credit with lending institutions that allows the retailer to borrow and pay back money in a manner similar to that of a revolving charge account with an established limit and regular payments with interest.

Cash flow is important to a retail organization's buyers in that payments to suppliers account for significant outlays of money within most retail accounting periods. Buyers can enhance a positive cash flow in two ways:

- By scheduling the delivery of goods as close as possible to their point of sale
- By negotiating payment terms that delay payments to suppliers as long as possible.

Shipments that arrive and are paid for far in advance of their selling season hinder cash flow.

BALANCE SHEETS

A **balance sheet** is a statement of an organization's assets, liabilities, and owners' equity at a particular point in time. (See Figure 10.2.) **Assets** are *owned* by an organization. Cash, inventory, and store fixtures are among a retailer's assets. Assets are classified according to their **liquidity**, or the likelihood of their conversion to cash. A *short-term*, or *current*, asset will be converted to cash within a year in the normal operation of business. Cash is a retailer's most liquid asset. A *long-term*, or *noncurrent*, *asset* will

---

Consolidated Financial Statements – 2000

Consolidated Balance Sheets (dollars in millions)

	January 30, 2000	January 31, 1999
ASSETS		
Current Assets:		
Cash	$ 307	$ 142
Accounts receivable	2,209	2,640
Merchandise inventories	3,259	3,239
Supplies and prepaid expenses	117	115
Deferred income tax assets	80	58
Total Current Assets	**5,972**	**6,194**
Property and Equipment – net	6,572	6,520
Intangible Assets – net	631	690
Other Assets	289	334
Total Assets	**$ 13,464**	**$ 13,738**
LIABILITIES AND SHAREHOLDERS' EQUITY		
Current Liabilities:		
Short-term debt	$ 524	$ 556
Accounts payable and accrued liabilities	2,446	2,416
Income taxes	98	88
Total Current Liabilities	**3,068**	**3,060**
Long-Term Debt	3,057	3,919
Deferred Income Taxes	1,060	939
Other Liabilities	570	564
Shareholders' Equity	5,709	5,256
Total Liabilities & Shareholders' Equity	**$ 13,464**	**$ 13,738**

Figure 10.2

A balance sheet is a statement of assets, liabilities, and owner's equity. *Courtesy of Federated Department Stores, Inc.*

not be converted to cash within a year in the normal operation of business. A retailer's long-term assets include store facilities and fixtures.

Inventory is a current asset that receives considerable attention in this text. Inventory is converted to cash as it is sold. The more quickly that inventory is converted to cash, the more quickly the cash can be again invested into new inventory which, in turn, will generate more sales. Inventory not quickly converted to cash often decreases in value as an asset, especially if it is perishable and becomes unsalable over time.

Liabilities are debts *owed* by an organization. Liabilities are classified according to the time in which they are due to be paid. Payment on a *short-term* liability is due within one year. Payment on a *long-term* liability is due in one year or longer. A retailer's short-term liabilities include payables to suppliers, and short-term debts to lending institutions for money borrowed to balance cash flow. Long-term liabilities include mortgages on land and buildings, and long-term financing for extensive expansion and renovation projects.

Owners' equity is the difference between assets and liabilities. Owners' equity is also called *shareowners' equity* and *shareholders' equity*. The relationship between assets, liabilities, and owners' equity is such that:

$$assets = liabilities + owners'\ equity$$

Balance-sheet components are in a constant state of flux and subject to momentary change. For instance, inventory increases and cash decreases whenever a shipment from a supplier is received and paid for. A balance sheet reflects neither sales nor profit performance. Two retailers with similar balance sheets can produce vastly different sales and profit results.

FINANCIAL RATIOS

Financial ratios are analytical tools based on the proportionate relationship between two balance-sheet components. Financial ratios are used to assess an organization's level of solvency or financial stability. A **current ratio** is the relationship between current assets and current liabilities. A current ratio measures an organization's short-term debt-paying ability, or ability to pay off current debts with current assets. The formula for the current ratio is:

$$current\ ratio = \frac{current\ assets}{current\ liabilities}$$

A current ratio less than 1.0 indicates that current liabilities are greater than current assets and that current assets are insufficient to pay off current liabilities, a highly undesirable financial position. A 2.0 current ratio indicates that current assets are twice current liabilities. (See Table 10.1.) Generally, 2.0 is considered an acceptable current ratio, though this standard varies by type of industry. Credit-rating services use financial ratios to determine an organization's credit worthiness.

Compiled by Dun and Bradstreet, the nation's largest credit-rating service, the *Business Information Report* compares organizations' financial ratios to industry benchmarks. Suppliers use the *Business Information Report* to determine the risk associated with extending credit to retailers.

Financial ratios are also important to factors. A **factor** is a financial intermediary peculiar to the apparel industry that assumes responsibility

Table 10.1 CURRENT RATIOS FOR SELECT RETAIL STORES

Department Stores	
Dillards	2.01
Federated Department Stores	1.62
Kohl's	2.44
Nordstrom	2.06
Full-line Discounters	
Ames	1.40
Kmart	1.67
Wal-Mart	1.69
Category Killers	
Barnes & Noble	1.50
Best Buy	1.37
Toys "R" Us	2.27
Furniture Stores	
Ethan Allen	2.63
Levitz	0.91
Home Accessories Stores	
Bed Bath & Beyond	2.81
Pier 1 Imports	2.51
Off-pricers	
Burlington Coat Factory	2.46
T.J. Maxx	1.81
Specialty Stores	
American Eagle	1.46
Ann Taylor	2.68
The Gap	1.90
The Limited	2.26
Nine West Group	1.46

Figure 10.3

A factor is a financial intermediary that collects manufacturers' receivables from retailers.

for collecting manufacturers' receivables from retailers. Factors buy receivables at discounted rates from manufacturers to cover the cost and financial risk associated with collecting them. Factors keep a watchful eye on the fiscal status of retailers and refuse to approve shipments to stores whose financial statements send signals of an inability to pay promptly.

Though factoring is typically associated with the apparel industry, the service is becoming more and more prevalent in nonapparel industries such as furniture, floor coverings, and consumer electronics.[1] The bankruptcies of many major retailers have caused factors to raise their credit-approval standards to protect themselves against the possibility of unpaid claims in recent years. Some of the major factoring firms include Capital Factors, Heller Financial, and Rosenthal and Rosenthal.[2, 3]

INCOME STATEMENTS

An **income statement** is a statement of an organization's profit performance for a specific period of time. The fundamental components of an income statement are revenue, expenses, and net income. The relationship among the components is expressed by the equation:

$$revenue - expenses = net\ income$$

The income statement is sometimes called a *statement of earnings*, or a *profit and loss (P&L) statement*. A **profit** results when expenses are less than revenue and net income is positive. A **loss** results when expenses are greater than revenue and net income is negative.

Unlike a balance sheet that represents a particular *point in time*, an income statement represents a specific *span of time*, such as a year, a six-month season, a quarter, or a month. Income statements can be computed for an entire organization or for a unit of business within an organization, such as an individual store, a group of stores, or a department. Profit or loss is based on the revenue and expenses directly associated with each unit of business.

Income Statement Components

Retail income statements have five major components: net revenue, cost-of-goods-sold, gross margin, expenses, and net profit. The relationship among the components is such that:

$$net\ revenue$$
$$\frac{-\ cost\ of\ goods\ sold}{gross\ margin}$$
$$\frac{-\ expenses}{net\ income\ (loss)}$$

Since sales are typically a retailer's major source of revenue, the term *net sales* often appears on retailers' income statements. Other sources of revenue may include rent from leasing or renting property, or interest on accounts receivable. Net sales are the "top line" of the income statement from which all other income-statement components are derived. High net sales attest to the ability of an organization's buyers to select assortments of goods that are appealing to the store's target customers.

Net sales are equal to **gross sales** minus customer returns:

$$net\ sales = gross\ sales - customer\ returns$$

Though never appearing on an income statement, records of gross sales are maintained for other reasons, such as determining customer-return rates:

$$customer\ return\ rate = \frac{customer\ returns}{gross\ sales} \times 100$$

Customer returns of $4000 on gross sales of $100,000 represents a return of 4 percent on net sales:

$$customer\ return\ rate = \frac{\$4000}{\$100,000} \times 100$$

$$customer\ return\ rate = 4\%$$

Customer-return rates are computed for stores, categories of merchandise, and brands. A high customer-return rate can be indicative of poor customer service, poor product quality, or fit.

The **cost of goods sold**, also called the *cost of merchandise sold* or the *cost of sales*, includes the billed cost of merchandise plus shipping and workroom costs, less cash discounts for early payment and returns to vendors.

$$billed\ cost\ of\ merchandise$$
$$+\ shipping\ costs$$
$$+\ workroom\ costs$$
$$-\ returns\ to\ vendors$$
$$\frac{-\ cash\ discounts}{cost\ of\ goods\ sold}$$

Consolidated Statements of Income
dollars in millions, except per share data

	52 weeks ended January 30, 2000	52 weeks ended January 30, 1999	52 weeks ended February 1, 1998
Net sales, including leased department sales	$ 15,833	$ 15,668	$ 15,229
Cost of sales:			
Recurring	9,616	9,581	9,289
Inventory valuation adjustments related to consolidation	—	—	65
Total cost of sales	**9,616**	**9,581**	**9,354**
Percent to sales	60.7%	61.1%	61.4%
Selling, general and administrative expenses:			
Recurring	4,762	4,746	4,739
Business integration and consolidation expenses	—	—	243
Total selling, general and administrative expenses	**4,762**	**4,746**	**4,982**
Percent to sales	30.1%	30.3%	32.7%
Operating income	1,455	1,341	893
Interest expense	(304)	(418)	(499)
Interest income	12	35	47
Income before income taxes and extraordinary items	1,163	958	441
Federal, state and local income tax expense	(478)	(383)	
Income before extraordinary items	685	575	266
Extraordinary items	(23)	(39)	—
Net income	$ 662	$ 536	$ 266
Net income before unusual items*	$ 685	$ 575	$ 453
Diluted earnings per share:			
Income before extraordinary items	$ 3.06	$ 2.58	$ 1.24
Extraordinary items	(.10)	(.17)	—
Net income	$ 2.96	$ 2.41	$ 1.24

*See Note (1) on page two for definition of unusual terms.

Figure 10.4

An income statement is a statement of revenue, expenses, and net income. *Courtesy of Federated Department Stores, Inc.*

Shipping costs are the inbound delivery costs for transporting goods from suppliers. **Workroom costs** represent activities that prepare merchandise for sale, such as steaming and pressing apparel, and repairing merchandise damaged during shipment. Workroom activities change the merchandise in some way. Expenses for ticketing, hanging, or presenting merchandise on fixtures are not workroom costs. **Returns to vendors**, or *RTVs*, are chargebacks to vendors for defective or slow-selling goods returned for credit. **Cash discounts** are invoice concessions from suppliers for prompt payment, a topic that will receive considerable attention in Chapter 14.

Expenses are incurred in the day-to-day operation of an organization. Expense categories include payroll, rent, utilities, advertising, and interest on debt. Expenses are classified as either direct or indirect. A **direct expense** is attributable to a specific unit of business; an **indirect expense** is not. Direct expenses cease to exist when the unit of business is eliminated. A store's rent is a direct expense that would no longer exist if the store were closed. Newspaper advertising for a region of stores is an indirect expense for each store that would continue to exist if one of the stores in the region were closed.

Most retailers make every effort to allocate expenses directly. For instance, the advertising expense for a region of stores might be allocated to the stores in the region based on the sales volume of each store. Most of a retail organization's expenses are operational in nature, their control falling within the realm of the finance division or store administration.

Gross margin, or *gross profit*, is the difference between sales and the cost of goods sold. Retailers rely on gross margin to cover operating expenses, and ultimately profit. Gross-margin expectations vary by retailing format and type of merchandise. A discount store's "no-frills" strategy yields lower operating expenses than those of a department store. In turn, a discount store's gross margins are typically lower than those of a department store. (See Table 10.2.) A men's shop expects higher gross margins from its sportswear category than its suit category in that gross margins for suits are often eroded by alteration-workroom costs. Generating gross margin is fundamental to a buyer's mission in a retail organization. Buyers maximize gross margin in two ways:

- by negotiating favorable prices with vendors thus maintaining a low cost of goods sold
- by managing retail prices in a way that will maximize net sales

Many retailers include buying and occupancy costs in the cost of goods sold that appears in their annual reports. The practice inflates the cost of goods sold and reduces gross margin, a tactic that camouflages the *real* cost of goods sold which is a carefully guarded secret in retail organizations. Though buying and occupancy costs are included in the cost of goods sold in public financial statements, most retailers follow the traditional format for internal management reports.

Net income, sometimes called *net earnings*, or *net profit*, *earnings before taxes*, or *bottom line*, is equal to gross margin minus expenses.

Table 10.2   **GROSS MARGIN PERCENTAGES FOR SELECT RETAIL STORES**

Department Stores

Dillards	31.8
Federated Department Stores	40.3
Kohl's	31.2
Nordstrom	33.5

Full-line Discounters

Ames	27.8
Kmart	21.8
Wal-Mart	20.8

Category Killers

Barnes & Noble	25.0
Best Buy	15.9
Toys "R" Us	28.0

Furniture Stores

Ethan Allen	43.4
Levitz	42.8

Home Accessories Stores

Bed Bath & Beyond	41.3
Lands' End	46.6
Pier 1 Imports	41.4

Off-pricers

Burlington Coat Factory	34.1
T.J. Maxx	23.2

Specialty Stores

Ann Taylor	42.5
American Eagle	38.2
The Gap	46.4
The Limited	31.9
Nine West Group	42.5

Because generating net income is fundamental to a company's existence, all of the activities of a retail organization are directly or indirectly pointed to this goal. From an income-statement perspective, net income can be increased by:

- increasing sales
- increasing gross margin

- decreasing cost of goods sold
- decreasing expenses
- any combination of the above

Component Percentages

A **component percentage** is a ratio of an income statement component, such as gross margin, expenses, or net income, to net sales expressed as a percentage. The following are formulas for computing four component percentages:

$$cost\ of\ goods\ sold\ \% = \frac{cost\ of\ goods\ sold}{net\ sales} \times 100$$

$$gross\ margin\ \% = \frac{gross\ margin}{net\ sales} \times 100$$

$$expenses\ \% = \frac{expenses}{net\ sales} \times 100$$

$$net\ income\ \% = \frac{net\ income}{net\ sales} \times 100$$

Component percentages are often used to evaluate performance between two time periods, a comparison called a **time-series comparison**. To demonstrate, refer to the information in Table 10.3 which was derived from two successive annual income statements of The Limited, Inc. The figures in the *percent columns* are based on the above formulas. Note that sales increased from year one to year two by $637,298,000, representing a gain of 11.5 percent. However, in spite of this sizable

Table 10.3   **A TIME-SERIES COMPARISON OF THE LIMITED'S INCOME STATEMENT COMPONENTS**

	Year 2	% Sales	Year 1	% Sales
Net Sales	$6,160,807	100.0%	$5,523,509	100.0%
Cost of Goods Sold	$4,367,264	70.9%	$3,893,070	70.5%
Gross Margin	$1,793,543	29.1%	$1,630,439	29.5%
Expenses	$1,133,241	18.4%	$ 977,001	17.7%
Net Income	$ 660,302	10.7%	$ 653,438	11.8%

Dollar figures are expressed in thousands

gain in sales, the company's net income as a percentage of sales slipped by 1.1 percent because of two factors: lower gross margin (-0.4%), and an increase in expenses ($+0.7\%$) Though the percentages are seemingly minuscule, the drop in net income amounted to $6,864,000.

Note that the component percentages converted multidigit dollar figures into more comprehensible numbers. Component percentages also facilitate comparing stores or organizations of vastly different volume. A meaningful comparison can be made between the performance of a *$6 million* dollar retailer to The Limited, a *$6 billion* retailer, since percentage ratios conveniently convert income statement components to a scale of 0 to ± 100 percent, regardless of the dollar magnitude of the components. Naturally, other factors must be considered when comparing the two retailers. As a multibillion-dollar organization, The Limited reaps economic advantage unattainable for small retailers.

GROSS MARGIN RETURN ON INVESTMENT (GMROI)

Prudent merchandising decisions are often based on multiple pieces of information. For instance, assume that a retailer is faced with the decision to eliminate one of two categories of merchandise from a store's assortment because of space constraints. Basing the decision solely on sales performance is an information-poor decision in that the lower sales producer might be generating more gross margin than the higher sales producer. Table 10.4 compares the sales and gross margin of the two categories. Note that Category A sales exceed category B sales by $50,000. However, Category B generates $30,000 more gross margin than Category A, and it is thus a larger contributor to the store's net income. The analysis suggests that Category B, the lower sales producer, should be retained in the assortment, not Category A. Naturally, factors other than sales and gross margin

Table 10.4   **GROSS MARGIN COMPARISON OF TWO CATEGORIES**

	Category A	Category B
Sales	$300,000	$250,000
Cost of Goods Sold	$180,000	$100,000
Gross Margin $	$120,000	$150,000
Gross Margin %	40%	60%

should be considered as well. Even high-gross-margin producers fall under scrutiny if they have high selling expenses or poor space productivity.[4]

Gross margin return on investment (GMROI) integrates two performance measures, gross margin and turnover, to create a single measure of performance. The formula for GMROI (pronounced *jim-roy*) is:

$$GMROI = \frac{gross\ margin\ dollars}{net\ sales} \times \frac{net\ sales}{average\ inventory}$$

Note that *gross margin/net sales* is the component percentage formula for gross margin (without the x *100*), while *net sales/average inventory* is the formula for turnover.[5] The formula can be simplified by canceling *net sales*.

$$GMROI = \frac{gross\ margin\ dollars}{average\ inventory}$$

The derived formula measures the amount of gross margin dollars generated per average dollar of inventory invested.

The following example demonstrates the use of GMROI: As a result of a store renovation, a gourmet-cooking shop will gain enough additional selling space to expand a single category of merchandise. The choice has been narrowed to three categories: specialty foods, countertop appliances, and open-stock glassware. The shop's annual volume is $2 million. Each category represents about 20 percent of the shop's business. The remaining business is generated by categories, such as cookbooks, cookware, and table and kitchen linens. Countertop appliances yield a 20 percent gross margin ($80,000), specialty foods a 30 percent gross margin ($120,000), and glassware a 50 percent gross margin ($200,000). Specialty foods turn fastest at 10.0 times a year with an average inventory of $40,000 at cost. Countertop appliances turn 4.0 times a year with an average inventory of $100,000 at cost. Glassware is the slowest-turning category at 2.5 times a year with an average inventory of $160,000 at cost. The GMROI for each category is computed by dividing gross margin dollars by average inventory. The results appear in Table 10.5.

Note that specialty foods yield the highest GMROI (3.0), and that countertop appliances yield the lowest GMROI (0.8). If the decision to expand a category of merchandise were based solely on the gross margin, glassware would be the chosen category. However, when turnover is considered, specialty foods fall under a favorable light. Though specialty foods generate fewer gross-margin dollars than countertop appliances or glassware, inventory investments for specialty foods are considerably less than inventory investments for the other two categories. In other

Table 10.5   GMROI FOR THREE MERCHANDISE CATEGORIES

	Gross Margin	Average Inventory	GMROI
Specialty Foods	$120,000	$ 40,000	3.0
Countertop Appliances	$ 80,000	$100,000	0.8
Glassware	$200,000	$160,000	1.25

Table 10.6   GMROI FOR SELECT RETAIL STORES

Department Stores

Federated Department Stores	1.1
Kohl's	1.4
Nordstrom	1.4

Full-line Discounters

Ames	2.7
Kmart	2.1
Wal-Mart	2.0

Furniture Stores

Ethan Allen	1.3
Levitz	1.5

Home Accessories Stores

Bed Bath & Beyond	1.1
Pier 1 Imports	1.1

Off-pricers

Burlington Coat Factory	1.0
T.J. Maxx	1.1

Specialty Stores

American Eagle	2.7
Ann Taylor	1.9
The Gap	2.3
The Limited	1.9
Nine West Group	0.8

words, specialty foods yield more gross-margin dollars per dollar of inventory carried than countertop appliances or glassware.

In general, *high* turnover and *high* gross margins yield *high* GMROI, while *low* turnover and *low* gross margins yield *low* GMROI. In the example, specialty foods' high turnover compensates for its low gross margin. Conversely, a high gross margin can also compensate for low turnover. Because high turnover and high gross margin are very desirable merchandising objectives, maximizing GMROI is a major objective for most buyers. (See Table 10.6.)

SUMMARY POINTS

- Cash flow is the balance of cash coming into and going out of an organization.
- A balance sheet is a statement of a retailer's assets, liabilities, and owner's equity. Assets are *owned* by a retailer. Liabilities are *owed*. Net worth is the difference between the two.
- Financial ratios combine two balance sheet components to assess financial stability. The current ratio is a measure of an organization's short-term debt-paying ability used by credit-rating organizations to determine credit worthiness.
- An income statement reflects a retailer's profit performance for a specific period. Its components include net sales, cost of goods sold, gross margin, and profit.
- Gross margin return on investment (GMROI) combines gross margin and turnover in a single measure of performance, measuring the amount of gross margin generated per dollar of average inventory invested.

KEY TERMS AND CONCEPTS

assests	financial ratios	loss
balance sheet	gross margin	net income
cash discount	gross margin return on	net sales
cash flow	investment (GMROI)	owners' equity
component percentage	gross sales	profit
cost of goods sold	income statement	return to vendor
current ratio	indirect expense	time-series comparison
direct expense	liabilities	workroom cost
factor	liquidity	

FOR DISCUSSION

1. Search the Internet for recent annual reports from several publicly held retail organizations in various retailing formats. Using the consolidated

income statements, compute gross margin, expense, and profit percentages. Compare the stores within one retailing format to the stores within another. Explain the reasons for the variances that you find. Compare the percentages for stores within the same format. Explain these variances.

2. GMROI combines two measures of performance to create a single comprehensive measure. Are there other measures of performance that can be combined to create a single measure? Could three measures be combined? What two measures will *not* create a valid measure when combined?

3. The current ratio uses two balance sheet components to create a measure of a retailer's ability to pay its short-term debt. What other balance sheet components can be used to create other ratios? What would the ratios measure?

4. How might the GMROI of an apparel department compare to the GMROI of a furniture department in the same store? Explain.

5. How does the cash flow of a warehouse club compare to the cash flow of a department store? Why?

ENDNOTES

1. Ryan, T. (September14,1998). Non-apparel helps lift factors. *Women's Wear Daily*.p. 18.

2. Ibid.

3. Ryan, T. (February 22, 1999). Factors grid for uneasy '99. *Women's Wear Daily*. p.24

4. Staff. (August 1997) Manage for your most productive customer. *Speciality Stores/The Business Newsletter,*a supplement to *Women's Wear Daily*. pp. 5–6.

5. It should be noted that in Chapter 9 discussion of turnover advocated using average inventory at retail to determine turnover. GMROI is based on average inventory at cost. Note that there are many variations of the GMROI formula. Some formulas include "× 100" in the gross-margin portion of the formula, thus multiplying turnover by gross margin as a percentage of sales instead of as a ratio of gross margin to sales.

chapter eleven

INVENTORY VALUATION

Inventory values have considerable impact on a retail organization's financial statements. On a balance sheet, inventory is an asset that impacts a company's net worth. On an income statement, gross margin and net income are both derived from the cost of goods sold. The maintenance of inventory records and the assessment of inventory value are important merchandising functions and the subject of Chapter 11.

After you have read this chapter, you will be able to discuss:

Perpetual-inventory systems.

The fiscal impact of shortage.

Last in, first out (LIFO) and first in, first out (FIFO) as methods of inventory valuation.

INVENTORY VALUES

Retailers periodically determine the value of their inventories to prepare financial statements. Preparing an income statement requires
computing the cost of goods sold. Cost of goods sold is equal to the
value of the inventory on hand at the beginning of the fiscal period,
plus the value of the inventory purchased during the period, minus the
value of the inventory on hand at the end of the period:

> *inventory on hand at the beginning of the fiscal period*
>
> + *purchases*
>
> − *inventory on hand at the end of the fiscal period*
> _____
>
> *cost of goods sold*

Retailers also determine inventory values to prepare balance sheets.

The most reliable method of determining the value of an inventory
is to count it. A **physical inventory** involves counting and valuating an
inventory item by item. Retailers conduct physical inventories at least
once a year to determine the cost of goods sold and gross margin for
annual financial statements. Most retailers conduct physical inventories twice a year.

To prepare interim monthly and quarterly financial statements,
most retailers need to establish the value of their inventory more often
than annually or semi-annually. To avoid having to physically count an
inventory more than twice a year, retailers maintain a perpetual inventory. A **perpetual inventory system** is an inventory accounting system
whereby the value of an inventory is maintained on a continual basis
by adjusting a beginning physical inventory by purchases, sales, and
price changes. The resulting figure is called the **book inventory**. The
nomenclature dates back to the days when inventory records were
maintained in ledgers. Today, the "book" value of an inventory is likely
to be maintained electronically on a computer.

In theory, a book inventory should always equal a physical inventory. The balance between a book and physical inventory is maintained
by adjusting the book inventory by any changes in inventory status.
When new goods are received, the book is adjusted upward by the value
of the goods received. When goods are sold, the book is adjusted downward by the value of the goods sold. The book is also adjusted by price
changes, such as markdowns, and any other factors that affect the value
of a store's inventory, such as returns to vendors and customer returns.

OVERAGE AND SHORTAGE

Though in theory a book inventory should always equal a physical inventory, the two seldom match. The discrepancy between the two is called an **overage** when the book inventory is *less* than the physical inventory. The discrepancy is called a **shortage** when the book inventory is *greater* than the physical inventory. A shortage is sometimes called *shrinkage*. Most retailers track shortages and overages by department, store, and category of merchandise.

External theft by customers and internal theft by employees are frequent causes of shortage. Shoplifted items remain on the book, causing the book value to exceed the physical value when a physical inventory is taken. However, shoplifting accounts for only a portion of shortage and does not explain overage. Virtually all overages as well as many shortages are rooted in paper or clerical errors as the following scenarios demonstrate:

- A vase is received into a gift shop's inventory and booked at a $28 retail. The item is ticketed at $28, but the *8* looks like a *6*. When the vase is sold, the sale is transacted at $26. The book inventory is adjusted downward by $26, resulting in an overstatement of $2, which will emerge as a $2 shortage at the next physical inventory.
- At the end of the selling season, a buyer marks down the remaining pieces of a swimwear group from current clearance prices to 75 percent off the original retails. Fifty pieces of swimwear were each marked down $15 from $44.99 to $29.99. The information was accurately recorded on a change-of-price form; however, the person responsible for entering price-change transactions into the inventory-management system entered the digit *5* on the keyboard instead of the digits *5* and *0* when inputing the number of units marked down. The book inventory was adjusted downward by $75 (5 units at $15) instead of $750 (50 units at $15). This resulted in a $675 overstatement of the book inventory that will emerge as a $675 shortage at the next physical inventory.
- A furniture store used optical-scanning sheets in conducting a physical inventory. A sheet recording a $150 lamp and a $350 table was mislaid and never optically scanned as part of the store's inventory. This resulted in a $500 understatement of the physical inventory and a $500 shortage.

The examples are just three of the innumerable scenarios that cause paper shortage in retail stores. Though shortages resulted in the

Figure 11.1

Sensormatic designs systems to protect a store's inventory against theft. *Sensormatic Electronics Corp.*

examples, overages would have been the outcome if circumstances had been changed slightly: if the vase had been sold at a price *higher* than booked; if a figure *greater* than the number of pieces that were marked down were input; or if the lamp and table were recorded twice on inventory sheets.

Shortage and overage are expressed as a percentage of net sales of the period between the current and previous physical inventories. Assume that a department has a book inventory of $92,525, a semi-annual physical inventory of $87,375, and net sales of $500,000 for the six-month period. The difference between the book and physical inventories is $5150. Since the book inventory is greater than the physical inventory, the result is a shortage. The shortage percentage is calculated by dividing the shortage by the net sales for the period and multiplying by 100:

$$shortage \ \% = \frac{shortage \ \$}{net \ sales} \times 100$$

$$shortage \ \% = \frac{\$5150}{\$500,000} \times 100$$

$$shortage \ \% = 0.0115 \times 100$$

$$shortage \ \% = 1\%$$

Shortage varies by category of merchandise relative to factors such as the size and desirability of the merchandise, and the number of units handled in inventory transactions. Fashion jewelry displayed on top of a counter has a high shortage risk because of its pilferable size. Polo/Ralph Lauren menswear is vulnerable to shoplifting because of its desirability as a product and high street value. Transactional errors are more likely to occur in a greeting card store where *hundreds* of sales transactions are typical of each day, than in a furniture store where *a hundred* sales transactions would represent a very busy day. Shortage also varies by retailing format.

PHYSICAL INVENTORY

A physical inventory involves identifying each unit of merchandise by price and compiling this information by category and store location. Additional information such as vendor, age, or style number is sometimes required to update management reports that track inventories at these levels. A physical inventory is a tedious function, requiring weeks of preparation that involves tasks such as reticketing merchandise and grouping goods together by price to expedite counting. Rigid controls, such as numbered inventory sheets and detailed floor plans, are used to guarantee the accuracy of a physical inventory.

Stores are often closed during a physical inventory to avoid distraction by the public. Closing stores adds to the cost of taking a physical inventory because of the loss of business during the store's closing. To minimize the loss of business, physical inventories are scheduled on the least productive days of the week and at the least productive time of day. To minimize counting, physical inventories are conducted at times when inventories are at their lowest point. Physical inventory data is compiled either internally by the store's finance division or externally by a contracted service. The results are compared to book inventories to determine shortages and overages.

Some retailers inventory selected departments or stores more often than semi-annually. A retailer may inventory a high shortage department, such as fashion jewelry, quarterly, or highly pilferable items, such as camcorders, weekly. A change in department or category structure may necessitate an interim inventory. If Liz Claiborne handbags are transferred from the moderate-handbag category to the better-handbag category, a physical inventory of the line is taken so that the better category can be charged for the merchandise and the moderate category credited.

Inventory reconciliation involves scrutinizing the discrepancies between book and physical inventories in search of possible resolutions. Consider an $11,347 shortage in one category in one store and an overage of the same amount in the same category in another store. The discrepancy may be attributed to the incorrect processing of (or failure to process) paperwork representing the transfer of goods from the overage store to the shortage store. Thus the problem can be resolved by charging the overage store $11,347 and likewise crediting the shortage store. When inventory reconciliation is complete, the remaining discrepancies between book and physical inventories are wiped away by adjusting the book inventories to match the reconciled physical inventories. For one brief moment in time, the book and physical inventories match.

Technological advancements have enhanced the accuracy and speed of physical inventories. Many retailers scan bar codes into computers that compile inventory information down to the stock-keeping unit, or *sku*, level. Some inventory-management systems generate lists of booked items identified by sku. The lists can then be compared to the inventory on hand, enabling the retailer to identify shortages, not only by a dollar amount within a category or store but by individual item.

THE FISCAL IMPACT OF SHORTAGE

Inventory shortages and overages affect net profit because of their impact on the cost of goods sold. Shortages *increase* the cost of goods sold and *reduce* gross margin and net income. Overages *decrease* the cost of goods sold and *increase* gross margin and net income. The following scenario demonstrates this principle: Assume that a gift shop's end-of-the-year physical inventory of $50,000 is equal to the book inventory. The cost of goods sold for the period is computed as follows:

beginning-of-year physical inventory	$75,000
merchandise receipts during the year	+ $575,000
merchandise available for sale	$650,000
end-of-year physical inventory	− $ 50,000
cost of goods sold	$600,000

The shop's income statement for the period is as follows:

net sales	$1,000,000	
cost of goods sold	600,000	60%
gross margin	400,000	40%
expenses	350,000	35%
net income	$50,000	5%

Assume that the end-of-the-year physical inventory was $30,000, indicating a $20,000 shortage. The cost of goods sold would be computed as follows:

beginning-of-year physical inventory	$ 75,000
merchandise receipts during the year	+ $575,000
merchandise available for sale	$650,000
end-of-year physical inventory	− $ 30,000
cost of goods sold	$620,000

The income statement reflecting this change is as follows:

net sales	$1,000,000	
cost of goods sold	620,000	62%
gross margin	380,000	38%
expenses	350,000	35%
net income	$30,000	3%

Note that the cost of goods sold increased from 60 percent to 62 percent of net sales, and that net income decreased from 5 percent of net sales to 3 percent. A $20,000 overage would have the reverse effect on the cost of goods sold and net income. The cost of goods sold would drop to $580,000 and 58 percent of net sales, while net income would increase by $70,000 to 7 percent of net sales.

The example demonstrates the effect of shortage in eroding net income. Though overage produces "paper profit," overage is destined to return as a shortage in subsequent accounting periods. Assume that a $1000 gold chain is listed at $1500 by an inventory-taker creating a $500 inventory overage. Since book and physical inventory discrepancies are corrected by adjusting the book inventory to match the physical, the chain will be carried on the book at $1500 until the next physical inventory. If the chain is sold at the correct price of $1000, the book will be adjusted downward by that amount, leaving $500 of unaccounted-for inventory; in other words, a shortage of $500. If the chain is not sold during the subsequent inventory period, a $500 shortage will appear at the next physical inventory if the chain is correctly listed at $1000.

Buyers prefer inventory overages to inventory shortages because of their positive impact on gross margin and net income. However, neither overages nor shortages are desirable in that both reflect inaccurate record keeping and/or poor inventory management. Shortage receives more attention than overage in that shortage is the more likely occurrence. In essence, the types of error that create shortage are often the same mistakes that create overage.

Shortage Control

Though retailers employ exhaustive efforts to curb theft and the paper errors that cause overage and shortage, inequities between book and physical inventories are inevitable. When retailers open their doors to the public, they become vulnerable to shoplifting. By relying on people to order merchandise, receive and ticket goods, effect price changes, and ring sales on registers, retailers become susceptible to the consequences of human error.

Buyers are accountable for shortage even though many have little control over the stores or distribution centers where many shortages originate. Buyers control shortage by monitoring the position and value of inventory through reports of inventory position, price change, and receipts. They foster good inventory management through clear communication regarding ticketing of merchandise, inventory counts, price changes, and returns to vendors.

Point-of-Sale Systems

Computerized inventory management systems that track thousands of inventory items by store, merchandise category, style number, or brand across hundreds of locations, from the point at which they are ordered to the point at which they are sold, have facilitated the maintenance of perpetual inventory systems. A **point-of-sale**, or *POS*, **system** is a network of computerized cash registers linked to a central processing point, often referred to as a *back office*. A POS system processes sales transactions and related functions, such as credit verification and sales tax computation. As goods are sold, product information, such as style, size, and vendor, is transmitted to the back office by a multidigit number keyed into the register or an electronically scanned bar code. The information is stored in a database and used to adjust book inventories and to compile reports of inventory status that are used to plan assortments, make reorder and markdown decisions, and balance inventories among stores.

At store level, POS information is used to track salespeople's productivity and customer transactions by hour of the day and day of the week for use in scheduling the sales staff. Some POS systems have an e-mail feature for communicating announcements of promotions and price changes from a central office to stores. As noted in Chapter 5, POS information also has marketing applications. Customers identified by store-issued shoppers' cards or credit cards can be profiled by their purchases and targeted for catalog mailings or other niche marketing strategies. Individual stores can be profiled by their best sellers so that store-specific assortments can be developed. Athlete's Foot, a group of more than 400 athletic-footwear stores, can identify a city's favorite sport by the most popular styles of athletic shoes: Detroit prefers

Figure 11.2

A point-of-sale system is a network of computerized cash registers linked to a central-ized location that facilitates the management of retail inventories. *Retail Pro is a regis-tered trademark of Retail Technologies International.*

basketball, Boston running, and Atlanta tennis. Once appropriate for only large volume, high-transaction retailers, POS systems are now affordable to small retailers at an affordable cost.[1]

LIFO AND FIFO

Determining the cost of goods sold at the end of a fiscal period is com-plicated by variations in the cost of merchandise bought during the period. Goods acquired at the beginning of a fiscal period are likely to have been purchased at lower prices than goods acquired at the end of a fiscal period. Two assumptions can be made relative to the cost of goods acquired and sold during the fiscal period:

- The goods acquired at the end of a fiscal period are sold before the goods purchased earlier in the fiscal period. This describes an inven-tory concept called last in, first out or **LIFO**.

- The goods acquired at the beginning of a fiscal period are sold before goods purchased later in a fiscal period. This describes an inventory valuation concept called first in, first out or **FIFO**.

Consider the following: A pro shop sells knit shirts in basic colors. The inventory is carried from one season to the next, and periodically replenished with new receipts. The shop began a fiscal year with an opening inventory of 1000 shirts at a unit cost of $25. The shirts retailed at $50. When the shop reordered 2000 units of the same shirt later in the year, the unit cost had increased to $26. These shirts were retailed at $52. The remaining original inventory was marked up $2 per unit to $52 to maintain price consistency. Assume that 2800 shirts were sold throughout the fiscal year: 900 at a $50 retail, and 1900 at a $52 retail.

The following is a computation for the cost of goods available for sale during the year:

beginning inventory at cost (1000 units at $25)	$25,000
additional receipts (2000 units at $26)	$52,000
total cost of goods available for sale	$77,000

The following is a computation for annual sales:

900 units at $50	$ 45,000
1900 units at $52	$ 98,800
2800 units representing retail sales of	$143,800

LIFO assumes that the receipts that arrived later in the year were sold prior to the beginning inventory. The following is a computation of the cost of goods sold based on LIFO:

2000 shirts at $26 each	$52,000
800 shirts at $25 each	$20,000
2800 shirts at total cost of goods sold	$72,000

LIFO assumes an ending inventory value of $5000 (200 shirts at $25 each).

FIFO assumes that the beginning inventory was sold prior to the receipts that arrived later in the year. The following is a computation of cost of goods sold based on FIFO:

1000 shirts at $25 each	$25,000
1800 shirts at $26 each	$46,800
2800 shirts at total cost of goods sold	$71,800

FIFO assumes an ending inventory value of $5200 (200 shirts at $26 each).

The following is a computation of gross margin based on LIFO:

sales	$143,800
cost of goods sold	$ 72,000
gross margin	$ 71,800

The following is a computation of gross margin based on FIFO:

sales	$143,800
cost of goods sold	$ 71,800
gross margin	$ 72,000

Note that FIFO generates a gross margin that is $200 higher than LIFO. The higher FIFO gross margin will ultimately yield higher net income. FIFO will consistently generate higher gross margin and net income than LIFO in periods of inflation when the cost of inventory rises from the beginning of the period to the end. In cases of price decreases, FIFO will yield lower gross margin and net income. Table 11.1 summarizes the effect of LIFO and FIFO during periods of inflation.

The effects of LIFO and FIFO are proportionate to the amount of inflation that occurs during an accounting period. In a period of *very high* inflation, FIFO will yield a *very low* cost of goods sold and *very high* gross margin and net income. LIFO will yield a *very high* cost of goods sold and a *very low* gross margin and net income. LIFO and FIFO are not intended to reflect the way in which merchandise is actually sold. Stores typically rotate inventories to ensure that older stock sells before becoming shopworn.

LIFO is adopted as an accounting strategy to improve cash flow through the deferral of income tax. Since corporate taxes are paid on net income, a LIFO-induced net income reduction results in the deferral of tax payment, which results in improved cash flow. The domino effect continues: Recall that a negative cash flow is balanced by borrowing money and that the related interest expense reduces net income. By improving cash flow, LIFO results in less borrowing, lower interest payments, and improved earnings. The adoption of LIFO in a period of relatively low inflation will have little impact on net income, however LIFO's impact on net income during a period of high inflation is significant. This is why many retailers adopted LIFO during the early 1970s, a period of double-digit inflation.

Table 11.1 **COMPARISON OF LIFO AND FIFO**

LIFO	FIFO
yields higher cost of goods sold	yields lower cost of goods sold
yields lower ending inventory values	yields higher ending inventory values
yields lower gross margin	yields higher gross margin
yields lower net income	yields higher net income

LIFO is a theoretical accounting assumption contrary to the actual physical flow of merchandise. LIFO retailers often maintain two sets of inventory figures: one for external financial reports that reflects inventory value using LIFO, and another for nonfinancial internal management reports using FIFO that more accurately reflects the actual movement of goods. Federal tax law revisions have encouraged retailers to adopt LIFO. Previously, the Internal Revenue Service required conformity between the statement of inventory on the balance sheet, the computation of cost of goods sold, and the preparation of tax statements. However, income-tax laws have been relaxed to allow LIFO calculations for the preparation of tax statements, and FIFO inventory calculations for financial statements. Thus, a retailer can *minimize* the amount of taxes paid by using LIFO for tax purposes, and *maximize* the statement of earnings on financial statements by using FIFO. Today more than 50 percent of all major retailers use LIFO as an inventory method. Some elect to use a combination of both LIFO and FIFO. Kmart, for instance, uses LIFO for domestic goods and FIFO for imports.

To assist retailers in determining cost of goods sold, the U.S. Department of Labor issues a semi-annual (January and July) *Department Store Price Index*, or *BLS*, that reflects price inflation on various categories of merchandise. Many companies develop their own indices to measure inflation within the fiscal year, finding internally derived data more accurate.

SUMMARY POINTS

- A physical inventory is the actual value of inventory determined by a physical count. An inventory's book value is its recorded value. In theory, the book value of inventory should equal the physical value.

- Overage occurs when the book inventory is less than the physical inventory. Shortage occurs when the book inventory is greater than the physical inventory. A physical inventory is conducted periodically to determine overage or shortage.
- Shortages and overages affect net income because of their impact on cost of goods sold.
- A POS system is a network of computerized registers linked to a central processing point.
- LIFO and FIFO are concepts used to determine inventory values for accounting purposes.

KEY TERMS AND CONCEPTS

book inventory	inventory reconciliation	physical inventory
external theft	LIFO	point-of-sale system
FIFO	overage	shortage
internal reconciliation	perpetual inventory	
internal theft	system	

FOR DISCUSSION

1. Besides the errors described in the section Overage and Shortage, what other errors might occur in a retailer's day-to-day operation that would create inventory shortage or overage?
2. Why are some retailers reluctant to use technologically sophisticated shoplifting prevention devices, such as those offered by Sensormatic?
3. Outline the bookkeeping procedures that are necessary in stores without a POS system. Discuss the value of a POS system relative to accuracy and cost effectiveness.

PROBLEMS

1. Determine the overage/shortage in dollars and/or units if:
   - A $100 dress is stolen from a store.
   - A markdown from $20 to $16.99 is recorded as 10 units instead of 50.
   - A sale of $100 is incorrectly transacted as $120.
   - Goods received on the books at $2 per unit are incorrectly ticketed as $3 per unit; there are 100 units.

- The return of a $50 blouse by a customer is transacted as $60.
- The return of a $50 blouse by a customer is transacted as a sale of $80.
- A broken $60 vase is thrown into the trash. No transaction is recorded to remove the vase from the books.
- A markup is taken on 200 items from $80 to $90; the data-entry person enters 20 items.
- Goods transferred from store #1 to store #2 were miscounted; 50 items at $20 each were recorded as 60 items.
- A salesperson guessed at a selling price of an $80 item and transacted it at $85.

2. In the LIFO/FIFO example given in the section LIFO and FIFO, assume all of the shirts were sold at $50. What is the effect on cost of goods sold? Gross margin?

ENDNOTES

1. Staff. (November 1990). Athletes' Foot steps up inventory control. *Chain Store Age Executive*. pp. 128–130.

PRICING, PLANNING, AND PURCHASING RETAIL INVENTORIES

- Retail Pricing

- Planning Sales and Inventory

- Purchase Terms

chapter twelve

RETAIL PRICING

W hat constitutes the "right" retail price? The simple answer to this complex question is that a retail price should be high enough to cover an organization's profit objectives, but low enough to entice customers to buy. The retail prices at which goods are sold become the net-sales component of an income statement. Thus, the higher the retail price the higher the gross margin and net profit. However, when merchandise is priced too high it doesn't sell. Today's savvy consumers are always on the lookout for low prices, and will quickly switch their patronage to the retailer with the best values. Setting retail prices is an important merchandising function and the topic of Chapter 12.

After you have read this chapter, you will be able to discuss:

The intricacies of retail pricing.

The interrelationship of retail pricing components.

Promotional pricing.

The impact of pricing on an organization's sales and profitability.

MARKUP

A **retail price** has two components: cost and markup. **Cost** is the portion of a retail price that is paid to the supplier. The terms *wholesale cost* and *wholesale price* are used synonymously with cost to refer to a supplier's price. **Markup**, or *markon*, is the amount added to cost to establish a retail price. The relationship between cost, markup, and retail price is such that:

$$retail\ price = cost + markup$$

When a retailer adds a $2 markup to an item purchased at a wholesale price of $6, the retail price is $8.

$$retail\ price = cost + markup$$
$$\$8 = \$6 + \$2$$

As is true of any algebraic expression, when any two elements of a formula are known the third can be derived. When retail price and cost are known, markup can be determined:

$$retail\ price = cost + markup$$
$$retail\ price = cost + x$$

Then:

$$x = retail - cost$$
$$x = \$8 - \$6$$
$$markup = \$2$$

When retail price and markup are known, cost can be determined:

$$retail\ price = cost + markup$$
$$retail\ price = x + markup$$

Then:

$$x = retail\ price - markup$$
$$x = \$8 - \$2$$
$$cost = \$6$$

Markup can be expressed as a percentage of cost or retail. The formula for expressing markup as a percentage of retail is:

$$markup\ percent = \frac{markup}{retail\ price} \times 100$$

$$markup\ percent = \frac{\$2}{\$8} \times 100$$

$$markup\ percent = 25\%$$

The formula for expressing markup as a percentage of cost is:

$$markup\ percent = \frac{markup}{cost} \times 100$$

$$markup\ percent = \frac{\$2}{\$6} \times 100$$

$$markup\ percent = 33\%$$

Thus, a $2 markup on an item priced at $8 can be expressed either as 25 percent or 33 percent.

Consumers and nonretailers in general are likely to refer to markup as a percentage of cost. They often speak of doubling an item's cost to establish a retail price, called *keystoning*, as a 100 percent markup. An item with a $5 cost that is retailed at $10 has a 100 percent markup when markup is expressed as a percentage of cost:

$$markup\ percent = \frac{markup}{cost} \times 100$$

$$markup\ percent = \frac{\$5}{\$5} \times 100$$

$$markup\ percent = 100\%$$

However, retailers refer to markup as a percentage of retail. The item with a $5 cost and that is retailed at $10 has a 50 percent markup when markup is expressed as a percentage of retail:

$$markup\ percent = \frac{markup}{retail\ price} \times 100$$

$$markup\ percent = \frac{\$5}{\$10} \times 100$$

$$markup\ percent = 50\%$$

In retailing vernacular, markup as percentage of retail is always assumed unless otherwise specified. Subsequent references to markup in this textbook will assume markup as a percentage of retail.

When any two components of the markup percent formula are known, the third can be derived. When markup percent and retail price are known, markup can be determined:

$$markup\ percent = \frac{x}{retail\ price} \times 100$$

$$x = \frac{markup\ percent \times retail\ price}{100}$$

$$x = 50 \times \frac{10}{100}$$

$$x = 5$$

When markup percent and markup dollars are known, the formula can be solved for retail price:

$$markup\ percent = \frac{markup}{x} \times 100$$

$$x = \frac{markup}{markup\ percent} \times 100$$

$$x = \frac{5}{50} \times 100$$

$$x = 10$$

Types of Markup

Markups fall into several descriptive categories. The most common markup categories are:

Initial Markup An **initial markup** is the markup added to cost to establish the first price at which an item will be offered for sale, often called the **regular**, or *original*, **price**.

Additional Markup An **additional markup** is the markup added to raise an existing retail price. Additional markups are often used to equate the retail prices of goods purchased at different costs. The following scenario demonstrates this application:

A men's store sells packaged underwear at a 50 percent markup. Presently, packaged T-shirts purchased at a $5 cost are retailing at $10 per package. A new shipment of T-shirts has just arrived with an invoice price of $5.25 per package reflecting a manufacturer's price increase of 25 cents per unit. To maintain the store's standard 50 percent markup, the new shipment of T-shirts will be retailed at $10.50 per package. To equate the retail prices of the old goods with the retail prices of the new goods, the store adds a $0.50 per package *additional markup* to the T-shirts that were in stock prior to the manufacturer's price increase.

An additional markup is expressed as a percentage of the retail onto which the markup is added:

$$additional\ markup\ percent = \frac{markup}{present\ retail} \times 100$$

In the case of the T-shirts, the $0.50 added to the existing $10.00 retail, represents a 5 percent additional markup.

$$additional\ markup\ percent = \frac{\$0.50}{\$10.00} \times 100$$

$$additional\ markup\ percent = 5\%$$

Cumulative Markup A **cumulative markup** is the aggregate markup percentage on a group of goods with varying markups. The cumulative markup percent is equal to the total markup dollars on all of the goods divided by the sum of the retail prices of all of the goods, multiplied by 100.

$$cumulative\ markup\ percent = \frac{total\ markup}{total\ retail\ dollars} \times 100$$

Assume that a menswear buyer purchases 500 silk neckties from three vendors at three different wholesale prices:

100 ties at $9.25

200 ties at $9.50

200 ties at $9.75

To facilitate presentation and signing, the buyer retails all of the ties at a single unit price of $20. The cumulative markup for the ties is computed as follows:

$$cumulative\ markup\ percent = \frac{total\ markup}{total\ retail\ dollars} \times 100$$

$$cumulative\ markup\ percent = \frac{100(\$10.75) + 200(\$10.50) + 200(\$10.25)}{500(\$20)}$$

$$cumulative\ markup\ percent = \frac{\$5225}{\$10,000} \times 100$$

$$cumulative\ markup\ percent = 52.3\%$$

Note that a cumulative markup cannot be determined by averaging multiple markup percentages. This calculation is valid only if equal units are associated with each markup. Such an erroneous calculation would have resulted in a cumulative markup of 52.5 percent not 52.3 percent.[1]

MARKDOWNS

A **markdown**, or *price reduction*, is a downward adjustment in a retail price. A markdown is often expressed as a percentage of the retail price on which the markdown is taken. The markdown percent formula is:

$$markdown\ percent = \frac{markdown\ dollars}{current\ retail\ price} \times 100$$

The markdown percent of a $10 markdown taken on a $50 sweater is computed as follows:

$$markdown\ percent = \frac{\$10}{\$50} \times 100$$

$$markdown\ percent = 20\%$$

Sometimes an **additional markdown** is applied to an item already marked down. The additional markdown is often stated as a percentage of the already marked down price. The markdown percent of an additional markdown of $10 on the $50 sweater already marked down to $40 is calculated as follows:

$$markdown\ percent = \frac{\$10}{\$40} \times 100$$

$$markdown\ percent = 25\%$$

Sometimes the total of all the markdowns on an item is expressed as a markdown percentage of the original retail price. Thus the total markdown of $20 ($10 + $10) in the example may be advertised as a 40 percent markdown:

$$markdown\ percent = \frac{total\ markdown\ dollars}{original\ retail\ price} \times 100$$

$$markdown\ percent = \frac{\$20}{\$50} \times 100$$

$$markdown\ percent = 40\%$$

Markdown dollars can be computed when a markdown percent and original retail price are known:

$$markdown\ dollars = original\ retail\ price \times markdown\ percent$$

A 30 percent markdown on a dress currently retailing at $80 is computed as follows:

$$markdown\ dollars = \$80 \times 0.30$$

$$markdown\ dollars = \$24$$

A new marked down retail price is computed by subtracting the markdown dollars from the original retail.

$$marked\ down\ retail\ price = original\ retail\ price - markdown\ dollars$$

$$marked\ down\ retail\ price = \$80 - \$24$$

$$marked\ down\ retail\ price = \$56$$

Because markdown goods are sold at lower-than-intended retail prices, markdowns have a negative impact on a company's gross margin and net profit. Therefore retail organizations monitor markdowns very carefully with the hope of minimizing them by keeping them under control. Companies often track markdowns by department, category, and/or vendor. As an evaluative tool, the total markdown dollars taken for a period is compared to the net sales for the same period. For instance, if the total markdowns taken during August in a junior dress department are $50,000, and net sales for the month are $500,000 markdowns for August are computed as follows:

$$markdown\ rate\ for\ a\ period = \frac{total\ markdown\ dollars\ for\ the\ period}{net\ sales\ for\ the\ period} \times 100$$

$$markdown\ rate = \frac{\$50,000}{\$500,000} \times 100$$

$$markdown\ rate = 10\%$$

Because markdowns should be minimized, a markdown figure less than 10 percent is more desirable than a markdown figure greater than 10 percent. Markdown expectations vary by category of merchandise and time of year. For instance, markdowns on cold-weather outerwear are high toward the end of the winter when goods are being marked down to clear the way for spring merchandise.

Types of Markdowns

Markdowns fall into several descriptive categories. The most common markdown categories are:

Damage A **damage markdown** is a price reduction on goods damaged after delivery from a vendor.[2] Some retailers sell damaged goods to customers "as is." A $100 dress with broken buttons reduced to $75 is a good buy for a customer willing to spend a few dollars and a little time sewing on a new set of buttons. Selling the dress at a markdown price may be also be advantageous to the retailer in that $25 markdown may be less costly in terms of time and effort than sending the garment out for repair. Damaged merchandise that is not salable, such as broken glassware, must be "marked out of stock" by a markdown to zero retail. When damaged goods are disposed of without being marked out of stock, their retail value remains on the book resulting in a shortage at the next physical inventory.

Employee Discount An **employee discount** is a price reduction on employee purchases, an employment benefit characteristic of the retail industry. Employee discounts usually range between 5 and 50 percent. The amount varies according to the markup on the goods being discounted which is why department stores typically offer higher employee discounts than discounters, and why stores are more generous with discounts on high-markup goods, such as apparel, than low-markup goods such as sale merchandise or consumer electronics.[3] Hefty employee discounts are typical of apparel retailers who hope to induce their employees to buy their merchandise and wear it to work as a way of promoting it.

Promotional A **promotional markdown** is a price reduction on merchandise featured in a promotional event, commonly called a *sale*. Promotional markdowns are called **temporary markdowns** since the promotional goods are marked back up to regular price after the promotional event has ended. The duration of a promotion can range from a few hours, such as a *Midnight Madness Sale*, to several weeks, such as a semi-annual *White Sale*. To ensure the credibility of an event, it is important that promoted merchandise is not offered at promotional prices during nonpromotional periods.

Clearance A **clearance markdown** is a price reduction that induces the sale of residual or slow-selling merchandise. Clearance markdowns are called **permanent markdowns** in that clearance goods do

Figure 12.1

A promotional markdown is a temporary price reduction on merchandise featured in a promotional event. *Macy's East.*

Table 12.1 **REPORT OF TEMPORARY AND PERMANENT MARKDOWNS**

DEPT 149	CLASS	WTD POS MKDNS	WTD PERM/TEMP	WTD TOTALS	MTD POS MKDNS	MTD PERM/TEMP	MTD TOTALS
	1	1177.2	.0	1177.2	3577.5	224.3	3801.8
	2	259.4	.0	259.4	1241.3	395.2	1636.5
	3	107.1	.0	107.1	416.9	286.7	703.6
	4	351.7	.0	351.7	968.5	.0	968.5
	5	619.3	60.0	679.3	2051.4	464.4	2515.8
	6	306.9	.0	306.9	720.2	36.0	756.2
	7	824.8	.0	824.8	2001.1	415.1	2416.1
	8	.0	.0	.0	.0	30.0	30.0
	ALL	3646.5	60.0	3706.5	10,976.8	1851.6	12,828.4

not return to a regular price, or any higher price, at a later date. Prices on clearance goods are reduced by subsequent additional markdowns until all of the merchandise has sold. A buyer of cold-weather accessories may take a 20 percent clearance markdown on gloves at the end of December. If the gloves do not sell out within a few weeks, the buyer will likely take additional markdowns of 35 percent, 50 percent, and eventually 75 percent off original prices until all of the gloves are sold.

CLEARANCE MERCHANDISE

Clearance markdowns are taken on various types of residual or "leftover" merchandise including:

Discontinued Goods Discontinued goods are goods that will not be part of future assortments. Discontinued goods can include a category, a product line, or a single style, pattern, or color. A department store may discontinue a slow-selling cosmetics line. A women's specialty store may discontinue dresses to devote more space to sportswear. A manufacturer may discontinue unpopular colors in an assortment of bath towels which, in turn, are discontinued by the retailers that carry them.

Seasonal Merchandise **Seasonal merchandise** is salable for a limited time period often defined by a season or holiday. Seasonal goods are marked down for clearance as their period of salability comes to a close. Velour shirts are marked down as the season for wearing warm clothing passes and customers begin to seek apparel for warmer weather. Examples of seasonal merchandise include swimwear, gloves, and Valentine's Day underwear.

Broken Assortments **Broken assortments** are residual items within a group or set of related or coordinated merchandise. Items within sets

Figure 12.2

Clearance markdowns on end-of-season goods are permanent markdowns.

Table 12.2   **MARKDOWN REPORT FOR A SLEEPWEAR DEPARTMENT**

RUN DATE: 05/22/01
WEEK ENDING: 05/21/01
PAGE 89
INTIMATE APPAREL
CCN: 540 SLEEPWEAR

VENDOR NAME	SALES				PUR MU%	STOCK		MARKDOWNS	
	TY	LY	%CHG	%TOTL	STD	$	%TOTL	$	%SLS
PRIVATE LABEL	577.3	285.4	102.3	30.7	51.8	474.1	26.8	75.2	13.0
MISS ELAINE	271.8	133.6	103.5	14.5	53.2	233.3	13.2	54.9	20.2
CAROLE HOCHMAN	116.4	37.3	212.2	6.2	54.4	69.2	3.9	15.7	13.5
DAMEA	129.5	54.9	136.0	6.9	57.3	101.0	5.7	15.8	12.2
KOMAR	145.8	81.6	78.7	7.8	52.3	119.8	6.8	24.5	16.8
VAL MODE	155.8	138.4	12.5	8.3	53.9	223.8	12.6	48.1	30.9
AUGUST SILK	85.8	50.8	69.1	4.6	53.8	100.9	5.7	19.4	22.6
LANZ	74.5	75.3	−1.1	4.0	51.9	97.4	5.5	31.7	42.6
EILEEN WEST	78.6	60.0	31.0	4.2	53.8	74.3	4.2	23.2	29.5
NICOLE	26.3	47.3	−44.4	1.4	54.4	67.4	3.8	5.8	22.2
LORRAINE	19.9	15.2	30.9	1.1	56.1	72.2	4.1	6.1	30.4
NATORI	32.0	35.1	−8.9	1.7	53.9	40.6	2.3	10.9	34.0
CINEMA	48.0	66.5	−27.9	2.6	48.2	24.6	1.4	7.0	14.6
DONNKENNY	32.1	.0	.0	1.7	53.0	25.4	1.4	18.4	57.4
VANITY FAIR	15.9	62.3	−74.4	.9	41.2	8.0	.5	5.5	34.4
SARA BETH	12.3	35.9	−65.8	.7	60.0	15.9	.9	5.9	48.0
RELIABLE MILWAUKEE	1.4	.5	193.9	.1	−1.4	−.1	.1	3.9	
KATHERINE	16.4	9.0	81.4	.9	48.9	16.3	.9	9.8	59.8
BODY DRAMA	10.8	58.6	−81.5	.6		6.6	.4	7.7	71.5
JENNIFER SMITH	1.2	53.5	−97.8	.1		.8	.1	.7	56.6
HOST	7.2	.0	.0	.4		3.1	.2	6.7	92.8
CAL DYNASTY	2.2	60.5	−96.3	.1		2.9	.2	1.4	62.8
EVE STILLMAN	3.3	5.0	−33.5	.2		2.6	.2	1.6	47.7
DIOR	6.8	12.5	−45.6	.4	103.2	7.2	.4	3.7	54.4
ALL BREED & HARTLAN	1.4	15.7	−90.8	.1		2.4	.1	.5	35.9
GILLIGAN	.0	116.8	.0	.0		1.4	.1	.5	.0
UNIDENTIFIED OTHER	.0	3.3	.0	.0		−22.1	−1.3	.4	.0
P.M. STORIES	.0	1.7	.0	.0		.0	.0	.1	.0
EVA DALE	1.9	.0	.0	.1	79.3	3.6	.2	1.9	100.5
N A P	1.9	24.8	−92.4	.1	56.7	.6	.0	2.1	109.8
CHARACTER	.0	3.6	.0	.0		.0	.0	.0	.0
TOSCA	.0	21.5	.0	.0		.2	.0	.1	.0
GROUND CONTROL	.0	3.9	.0	.0		.0	.0	.0	.0
ROBERT KLIEN	.0	4.2	.0	.0		.0	.0	.0	.0
INTIMATES	.0	7.2	.0	.0		.0	.0	.0	.0
ME AND MY PALS	.0	2.2	.0	.0		.0	.0	.0	.0
VALERIE JONES	.0	16.5	.0	.0		.0	.0	.1	.0
MISS DIOR	.0	13.4	.0	.0		.1	.0	.0	.0
OTHERS	2.3	1.3	73.4	.1		−1.1	−.1	.8	36.6
TOTAL	1878.7	1615.5	16.3	100.0	53.1	1772.4	100.0	406.4	21.6

or groups become candidates for clearance markdowns when assortments become "piecy." The remaining pieces of a Liz Claiborne jacket/blouse/skirt coordinate group are marked down when so few pieces of the group remain that it is no longer possible to coordinate an ensemble in any one size or color.

Slow Sellers

Clearance markdowns are also taken on goods that sell at slower than anticipated rates of sale. There are innumerable factors that can cause slow selling. Some of the more common problems relate to:

Weather Unseasonable weather that is atypical of a season affects the sale of seasonal goods such as boots, wool sweaters, patio furniture, and shorts. Buyers are often quick to blame poor sales on the weather, since weather is a variable beyond their control.

Poor Assortment Most buyers are diligent in their efforts to choose assortments that will appeal to their target customers. However, the process is far from foolproof, and even the most carefully chosen assortments of items, brands, price-points, sizes, styles, fabrics, and colors become slow sellers when customers determine that the hemlines are too short, the colors are garish, or the prices are too high.

Poor Presentation A sportswear group that is placed on a main aisle in one store may sell out in a week, while the same group remotely placed in the rear of a selling area in another store may not sell a single piece in two weeks. Unfortunately, not all of the merchandise in a store can be presented in prime locations. However, the way in which goods are fixtured, faced, folded, hung, sized, or colorized can greatly enhance their rate of sale.

Late Delivery Seasonal and trend-sensitive goods that arrive after their selling peak become slow sellers. Velvet special-occasion dresses are salable for New Year's Eve celebrations. They are useless if they arrive on December 28. To avoid this dilemma, purchase orders include a *do not ship later than* date as a caution to vendors not to ship too late in the selling season.

Clearance markdowns induce the sale of even the slowest selling merchandise. The dress that a customer perceived as a "dog" at $200 becomes ever so attractive at $149.99. Though clearance markdowns are heaviest at the ends of selling seasons, most buyers regularly review inventories to edit slow sellers and broken assortments which is why clearance racks or clearance sections have become ubiquitous in many retail stores. Clearance prices traditionally have a "9 ending," such as $29.99, indicated in red. It is wise to show the original price of clearance markdowns so that customers can appreciate the value of the markdown.

In spite of their negative impact on gross margin, clearance markdowns are an important element in a buyer's effort to maintain clean assortments and to free up inventory dollars and fixtures for new goods. Clearance markdowns have a positive impact on turnover in that they decrease the value of inventory and induce sales. A buyer can be subject to as much criticism for taking too few clearance markdowns as for taking too many.

Figure 12.3

Clearance markdowns induce the sale of even the slowest-selling merchandise. *CATHY* © *Cathy Guisewhite. Reprinted with permission of UNIVERSAL PRESS SYNDICATE. All rights reserved.*

MAINTAINED MARKUP

Maintained markup is the difference between the cost of merchandise and the actual retail selling price. It is the net markup that remains after markdowns and additional markups have been subtracted or added to an initial markup. The formula for maintained markup is:

maintained markup = initial markup + additional markups − markdowns

Since reductions are more likely to exceed additional markups, the formula is often stated:

maintained markup = initial markup − net markdowns

Gross margin can be derived from maintained markup by subtracting transportation and workroom costs and adding cash discounts:

gross margin = maintained markup − transportation costs − workroom costs + cash discounts

Therefore maintained markup is equal to gross margin before transportation and workroom costs and cash discounts are considered:

maintained markup = gross margin + transportation costs + workroom costs − cash discounts

Maintained markup and initial markup are equal when goods are sold at original price. Maintained markup and gross margin are equal when:

- There are no transportation costs, workroom costs, or discounts
- The net value of all three is zero

Maintained markup is an indicator of how well merchandise sustains markup.

The following scenario demonstrates the use of maintained markup as an evaluative tool:

A sportswear buyer purchased cotton sweaters from two resources. Group A was purchased at $20 per unit and initially retailed at $40. Of the 2000 sweaters in this group, 1500 sold at regular price. At the end of the season, the remaining 500 sweaters were marked down; 300 sold at a first markdown price of $30; 150 sold at a further marked down price of $20; and the remaining 50 sold at a final markdown price of $10. Group B was purchased at a $17 per unit and initially retailed at $40 also. Of the

3000 sweaters in this group, 1200 sold at regular price. At the end of the season, the remaining 1800 sweaters were marked down; 800 sold at a first markdown price of $30; 500 at a further marked down price of $20; and the remaining 500 sold at a final markdown price of $10.

After all of the sweaters sold out the buyer computed the maintained markup *dollars* for each group of sweaters as reflected in Table 12.3. Table 12.4 reflects the computation of the maintained markup *percentage* for each group of sweaters. Note the following relative to the data in Tables 12.3 and 12.4:

- The initial markup of Group A was 50 percent and that the initial markup of Group B was 57.5 percent. However, subsequent markdowns eroded the initial markup of each group resulting in an average maintained markup of 44.8 percent for Group A and 41.4 percent for Group B.
- Though the initial markup of Group A was *lower* than the initial markup of Group B, the maintained markup of Group A was *higher* than the maintained markup of Group B.

Table 12.3 **MAINTAINED MARKUP DOLLARS FOR TWO GROUPS OF SWEATERS**

	Group A	**Cost = $20/unit**			**Group B**	**Cost = $17/unit**		
Price	**# Sold**	**Sales $**	**MU$/Unit**	**Total MU$**	**# Sold**	**Sales $**	**MU$/Unit**	**Total MU$**
$40	1500	$60,000	$ 20	$30,000	1200	$48,000	$23	$27,600
$30	300	$ 9,000	$ 10	$ 3,000	800	$24,000	$13	$10,400
$20	150	$ 3,000	0	0	500	$10,000	$ 3	$ 1,500
$10	50	$ 500	−$ 10	−$ 500	500	$ 5,000	−$ 7	−$ 3,500
TOTAL	2000	$72,500	$16.25	$32,500	3000	$87,000	$12	$36,000

Table 12.4 **MAINTAINED MARKUP PERCENTAGES**
          FOR TWO GROUPS OF SWEATERS

	Group A	**Group B**
Total initial markup dollars	$40,000	$ 69,000
Total original retail dollars	$80,000	$120,000
Initial markup percent	50%	57.5%
Total maintained markup dollars	$32,500	$ 36,000
Total actual retail dollars	$72,500	$ 87,000
Maintained markup percent	44.8%	41.4%

- Though 75 percent of Group A (1500 of 2000 units) sold at the original $40 retail, only 40 percent of Group B (1200 of 3000 units) sold at the original price of $40.
- Only 2.5 percent of Group A sold at a below-cost retail (50 of 2000 units), whereas more than 16 percent of Group B (500 of 3000 units) were sold below cost.

The buyer priced the Group-B sweaters at a higher initial markup than the Group-A sweaters hoping to yield a higher maintained markup. However, it was the Group-A sweaters that sustained higher markup over time. Seemingly customers resisted the $40 original price on the Group-B sweaters. However, they perceived the same price for the Group-A sweaters as a good value. Perhaps Group B would have sold better at an original price based on a more modest initial markup.

Tactical Price Changes

A **tactical price change** is a strategic markup or markdown that falls within a retail price zone defined at one end by a retail price with a standard markup, and at the other end a retail price with an inflated markup. A markup within the zone is called a **markdown cancellation**. A markdown within the zone is called a **markup cancellation**.

The concept of tactical price changes is best explained by an example: A sales representative has offered a retail buyer a closeout price of $15 per pair on a popular pant style. The original wholesale price was $20. The buyer identifies this as a great promotional opportunity in that, at $15 a pair, the pants can be retailed at $29.99 and still yield the department's standard initial markup of 50 percent. The buyer wrote an order for the pants with instructions to the store's distribution center to book and ticket the goods at a $40 retail. The buyer plans to offer the pants at the $40 retail for a few weeks before reducing them to $29.99. By so doing, he hopes to validate the comparative price and to enhance customer perception of the promotional price as a real bargain.

The tactical retail price zone in this scenario is $29.99 at the low end, a point of normal markup, and $40 at the high end, an inflated retail price. Price changes within this zone are called markup cancellations and markdown cancellations. A price reduction from $40 to $29.99 is a markup cancellation, not a markdown, because the new price of $29.99 falls within the tactical price zone. A price increase from $29.99 to $40 is a markdown cancellation, not a markup. Price changes to points lower than $29.99, are classified as markdowns.

Markup cancellations are unlike typical markdowns in that markdowns taken within the tactical zone are a reflection of a buyer's pricing strategy and not a result of poorly chosen assortments. Tracking markup cancellations and markdowns separately ensures that a buyer's ability to control markdowns isn't tainted by strategic planning.

Not all retailers make a distinction between markdowns and markup cancellations and markup and markdown cancellations, feeling that the effort to track them outweighs its worth. Also, there is difficulty in defining "normal" and "inflated" markup in many retail organizations.

Managing Markdowns

Like sales and inventory, markdowns are planned and tracked over time by department and/or category of merchandise and markdown type. Last year's markdowns for the same time-period are used to project this year's markdowns since, like sales, markdowns fall into cyclical patterns. Markdown projections are also validated against industry standards for comparable types of stores and categories of merchandise. Markdowns are monitored throughout the season to ensure that actual markdowns do not exceed projections. Excessive markdowns may yield high sales due to the attractive prices of the reduced merchandise, however, gross margin and net income will be negatively affected.

ESTABLISIHNG AN INITIAL MARKUP

Buyers must price goods at an initial markup that will ensure final selling prices consistent with the organization's profit objectives. In essence, an initial markup must be high enough to cover:

- Transportation and workroom costs (less cash discounts)
- Expenses and net profit
- Markdowns

The formula for establishing an initial markup percentage reflects the notion that a markup percentage is equal to markup divided by retail. For the case in point, initial markup is the numerator. Its computation reflects the fact that an initial markup must cover the aforementioned:

*transportation + workroom costs − cash discounts + expenses
+ net profit + markdowns*

Company Profile 12.1

Managing Markdowns at Target

More and more retailers are turning to decision-support systems to control markdowns. Target worked with the Retail Management Institution of Santa Clara, California, to develop a system that controls the timing and amount of markdowns. Before the system was implemented, buyers set clearance dates and prices according to established precedents without reference to how well the goods were selling just prior to the markdown. Though buyers still determine when goods should be marked down, the new system uses recent sales histories to determine how much of a markdown to take.

For instance, the system tracks sweater sales from the time they arrive on the floor in October to the time that they are ready to be cleared in late December. When the clearance date hits, the system determines how much the prices should be cut based on the past month's sales. If the sweaters don't sell well on the first round of markdowns, the system generates a second round.

Other parameters can be introduced into the system. Although swimsuits are first marked down on July 4, the decision-support system will stipulate a low markdown in California where the selling season for swimwear is long, and a high mark down rate in Minnesota where the selling season for swimwear is short.[1]

Source:
1 Thilmany, J. (January 27, 1999). Systemizing the markdowns. Women's Wear Daily. p. 16

The numerator can be simplified by recalling from Chapter 10 that:

$$gross\ margin = expenses + net\ profit$$

Therefore, gross margin can be substituted for expenses and profit in the numerator:

$$gross\ margin + transportation + workroom\ costs$$
$$-\ cash\ discounts + markdowns$$

Recall also that:

$$maintained\ markup = gross\ margin + transportation$$
$$+\ workroom\ costs - cash\ discounts.$$

Therefore the numerator can be further simplified by substituting maintained markup for transportation costs, workroom costs, cash discounts, and gross margin.

$$maintained\ markup + markdowns$$

The denominator of the formula reflects the fact that initial retail prices will be eroded by markdowns before becoming net sales:

$$net\ sales\ +\ markdowns$$

Thus the formula for computing an initial markup percent is:

$$initial\ markup\ \% = \frac{maintained\ markup\ +\ markdowns}{net\ sales\ +\ markdowns} \times 100$$

Factors That Drive Initial Markup

In general, high figures in the numerator of the initial-markup formula will yield a high initial markup percentage, while low figures will yield a low percentage. The following factors have an impact on how high or low an initial markup will be:

- *Markdowns.* An apparel department requires a higher initial markup to achieve the same maintained markup as the cosmetics department because of the apparel department's high clearance-markdown rate. Reductions are virtually nonexistent in the cosmetics department where damages and residual merchandise, such as unsold holiday gift sets, are returned to vendors for credit.
- *Transportation costs.* Bulky items, such as furniture, necessitate a high initial markup to cover high transportation costs.
- *Workroom costs.* A bridal shop that offers free alterations requires a higher initial markup to achieve the same maintained markup as a dress shop. The workroom costs for turning a hem on very full, multitiered wedding dresses are considerably greater than the workroom costs for turning hems on straight skirts.
- *Direct expenses.* Direct expenses can include commissions or specialized supplies, such as velvet jewelry boxes. Wal-Mart abandoned its small pet business because of high direct expenses. Though birds, hamsters, and gerbils had the same initial markup as tropical fish, the cost of feeding and caring for a small animal completely erodes its markup if the animal isn't sold within two weeks.[4]

Calculating an Initial Markup Percentage

The following scenario demonstrates the calculation of an initial markup percentage:

Table 12.5 **MARKDOWN PERCENTAGES FOR MEN'S SPECIALTY STORES BY CATEGORY OF MERCHANDISE**

CATEGORY	% MARKDOWN
Men's Clothing	
Men's Suits	18.9%
Men's Coats	24.3
Sport Coats	22.5
Dress Slacks	13.3
Total Men's Clothing	19.2
Men's Sportswear	
Sport Shirts	20.9
Sweaters	24.2
Activewear	25.2
Casual Slacks	19.5
Jeans	8.4
Jackets & Heavy Outerwear	25.6
Coordinated Leisurewear	20.4
Total Men's Sportswear	21.7
Men's Furnishings	
Dress Shirts	12.8
Neckwear	11.9
Hosiery	6.0
Men's Belts	5.4
Men's Accessories	8.7
Underwear	5.3
Sleepwear	8.7
Men's Headwear	15.1
Total Men's Furnishings	10.8

A shoe buyer's maintained markup objective for a season is 40 percent. The buyer anticipates seasonal markdowns of 20 percent. An initial markup for the season is calculated as follows:

$$\textit{initial markup \%} = \frac{\textit{maintained markup \%} + \textit{markdown \%}}{\textit{net sales} + \textit{markdown \%}} \times 100$$

$$\textit{initial markup \%} = \frac{40\% + 20\%}{100\% + 20\%} \times 100$$

$$\textit{initial markup \%} = \frac{0.40 + 0.20}{1.00 + 0.20} \times 100$$

$$\textit{initial markup \%} = \frac{0.6}{1.2} \times 100$$

$$\textit{initial markup \%} = 50\%$$

Thus, a buyer who anticipates a 20 percent markdown rate for the season must price goods at an initial markup of 50 percent to maintain a 40 percent markup. Though the above formula is preferable because of its simplicity, any of the formulas from which it was derived may be used to calculate an initial markup. Either dollars or percentages can be used in the computation. Note that net sales is always 100 percent when using percentages in the computation.

Computing an Initial Retail Price

Converting an initial-markup percentage to a retail price requires the use of a simple formula based on a **cost complement**, the difference between the initial-markup percentage and 100 percent, and the wholesale cost of the item being priced:

$$Retail\ price = \frac{cost}{100\% - initial\ markup\ \%}$$

Assume that a buyer sees an interesting item at a trade show priced at $12.50. The buyer needs to retail goods at a 55 percent initial markup to achieve a desired maintained markup for the department. The buyer calculates the retail price of the $12.50 item at a 55 percent markup as follows:

$$Retail\ price = \frac{cost}{100\% - initial\ markup\ \%}$$

$$Retail\ price = \frac{\$12.50}{1.0 - 0.55}$$

$$Retail\ price = \frac{\$12.50}{\$0.45}$$

$$Retail\ price = \$27.78$$

The retail price of a $12.50 item at a 55 percent markup is $27.78. For the sake of simplicity and a little extra markup, odd-ending prices are typically rounded up to the nearest 0-ending price ($27.80) or whole dollar price ($28.00).

PROMOTIONAL PRICING

A promotional price is a discounted price that is less than a conventional or regular price. Once the hallmark of discounters, promotional pricing has become an important element in the merchandising strategies of many department and specialty stores. Promotional pricing is often linked to one of the advertised events discussed in Chapter 5.

Retailers conduct price promotions to:

- Generate customer traffic
- Stimulate sales during a slow-selling period
- Induce the sale of related nonpromotional merchandise
- Engage in competitive pricing with other retailers
- Establish an image as a value-oriented retailer

Price changes require book inventory adjustments to maintain the balance between book and physical inventory values. Because promotional prices are temporary, they require two adjustments: markdowns at the beginning of a promotion, and markups at the end of a promotion. Computerized **price lookup** (PLU) technology has facilitated this process. PLU involves maintaining a system file of every stock-keeping unit (sku) in inventory and a corresponding retail price. When the sku is identified at point-of-sale by a number or bar code, the system "looks up" the price and transmits it to a cash register display or monitor while processing the transaction at the looked-up price. The prices in the file can be changed to promotional prices for promotional events eliminating the need for a physical count of inventory before or after the promotion. Preparing for a promotional event merely involves identifying promoted merchandise with the appropriate signage indicating that the reduction will be taken at the register. This permits retailers to increase the frequency of promotions by reducing the stock-handling costs associated with event preparation and recovery. A PLU system also allows more rigid price control by preventing salespeople from discounting nonpromotional items.[5, 6]

Everyday Low Pricing

Though promotional events produce immediate sales results, their long-term effect is questionable. Frequent promotions encourage customers to wait for sales and to buy only at promotional prices. This can be devastating to gross margin and net income since promotional goods carry lower markup. An intense promotional schedule may also cause customers to question the "real" price of goods, assuming that retailers cover promotional markdowns with inflated markups. One study showed that three-quarters of consumers believed that department stores intentionally inflated prices so that their promotional markdowns appear to be more significant.[7]

Source:

1 Haran, L. (June 24, 1996). *Dollar General: Angela Martin.* Advertising Age. p. S26.

Company Profile 12.2

Dollar General and EDLP

"Easy-to-shop neighborhood stores" is the how people often characterize Dollar General stores. Consistent with this image of convenience, the extreme-value retailer has simplified its marketing strategy with an even-dollar pricing structure that doesn't fluctuate from week to week.

The chain relies on just two direct-mail pieces a year to convey its simple-pricing message. Word-of-mouth has become Dollar General's most effective advertising. The "what-you-see-is-what-you-get" pricing strategy is what attracts Dollar General's loyal customer base of low- to middle-income households. This marks a change from Dollar General's previous marketing strategy that included extensive radio advertising.

However, the company began to realize that its message was being confused with those of other extreme-value stores, and that many of its customers didn't drive cars and were not radio listeners. The shift in strategy proved to be a good move for Dollar General. With sales increases that have exceeded 20 percent in recent years, the company has shown that you don't need glitzy advertising to satisfy customers—just good consistent value.[1]

Everyday low pricing (EDLP) is a value-oriented pricing strategy involving continuous promotional pricing without the support of advertised events. Everyday low prices are either a retailer's lowest promotional price, or a price between the retailer's highest regular price and lowest promotional price. EDLP facilitates inventory management since product demand is more stable when not driven by sporadic sales. The lower gross margins associated with EDLP strategy are often offset by reduced advertising expenses, as well as reduced labor expenses since fewer floor moves are required for sale setup and recovery. EDLP is a shopping advantage for customers too busy to chase promotions.

EDLP is fundamental to the warehouse club concept and to the success of discounters such as Wal-Mart and Toys "R" Us, both of which have employed an EDLP strategy since their inception.[8] However, EDLP has not been successful for every retailer.[9] Sears once closed its stores for two days to retag every piece of merchandise with permanently reduced prices. A year later, Sears abandoned EDLP because sales increases were not significant enough to offset the decreases in gross margin.[10] Feeling that their customers enjoy the excitement of promotional events, Target combines its EDLP program with advertised promotions.[11]

DECEPTIVE PRICING

The Federal Trade Commission (FTC) is a regulatory agency that prevents unfair competition in the marketplace by protecting consumers from abuses such as constraint of trade and deceptive advertising. The FTC issues guidelines that prescribe standards of conduct for various industry segments, including retailers. In addition to FTC guidelines, each state has specific statutes that govern retail trade practices. Because laws vary by state, retailers that conduct business in several states often ensure compliance to the statutes in all states by conforming to the guidelines of the most stringent state. To avoid embarrassment and/or penalty, retailers should be familiar with topics governed by various forms of protective legislation.

Regular-Price Comparisons A stated reduction from an original or regular price is a common form of price promotion. However, the strategy is legitimate only if the promoted items are offered at regular price for a sufficient period of time. That "sufficient period of time" varies by state.[12] One state attorney general's office offers the following guidelines for determining the legitimacy of a regular-price comparison:

- That at least 25 percent of the goods were sold at the regular price during the previous six months, or
- That the goods were offered at the regular price for at least 70 percent of the time during the previous six months. This allows approximately 55 promotional days in a six-month period, or 10 promotional days a month.

A nonpromotional price should be effected within a reasonable amount of time after a promotion has ended, and it should be maintained for a sufficient amount of time thereafter. One state attorney general's office recommends effecting the regular price within 60 days after the end of a promotion and maintaining the regular price for a minimum of 90 days.

If criteria such as these are not met, it may be determined that a promotional price is, in fact, the regular price, and that promoting the goods as a "sale" is a deceptive practice. A Colorado appeals court upheld the state attorney general's allegations that advertising by May Department Stores was deceptive and that the company had no intention of selling some of its advertised goods at regular price. Levitz Furniture Corporation once paid $1 million to settle claims in eight states when it tricked customers into thinking that they were saving on fictitious "regular" prices at which the goods were never sold.[13]

In general, regular-price comparisons should be genuine and not based on exaggerated prices. A retailer should not cushion high promotional markdowns with an excessively high initial markup that exceeds the initial markup customarily taken on the item or merchandise category.

Comparisons to Competitors' Prices Price comparisons to competitors' offerings must be for identical merchandise. Comparing one style or grade of merchandise to another style or grade is deceptive.

Lowest Price A retailer must validate a *lowest price* claim with proof of the customary prices of competitors, a difficult substantiation when competitors have frequent price promotions.[14] Wal-Mart's claim of "Always low prices" avoids the use of the superlative "lowest" for this reason.

Free Merchandise Retailers sometimes offer customers free merchandise, frequently on condition of a purchase. Advertising for this type of promotion often reads:

- "Buy one, get one free"
- "One-cent sale"
- "Two-for-one sale"
- "Gift with purchase"

In general, the offer of free merchandise must be temporary, otherwise the "gift" becomes part of the retailer's everyday offerings. Also, raising the regular price of the required purchase to cover the cost of the free merchandise is a deceptive practice.

Going Out of Business A company should not be established with the intent of going out of business to have a liquidation sale. Many states ensure adherence to this principle by requiring that a business operate

Figure 12.4

Wal-Mart's claim of "Always Low Prices" avoids the use of the superlative "lowest."

Figure 12.5

Retailers sometimes offer
customers free merchandise
on condition of purchase.
Courtesy of Bloomingdales, Inc.

for a minimum time period, such as a year, before conducting a going-out-of-business sale (GOB).

A GOB must be validated by a planned cessation of business. The sale inventory should not be salted with lower-quality goods at higher than normal markup that appears to be part of the regular inventory. States ensure adherence to this guideline by requiring a complete list of inventory on hand at the point at which a going-out-of-business notice is filed.

Bait and Switch Promoting an item as *bait* to lure customers into a store to sell them a higher-margin item is illegal. Retailers guilty of **bait and switch** have even penalized salespeople who sold the advertised merchandise instead of a substitute. To avoid bait-and-switch implications, retailers should have a sufficient quantity of advertised promotional merchandise on hand to meet anticipated demand, unless the advertisement discloses the number of items available, or states "while supply lasts." A key factor in determining the existence of bait and switch is the number of times that an item was advertised compared to the number of times it was actually sold.

The Raincheck Rule The Federal Trade Commission's *Unavailability Rule* or *Raincheck Rule* is a guide for handling cases of out-of-stock advertised merchandise. The guide suggests that retailers:

- Issue a **raincheck** that will allow customers to buy the advertised merchandise at a later date at the sale price
- Offer substitute merchandise of comparable value to the promoted item
- Offer a compensation that is at least equal in value to the reduction on the promoted merchandise

Predatory Pricing Some states have antitrust laws that prohibit **predatory pricing**, a low-pricing strategy designed to put competitors out of business.[15] Small independent retailers claim that large retailers engage in predatory pricing when they sell **loss leaders**, goods priced

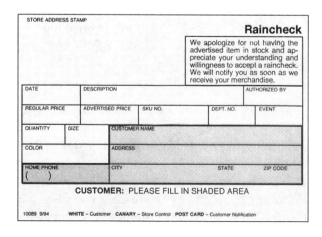

Figure 12.6

A raincheck allows a customer to buy out-of-stock advertised merchandise at sale price a later date.

below cost. Volume discounts enable large retailers to sell an item at a price that is often lower than the wholesale price charged the small retailer. Wal-Mart was found guilty of violating the Arkansas Unfair Practice Act and ordered to pay nearly $300,000 in punitive damages to three Arkansas pharmacies for selling some 200 items ranging from prescription drugs to cosmetics below cost.[16]

RESALE PRICE MAINTENANCE

Resale price maintenance (RPM), or vertical price fixing, is the practice whereby producers enforce the sale of their products at a prescribed **manufacturer's suggested retail price** (MSRP). The Miller Tidings Act (1936) permitted the practice of **fair trade** to insulate small independent retailers from price competition with large chains that paid lower wholesale prices because of quantity discounts. Fair trade allegedly sheltered the image of a product in that a consumer's perception of a product's quality is often tied to its retail price. Fair trade was highly criticized by discounters and consumer-advocacy groups as a form of price fixing and a violation of the Sherman Antitrust Act of 1890 which prohibits constraint of trade. In 1975, the Consumer Goods Pricing Act made RPM and fair trade illegal.[17, 18]

However, the definition of *price fixing* is ambiguous, leading some to conclude that certain industry practices constitute illegal acts. A manufacturer can choose to channel its products to retailers on the basis of service, training, warranties, and repair and thus refuse to sell to discounters that offer limited service.[19] Upon the complaint of a retailer that a competitor is failing to maintain suggested price levels, a supplier can cut shipment to the price cutter, as long as the supplier does not coerce the discounter to sell at a suggested price. Producers can also structure their cooperative advertisement agreements around a **minimum advertised price** (MAP) to make retailers that sell below the MAP ineligible for cooperative advertising dollars.

The most aggressive opponents of RPM are discount retailers who claim that RPM is contrary to the free market system, and that consumers have the right to buy products at competitive prices through multiple retail channels. Manufacturers of prestige products support RPM because they fear that their products will lose their cachet in consumers' eyes if discounted by mass merchandisers.

These suppliers fear that the conventional retail channels will discontinue their product lines sooner than engage in price competition with discounters.

Supreme Court rulings and the prevailing political climates have influenced the enforcement of price-fixing legislation by the Justice Department's Antitrust Division and the Federal Trade Commission's Bureau of Competition.[20, 21] In 1993, the Stride Rite Corporation paid $7.2 million in damages to settle a price-fixing suit brought by the attorneys general of 50 states and the Federal Trade Commission. Stride Rite had threatened to stop supplying its most popular Keds sneaker styles to retailers that discounted prices. The company was found guilty of price conspiracy when it encouraged retailers to report competitors' price-cutting.[22, 23] Reebok International once paid a $9.5 million settlement for threatening to terminate shipment to retailers that violated Reebok's pricing policy.[24]

PRICING: A SCIENCE AND AN ART

Pricing has been called a science and an art. As a science, price is a quantitative decision based on the numeric relationships among various pricing components. As an art, price is a qualitative decision based on intuition and creativity.[25] The following two scenarios demonstrate the nonquantitive considerations that surround pricing decisions.

Right Price, Wrong Customer A menswear buyer came across a well-styled and constructed, nicely fabricated dress shirt during a market visit. The buyer perceived the shirt as an exceptionally good value at a $20 wholesale cost, but realized that the shirt needed to be priced at $45 retail to meet the department's maintained-markup objective. Because the store's customers have historically resisted shirts priced higher than $35, the buyer is faced with a dilemma. If the shirts are retailed at $45, they are not likely to sell. If the shirts are retailed at $35, they are likely to sell, but the department's maintained-markup expectations will not be met. The decision is clear. The buyer must pass up the shirts and continue the quest for goods that will allow a retail price consistent with customers' price expectations and the store's profit objectives.

THE SUGGESTED
RETAIL PRICE
OF THIS SHIRT IS
$125. WE HAVE A
SUGGESTION FOR
WHOEVER
SUGGESTED IT.

Men's, women's and children's fashion & designer clothing 40-75% off, every day. New York City: Manhasset, NY. 17th and Chestnut St., Philadelphia; Elizabeth, East Hanover, Paramus and Wayne, NJ and Potomac Mills Mall, VA.

DAFFY'S
CLOTHES THAT WILL MAKE YOU, NOT BREAK YOU.

Figure 12.7

Daffy's is positioned as a price leader in the greater New York metropolitan area. *Devito/Verdi*

No Easy Answer A buyer has computed an initial markup percentage objective for the handbag department but realizes that the figure is not an immediate answer to every pricing decision. Factors relative to the type of goods, accepted pricing standards, and competition bear considerable weight on the pricing of individual classes or items as the following considerations for pricing four groups of handbags demonstrates. The four groups are Dooney & Bourke, a seasonal straw and canvas group, a private-label group, and an assortment of hand-crafted novelty evening bags.

- The pricing of Dooney & Bourke is restricted by the fact that the prestigious line is heavily branded and sold by other stores in the shopping center.
- The prices for the seasonal bags must include a generous provision for seasonal markdowns.
- The private-label goods afford considerable pricing flexibility and healthy markup opportunity since customers have no basis for price comparisons.

- Similarly, hand-crafted evening bags afford considerable pricing latitude as **blind items**, goods for which consumers have no frame of reference, because of the absence of brand identity and/or infrequent purchase.

SUMMARY POINTS

- Retail prices must be high enough to cover profit objectives, but low enough to stimulate customer purchase.
- A retail price has two components: cost and markup. Markup is expressed as a percentage of the retail price.
- The various types of markup include initial markup, additional markup, and cumulative markup.
- Markdowns are downward adjustments in retail prices. Four categories of reductions include: damaged merchandise, employee discounts, clearance markdowns, and promotional markdowns.
- Clearance markdowns are permanent reductions used to liquidate residual merchandise and slow sellers.
- Maintained markup is the difference between the cost of merchandise and the actual selling price.
- Tactical price changes involve a strategy for manipulating markup and markdown within a tactical price zone.
- A retail price can be computed when a desired markup and cost are known.
- Promotional markdowns are temporary reductions for sale events.
- Everyday low pricing is a value-oriented pricing strategy that eliminates the need for extensive promotional advertising.
- Each state has guidelines for valid price referencing to avoid deceptive pricing.
- Resale price maintenance (RPM) is the control of retail prices by a supplier. Under certain circumstances RPM is illegal.

KEY TERMS AND CONCEPTS

additional markdown	clearance markdown	discontinued goods
additional markup	cost	employee discount
bait and switch	cost complement	everyday low pricing
blind item	cumulative markup	(EDLP)
broken assortments	damage markdown	fair trade

initial markup

loss leader

maintained markup

manufacturer's

   suggested retail price

markdown

markdown cancellation

markup

markup cancellation

minimum advertised price

permanent markdown

predatory pricing

price lookup (PLU)

promotional markdown

raincheck

regular price

resale price maintenance

   (RPM)

retail price

seasonal merchandise

tactical price change

temporary markdown

FOR DISCUSSION

1. Give examples of goods that have the potential to become "residual" or "slow-selling" and vulnerable to clearance markdowns. What can be done to minimize the clearance markdowns taken on these goods?

2. A hosiery buyer is writing orders for two groups of cotton socks. One group is an assortment of basic colors. The other group is a holiday assortment with Christmas tree and snowman motifs. The buyer wants to generate the same maintained-markup percentage from each group. Which group will require a higher initial markup and why?

3. A furniture retailer operates stores in California, Maine, and Georgia. Most of the retailer's resources ship from High Point, North Carolina. Which stores will require the highest markup if the retailer wants to generate equal maintained markup from all stores? What workroom costs might have to be considered in the computation of initial markup?

4. Compare the promotional pricing strategies of several retailers within different retail formats. What differences/similarities do you note in terms of promotion frequency, advertising vehicles, and the types of merchandise promoted? Compare the promotional pricing strategies of several retailers within the same format. What differences/similarities do you note?

PROBLEMS

1. A sportswear buyer needs to maintain a 50 percent markup. Markdowns are projected at 25 percent. What should initial markup be?

2. What is maintained markup when:

   - gross margin is $50,000
   - workroom costs are $2,000
   - cash discounts are $3,000

3. Cost is $8, retail is $12. What is markup as a percentage of cost? As a percentage of retail?

4. Give an example of a 99 percent markup (as a percentage of retail). Give an example of a 1 percent markup.

5. What is the markdown price of a $20 item that has been marked down 35 percent. What is the price when an additional 20 percent markdown is taken?

ENDNOTES

1. There was a 53.75 percent markup on the $9.25 ties; a 52.50 markup on the $9.50 ties; and a 51.25 percent markup on the $9.75 ties. The total of all three markup percentages is 157.50. This number divided by three is 52.5.

2. Goods damaged in delivery are the responsibility of either the vendor or the shipper and should be charged back to the vendor for credit

3. Some retailers give no discount on sale or low-markup merchandise.

4. Halverson, R. (August 15, 1994). Wal-Mart's live pet biz: Bye-bye birdie. *Discount Store News*. pp. 3, 100.

5. Robbins, G. (February 1991). New POS power at Talbots. *Stores*. pp. 44–47.

6. Staff. (December 1990). Beyond the challenge: Strawbridge & Clothier builds PLU department. *Chain Store Age Executive*. pp. 86–89.

7. Negley, J. (January 5, 1998). Putting the value back in value-added retailing. *Discount Store News*. p. 13.

8. Troy, M. (November 3, 1997) 'Sales" could undercut Wal-Mart's EDLP image. *Discount Store News*.

9. Weiner, S. (February 20, 1989). Price is the object. *Forbes*. pp. 123–124.

10. Gallanis, P. Sears' new "Good Life" campaign to caplitalize on EDLP craze. *Discount Store News*. p. 33.

11. Urbonya, T. (December 4, 1989). Target takes aim with "everyday" prices. (Minneapolis/St. Paul) *Citybusiness*.

12. Cuneo, A. Ad group opposes N.Y. retail sales rules. *Advertising Age*. pp. 4, 54.

13. Staff. (June 26, 1996). Levitz to pay in settlement. (Springfield, Mass.) *Union News*.

14. Wen, P. & Mohl, B. (August 16, 1998). "Lowest-price" isn't right in grocery circular, survey shows. *The Boston Sunday Globe*. p. B2.

15. Ramey, J. (September 11, 1993). Smart strategy or unfair pricing? *Women's Wear Daily*. p. 14.

16. Brookman, F. (October 22, 1993). Rivals don't see Wal-Mart easing its price cutting. *Women's Wear Daily*. pp. 1, 7.

17. Rankin, K. (May 7, 1990). RPM bill sails through House; Still faces rough seas in Senate. *Discount Store News*. pp. 5, 202.

18. Verdisco, R. (March 15, 1993). Enforce the law against retail price-fixing. *Discount Store News*. p. 12.

19. Gannon, V. (May 10, 1991). Price maintenance bill approved by Senate. *Daily News Record.* p. 8.

20. Rankin, K. (May 7, 1990). Bush may still veto RPM. *Discount Store News.* p. 10.

21. Rosenberg, A. (May 1, 1991). Retail "price-fixing" is target of proposal. *Aftermarket Business.* pp. 1, 11.

22. Staff. (September 28, 1993). Keds to pay to settle suits. *New York Times.* p. D7.

23. Pereira, J. (September 28, 1993). Stride Rite agrees to settle charges it tried to force pricing by retailers. *Wall Street Journal.* p. A5.

24. Ramey, J. (May 15, 1995). Reebok pays to settle price-fixing lawsuit. *Women's Wear Daily.* p. 9.

25. Verdi, E. (May 15, 1995). Mingling the price message with a quality image. *Discount Store News.* p. 71.

chapter thirteen

PLANNING SALES AND INVENTORY

Planning involves establishing an organization's goals or objectives and strategies to achieve them. The planning process often includes **forecasting**, the attempt to predict trends or outcomes. Planning occurs at all organizational levels and is critical to a company's success. The absence of planning has been likened to taking a trip without a road map. Chapter 13 covers sales planning and inventory planning, two forecasting functions that are germane to the merchandising function of a retail organization.

After you have read this chapter, you will be able to discuss:

The importance of planning in a retail organization.

Sales planning and the relevance of sales plans to other organizational plans.

Inventory planning methods.

Assortment planning.

Resources of information for planning decisions.

TYPES OF PLANS

Plans are categorized by the time period that they cover. A **long-range plan** covers a three-to-five-year period or longer. Developed by top management, long-range plans have significant impact on an organization and include strategies for expansion, market position, and major capital expenditures. A **short-term plan** covers periods shorter than a year. Developed by lower-level managers, short-term plans are narrower in scope than long-range plans. Schedules and budgets are two common forms of short-term plans.

Plans are categorized by their point of origin and the direction that they travel within a table of organization. A **top-down plan** originates at the upper levels of an organization and impacts planning at lower levels. For instance, the top management of a retail organization may project a corporate sales objective for the forthcoming year. The sales plan is then broken down by merchandise division. Sales are then planned for each department within the division. Buyers and planners then determine the categories, vendors, and items that will best support departmental sales plans and ultimately the organization's sales goal.

A **bottom-up plan** is developed at lower levels of the organization as a building block of an organization-wide plan. An organizational sales objective based on the sum total of plans developed at departmental level would reflect bottom-up planning. Most organizations combine top-down and bottom-up planning, recognizing that planning is a two-way street that requires input at every managerial level.[1]

THE 4-5-4 PLANNING CALENDAR

The **4-5-4 calendar** is an accounting calendar universally adopted by retailers. The calendar is called *4-5-4* because each month has exactly *four* weeks (28 days) or *five* weeks (35 days). Months are chronologically arranged in a *4-week month, 5-week month, 4-week month* sequence. Within the 4-5-4 calendar, four months have five weeks: March, June, September, and December. The remaining eight months have four weeks. The beginning and end of a month on the 4-5-4 calendar do not necessarily coincide with the beginning and end of the same month on

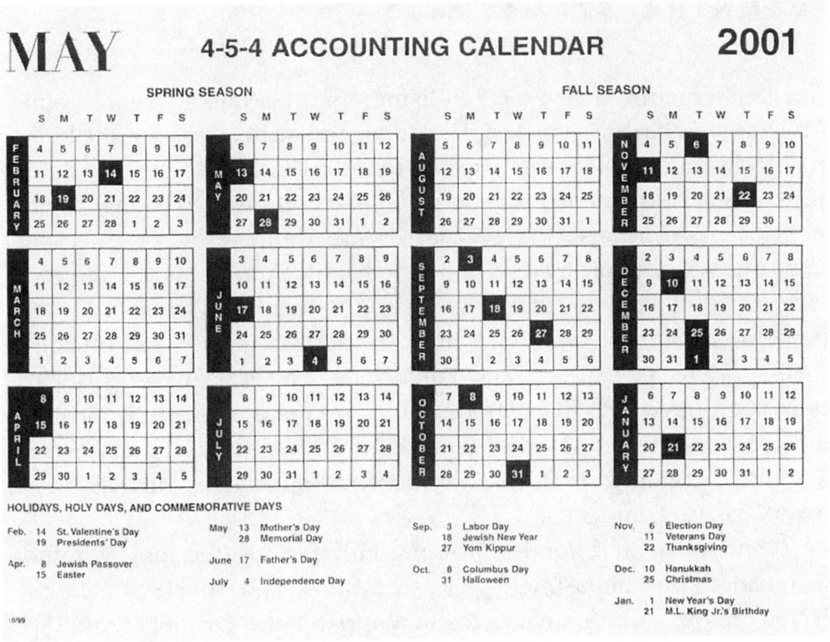

Figure 13.1

The 4-5-4 calendar is an accounting calendar used by retailers to structure their fiscal year. *The May Department Stores Company.*

a conventional Gregorian calendar. Note that in Figure 13.1, June begins on June 3 and ends on July 7.

The 4-5-4 calendar has two six-month seasons: **spring** which runs from February through July; and **fall** which runs from August through January. The weeks of a month on the 4-5-4 calendar are referred to ordinally. In Figure 13.1, April 8 through April 14 is *the first week of April*, or *Week 1 of April*. A year on the 4-5-4 calendar has 364 days and exactly 52 weeks. The Gregorian calendar has 365 days and 52 weeks and a day. Thus, an additional week is added to January in the 4-5-4 calendar every five or six years to account for this extra day and for the 366th day of leap years. The nearly universal adoption of the 4-5-4 calendar has ensured that everyone is "on the same page" when referring to time periods such as "the last week of December." The one-calendar concept enhances communication within the retailing industry and between retailers and their suppliers.

PLANNING STRUCTURES

Retailers structure their merchandising organizations by product line. **Divisions, departments, classifications,** and **subclasses** are the building blocks that retailers use to create pyramid-like hierarchies to define units of business and organizational responsibilities. Divisions, departments, classifications, and subclasses are defined by product line. Divisions are the most broadly defined unit. Subclasses are the most narrowly defined unit. In Figure 13.2, The men's division of Dolan's Department Store is organized into five departments: basics, furnishings, sportswear, clothing and collections. The men's basics department is grouped into five classifications: underwear, hosiery, pajamas, and robes. Though not indicated in Figure 13.2, the men's underwear classification might be further divided into subclasses such as briefs, boxers, T-shirts, and so on.

Item (shirts) and vendor (Tommy Hilfiger) are the most common designations for departments, classifications, and subclasses. Brand-driven business units, such as fashion apparel and cosmetics, are typically identified by vendor. Other designations are based on:

- Price range (moderate)
- Size range (junior)
- End use (sportswear)
- Lifestyle (active)
- Selling season (holiday)
- Product composition/fabrication (brass/silk)
- Customer (female)

Multiple designations are often combined to create a single business-unit identity such as *misses better sportswear*. Designations need not be consistent from one business unit to another. A store may identify high-fashion handbags by vendor (Coach, and Dooney & Bourke) and less fashion-oriented handbags by fabrication (leather, vinyl, fabric, straw), or style (evening, shoulder, clutch, briefcase, satchel). Business-unit identities within a retail organization often parallel those of the wholesale market. A *housewares* buyer buys for a *housewares department* at a *housewares market*.

There are no universal standards for structuring a merchandise hierarchy. Knit shirts may be a *department* in the men's sportswear *division* in one retail organization, and a *subclass* of the men's sportswear *classification* in another retail organization. In general, merchandise hierarchies in

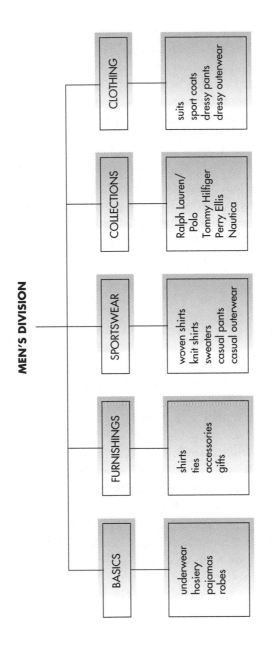

Figure 13.2

A system of departments and classes for the men's division in a retail store.

large retail organizations have a greater number of precisely defined business units than the merchandise hierarchies of small retail organizations. A large organization's *knit shirt* volume is high enough to stand alone as a department, whereas a small organization's *knit shirt* volume is not. Assortment diversity affects the number of units within a hierarchy. A department with a few homogeneous products has fewer classifications than a department with many heterogeneous products.

Business-unit hierarchies are used as a basis for planning and tracking sales and inventory. Each defined unit must represent enough sales volume to warrant being planned and tracked separately. Defining merchandising hierarchies by division, department, classification, and subclass is a common but not universal practice within the retail industry. Some retailers use closely related terms such as *category* or *product group*. One major retailer groups merchandise into *fine departments* and *major departments*.

PLANNING SALES

Sales planning is a critically important function in a retail organization in that expense plans, inventory purchases, and profit objectives are all predicated upon plan sales. A store's seasonal selling payroll budget is based on projected sales. Planning sales too low will result in an understaffed store, while planning sales too high will result in an overstaffed store. Sales plans also drive inventory purchases. Sales plans that are too high will yield an overstocked condition and poor turnover; sales plans that are too low will yield an understocked condition and lost sales. Sales plans often include growth strategies for cultivating additional business through new items, vendors, and categories.

Retailers look to the past and present to predict future sales. Last year's sales are often used as a base for planning this year's sales, anticipating that recurring conditions and events that drove sales last year will drive them again this year. Examples include seasonal weather conditions that stimulate the sale of swimwear, lawn furniture, wool coats, and boots, and annual gift-giving occasions, such as Valentine's Day, Fathers' Day, and Christmas that drive sales of chocolates, shirts and ties, and toys.

The past sales upon which future sales are projected must be a **comparable**, or valid, **reference point**. Easter may fall as early as late March or as late as the end of April. Sales for the week prior to Easter last year are *comparable* to sales for the week prior to Easter this year, even though the weeks may fall in different months. Changes in back-to-school dates (based on when Labor Day falls), a store's promotional calendar, and the number of days between Thanksgiving and Christmas are other factors that must be considered when determining comparable, or *comp*, sales. Business units must also be comparable. A "12 percent sales increase over last year for comparable stores" implies that a comparison is being made between stores that were open for business this year and last year, and that new stores opened since last year, and/or stores closed since last year are not included in the comparison.

Historical sales used as a planning base should be typical of the period. Last year's cold-weather-accessories sales for November are an invalid reference for projecting this November's sales if last November was atypically warm. Using last year's sales to project this year's sales will yield an understocked condition if this November's weather is typical of the season. When there is no historical reference point on which to project sales, as in the case of a new store or a new category of merchandise or vendor, the sales history of a similar business unit is often used until a history is developed.

Current trends are valid predictors of future sales in that recent trends are chronologically closer to the future than the distant past. Assume that it is fall and that a planner is using information from a trailing-nine-months sales report to project sales for a sportswear line for the forthcoming spring season (see Table 13.1). The planner's immediate reaction is to base this

Table 13.1   **TRAILING NINE MONTHS SALES REPORT**

Month	Plan	Actual	Percent +/-
February	$ 18,000	$ 18,218	+1%
March	$ 24,000	$ 24,676	+3%
April	$ 28,000	$ 28,795	+3%
May	$ 40,000	$ 41,446	+4%
June	$ 20,000	$ 21,267	+6%
July	$ 15,000	$ 15,311	+2%
August	$ 25,000	$ 27,428	+10%
September	$ 30,000	$ 34,654	+16%
October	$ 35,000	$ 42,659	+21%
TOTAL	$235,000	$254,454	+8%

spring's plan on last spring's sales with a modest increase to reflect higher wholesale prices. However, the planner notices that last spring's sales were relatively flat, but that impressive gains have been posted since the beginning of the current season. The planner decides to plan more aggressively, interpreting the current sales trends as an indicator that the line is garnering a loyal following.

Innumerable internal and external factors influence an organization's sales plans. A store's decision to become more upscale will be supported by aggressive sales plans for better goods, and modest sales plans for moderate goods. Economic conditions, such as inflation, interest rates, and the general state of the economy, are also evaluated for their potential impact on sales. Slumps in housing construction reduce demand for window treatments. The impact of economic factors varies by type of goods and customer profile. Sales of trendy fashion goods are affected more dramatically by negative economic conditions than sales of functional items, such as refrigerators. The spending patterns of lower-income groups are more sensitive to economic shifts than those of upper-income groups. Sometimes economic factors have regional impact. For example, layoffs in the aerospace industry caused a retail slump in Southern California a few years back.

Demographic shifts, fashion trends, and changes in competition impact a retail organization's sales plans. A decline in the teenage population during the 1980s led to downsized junior departments. However, a blossoming teenage population in the 1990s caused many retailers to recapture the junior business with aggressive sales plans and larger inventory commitments. Fashion trends impact sales. A shift toward casual dress in the workplace will have a negative effect on the sale of men's ties and women's hosiery, but a positive impact on the sale of men's twill pants and female sportswear. Changes in competition affect sales plans. The addition of complementary stores in a shopping area may increase customer traffic and positively impact sales, while new direct competition will have a negative impact on sales.

Unpredictable and uncontrollable factors make sales planning an inexact process. When Sunglass Hut International investors chided company executives for lackluster sales and profit in their more than 2000 stores, the only retort was cloudy skies.[2] Though objective indicators, such as current sales trends and inflation, are used to project sales, determining the impact of these indicators as well their interaction is often a best guess. Will a manufacturer's price increase induce customers to explore substitute brands? How much will new competition

SWS and The Whims of Weather

Weather has a profound impact on a retailer's business affecting store traffic, sales volume, and the demand for weather-sensitive products. The impact can be significant ranging anywhere from 10 to 30 percent of sales. However, most retailers do not strategically factor weather into their sales or inventory plans. Instead they assume that last year's weather will repeat from one year to the next, when in fact weather is similar from one year to another only about one-third of the time. The result: two-thirds of the time retailers have either too little or too much seasonal inventory on hand.

Strategic Weather Services (SWS) is an international consulting firm that specializes in long-range weather forecasting and its application to business. The company works with clients to look at weather as both a risk factor and an opportunity for business. For instance, SWS advised one apparel-retailer client that the back-to-school season would be unseasonably warm in the Midwest and Northeast. The retailer shifted its mix of heavy versus lightweight outerwear in its back-to-school assortments resulting in a significant increase in sales over the previous year. In another instance, SWS advised a national retailer of unseasonably heavy rain in the company's West Coast markets. The retailer altered its mix of humidifiers and dehumidifiers and increased dehumidifier sales from 10,000 units to 30,000 units.

SWS uses proprietary software to conduct weather analyses in its Palm Springs weather lab, the only private weather-research facility in the nation. The lab is staffed by a cohort of 12 meteorologists who are responsible for maintaining weather-prediction databases for all of North America and Europe. Strategic Weather Services' client list includes Wal-Mart, Kmart, Target, J.C. Penney, Eastern Mountain Sports, Eddie Bauer L.L. Bean, and Charming Shoppes.[1,2]

Sources:

1 Reda, S. (September 1997). *Apparel Merchants: Aiming for fall with weather forecasting. Stores. pp. 66-68.*
2 Mander, E. (March 1996) *Firm makes weather its guessing game. Retailing Today. p. 15*

impact sales? For how long? The best plans are the flexible ones that allow for the unforeseen circumstances that might affect them.[3]

PLANNING INVENTORY

Attaining a sales objective is contingent upon having sufficient inventory to support the plan. However, having too much inventory poses problems such as slow turnover and high clearance markdowns.

| Buyer | DIV MGR | GEN MGR | DEPT |

6-MONTH MERCHANDISING PLAN FOR PERIOD FROM .... TO .... YEAR ....

STORE NO.

ACT LY	PLANNED THIS YEAR	ACT TY	NET SALES	FEB/AUG	MAR/SEP	APR/OCT	MAY/NOV	JUN/DEC	JUL/JAN
	NET SALES		LAST YEAR						
	AV MO STOCK		PLAN						
	STOCK TURN		THIS YEAR						
	MARK DN %		EOM STOCK	JAN/JUL	FEB/AUG	MAR/SEP	APR/OCT	MAY/NOV	JUN/DEC	JUL/JAN
	GROSS MARG		ACT LY						
	MAINT M/U		PLAN TY						
			ACT TY						
			MD LY						
			MD TY						

STORE NO.

ACT LY	PLANNED THIS YEAR	ACT TY	NET SALES	FEB/AUG	MAR/SEP	APR/OCT	MAY/NOV	JUN/DEC	JUL/JAN
	NET SALES		LAST YEAR						
	AV MO STOCK		PLAN						
	STOCK TURN		THIS YEAR						
	MARK DN %		EOM STOCK	JAN/JUL	FEB/AUG	MAR/SEP	APR/OCT	MAY/NOV	JUN/DEC	JUL/JAN
	GROSS MARG		ACT LY						
	MAINT M/U		PLAN TY						
			ACT TY						
			MD LY						
			MD TY						

STORE NO.

ACT LY	PLANNED THIS YEAR	ACT TY	NET SALES	FEB/AUG	MAR/SEP	APR/OCT	MAY/NOV	JUN/DEC	JUL/JAN
	NET SALES		LAST YEAR						
	AV MO STOCK		PLAN						
	STOCK TURN		THIS YEAR						
	MARK DN %		EOM STOCK	JAN/JUL	FEB/AUG	MAR/SEP	APR/OCT	MAY/NOV	JUN/DEC	JUL/JAN
	GROSS MARG		ACT LY						
	MAINT M/U		PLAN TY						
			ACT TY						
			MD LY						
			MD TY						

STORE NO.

ACT LY	PLANNED THIS YEAR	ACT TY	NET SALES	FEB/AUG	MAR/SEP	APR/OCT	MAY/NOV	JUN/DEC	JUL/JAN
	NET SALES		LAST YEAR						
	AV MO STOCK		PLAN						
	STOCK TURN		THIS YEAR						
	MARK DN %		EOM STOCK	JAN/JUL	FEB/AUG	MAR/SEP	APR/OCT	MAY/NOV	JUN/DEC	JUL/JAN
	GROSS MARG		ACT LY						
	MAINT M/U		PLAN TY						
			ACT TY						
			MD LY						
			MD TY						

STORE NO.

ACT LY	PLANNED THIS YEAR	ACT TY	NET SALES	FEB/AUG	MAR/SEP	APR/OCT	MAY/NOV	JUN/DEC	JUL/JAN
	NET SALES		LAST YEAR						
	AV MO STOCK		PLAN						
	STOCK TURN		THIS YEAR						
	MARK DN %		EOM STOCK	JAN/JUL	FEB/AUG	MAR/SEP	APR/OCT	MAY/NOV	JUN/DEC	JUL/JAN
	GROSS MARG		ACT LY						
	MAINT M/U		PLAN TY						
			ACT TY						
			MD LY						
			MD TY						

Figure 13.3

A six-month merchandising plan.

Inventories must be strategically planned so that sales objectives are met with minimum inventory investments.

A buyer's purchase and delivery decisions are predicated on inventory projections based on the interaction of two factors: plan sales and desired turnover. To understand the relationship of plan sales and turnover to purchase and delivery decisions, recall the jeweler from Chapter 9 who sold 600 gold chains a year. The jeweler found that purchasing 600 chains at the beginning of the year resulted in an annual turnover of 2.0. The jeweler determined limiting purchases to 50 chains each month would increase turnover to 13.0.

Five methods of planning inventory are presented in this chapter. They include the:

- Basic stock method
- Percentage variation method
- Stock-to-sales ratio method
- Weeks-of-supply method
- Formula for replenishment of staple merchandise

All five formulas combine sales projections and some variation of turnover to determine the amount of inventory needed to achieve a desired sales goal for a certain time period.

The Basic Stock Method The **basic stock method** asserts that a beginning-of-month (BOM) inventory should be equal to the plan sales for the month plus a basic inventory. The basic stock method formula is:

BOM = plan monthly sales + (average inventory − average monthly sales)

The following example demonstrates using the basic stock method to plan the BOMs for a year for a store with a monthly sales plan as indicated in Table 13.2 and a desired turnover of 4.0.

Average inventory is computed by dividing annual sales by turnover.

$$turnover = \frac{sales}{average\ inventory}$$

$$4.0 = \frac{\$720,000}{average\ inventory}$$

$$average\ inventory = \$180,000$$

Table 13.2 **PLAN SALES FOR A YEAR**

Month	Plan Sales
February	$ 30,000
March	$ 60,000
April	$ 90,000
May	$ 60,000
June	$ 60,000
July	$ 30,000
August	$ 30,000
September	$ 60,000
October	$ 60,000
November	$ 90,000
December	$120,000
January	$ 30,000
TOTAL	$720,000

Average monthly sales is computed by dividing annual sales by 12:

$$average\ monthly\ sales = \frac{annual\ sales}{12}$$

$$average\ monthly\ sales = \frac{\$720,000}{12}$$

$$average\ monthly\ sales = \$60,000$$

The difference between average inventory and average monthly sales is the basic inventory.

$$basic\ inventory = average\ inventory - average\ monthly\ sales$$

$$basic\ inventory = \$180,000 - \$60,000$$

$$basic\ inventory = \$120,000$$

The basic inventory is added to each month's planned sales to compute BOM. The results are tabulated in Table 13.3.

When turnover is 12.0 the average monthly sales and the average inventory will be equal in the basic stock method. The basic stock will be zero and BOM will always equal plan sales. When turnover is greater than 12.0, the average monthly sales will be greater than the average inventory. The basic stock will be a negative number and BOM

Table 13.3   **PLAN SALES AND BOMs FOR A YEAR USING THE BASIC STOCK METHOD**

Month	Plan Sales	Plan BOM Inventory
February	$ 30,000	$150,000
March	$ 60,000	$180,000
April	$ 90,000	$210,000
May	$ 60,000	$180,000
June	$ 60,000	$180,000
July	$ 30,000	$150,000
August	$ 30,000	$150,000
September	$ 60,000	$180,000
October	$ 60,000	$180,000
November	$ 90,000	$210,000
December	$120,000	$240,000
January	$ 30,000	$150,000

will be less than plan sales. Thus, the basic stock method can only be used when turnover is less than 12.0. The method can be adapted to a six-month or three-month planning period by using the desired turnover for the period and computing average monthly sales based on either three or six months.

The Percentage Variation Method The **percentage variation method** asserts that a BOM should be a percentage of average inventory. The percentage will vary each month based on plan sales. The percentage variation method formula is:

$$BOM = average\ inventory \times 0.5 \left(1 + \frac{plan\ sales\ for\ the\ month}{average\ monthly\ sales} \right)$$

The following applies the percentage variation method to the data in Table 13.2. The calculation of the BOM for February is:

$$BOM = \$180,000 \times 0.5 \left(1 + \frac{\$30,000}{\$60,000} \right)$$

$$BOM = \$180,000 \times 0.5\ (1 + 0.5)$$

$$BOM = \$180,000 \times 0.75$$

$$BOM = \$135,000$$

Table 13.4   PLAN SALES AND BOMs FOR A YEAR USING THE
PERCENTAGE VARIATION METHOD

Month	Plan Sales	Plan BOM Inventory
February	$ 30,000	$135,000
March	$ 60,000	$180,000
April	$ 90,000	$225,000
May	$ 60,000	$180,000
June	$ 60,000	$180,000
July	$ 30,000	$135,000
August	$ 30,000	$135,000
September	$ 60,000	$180,000
October	$ 60,000	$180,000
November	$ 90,000	$225,000
December	$120,000	$270,000
January	$ 30,000	$135,000

Table 13.4 lists BOMs for a year computed by the percentage variation method. Note that when plan sales are *equal* to average monthly
sales, the BOM is equal to the average inventory. When plan sales are
less than average monthly sales, the BOM is *less* than the average inventory. When plan sales are *greater* than average monthly sales, the BOM
is *greater* than average inventory. Thus, an *average* sales plan will
require an *average* inventory as a BOM. A *lower* than average sales plan
will require a BOM less than average inventory. A *higher* than average
sales plan will require a BOM *greater* than average inventory.

Though the basic stock method is simpler than the percentage variation method the latter is more sensitive to fluctuations in plan sales.
Table 13.5 compares the BOMs generated from both methods. Note that
the range between the highest and lowest BOM in the percentage variation method ($135,000) is greater than the range between the highest
and lowest BOM in the basic stock method ($90,000). The percentage
variation method yields higher BOMs than the basic stock method
when sales plans are high, and lower BOMs than the basic stock
method when sales plans are low.

The Stock-to-Sales Ratio Method The BOMs generated by the **stock-to-
sales-ratio method** are based on a desired stock-to-sales ratio for a
month. The stock-to-sales ratio method formula is:

Table 13.5 **A COMPARISON OF BOMs USING THE BASIC STOCK METHOD AND THE PERCENTAGE VARIATION METHOD**

Month	Plan Sales	BOM-Basic Stock Method	BOM-Percentage Variation Method
February	$ 30,000	$ 150,000	$ 135,000
March	$ 60,000	$ 180,000	$ 180,000
April	$ 90,000	$ 210,000	$ 225,000
May	$ 60,000	$ 180,000	$ 180,000
June	$ 60,000	$ 180,000	$ 180,000
July	$ 30,000	$ 150,000	$ 135,000
August	$ 30,000	$ 150,000	$ 135,000
September	$ 60,000	$ 180,000	$ 180,000
October	$ 60,000	$ 180,000	$ 180,000
November	$ 90,000	$ 210,000	$ 225,000
December	$120,000	$ 240,000	$ 270,000
January	$ 30,000	$ 150,000	$ 135,000
TOTAL	$720,000	$2,160,000	$2,160,000

$$BOM = plan\ sales \times desired\ stock\text{-}to\text{-}sales\ ratio$$

If a desired stock-to-sales ratio is 3.0 and plan sales are $8000, the BOM is computed as follows:

$$BOM = \$8000 \times 3.0$$

$$BOM = \$24,000$$

Recall from Chapter 9 that peak selling periods require lower stock-to-sales ratios than slow selling periods. To demonstrate this principle, the BOMs generated by the percentage variation method were divided by plan sales to calculate the stock-to-sales ratios for each month. The results are tabulated in Table 13.6.

Note that months with high sales plans have low stock-to-sales ratios, while months with low sales plans have high stock-to-sales ratios. Therefore, the stock-to-sales ratios used in the stock-to-sales-ratio method should vary relative to the sales volume each month. The stock-to-sales-ratio method is inappropriately applied when an annualized stock-to-sales ratio is used to plan each month's BOM. A range of stock-to-sales ratios should be used unless there is little sales fluctuation from month to month.

Table 13.6   **PLAN SALES AND BOMs USING THE STOCK-TO-SALES RATIO METHOD**

Month	Plan Sales	S/S Ratio	BOM
January	$ 30,000	4.5	$ 135,000
February	$ 30,000	4.5	$ 135,000
March	$ 60,000	3.0	$ 180,000
April	$ 90,000	2.5	$ 225,000
May	$ 60,000	3.0	$ 180,000
June	$ 60,000	3.0	$ 180,000
July	$ 30,000	4.5	$ 135,000
August	$ 30,000	4.5	$ 135,000
September	$ 60,000	3.0	$ 180,000
October	$ 60,000	3.0	$ 180,000
November	$ 90,000	2.5	$ 225,000
December	$120,000	2.3	$ 270,000
TOTAL	$720,000	3.0	$2,160,000

The Weeks-of-Supply Method The three inventory-planning methods covered thus far assume that inventories are planned by month. However, fast-turning inventories are planned for shorter periods because fast-turning goods require more frequent replenishment than slow-turning goods.

The weeks-of-supply method asserts that the amount of inventory required to support plan sales for a week is driven by the number of weeks that the inventory will last based on a projected turnover. The weeks-of-supply formula is:

$$weeks\ of\ supply = \frac{52}{turnover}$$

If the desired turnover is 6.0, then weeks of supply is calculated as follows:

$$weeks\ of\ supply = \frac{52}{6.0}$$

$$weeks\ of\ supply = 8.7$$

An implication of the formula is that at any point throughout the year a buyer must have enough inventory on hand to support 8.7 weeks of sales if he or she intends to achieve an annual turnover of 6.0. A further implication is that to achieve a certain sales objective, a buyer needs enough inventory to last 8.7 weeks. Therefore, the formula for projecting an inventory based on the weeks-of-supply method is:

$$plan\ inventory = plan\ sales \times weeks\ of\ supply$$

If plan sales are $5000 and weeks of supply is 8.7, then

$$plan\ inventory = plan\ sales \times weeks\ of\ supply$$

$$plan\ inventory = \$5000 \times 8.7$$

$$plan\ inventory = \$43,500$$

Based on a 6.0 turnover, the amount of inventory required to support a sales plan of $5000 is $43,500. Note that as turnover increases, weeks of supply decreases and that as turnover decreases, weeks of supply increases. The weeks-of-supply numerator is adjusted accordingly when turnover for a period other than a year is used in the computation. The numerator would be 26 if turnover were for a half year. The weeks' supply method is best applied when sales are relatively stable.

Weeks of supply, or *weeks' supply*, is frequently used to evaluate inventory levels. In this case, weeks' supply is an indicator of the number of days an inventory will last if sold at a current rate of sale. The higher the weeks' supply, the longer the inventory will last and the slower it will turn. Thus, weeks' supply can be used as an indicator of too much or too little inventory.

The weeks-of-supply concept has many derivations. **Days of supply**, or *days' supply*, is a close cousin of weeks' supply. Days' supply is the number of days an inventory will last if sold at a current rate of sale. Some stores use a *weekly percent sell* as a weeks-of-supply indicator. The weekly percent sell is the percent of stock on hand that will sell in one week at a current rate of sale. The higher the percentage the faster the inventory will turn. (See Table 13.7.)

Formula for Periodic Replenishment of Staple Merchandise The formula for periodic replenishment of staple merchandise asserts that staples should be replenished based on the amount of units sold during a typical selling period, the time lapse between the arrival of reorders, and a safety, or reserve, stock. The formula for the periodic replenishment of staples is:

$$M = (RP + DP)\ S + R$$

- M (maximum) is the amount of inventory needed for the period.
- RP (reorder period) is the time period that defines the frequency with which orders are placed.
- DP (delivery period) is the time period between the point at which an order is placed and the point at which the goods are available for sale.

Table 13.7   **WEEKS OF SUPPLY AND WEEKLY PERCENT
SELL FOR VARIOUS TURNOVER RATES**

Annual Turnover	Six-Month Turnover	Weeks of Supply	Weekly % Sell
12.0	6.0	4	23
11.0	5.5	5	21
10.0	5.0	5	19
9.0	4.5	6	17
8.0	4.0	7	15
7.0	3.5	8	14
6.0	3.0	9	12
5.5	2.75	10	11
5.0	2.5	11	10
4.5	2.25	12	9
4.0	2.0	13	8
3.5	1.75	15	7
3.0	1.5	17	6
2.5	1.25	21	5
2.0	1.0	26	4

- S (rate of sale) is the number of units that are typically sold during the reorder period.
- R (reserve stock) is additional stock to avoid stockouts if sales exceed plan. The formula for reserve stock is $2.3\sqrt{(LT)S}$. LT (lead time) is the sum of RP and DP.

The following demonstrates using the formula to replenish goods ordered biweekly and delivered in a week, in a store that sells 100 items per week.

$$M = (RP + DP)S + R$$

$$M = (2\ weeks + 1\ week) \times 100\ units\ per\ week + R$$

$$R = 2.3\sqrt{(2\ weeks + 1\ week) \times 100\ units\ per\ week}$$

$$R = 40$$

$$M = 300 + 40$$

$$M = 340$$

OPEN-TO-BUY

Open-to-buy is the amount of merchandise that a buyer needs to order to support plan sales for a period. Open-to-buy is derived from **plan purchases**. Plan purchases are based on the:

- Amount of inventory brought forward from the previous period (BOM)
- Plan sales for the period
- Amount of inventory that must be rolled over to the next period (EOM)
- Plan markdowns for the period[4]

The formula for plan purchases is:

> *plan sales for month*
> *+ plan markdowns*
> *+ plan EOM*
> *− plan BOM*
> _____
> *plan purchases*

Open-to-buy is the difference between plan purchases and merchandise on-order. The formula for open-to-buy is:

> *plan purchases*
> *− on order*
> _____
> *open-to-buy*

Open-to-buy can be likened to a checkbook balance. Plan purchases are like a beginning checkbook balance. Placing an order is like writing a check. The buyer begins each month with a new balance. The balance decreases as the buyer writes orders. A buyer with "no open-to-buy" has a zero open-to-buy balance. A buyer who has exhausted one month's open-to-buy can write orders against the next month's open-to-buy. A buyer "bought up through March" can place orders against April's open-to-buy.

A buyer is "overbought" when on-order exceeds plan purchases, a condition comparable to an overdrawn checking account. Some buyers overbuy anticipating that some orders will be short shipped or not shipped at all. Order cancellation is the most common remedy for an overbought condition. Like sales, open-to-buy is planned at various organizational levels such as department and classification.

JARROD & YOUNG		-SALES	-SALES	-SALES	-SALES	-SALES	-SALES	-SALES	-SALES
(a.) SALES									
(a1.) APR	PERIOD PLN	13.9	10.6	21.6	27.9	12.2	11.5	17.9	2.7
(a2.) MAR	PTD TY	17.4	13.0	32.3	27.3	18.9	14.6	19.8	3.0
(a3.)	LY	19.4	14.9	25.3	29.0	15.0	14.0	21.6	3.1
(a4.) MAR TY-LY	%CHG	-7.7	-12.8	58.6	-5.9	26.0	4.3	-8.3	-3.2
(a5.) YR TD BOP	MAR TY	12.3	12.0	23.1	19.1	10.2	9.8	13.9	2.3
(a6.)	LY	12.4	9.5	8.5	15.0	8.1	6.5	9.9	1.6
(a7.) YR TY-LY	%CHG	-0.5	26.3	171.8	27.3	25.9	50.8	40.4	43.8
(b.)	STOCK	STK	STK	STK	STK	STK	STK	STK	STK
(b1.) MAR AUDIT	OH BOP	62.6	65.0	74.8	80.2	58.4	47.6	71.0	23.5
(b2.) MAR -MEMO-BNJ	BOP	23.1	5.9	17.0	14.9	4.9	7.2	10.0	1.1
(b3.) MAR NET RCPTS	PTD	37.5	34.2	60.0	76.8	50.1	36.3	53.1	14.3
(b4.) MAR TRANSFERS	IN	0.2	0.8	12.1	2.4	0.3	1.0	3.1	0.2
(b5.)	OUT	-3.2	-5.4	-0.7	-2.4	-5.8	-2.6	-5.6	-0.2
(b6.) LAST WK ON HND	TY	81.8	82.4	105.1	126.3	72.1	64.8	92.4	32.9
(b7.) APR BOP STOCK	PLN	95.3	49.4	86.0	77.0	47.9	59.8	67.8	15.2
(b8.) THIS WK ON HND	TY	88.0	81.6	114.0	129.7	84.1	67.7	101.8	34.8
(b9.)	LY	108.7	57.8	104.3	89.2	54.9	67.5	79.8	17.3
(b10.) TY-LY	%CHG	-20.7	23.8	9.7	40.5	29.2	0.2	22.0	17.5
(b11.) MAY BOP STOCK	PLN	105.5	51.4	91.2	77.2	51.7	56.4	70.0	18.0
(c.) OUTSTANDING	OTB	OUTST	OUTST	OUTST	OUTST	OUTST	OUTST	OUTST	OUTST
MAR	OUTST	1.6	6.3	19.3	12.1	4.8	11.7	15.8	8.6
APR	OUTST	34.9	16.8	22.7	21.3	5.1	17.1	20.0	9.4
MAY	OUTST	14.0	11.5	17.5	17.5	13.0	10.1	14.7	7.0
(c1.) JUN	OUTST								
(c2.) AFTER JUN	OUTST								
(d.) APR OP-TO-BUY	BAL	-3.6	-42.1	-41.5	-54.7	-28.4	-27.4	-43.9	-32.1
(e.)	MARKUP								
(e1.) FEB	ACT %	47.2	47.1	48.4	51.1	47.1	46.9	47.1	47.3
(e2.) FEB	PLAN %								
(e3.) MMU—SEAS TD	TY								
(e4.) BOP MAR	LY								
(f.)	MARKDOWNS	MKD	MKD	MKD	MKD	MKD	MKD	MKD	MKD
(f1.) MAR	PTD								
(f2.) MAR	PLN	0.9	0.8	1.3	1.0	0.9	1.2	1.0	0.4
(f3.) YR TD BOP MAR	TY$	0.2	0.2	1.0	0.4	0.4	0.5	0.4	0.1
	TY%	1.6	1.7	4.3	2.1	3.9	5.1	2.9	4.3
		DEPT	DEPT	DEPT	DEPT	DEPT	DEPT	DEPT	DEPT
		04-02-	04-02-	04-02-	04-02-	04-02-	04-02-	04-02-	04-02-

Figure 13.4

An open-to-buy report.

Discrepancies between plan and actual sales necessitate frequent open-to-buy adjustments. Poor sales for a month will increase the EOM carried into the subsequent month (BOM) necessitating a reduction in open-to-buy. Favorable sales will decrease the EOM carried into the subsequent month necessitating an increase in open-to-buy. Failure to adjust open-to-buy as needed will result in overinventoried or underinventoried conditions. Open-to-buy can be expressed as dollars or units.

cathy®   **by Cathy Guisewite**

Figure 13.5

A buyer is "overbought" when on-order exceeds plan purchases. *CATHY © Cathy Guisewhite. Reprinted with permission of UNIVERSAL PRESS SYNDICATE. All rights reserved.*

Like open-to-buy, **open-to-ship** is a figure that defines inventory needs. Merchandise allocators use open-to-ship to determine the type and amount of merchandise to ship to stores from a distribution center. Open-to-ship is the difference between a store's projected inventory needs and inventory on hand.

ASSORTMENT PLANNING

Plan purchases is the amount of inventory that needs to be bought to support a sales goal. However, this *right amount* of inventory is only the first step in determining the *right* inventory. Plan purchases must be translated into an assortment plan that defines the goods by product characteristics. The characteristics most used to plan assortments include:

Price The price range of an assortment is defined by its **opening**, or lowest, **price-point** and its **ending**, or highest, **price-point**. An assortment can be planned with multiple price ranges. For instance, a gift shop might define its assortments within three price categories:

- Gifts under $10
- Gifts between $10 and $100
- Gifts over $100

BRAND	CLASS.	AVAIL.			RETAIL PRICE RANGE	ORDER MINIMUM	U.P.C. CODE	E.D.I. READY	SIZES & WIDTHS			
		PRE-PACK	MAKE UP	OPEN STOCK					Narrow	Medium	Wide	Extra Widths
A'MANO	D	•	•	•	$35-600	12	•	•	4-12	4-12	4-12	
Accessoire Diffusion	D, C, B, HB		•		$145-300	60				4-12		
Accessory Group Inc.,Clip-Ons	AC		•	•	$4-12	4						
Acme	B			•	$80-150	None	•	•	6-9	5-10		
Adirondack Collection	C, S, AC		•		$40-75	12	•	•		5-11 full sizes		
Aerosoles · Women	C, B, S	•	•	•	$30-60	None	•	•	7.5-9	5-12		
Alfie's Original Souliers	D, C, B		•		$49-79	12				5-12		
Allure	D, C, B	•	•	•	$60-120	72	•	•	5-10	4-12	6-10	
Amalfi	D, C	•	•	•	$79-150	12	•	•	5-12	4-12	4-10	4A-C
Amante	D, C		•		$60-125	500			4-12	4-12	4-12	
American Eagle	D, C, B	•		•	$20-70	12	•	•		5-11		
Amiana (For Women)	D, S		•		$100-200	36		•	5-10	4-11		
Amour By Pepe Jimenez	D		•		$60-125	None			6-11	3.5-12		S
André Assous	C, B	•	•		$22-200	12			7-9	4-11		
Andrea Cecconi	D, C		•		$115-250	12				5-11		
Andrea Pfister S.R.L.	D, B, AC, HB		•		$200-450	100				36-40		
Ann-Marino	D, C	•		•	$38-90	12	•	•	7-9	5.5-11		
Anne Jordan	D, C		•		$40-80	12				5-12	7-10	
Anne Klein	D, C, B	•	•		$120-240	108		•	7-10	4-10		
Anne Klein II	D, C, B	•	•	•	$80-145	108		•	7-10	4-10		
Aqua-Talia By Bootlegger	B		•		$80-120	36				5-11		
Archie	C, B, HB		•		$145-210	100				5-12		
Atsco/Private Labels	D, C, B, AC,S	•	•	•	$20-150	None	•	•	4-12	4-12	4-12	XW
Auditions	D, C, B			•	$40-100	None	•		5-11,12,13	5-12,13	4-12,13	SS-WW

Abbreviations & Symbols: Classifications: **D** - Dress Shoes / **C** - Casuals / **B** - Boots / **AT** - Athletics / **S** - Slippers / **SV** - Service Footwear
AC - Accessories / **HB** - Handbags / **LG** - Leather Goods / **AP** - Apparel / **SC** - Shoe Care Products
• – Available

Figure 13.6

Buyers use vendor profiles such as this to plan shoe assortments by style, price, and size. *Provided by Fashion Footwear Association of New York (FFANY).*

Assortments are sometimes characterized by more general pricing terms, such as *moderate* or *better*. An assortment's price range must be consistent with a store's image and target customer. Thousand-dollar dresses at Sears and washable polyester suits at Brooks Brothers are inconsistent with each store's image and customer. There is no consistent method for defining assortment by price. One store may consider leather handbags as better, and vinyl handbags as moderate. Another store may include low-end leathers in its moderate assortment, and high-end vinyls in its better assortment.

Brand Sometimes assortments are planned by brand. A department store may define its cosmetics assortment as Estee Lauder, Clinique, Chanel, Lancome, Origins, and so on. Like price, the brands within an

JARROD & YOUNG			
	Sub-Classification	**% to Stock**	**Open-to-Buy in $**
A. SUB-CLASSIFICATION	Straight line	20	20,000
	Side pleat	20	20,000
	A-line	15	15,000
	Wrap	15	15,000
	Trouser	15	15,000
	Full	5	5,000
	Dirndl	10	10,000
		100%	$100,000 (OTB share)
	Price Range	**% to Stock**	
B. PRICES	$130.00	5	
	120.00	10	
	100.00	30	
	80.00	30	
	75.00	15	
	65.00	10	
		100%	
	Colors	**% to Stock**	
C. COLORS	Gray heather	10	
	Navy	10	
	Black	25	
	Brown	10	
	Red	10	
	Taupe	15	
	Novelty	20	
		100%	
	Sizes	**% to Stock**	
D. SIZES	4	8	
	6	16	
	8	25	
	10	25	
	12	18	
	14	8	
	16	–	
	18	–	
	20	–	
		100%	
	Fabrics	**% to Stock**	
E. FABRICS	Wool/gabardine and/or crepe	25	
	Wool/flannel	40	
	Wool/silk	10	
	Poly/wool	20	
	Acrylic/rayon	5	
		100%	

Figure 13.7

Assortments can be planned as percentages of total inventory by factors such as price, color, size, and fabric.

assortment must be consistent with a store's image. Within the context of planning an assortment by brand, buyers also consider private labels. Buyers often seek private-label substitutes for basic items with weak brand identity, since private-label goods generate more gross margin than branded goods. However, the mix of private labels and brands must be carefully balanced. An extensive choice of brands is often an assortment feature that draws many customers to a store, especially for brand-driven purchases.

Size Since sized merchandise seldom sells in equal quantities, buyers must be careful to plan assortments according to the sizes in greatest demand. An end-of-season clearance rack with a disproportionate number of *smalls* is often indicative of an overabundance of one size, and lost sales to customers seeking other sizes. Suppliers often recommend size distributions based on historical sales records. Shoe manufacturers pack individual shoe styles in case lots, called size runs, that include specific size assortments.

Color Though assortments are not often planned by specific colors such as "blue," color categories, such as *basic, fashion, or neutral*, are often used as a basis for planning assortments. A men's dress-shirt assortment may be planned as *solids* and *fancies*.

Fabrication Sometimes fabric is an important assortment distinction. *Silk* is an important assortment characteristics in women's dresses and men's neckties. A men's dress-shirt assortment may be planned as *cottons* and *blends* (of polyester and cotton). A sweater assortment might be planned as wool, cotton, and acrylic.

Style The style or look of product may determine its significance in an assortment. A sweater assortment may be defined as:

- Crew neck
- Cardgian
- Vest

A dress assortment may be planned as *casual* and *special occasion*. Some assortments are planned by item. Assortments of small leather goods include key chains, wallets, checkbooks, and change purses. Items are sometimes identified as classifications or subclasses within department/class structures.

Assortment plans vary by month and season. Cotton sweaters give way to wool sweaters as seasons change. Lacy teddies become an important women's sleepwear item in February for Valentine's Day. The demand for table linens surges just before Thanksgiving. A full-line discounter reports of planning large inventories of cup hooks in November to respond to a demand by customers who use them to hang holiday lights! Assortment plans are also linked to a store's promotional calendar. A store-wide *Anniversary Sale* requires extensive quantities of goods with broad appeal that can be promotionally priced.

Buyers constantly review their assortment to ensure that they are satisfying customers' needs and, in turn, the store's sales objectives. For instance, buyers replace lackluster brands with brands that show promise of being better investments of inventory and space. Naturally, profit objectives must also be considered. The brands that generate the most sales are not necessarily the most productive in terms of gross margin. Some of the best-selling brands sell only at promotional prices. These brands are good volume generators but poor gross-margin producers.

Factors external to the organization, such as fashion and economic trends, impact assortment plans. Strapless dresses becoming fashionable will encourage an innerwear buyer to maintain a selection of strapless bras. During trying economic times, buyers will slant assortments toward basic practical items at the expense of trendy frivolous items. One fabric mill reports that black-velvet special-occasion dresses become very popular during poor economic times because of their fashion durability. Assortment plans are driven by a store's merchandising objectives. A desire to upgrade a store's image will affect the selection of price and brand. A desire for exclusivity will influence the selection of brands and styles.

Recall from Chapter 2 that assortments are characterized by depth and breadth and that there is often a trade-off between the two. A store with a wide assortment of cosmetics brands limits the amount of space that can be dedicated to the selection within each line. By discontinuing brands, the store will free up space for greater depth within the lines that are retained. In general, narrow and deep assortments are more desirable than broad and shallow assortments. It is better to carry full assortments of a few product lines than piecy assortments of many product lines. A selection is *overassorted* when it has too much breadth and too little depth. Exclusive specialty shops are an exception to this generalization where uniqueness is a fundamental assortment characteristic.

Assortment Plan

	Store A	Store B	Store C
Bath & Body	360	720	720
Gift Sets	240	300	336
Accessories	72	114	216
Candles	72	96	96
Soaps	72	144	216
Total Units	816	1374	1584

Figure 13.8

A unit assortment plan for body care products provided by a vendor.

Assortment plans can be quantified by units, dollars, or percentages. An assortment of small, medium, large, and extra-large knits may be planned in a unit ratio of 2:3:2:1. A misses sportswear assortment may be planned as 40 percent better and 60 percent moderate. The assortment of a men's collections department may be 50 percent Polo, 25 percent Tommy Hilfiger, and 25 percent Claiborne.

Trends in Planning

Because planning involves the interaction of so many inexact variables, efforts have been made to computerize functions with the hope of making the process more precise. Computerized planning systems have facilitated the planning of assortments by individual sku and store. "What if" capabilities allow planners to observe instantly the effect of adjusting various planning variables. Because tedious calculations are eliminated, planners devote more time to analytical functions, and less time to computational functions. Computerized planning also integrates plans from various organizational levels to ensure a match between financial and merchandise plans, bottom-up and top-down plans, and unit and dollar plans.[5]

Category management involves managing a product category as if it were a separate business entity, such as a store or department. Category management is a customer-driven concept that uses planning technology and historical sales data to develop ideal space allocation and assortments by store. Some observers warn of the dangers of category management in that only the highest turning and highest margin goods are retained in assortments at the expense of core products that may not be profitable but are popular with consumers. Critics also fear that running a store as a collection of disjointed businesses will disrupt the store's cohesiveness and sales synergy.[6]

Though computerized planning systems have become common, even in small retail organizations, an understanding of manual systems is fundamental to understanding automated systems, since computerized systems are based on the same theoretical constructs as manual systems.

PLANNING INFORMATION

Planning involves integrating information from a diverse group of sources. Information on a store's sales history, current sales trends, and inventory status is obtained from internal organizational sources. However, information pertaining to fashion trends, market conditions, and the status of competitors must be obtained from sources external to the organization. The following is a discussion of several external information sources often tapped by retailers, including consumer publications, trade publications, trade associations, forecasting services, and reporting services.

Consumer publications are magazines and newspapers available to the public at newsstands. Targeted to clearly defined market niches, the editorial content of consumer publications provides retailers with insight into the lifestyles, tastes, and needs of specific market segments. Fashion magazines such as *Vogue, Mademoiselle,* and *GQ* are sources of information on current fashion trends for women and men. Newspapers such as *The Wall Street Journal,* and magazines such as *Business Week, Fortune,* and *Forbes,* offer timely information on the general business climate.

Trade publications are targeted to members of a specific industry segment. They feature editorials, business analyses, and information on the current status of major industry players, new products, and governmental legislation relative to the industry. Trade publication advertising

Figure 13.9

Consumer magazines are
sources of information on
current fashion trends.

provides retailers with information on merchandise resources, trade shows, and trade services. Trade publications often conduct studies of interest to their readership.

Fairchild Publications is the leading source of apparel industry publications including *Women's Wear Daily (WWD)*, for the women's apparel industry; *Daily News Record (DNR)*, for the textile and men's apparel industries; and *Home Furnishings Network (HFN)* for the home furnishings and accessories industries. *Buyer's guides* are supplements to *HFN* that cover specific merchandise categories. A typical *buyer's guide* includes sections such as:

- *State of the Market*: statistics on a category's growth potential, major resources, and market share by retail channel of distribution.
- *Products Inside and Out*: information on materials and production processes, and glossaries of terms related to the product.
- *Merchandising the Category*: suggestions for pricing, promoting, and presenting the category.

Other retail-trade publications include *Retailing Today*, a monthly newspaper for discounters published by Lebhar-Freidman, and *Chain Store Age Executive*, a monthly magazine for general retail readership.

 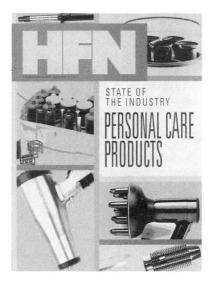

Figure 13.10

Planning involves integrating information from a diverse group of sources including trade publications such as *Women's Wear Daily* and *Home Furnishings News*.

Trade publications are often targeted to specific product categories. *Gifts & Decorative Accessories* is a monthly publication for gifts, tabletop, gourmet, home accessories, greeting cards, and stationery published by Geyer-McAllister Publications.

Trade associations represent the interests of a particular industry segment. Supported by dues-paying members, trade associations promote goodwill, lobby before legislatures, conduct research, produce trade shows, sponsor conferences, and publish newsletters. The largest trade associations for retailers include the National Retail Federation (NRF), the International Mass Retail Association (IMRA), and the International Council of Shopping Centers (ICSC). Some trade associations represent narrow segments of the retail industry such as the National Association of Menswear Sportswear Buyers (NAMSB) and the Apparel Retailers Association.

Manufacturers' trade associations, such as the Cosmetics, Toiletry, and Fragrance Association and the American Apparel Manufacturers Association, are authoritative sources of information on the product lines produced by their constituents. The research laboratory of the Leather Industries of America at the University of Cincinnati publishes the *Directory of Leather Terminology*. The association also distributes *Leather Facts*, a comprehensive booklet on the qualities and manufacturing of leather published by the New England Tanners Club.

Forecasting services study history and prevailing socioeconomic and market conditions to predict trends in advance of a selling season. The Color Association of the United States (CAUS) and Intercolor are color-forecasting services subscribed to by fiber, textile, and apparel producers, and retailers that develop their own private-label merchandise. **Reporting services** survey and analyze specific industry segments, reporting their findings to service subscribers. The *Tobe Report* is a heavily illustrated fashion report that dates back to 1927. The report is a merchandising guide for apparel retailers used to identify the hottest fashion trends and merchandise resources. Johnson's Redbook Service is a reporting service that tracks the sales of leading apparel and textiles producers, chemical companies, and department, specialty, and discount stores.

Other Information Sources

Suppliers often provide retailers product information and market studies designed to support the sale of their product. Though the information is

Figure 13.11

Fashion Watch is a report of new trends, items, and resources published for retailers of female apparel by Retail Reporting. *Courtesy of Retail Reporting.*

biased, it is free and readily available. **Consultants** are advisers who offer expertise, analyze issues, or resolve problems on a contractual fee basis. A division of Price Waterhouse, Management Horizons is a consulting firm that specializes in strategy development, market positioning, new-concept development, merchandising, operations, and retail growth and expansion. Barnard's Consulting Group is a retail forecasting and consulting firm that performs market analyses, develops marketing strategies, and conducts seminars for retailers in the United States and Europe. Local, state, and federal governments are reliable sources of information on population, consumer spending, and economic conditions. The *Retail*

Figure 13.12

The Center for Retailing Studies at Texas A&M University sponsors symposiums for retailing executives and professors who teach and conduct research in retailing. *Reprinted with permission. Copyright © 2000 Center for Retailing Studies, Department of Marketing, Texas A&M University, College Station, Texas. All rights reserved.*

Trade Area Statistics is a document prepared by the federal government that is very useful to retailers.

Academic institutions are other sources of information. The Center for Retailing Studies (CRS) at Texas A&M University is a corporately sponsored organization, which sponsors an annual symposium for retailing executives and professors who teach and conduct research in retailing. The CRS copublishes the *Retailing Issues Letter* with Arthur Andersen & Co., a bimonthly essay on critical issues facing retailers. Academic publications available at college and university libraries, such as the *Journal of Retailing* and *Journal of Marketing,* are other sources of helpful information. The American Collegiate Retail Association and the International Textiles and Apparel Association are professional associations of college professors, many of whom conduct and publish scholarly research on merchandising topics.

SUMMARY POINTS

- Planning involves establishing an organization's goals or objectives and the strategies to achieve them.
- The 4-5-4 calendar is an accounting calendar used by retailers to structure their fiscal year.
- Divisions, departments, classifications, and subclasses define related groups of merchandise as manageable units of businesses.
- Sales plans are based on history and the current trends that may impact future sales.
- The attainment of sales objectives is contingent upon having a sufficient amount of inventory to support plan sales. Inventory planning methods are based on plan sales and a desired turnover objective.
- Open-to-buy is the amount of inventory that needs to be purchased for a specific selling period.
- Merchandise assortments are planned by brand, size, price, color, style, lifestyle, and various other factors.
- External information sources include consumer publications, trade publications, trade associations, forecasting services, and reporting services.

KEY TERMS AND CONCEPTS

basic stock method
bottom-up plan
category management
classification
comparable reference point
consumer publication
consultant
days-of-supply method
department
division
ending price-point
fall

forecasting
forecasting service
4-5-4 calendar
long-range plan
opening price-point
open-to-buy
open-to-ship
percentage variation
  method
planning
plan purchases
reporting service

short-term plan
spring
stock-to-sales ratio
  method
subclass
top-down plan
trade association
trade publication
weeks-of-supply
  method

FOR DISCUSSION

1. Develop a structure of departments, classes, and subclasses for the following merchandise divisions. Justify each segmentation as a unit of business:

   intimate apparel
   ready-to-wear
   home division
   accessories
   children's

2. Make a list of cyclical factors that affect the sale of apparel. Classify each relative to their reliability as a predictor. Explain how the impact of these factors will vary by category of merchandise.

3. Make a list of current economic, demographic, lifestyle, and fashion trends that should be considered when planning sales for a forthcoming season for the following departments:

   cosmetics
   activewear
   infants and toddlers
   china and crystal

4. What problems do you perceive in a sales planning method that is exclusively top down? Exclusively bottom up?

PROBLEMS

1. Spring sales for a department have been planned as follows:

February	$4000
March	$8000
April	$9000
May	$7000
June	$5000
July	$3000

   The turnover for the season is 4.0. Plan BOM inventories for each month using the basic stock and percentage variation methods. Compare the results of the two methods.

   Compute monthly stock-to-sales ratios using the BOMs from each method. Compare the stock-to-sales ratios that result from each set of BOMs.

2. Assume that markdowns for the season are 15 percent of sales and that markdowns are distributed by month according to the following percentages:

February   20%
March   10%
April   5%
May   15%
June   20%
July   30%

Compute plan purchases for each month. Assume that the EOM for July is the BOM of February.

3. Using the formula for the periodic replenishment of staples, compute M when the rate of sale is 50 units:

DP = 2 weeks
RP = 1 week
S = 50 units per week

4. Develop the following assortments:

A vendor assortment of prestige cosmetics lines for a department store by percent.
A vendor assortment of mass market cosmetics for a full-line discounter by percent.
A size and color assortment for 2500 wool crew-neck sweaters available in S/M/L/XL and in ecru, navy, burgundy, black, and gray.
An item assortment for a fine jewelry case featuring onyx.
A knit/woven, size, style assortment of 5000 junior tops.
Style, color, and size assortment of a major brand of blue jeans.

ENDNOTES

1. Allen, R. (1984). *Bottom Line Issues in Retailing.* Chilton Book Company. Radnor, Penn.: 1984. p. 5.
2. DeGeorge, G. (June 9, 1997). Sunglass Hut is feeling the glare. *Business Week.* pp. 89–91.
3. Mahaffie, J. (March 1995). Why forecasts fail. *American Demographics.* pp. 34–40.
4. Reductions are included in the computation since reductions reduce the value of the inventory.
5. Reda, S. (March 1994). Planning systems. *Stores.* pp. 34–37.
6. Brookman, F. (June 1997). Drug chains make progress on category management. *Stores.* pp. 45–46.

chapter fourteen

PURCHASE TERMS

A retail buyer's task of seeking quality products at favorable prices is not unlike a consumer's quest for the best values in the retail marketplace. Though consumers have considerable product options, price is rarely negotiable. A greater degree of pricing flexibility exists in the wholesale marketplace where price and other purchase agreements are often negotiable. Retailers who negotiate favorable wholesale prices can pass their savings on to consumers in the form of lower retail prices, and thus compete more effectively with other retailers. Favorable nonprice vendor agreements can increase gross margin, decrease processing expenses, and improve cash flow. Chapter 14 covers the negotiable points of wholesale purchase agreements and their effect on a retailer's pricing and profitability.

After you have read this chapter, you will be able to discuss:

The retail buyer's role as a negotiator.

The impact of vendor payment terms on cash flow and gross margin.

Basic transportation terms.

The importance of strategic partnerships between retailers and their vendors.

PURCHASE ORDERS

A **purchase order** is a contractual sales agreement between a retailer and a vendor in which items of merchandise, prices, delivery dates, and payment terms are specified. Purchase orders are often categorized by factors such as the type of goods ordered and order status. Purchase orders for merchandise are often categorized relative to the certain characteristics of the order:

Advance Order An advance order is an advance commitment to buy merchandise that may not be available for delivery until the distant future. Producers use advance orders as a barometer to gauge production.

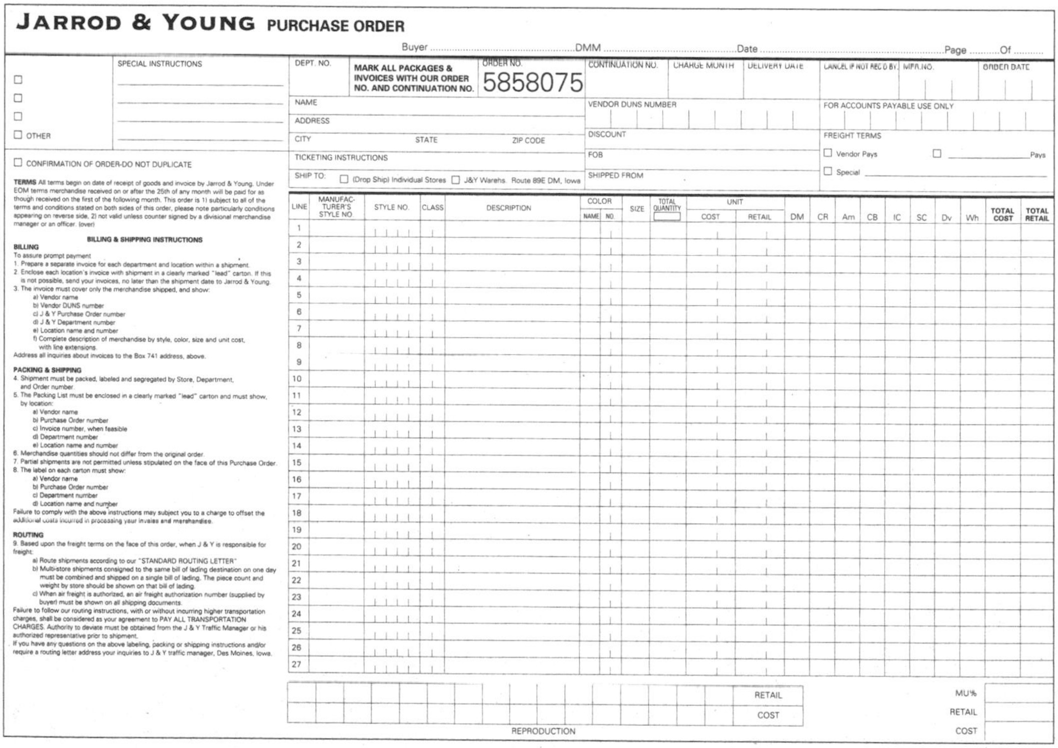

Figure 14.1

A sample purchase order.

Back Order A back order is an order for merchandise that was ordered but never shipped. Vendors *short ship* orders when they run out of the styles, colors, or sizes ordered by the retailer. Some vendors substitute out-of-stock goods with other styles, colors, or sizes, much to the dismay of retailers.

Complete Order A complete, or filled, order is an order that has been totally shipped by the vendor.

Fill-In Order A fill-in order is an order to replenish sold-out sizes/styles/colors of a basic-inventory assortment.

No-Order A no-order refers to merchandise that arrives at a retailer's distribution center without a supporting purchase order.

Past Due Order A past due order is an order not yet received by the specified delivery date on the purchase order.

Reorder A reorder is an order for previously ordered goods. Reorders are typical of fast-selling items. Not all merchandise may be reordered. Because fashion goods change so quickly, basic goods are more likely to be reordered than fashion goods.

Rush Order A rush, or priority, order is an order expedited by the vendor and the retail distribution center, often to replenish a low assortment of fast-selling merchandise, to cover a breaking advertisement, or for the grand opening of a new store.

Special Order A special order is an order placed for an individual customer. Special orders are often restricted by a vendor's minimum order specifications. Some retailers wait until enough special orders have accrued to satisfy the minimum. However, this delay in filling the order can lead to customer frustration.

Standing Order A standing, or open, order is an outstanding order to which additional items can be added without generating new paper.

Purchase order management (POM) systems have transformed purchase order processing from an inefficient superintensive procedure involving handwritten documents into a computerized system

```
PM278(16.00)          PO WITHIN VENDOR INQUIRY            02/25/93   15:15:23
19 - FILENES                     VENDOR DUNS NUMBER:   51318665  USER: T01
  VENDOR NAME: SAHARA
   PO             SHIP                        PO              SHIP
 NUMBER  DEPT POM  DATE   PO STATUS         NUMBER  DEPT POM  DATE   PO STATUS
01002476 0390  Y  12/03/92 OPEN ORDER     01017326 0390  Y  03/05/93 OPEN ORDER
01022375 0390  Y  04/01/93 OPEN ORDER     01022607 0390  Y  03/20/93 OPEN ORDER
01025071 0390  Y  04/10/93 PEND W/ERR     01025766 0390  Y  03/20/93 PEND W/ERR
01026012 0390  Y  04/12/93 OPEN ORDER     01026400 0390  Y  04/10/93 CANCELED
09008307 0390  Y  03/25/93 PEND MGMT      39005262 0390  Y  02/01/92 CANCELED
39005353 0390  Y  02/15/92 CANCELED       39005767 0390  Y  10/01/92 CANCELED
39005791 0390  Y  11/20/92 CANCELED       39005809 0390  Y  04/01/93 OPEN ORDER
39005825 0390  Y  02/20/93 OPEN ORDER     39005833 0390  Y  02/10/93 OPEN ORDER
39005841 0390  Y  01/15/93 OPEN ORDER     39005858 0390  Y  03/01/93 OPEN ORDER
39005866 0390  Y  01/25/93 OPEN ORDER     39005874 0390  Y  02/20/93 OPEN ORDER
39005882 0390  Y  12/15/92 OPEN ORDER     39005916 0390  Y  11/13/92 CANCELED
39005932 0390  Y  03/01/93 OPEN ORDER     71025766 0390  Y  03/20/93 CANCELED
76138226 0390  Y  04/01/93 OPEN ORDER     76138234 0390  Y  03/10/93 OPEN ORDER
76138242 0390  Y  02/04/93 OPEN ORDER     76138259 0390  Y  11/25/92 OPEN ORDER
76138267 0390  Y  11/25/92 OPEN ORDER     76138275 0390  Y  01/29/93 OPEN ORDER
76216790 0390  Y  11/25/92 OPEN ORDER     76216808 0390  Y  11/25/92 PEND W/ERR

           PF1=MENU      PF2=HELP     PF3=RECOVER    ENTER=CONTINUE
 ** 968 ** PRESS ENTER FOR MORE POS
```

Figure 14.2

POM systems track open-to-buy and purchase orders by number, ship date, and status.

for preparing and transmitting orders electronically. POM systems also track purchase orders by factors such as order number, delivery date, vendor, and category of merchandise.

DISCOUNTS

Buyers often receive special price reductions in the cost of merchandise called **discounts.** A **quantity discount** is a reduction in cost based on the amount of merchandise purchased. A *noncumulative discount* applies to each order placed. A *cumulative discount* applies to orders placed over time. The discount increases as the accumulated value of the orders increases. Noncumulative discounts encourage large individual orders while cumulative discounts encourage a steady flow of repeat orders. A quantity discount can be stated as a percentage applied to a total invoice, or as a reduction in unit cost. The unit cost of an item may be $1, however if more than 500 units are purchased, the unit price becomes $0.98; if 1000 units are purchased, the unit price becomes $0.95; and so on.

Vendors offer quantity discounts as sales inducements and to encourage the placement of large orders since it is less costly to pick, pack, ship, and invoice a few large orders than many small orders. Most vendors have a **minimum order** requirement, a dollar or unit

Phone: 773.890.1466
Fax: 773.890.1467
E mail: sales@hoohobbers.com

2847 West 47th Place   Chicago, IL 60632

Hoohobbers
Innovations for children ♦♦♦

Effective: 9/22/00

2000/2001 Price List, Specifications and Conditions

•*Opening Order Minimum: $350.00 (with account approval)*

•*Reorder Minimum: $150.00*

•*Freight is F.O.B. Factory. All orders ship UPS, unless specified otherwise. Actual shipping charges are added to your invoice. Truck orders ship freight collect.*

•*Payment for initial orders may be by credit card (MC, VISA, Discover), COD or cash in advance.*

•*Open account status (net 30) is available upon completion and approval of Credit Application.*

•*All returns must have prior approval from our Customer Service Department. An authorization number will be issued. The authorization number must appear on all cartons. No merchandise will be accepted without authorization.*

•*We will replace any defective item or part. Feel free to have your customer call us with any problem.*

•*Case weight & cube information is not available on softgoods. These items are boxed at time of shipment. Actual case weight and size varies dependent upon the particular mix of softgoods ordered.*

we manufacture all our products in Chicago
made in the
USA

Figure 14.3

One vendor's purchase terms and conditions.

amount that defines the smallest order that the vendor is willing to accept. Levi Strauss' minimum order requirement is $10,000. Quantity discounts give large retailers a significant competitive pricing advantage over small independent retailers. Wal-Mart profitably retails some items at prices lower than the wholesale cost paid by small independents. However, retailers should avoid the temptation to buy excessive amounts of merchandise for the sake of obtaining quantity discounts. Markdowns on excessive inventory can more than negate the advantage of the discounts.

A **seasonal discount** is a reduction in cost for orders placed in advance of the normal ordering period. Seasonal discounts are sometimes stated as price schedules of discounted unit costs for orders placed before specified dates. Pricing programs such as these are often dubbed *Early Bird Specials* or *Preseason Incentive Programs*. Seasonal discounts often involve long-term purchase commitments over time. A retailer that commits to seasonal orders of $2 million may receive a discount after orders of $1 million have been placed. Long-term purchase commitments allow producers to plan production strategically and to balance the peaks and valleys of the production cycles of seasonal goods. However, retailers assume risk by committing to goods far in advance of a selling season, especially fashion goods. To minimize this risk, some producers offer seasonal discounts based on dollar commitments, allowing buyers to select specific styles closer to the selling season.

Just as the retailer offers slow-selling, end-of-season merchandise at markdown prices to consumers, vendors offer retailers their slow sellers, closeouts, and overruns at off-price at the end of a season. These opportunistic buys are often referred to as end-of-season discounts.

DATING

Part of the buying process involves negotiating arrangements for payment. Payment terms are stated on the vendor's **invoice,** an itemized statement that lists the goods shipped, the unit and extended cost, and any additional charges for transportation and/or insurance.[1] The term **dating** refers to the period allowed for the payment of an invoice. *Net 30* is a common dating expression meaning that full payment of the invoice is due within 30 days of the **date of invoice** (DOI), the date that the invoice was issued.

A **cash discount** is a reduction in the amount due on an invoice when payment is made on or before a specified date. Unless otherwise specified, the **cash discount period** begins on the DOI and expires on the designated cash discount date. The **net-payment period** begins on the **cash discount date** and ends on the specified **net payment date.** A cash discount is not applied until all other discounts have been deducted. Cash discounts are applied to merchandise charges only. Shipping and insurance charges are not discountable.

A common expression of cash discount terms is *2/10 net 30,* read "two ten net 30." This means that a 2 percent discount may be deducted from an invoice paid within 10 days of the DOI. Once the cash-discount period has expired, the full amount of the invoice is due within 30 days of the DOI. The expression *2/10, 1/15, net 30* means that a 2 percent discount may be deducted from an invoice paid within 10 days of the DOI, or a 1 percent discount if paid between 11 and 15 days. Once both discount periods have expired, the full amount of the invoice is due within 30 days of the date of invoice. The expression *2/10 net 30* may also be written as *2/10, n/30*. When terms are not stated, it is assumed that full payment is due in 30 days.

Regular, or *ordinary,* **dating** assumes the DOI as the first day of the payment period. Discount and payment periods can be extended by beginning the period later than the DOI. An **EOM notation** means that the periods begin at the end of the month in which the invoice is dated. If the terms of an August 15 invoice are *2/10 net 30 EOM,* the discount period begins August 31 and a 2 percent discount may be deducted until September 10. Full payment is due through September 30.

Some vendors consider invoices dated the 25th of a month or after as if they were dated the first of the following month. In the case of an August 25 invoice dated *2/10 EOM,* a 2 percent discount may be deducted through October 10. Full payment is due by October 30. These are highly favorable terms for the retailer who has approximately six weeks to generate cash from the sale of the merchandise and still take advantage of the discount.

There are a number of special types of dating:

- **Proximo,** or *prox,* **dating** specifies the day of the following month by which the cash discount must be taken; *2% 15th prox. net 30* means that a 2 percent discount may be deducted through the 15th of the following month. Full payment is due within 30 days of the DOI.
- **Advance dating** delays the beginning of discount and payment periods until a future date noted "as of." If the terms of an August 15 invoice are *2/10, net 30, as of December 1,* a 2 percent discount may be deducted through December 11. Full payment is due by December 31. Advance dating is also called *post* or *seasonal* dating and is common in the menswear industry.
- **Extra dating** adds additional days to the discount and payment periods. If the terms of an August 15 invoice are *2/10, 60X* or *2/10, 60 ex.,* a 2 percent discount may be deducted until October 25. Full payment is due November 15. Suppliers use advance and extra dating to induce retailers to accept early shipments of merchandise, preferring to show high receivables on their balance sheets rather than high inventories. A vendor may use these forms of dating to test merchandise in certain stores as early predictors of a season's selling trends.

- **ROG,** or receipt-of-goods, **dating** delays the beginning of the discount and payment periods until the goods are received by the retailer. If the terms of a shipment invoiced August 15 are *2/10 ROG,* and the goods arrive on September 1, a 2 percent discount may be deducted through September 11. Full payment is due by October 1. ROG dating compensates for extended shipping time due to slow transportation modes or the transportation of goods over a considerable distance. ROG dating is not used frequently.

- **Cash,** or *immediate,* **dating** are payment arrangements with no provision for discount or payment periods. **COD,** or cash on delivery, means that cash payment is due upon the delivery of the goods. Suppliers ship COD to new retailers with no established credit, or to retailers with poor credit histories. *Cash in advance* (CIA) and *cash before delivery* (CBD) are other forms of cash dating.

Goods sold on **consignment** are not paid for until they are sold. Consignment arrangements are not common but are sometimes used to sell big-ticket items with a slow or unpredictable rate of sale, such as works of art, to minimize the retailer's risk:

- A positive cash flow is ensured since goods are not paid for until after they are sold.
- The retailer's capital is not tied up in inventory.
- Goods are returned to the vendor if not sold within an agreed upon time period.

Though arrangements are similar, there is a distinction between goods sold on consignment and goods sold on **memorandum.** The title of consignment goods passes from the vendor to the consumer but never passes to the retailer. The title of memorandum goods passes from the vendor to the retailer, usually when the goods are shipped, and then passes to the consumer at the point of sale.

Dating is a frequent point of negotiation between retailers and their vendors. Lengthy payment periods allow a retailer to generate a considerable amount of cash from the sale of goods before having to pay for them, thus enhancing a positive cash flow. Vendors, on the other hand, prefer shorter payment periods, wishing to balance their own cash flow and to meet financial obligations, such as payroll and payments to their suppliers. Some vendors offer incentive programs that combine both discount and dating terms. One footwear resource offers multiple-discount and extended-payment-period programs for replenishment orders based on quantities purchased. The program qualifies retailers for:

- A 1 percent discount and 30-day credit terms with a minimum purchase of 3600 pairs per year
- A 2 percent discount and 60-day credit terms with a minimum purchase of 9600 pairs per year
- A 3 percent discount and 60-day credit terms with a minimum purchase of 12,500 pairs per year[2]

COMPUTING DISCOUNTS

Cash discounts are computed by multiplying the discount rate by the cost of the goods as billed on the invoice:

$$cash\ discount = discount\ rate \times billed\ cost$$

A 2 percent discount on a $100,000 shipment is computed as follows:

$$cash\ discount = 2\% \times \$100,000$$

$$cash\ discount = 0.02 \times \$100,000$$

$$cash\ discount = \$2000$$

The cash discount is then subtracted from the billed cost to determine the balance due:

$$balance\ due = billed\ cost - cash\ discount$$

$$balance\ due = \$100,000 - \$2000$$

$$balance\ due = \$98,000$$

A balance due can be computed with a single step formula:

$$balance\ due = (100\% - discount\ rate) \times billed\ cost$$

$$balance\ due = (100\% - 2\%) \times \$100,000$$

$$balance\ due = 0.98 \times \$100,000$$

$$balance\ due = \$98,000$$

NINE TECHNIQUES OF SUCCESSFUL VENDOR NEGOTIATIONS

1. *Act Collaboratively, Not Competitively.* Negotiation is not "me against you." Recognize that the other party has to come away with a benefit, too. Show them how giving you what you want will help them get what they want.
2. *Prepare.* Do your homework about the other party; gather as much information about them as possible. Even rehearse and outline your remarks.
3. *Know What You Want.* Being able to state specific proposals or plans gives you strength. Don't wait to "see what they offer us." Know in advance what you must have, and what you can afford to give up. Each time you make a concession, get something in return.
4. *Don't Let Your Ego Get in the Way.* When you think of the negotiating process as winning or losing, you have too much ego involved. Don't get sidetracked by personalities or emotions. Stick to the issues.
5. *Learn to Make Time Your Ally.* Time is at the heart of every negotiation. Learn to make it work for you. Try to learn the other party's deadline without giving away yours. Most concessions occur at somebody's deadline.
6. *If You Can't Agree on Point One, Go to Point Two.* Agree even in small increments. Don't get hung up on one issue. It is easier to come back to an issue after you have reached some agreement, and the other person has invested time and energy in working with you.
7. *Be a Creative Risk-Taker.* If you are known to not take risks, you are predictable and can be easily manipulated. Create your own solutions; there is usually more than one way to get the results you want.
8. *Closing the Negotiation: Wrap it Up.* Don't stay around and chat after you have reached an agreement. If you have what you want, close the negotiation. Don't linger too long, or it may unravel.
9. *Develop Long-term Relationships.* Focusing on long-term goals will keep both parties from being sidetracked by short-term frustrations. Knowing you are both in for the long haul means you can solve any problem that arises.

Source:
Prepared by Elizabeth Tahir, president of Liz Tahir Consulting, a retail marketing and management consulting and training firm in New Orleans, Louisiana.

Anticipation is an additional discount for paying an invoice prior to a cash discount date. The discount is based on the prevailing prime rate of business interest, the number of days that the payment is made prior to the cash-discount date, and the balance of the invoice after discount. The formula for computing the additional discount is:

$$additional\ discount = invoice\ balance \times interest\ rate \times time\ ^3$$

Assume that the DOI on the above invoice was August 15 and that payment was made on August 20, five days in advance of the August 25 cash discount date. If the prevailing interest rate is 3 percent, the additional discount is computed as follows:

$$additional\ discount = invoice\ balance \times interest\ rate \times time$$

$$additional\ discount = \$98,000 \times 0.03 \times 5/360$$

$$additional\ discount = \$40.83$$

The additional discount is deducted from the $98,000 invoice balance leaving a new balance due of $97,959.17. Anticipation is not a common discounting practice. Many suppliers stipulate "no anticipation" as part of their dating terms.

The Long-Term Impact of Discounts

Discounts can dramatically impact a retailer's profitability over time. Consider the retailer who forfeits a $2000 discount on a $100,000 shipment invoiced *2/10 net 30*. The retailer has effectively paid an annual interest rate of 35.7 percent to use $100,000 for the 20 days between the cash discount date and the net payment date as the following calculation demonstrates:

$$interest = principal \times rate \times time$$

$$\$2000 = \$100,000 \times rate \times 20/360$$

$$\$2000 = \$100,000 \times rate \times 0.056$$

$$\$2000 = \$5600 \times rate$$

$$\$2000/5600 = rate$$

$$0.35714 = rate$$

$$35.7\% = rate$$

When a negative cash flow prevents a retailer from taking advantage within their cash discount, it is often wise to borrow money. The cash-discount savings will exceed the interest paid on the loan, since annual borrowing rates are lower than annualized cash-discount rates. Borrowing for short periods to take advantage of cash discounts is a common retailing practice. Favorable dating arrangements yield another important fiscal advantage. Since cash discounts decrease the cost of goods sold, they increase gross margin and ultimately net profit.

TRANSPORTATION

Arrangements for transporting goods from the vendor to a retail distribution center is a function of the retailer's traffic department. Cost-effective transportation arrangements will effectively minimize the cost of goods sold, and maximize gross margin and net profit. Transportation costs are a function of the weight and bulk of the merchandise shipped, the distance between the supplier's and retailer's distribution centers, and the mode of transportation used.

The rates charged by the transportation industry were once regulated by federal agencies, such as the Interstate Commerce Commission and the Civil Aeronautics Board. However, legislation, such as the Motor Carrier Act and the Staggers Rail Act, has significantly deregulated the transportation industry. Deregulation has fostered intense competition among transporters of goods, or carriers, who can now tailor rates and services to match the needs of individual shippers. The complexities of a deregulated transportation environment have increased the importance of the traffic function in retail organizations. Traffic managers now have the ability to increase service and decrease costs by favorable negotiations with carriers just as buyers negotiate favorable terms with their vendors.

Transportation Terms

Transportation terms identify the bearer of the cost of shipping goods from the supplier to the retailer, as well as the point at which the title of the goods passes from one to the other. Though transportation arrangements are the responsibility of a store's traffic department, transportation terms are the responsibility of the buyer. The cost of transporting goods from suppliers is typically absorbed by the retailer. However, transportation terms are sometimes negotiated whereby the supplier absorbs all or part of the transportation costs. Since transportation costs increase the cost of goods sold, favorable transportation terms maximize gross margin and net profit.

FOB stands for *free on board*. Words, such as *origin, factory, destination,* or the name of a city, that follow FOB refer to the point to which a supplier pays transportation charges, and the point at which the title of the goods passes from the supplier to the retailer. *FOB factory* means that the retailer pays the transportation charges from the vendor's *factory* and assumes title to the goods at that point. *FOB destination* means that the vendor pays the transportation charges to the retail *destination* without relinquishing title until that point.

The point at which title transfers from the supplier to the retailer is important when determining the responsibility of lost or damaged goods. When title is transferred to the retailer at the point at which the goods are shipped, the retailer must pay for all of the goods shipped and obtain compensation from the freight carrier for lost or damaged goods. When title is not transferred to the retailer until the goods reach the store, the supplier is responsible for replacing lost or damaged goods and for recovering the loss from the carrier.

Sometimes suppliers establish an FOB point that equates the cost of transporting their goods to the cost of transporting competitors' goods. A Los Angeles-based supplier competing with a Chicago-based supplier for a Philadelphia retailer's business may ship goods *FOB Chicago*. Shared shipping responsibility can also be expressed as:

FOB factory (or store), charges shared: __ % factory, __ % store

The following is a list of agreements between retailers and their vendors that indicate payment responsibility for transportation costs, and the point at which the title of goods is transferred from the vendor to the retailer:

- *FOB origin, freight collect.* The retailer pays the freight charges and owns the goods while in transit.
- *FOB origin, freight prepaid.* The vendor pays the freight charges, but the retailer owns the goods while in transit.
- *FOB origin, freight prepaid and charged back.* The vendor pays the freight charges but is reimbursed for them by invoicing the retailer for the freight charges along with the merchandise. The retailer owns the goods while in transit.
- *FOB destination, freight collect.* The retailer pays the freight charges but the vendor owns the goods while in transit.
- *FOB destination, freight prepaid.* The vendor pays the freight charges and owns the goods while in transit.

- *FOB destination, freight collect and allowed.* The retailer pays the freight charges but is reimbursed for them by a charge-back deducted from the vendor's invoice. The vendor owns the goods while in transit.

Timing the shipment of goods is an important part of a merchandising strategy. Since orders are placed against an open-to-buy planned for a specific period, the timely arrival of merchandise ensures that inventory levels are appropriate to planned sales. Most purchase orders specify two dates to define the delivery parameters: a *do not ship before* date and a *do not ship after* date. Early arrival of goods can be as devastating as late arrival. Unless extra dating has been arranged, early shipments can lead to imbalanced cash flow. Storage is also an issue related to early shipments.

Transportation Arrangements

Transportation terms are a function of the retail buyer. Four transportation modes are used to transport goods from suppliers to retailers.

- *Motor carriers,* or truckers, are the most common form of transportation used to transport domestic goods from suppliers to retailers.[4] Motor carriers provide door-to-door service by picking up shipments from a supplier and delivering them directly to a retailer's distribution center. Motor carriers are also used to supplement other forms of transportation that do not offer door-to-door service. Consolidated Freightways and Roadway Express are among the nation's largest motor carriers.
- *Railroads* are an economical transportation mode used for long hauls of heavy, bulky commodities. Retailers transport goods by rail in conjunction with other transportation modes, such as trucks, reaping the economic advantages of rail and the door-to-door efficiencies of truck. The combination of two or more modes of transportation is called **intermodal transportation.**
- *Airlines* are the most rapid and most expensive transportation mode. Airlines expose shipments to the least potential for damage, pilferage, or obsolescence. They are only used to transport valuable or highly perishable goods.
- *Water carriers* are a slow but economic transportation mode used by retailers to import goods directly from foreign sources.

If you want your next apparel sail to take place without a wrinkle, try Seaboard Marine on for size.

Because with Seaboard Marine, your apparel gets quick clearance through customs, intermodal facilities which operate 24-hours a day and a computer tracking system which guarantees prompt and efficient delivery. In addition, Seaboard Marine offers the expertise which has made us a leading carrier at the Port of Miami for apparel and other 807/9802 commodities such as pharmaceuticals and electronics components.

So, set sail with the ocean transport company that's leading the way to and from Central America, Panama, Colombia, Peru, Chile, Venezuela, the Dominican Republic, and the Eastern Caribbean Islands.

Apparel Sail

SEABOARD
M A R I N E

3401-A NW 72nd Avenue, Miami, FL 33122
Phone: (305) 591-2521 • Fax: (305) 594-4534

Figure 14.4

Retailers use water carriers to directly import goods from foreign resources.

Several services are also available for shipping small packages, including the parcel-post service of the U.S. Postal Service and United Parcel Service, a private door-to-door service for transporting packages under 70 pounds. Federal Express and Emery Air Freight also provide expedient delivery of very small packages and documents, as do intercity bus lines such as Greyhound.

Transportation firms are categorized as common, contract, and private.

- **Common Carrier** A common carrier establishes uniform rates and schedules for all shippers.
- **Contract Carrier** A contract carrier negotiates individual agreements with shippers or small groups of shippers.
- **Private Carrier** Some organizations operate as private carriers, shipping goods with their own transportation equipment.

Figure 14.5

Ames is a retailer that operates as a private carrier, shipping goods from their distribution centers to stores with their own transportation equipment. *Photos courtesy of Ames Department Stores, Inc.*

Retailers sometimes contract the services of transportation intermediaries called **consolidators,** or *freight forwarders*. Consolidators combine less-than-truckload (ltl) shipments from multiple suppliers into truckload (tl) shipments, and then contract carriers to deliver the tl shipments to their retail destinations. Since ltl rates are higher than the tl rates, a consolidator makes a profit by charging shippers rates that are lower than the ltl rates, but higher than tl rates.

Time and cost are the two major factors considered when determining a transportation mode. In general, slower modes of transportation are more economical than more expeditious modes and are appropriate for transporting goods shipped in advance of their selling season. However, retailers often pay premium transportation rates to expedite the delivery of perishable goods or goods with immediate consumer demand. A retailer that desperately needs goods for an ad breaking in 48 hours will pay premium transportation rates to ensure delivery to cover the ad. Rapid transportation also decreases the amount of time that goods remain in the merchandise pipeline.

DISTRIBUTION CENTERS

Single-unit retail operations ship goods from suppliers directly to their stores at which point they are unpacked, ticketed, and prepared for the selling floor. Most multiunit retailers ship goods to a central distribution

Company Profile 14.1

Bon-Ton—The Shortest Distance Between Two Points

Some retailers use sophisticated software systems to determine optimal route and load combinations for the shipment of merchandise to their stores.

Bon-Ton Stores, a York, Pennsylvania-based department-store chain that operates stores in the Northeast, has achieved considerable benefits through the use of an inbound-outbound freight-optimization and logistical-management software package called Maxpayload. Based upon a library of transportation algorithms, the system creates optimal combinations of shipments to develop multiple origin-destination shipment plans. A mileage calculation engine determines point-to-point mileage using map and mileage software packages. A carrier selection/assignment module determines shipping costs and then selects a list of transportation firms offering the lowest prices and best service ranked in order of preference. Other system features include a purchase-order verification and tracking manager, a cost allocator, and the ability to manage seasonal delivery patterns. Another module simplifies the freight-auditing process by tracking carrier invoice payments, vendor charge-backs against violations of shipping terms, and claims against missing or damaged shipments.

After implementing the system, Bon-Ton shaved an average of two days off its deliveries from manufacturers to its distribution centers. By identifying the lowest-cost carriers and modes of transportation, the software paid for itself in less than seven months.[1]

Source:
1 Ross, J. (August 1998). Routing software helps retailers curb transportation costs. Stores. pp. 98-99.

point where they are processed and then distributed to stores. The **distribution center** (DC) performs critical inventory-management functions by expediting processing to ensure the timely arrival of goods in stores, and by working closely with buyers to resolve issues related to damaged receipts, short shipments, and supplier substitutions. The following is a list of the major functions performed by retail distribution centers:

- *Receiving*—Unloading shipments at the dock.
- *Checking*—Matching the contents of shipments against a packing slip. Quality assurance is often a part of this function.
- *Marking*—Price labeling or ticketing the merchandise.
- *Putaway*—Warehousing basic merchandise for future replenishment of stores, or bulk items, such as furniture, for direct shipment to customers.

- *Picking*—Distributing putaway goods to stores or customers.
- *Distribution*—Allocating shipments to stores.
- *Shipping*—Routing merchandise to stores.
- *Vendor Return*—Processing returns of damaged or slow-selling goods to suppliers for credit.
- *Traffic*—Coordinating the inbound delivery from suppliers and outbound shipments to stores.

VENDOR PARTNERSHIPS

Vendor partnerships are collaborations between retailers and their suppliers that go beyond the traditional interactions between the two. These partnerships often involve strategies for pumping goods through the distribution channel more rapidly and efficiently than in nonpartnered interactions. The net results are often reduced distribution costs, better inventory control, increased sales, and improved gross margin and GMROI.

Floor-Ready Merchandise

Floor-ready merchandise (FRM) involves a negotiated agreement whereby the vendor agrees to package, case, fold, hang, and /or ticket merchandise in a such a way that it is ready for the selling floor upon its arrival at the store's distribution center. FRM eliminates redundancies. For instance, hanging goods are sometime shipped to retailers on flimsy shipping hangers that are then replaced with higher-quality selling-floor hangers at the retailer's distribution center. FRM is shipped on selling-floor hangers thus eliminating the labor-intensive hanger changing process at the distribution center.[5]

FRM also involves **source tagging** of goods with antitheft or price tags. Tagging is a function that a vendor can perform more cost effectively than a retailer as part of its own ticketing or packaging process. Source tagging expedites the processing of goods at the retail distribution center.[6] Mervyn's, a division of Target, requires source tagging of all of its more than 1200 vendors.[7]

FRM can also extend to the manner in which goods are packed for shipment to the retailer. Though some vendors **case pack,** or *prepack,* shipments with a standard assortment of sizes, colors, and styles, FRM assortments are packed specific to the replenishment needs of individ-

MOOTSIES TOOTSIES			
Shoes to Die For			
SIZE RUN AND BREAKDOWN INFORMATION:			
RUN	**WIDTH**	**SIZE RUN**	**BREAKDOWN**
			5 - 6 - 7 - 8 - 9 - 10
D	M	6/10 × 12	1 1 1 2 2 2 2 1
R	M	6/10 × 18	1 2 2 3 3 3 2 2
G	M	5/10 × 18	1 2 5 5 3 2
CD	M	6/10 × 18	2 5 5 4 2
KT	M	6/10 × 12	1 3 3 3 2
AA	N	7/10 × 6	1 1 1 1 1 1

Figure 14.6

Shoe vendors case pack shipments with standard assortments of sizes.

ual stores. These shipments can be sent directly to stores without being sorted at retail distribution centers. This facilitates **cross docking** whereby the distribution center functions like a trucking terminal with merchandise arriving in a truck in one bay, and going out in another truck in another bay with virtually no processing in between.[8]

The benefits of FRM are far-reaching. Distribution center operating costs can be reduced by as much as 80 percent and the average amount of time that goods remain in a DC can decrease from a few days to a few hours. The long-term result is an increase in turnover and GMROI.[9]

Markdown Allowances

Though buyers hope that goods will sell at prices consistent with their gross-margin objectives, each order is a gamble in that some of goods may eventually require drastic markdowns. Vendors can share this risk in two ways:

- Return agreements whereby the retailer is allowed to return unsold goods after a specified period.

- Markdown allowances whereby the vendor compensates the retailer for markdowns. The compensation is often based on the difference between a guaranteed gross margin and the actual gross margin with an allowance against future purchases.

S P I   a n d   F l o o r - R e a d y   M e r c h a n d i s e

Seattle Pacific Industries uses a supply-chain management system to bolster its floor-ready-merchandise effort. The Seattle-based supplier of men's and women's jeans and sportswear distributes products under labels such as Unionbay, ReUnion, Nautica Marine Denim, and Sergio Valente.

SPI's inventory-management system enables the company to track floor-ready requirements from point of production through point of distribution. In so doing, SPI can often pass the responsibility for certain floor-ready requirements back to the manufacturer instead of performing all of the floor-ready functions as goods are being distributed to stores. For instance, assume that 2000 shirts are ordered from a single manufacturer for several retailers, and that some of those retailers want the shirt on the same hanger. This specification can be integrated into the production requirements so that the shirts can be put on hangers at the factory-level instead of by SPI at distribution level. The system works with radio-frequency scanners that scan products as they are shipped from manufacturing operations throughout North America and Asia. This provides information about the location of product far back in the supply chain, thus allowing for better reaction to customer needs throughout the entire distribution process.

SPI customers include Dillard's, Federated Department Stores, and Nordstrom.[1]

Source:
1 Hye, J. (June 10, 1998). SPI Focus: Getting floor-ready. Women's Wear Daily. p. 16.

In essence, markdown allowances are a strategy through which a retailer negotiates more favorable wholesale prices. Markdown allowances are a sensitive issue between retailers and their vendors. New vendors feel that the only way that they will ever conduct business with some retailers is with the promise of markdown dollars. Retailers claim that they need the insurance of markdown dollars until a new vendor proves its worth. Vendors resent sharing markdown expenses feeling that markdowns are often attributable to factors controllable by the retailer, such as poor merchandise presentation and inadequate selling floor coverage.[10]

Promotional Support

Many vendors offer retailers promotional opportunities to enhance the recognition and sale of their products in stores. **Cooperative advertising**

Company Profile 14.3

Sensomatic—A Floor-Ready Advantage

Sensormatic, the Deerfield Beach, Florida-based purveyor of electronic article surveillance (EAS) antitheft tags, has developed new technology that may revolutionize the way that apparel retailers protect their goods from shoplifters.

The Ultra-Max system uses acousto-magnetic technology in a 1.5" x 0.5" tag designed to be embedded within a garment label, waist ticket, or pocket splashers. Some suppliers "double-tag" for extra security placing EAS devices in more than one location on the same item. Ultra-Max tags are supersensitive and detectable in metal shopping carts, foil-lined bags, and clothing that professional shoplifters use to shield hard-tagged merchandise from being detected.

The new tags are a marked improvement over Sensormatic's hard tags that detract from a garment's appearance, can damage fabric, and are cumbersome to customers who try on the garment. There are other advantages to the retailer. Acousto-magnetic tags can be deactivated without being removed thereby increasing processing time at point of sale. Because the tags are applied by the vendor, retailers avoid the labor-intensive cost of tagging goods at their distribution centers.

The cost of source tagging is a point of negotiation between retailers and suppliers. Suppliers with little leverage often assume the entire cost of tagging as an incentive for retailers to carry their lines. In other cases retailers often split the cost with the supplier.[1]

Source:

1 Staffs. (June 1996). *Retailers Test Source-Tagging of Apparel.* Stores. *pp. 60-61.*

is an agreement between a retailer and a vendor to share advertising expense. The level of a vendor's participation in a cooperative-advertising program is based on a retailer's purchases over a specified time period, usually a year. Most cooperative-advertising programs place restrictions on the items advertised and the advertising medium and schedule. Some vendors prepare generic advertising for their products that retailers can adapt for their use with tag lines, such as "Available at all Jacobson's stores," dubbed onto electronic ads or store logos pasted onto print ads. Retailers save considerable advertising production costs by using vendor-prepared advertising.

Other forms of promotional support by vendors include:

- *Product demonstrations:* Some vendors provide demonstrators to show the effective use of their product or product line in stores. Cosmetic makeovers and countertop-appliance demonstrations are common vendor-sponsored demonstrations in department stores.

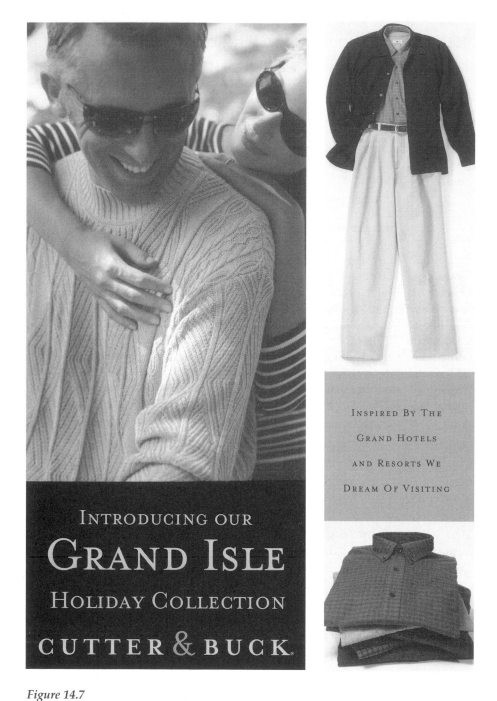

INTRODUCING OUR

GRAND ISLE

HOLIDAY COLLECTION

CUTTER & BUCK.

INSPIRED BY THE
GRAND HOTELS
AND RESORTS WE
DREAM OF VISITING

Figure 14.7

An example of a cooperative advertising program from Cutter and Buck. *Courtesy of Cutter and Buck.*

- *Premiums:* A **premium** is a product offered without charge or at a very low retail price to customers who have made a minimum purchase within a product line. Advertising for premiums often reads: "Yours free with any $__ purchase of__" or "Yours for $__ with any $___ purchase of__." Premiums are common in the prestige cosmetics industry where a free premium is called a **gift with purchase,** or *GWP,* and a paid-for premium is called a **purchase with purchase,** or *PWP.*
- *Samples:* Samples are small quantities of a product offered without charge to customers independent of a purchase within a line. Samples are common in the prestige fragrance industry.
- *Contest and drawings:* **Contests** are promotional activities that require the demonstration of a skill. **Drawings,** or *sweepstakes* are games of chance. Contests are popular for children's products.
- *Displays and exhibits:* Some vendors loan retailers museum-like exhibits for use in displays or in conjunction with a vendor promotion.

Some vendors provide point-of-purchase signage and fixtures to enhance the sale of their product line in stores, a topic of discussion in Chapter 16. Other vendors sponsor training schools for salespeople to highlight new products and provide selling tips. Some vendors pay commissions or other incentives to the retail salespeople who sell their product line.

Electronic Data Interchange

Electronic data interchange (EDI) is a partnership between a retailer and a supplier that involves a backward flow of customer-purchase information through the distribution pipeline beginning at the retailer's point of sale. The partners use the information to execute their function more efficiently. EDI is sometimes extended to include vendors' suppliers, such as fabric mills.

EDI involves developing model assortments of product styles, sizes, and colors by store based on sales histories, sales projections, desired turnover, and lead time for delivery. Product information is captured electronically at point of sale and is periodically transmitted to suppliers who then replenish the depleted inventory. EDI is most often used for basic reorderable goods with broad assortments of styles, sizes, or colors, such as cosmetics and hosiery. Dillard's also uses EDI to test fashion goods at the beginning of the season and then reorders the best-selling items.

QUICK RESPONSE — PILOT PROGRAM									
Actual Results									
	On-	On-	**Sales**		Weeks	Inventory	Stock-	Lost	New
Date	hand	Order	Curr.	Avg.	Supply	Turns	Outs	Sales	Order
3/11	1,120	0	50	69.0	16.2	2.7	0	0	33
3/18	799	93	325	94.6	8.4	4.1	1	3	105
3/26	924	138	29	88.6	10.4	4.1	1	2	6
4/3	836	111	95	89.2	9.4	4.3	0	1	36
4/10	857	36	38	85.2	10.0	4.2	0	0	15
4/17	831	51	37	81.8	10.2	4.2	0	0	174
4/24	674	39	193	89.2	7.6	4.7	0	0	174
5/3	816	198	79	88.6	9.2	4.8	0	0	45
5/9	726	207	89	88.6	8.2	4.9	0	0	57

Figure 14.8

EDI increased the turnover of a major retailer's hosiery department from 2.7 to 4.9 while reducing stock-outs and lost sales. *Reprinted by permission.* Chain Store Age, *March 1991. Copyright Lebhar-Friedman, Inc. 425 Park Avenue, New York, NY 10022.*

There are several positive outcomes associated with EDI including:

- *Improved in-stock position.* The in-stock position of EDI merchandise is 95 percent or better since assortments are rapidly replenished as merchandise is sold.[11] The in-stock position of non-EDI merchandise is often as low as 50 percent. Fewer stockouts result in increased sales, since customers are likely to find their choice of size, color, and style.[12]
- *Better inventory management.* EDI improves turnover since fast-selling goods are re-ordered while slow-turning goods are not. EDI also enhances space productivity since slow sellers are edited from assortments freeing up valuable shelf and floor space for more productive goods. Frequent small orders also reduce the amount of inventory carried.
- *Shortened lead time.* Because time-consuming manual ordering tasks are eliminated, some retailers experience as much as a 50 percent reduction in lead time by implementing EDI. J.C. Penney developed an EDI program with Haggar Apparel that accelerated delivery to the selling floor by ten days. Sales increased by 11 percent with 19 percent less inventory on hand.[13]
- *Greater efficiency.* EDI eliminates errors due to manual counts, data entry, and illegible orders. By reducing administrative tasks, EDI

permits buyers to concentrate on selecting merchandise and developing merchandising programs.

• *Increased profitability.* A higher markup is maintained on EDI merchandise since only merchandise that is selling is reordered. Dillard's estimates that the maintained markup on EDI merchandise is 3 to 4 percent higher than on non-EDI merchandise, and that every dollar invested in EDI-replenished goods is 16.3 percent more profitable than non-EDI goods.

Advance shipping notices (ASN) and shippers container marking (SCM) are two technologically advanced concepts that have enhanced EDI's success. An ASN is a supplier's electronic notification to a retailer that an order has been shipped. SCM involves identifying the contents of cartons by bar codes that are scanned into a retailer's inventory upon receipt. The cartons are then sent directly to stores without further distribution and processing. This paperless transaction speeds up the flow of merchandise while significantly reducing processing expenses.[14]

Suppliers also benefit from EDI. EDI provides them with sales information that can be used to manage inventories and plan production. To complete the trading linkage, some suppliers develop similar partnerships with their own suppliers matching consumer demand at one end of the merchandise pipeline to the availability of raw materials at the other. The standardization of EDI forms and procedures has facilitated the widespread application of EDI. Once the property of large retailers and suppliers, EDI is now technologically and fiscally feasible for small retailers and suppliers.

EDI requires a bond of trust between the retailer and supplier. The retailer must feel confident that a vendor will not share its sales information with competitive retailers and that the actual carton content matches what is indicated on the SCM. Some predict that EDI will eventually become a condition of transacting business with many retailers. Dillard's encourages EDI partnerships by charging vendors a handling fee for every purchase order not generated through EDI.[15]

The Vendor Matrix

A **vendor matrix** is a list of preferred vendors selected at conglomerate level. The decision to include a vendor in a matrix is based on the product line's compatibility with the organization's merchandising objectives,

Federated Merchandising

VENDOR FAIR

New Vendors Welcome

While we continue to strengthen and expand our relationships with existing vendors on behalf of all Federated divisions except Bloomingdale's, Federated Merchandising is reaching out to identify new resources (excluding private label) who can also supply us with quality merchandise for our customer, as well as fill gaps in our vendor palette. So we're hosting our first-ever Federated Merchandise New Vendor Fair during the week of March 27. This event is open exclusively to resources not currently shipping to Federated or Macy's -- including those who have never done business with Federated or Macy's, as well as those who are not holding orders or who have not shipped to Federated or Macy's in the last six months.

We'll provide space in our New York offices to potential new vendors who want to show us their goods. Appointments will be set for one-hour blocks between 8 a.m. and 7 p.m. throughout the week of March 27, with each day set aside for a different family of business. Shopping the merchandise will be merchants from Federated Merchandising, who are responsible for identifying and evaluating goods bought by most Federated divisions (excluding Bloomingdale's.)

The following schedule has been established for each family of business:

-    **Monday, March 27**   **Men's and Children's**
-    **Tuesday, March 28**   **Home Merchandise (home textiles, tabletop, furniture, housewares, gifts, electronics)**
-    **Wednesday, March 29**   **Ready-to-Wear**
-    **Thursday, March 30**   **Ready-to-Wear (a.m.) Center Core (p.m.)**
-    **Friday, March 31**   **Center Core (shoes, accessories, cosmetics and intimate)**

Figure 14.9

Federated Department Stores hosts periodic vendor fairs to recruit new vendors.

favorable price negotiations, and various forms of vendor support, in exchange for a retailer's commitment to space and established inventory levels. Some organizations limit their buyers to conducting business only with matrix vendors. Retailers have reduced the number of vendors with whom they conduct business by as much as 50 percent as a result of adopting a matrix. These streamlined vendor structures are criticized as unholy alliances between large retailers and large suppliers that limit business opportunities for small suppliers. Some feel that a matrix transforms a buying function into an order-filling function by limiting a buyer's autonomy.[16] To negate this criticism, some retailers host periodic vendor fairs to give vendors outside the matrix the opportunity to pitch their goods to buyers for possible inclusion in their assortments.[17]

Vendor Relations

Maximizing consumer sales is an objective that is common to both retailers and their suppliers. Many vendors realize the importance of teamwork in achieving this common objective. To deal with the prob-

THE TJX COMPANIES, INC.
Framingham, Massachusetts

T·J·MAXX   Marshalls·   HomeGoods·   WINNERS   TKMAXX   A.J.Wright·

To Our Manufacturers And Suppliers: Statement of Policy Concerning Gifts

We are taking this opportunity to restate our policy concerning gift-giving, not only during the forthcoming holiday season, but at all times of the year, on any occasion. Gifts, no matter how well intentioned by the donor, tend to shake the moral structure of the firmest business foundations by substituting subjective emotions and motives for objective judgment based on service, quality and price.

Accordingly, for the mutual protection of our suppliers, our associates and the Company, we prohibit our associates from accepting gifts, gratuities, payments or favors of any kind. Any gifts received by our associates will be returned to the donor or donated to charitable organizations. Our associates are advised that violation of this policy is considered to be a grievous matter.

We call upon you to assist us and our associates by refraining from giving or offering such gifts. Your awareness of and cooperation with this policy will foster the continuation of fair business practices that favor our close association.

Best wishes for a happy holiday season and a prosperous New Year.

Bernard Cammarata
Chairman of the Board

Edmond J. English
President and Chief Executive Officer

The Marmaxx Group/T.J. Maxx/Marshalls
HG Buying, Inc./HomeGoods, Inc.
Winners Apparel, Ltd.   T.K. Maxx
Concord Buying Group Inc./A. J. Wright

Figure 14.10

To avoid conflicts of interest, most retailers prohibit buyers from accepting gifts from vendors. © 2000 *The TJX Companies, Inc.*

lem of buyer turnover, Liz Claiborne Hosiery helps new buyers through their period of adjustment by assisting them with six-month plans, writing orders, and monitoring sales and inventory.[18]

Though retailers and their suppliers share common sales goals, their individual profit objectives are sometimes a source of conflict. A supplier's profit is derived from selling goods to retailers at the *highest* possible prices, while a retailer's profit is derived from purchasing goods from suppliers at the *lowest* possible prices. To circumvent conflict, some retailers publish vendor-relations guidelines that establish parameters for professional interactions. For instance, to avoid conflicts of interest, many retailers prohibit buyers from accepting gifts or any form of hospitality from vendors, other than an occasional lunch.

In spite of these provisions, interactions between retailers and their suppliers are sometimes adversarial. Vendors provoke retailers by shipping short, shipping late, or making random substitutes for out-of-stock goods. Retailers often retaliate by levying charge-back penalties for incomplete orders or damaged or mislabeled goods. A vendor once reported a $50.50 charge back on an item with an upside down label: $0.50 was for the error and $50 was for a minimum penalty charge. Another supplier reported a $10,000 charge back on a $20,000 order for goods that arrived two weeks late. The vendor disputed the charge back because the goods eventually sold out at regular price, even though they arrived late.[19, 20]

Other transgressions can be traced to the retailer. Common abuses to vendors include taking cash discounts on invoices after cash-discount periods have expired, returning as flawed merchandise that was damaged on the selling floor, and canceling ready-to-be-shipped orders with little notice. A New York State Supreme Court judge found Wal-Mart's cancellation clause in its purchase order "unconscionable" due to the financial ramifications to the vendor. The clause gave Wal-Mart the right to cancel an order any time prior to shipment, regardless of the stage of production.[21] In 1997, 44 states and the District of Columbia and Puerto Rico filed an antitrust lawsuit against Toys "R" Us for using its clout as the nation's second largest toy retailer to intimidate its suppliers. The suit alleged that Toys "R" Us threatened to discontinue goods that suppliers shipped to warehouse clubs to avoid being undersold.[22]

SUMMARY POINTS

- Quantity and seasonal discounts are reductions in the cost of merchandise that are mutually advantageous to the vendor and the retailer.
- Dating is the time period allowed for the payment of an invoice. Favorable dating terms reduce the cost of goods sold and improve a retailer's cash flow.

- Transportation terms identify the bearer of the cost of shipping goods from the vendor to the retailer, as well as the point at which the title of the goods passes from one to the other. Time and cost are the two factors that are considered when determining a transportation mode.
- Vendor partnerships are collaborations between retailers and their suppliers to reduce distribution costs, control inventory, increase sales, and improve gross margin and GMROI.
- Electronic data interchange is a trading partnership among marketing channel members whereby each member can access customer purchase information to execute more efficiently their function in the supply pipeline.
- A vendor matrix is a list of a retailer's preferred merchandise resources.
- Retailers and vendors should work together cooperatively to achieve their goals.

KEY TERMS AND CONCEPTS

advance dating	discount	premium
anticipation	distribution center	private carrier
case pack	drawing	proximo dating
cash dating	EOM notation	purchase order
cash discount	electronic data	purchase with
cash discount date	interchange (EDI)	purchase (PWP)
cash discount period	extra dating	quantity discount
cash on delivery (COD)	floor-ready	receipt-of-goods
common carrier	merchandise (FRM)	(ROG) dating
consignment	free on board (FOB)	regular dating
consolidator	gift with purchase (GWP)	seasonal discount
contest	intermodal transportation	source tagging
contract carrier	invoice	vendor matrix
cooperative advertising	memorandum	vendor partnership
cross docking	minimum order	
date of invoice (DOI)	net payment date	
dating	net payment period	

FOR DISCUSSION

1. Discuss several categories of merchandise and the characteristics of each that determine how they are transported such as size, value, perishability, and source.
2. Though dating varies significantly by category of merchandise, it is relatively consistent within a category. Can you think of reasons for the discrepancies among product categories?
3. What are the long-term disadvantages of poor vendor relationships?
4. Ask a local retailer to identify some EDI-linked product lines. Compare the retailer's in-stock position of EDI and non-EDI merchandise in the same category relative to color, size, and style assortments. What do you observe?

ENDNOTES

1. Units shipped times unit cost.
2. Staff. (December 9, 1991). K-Swiss offers fill-in terms for volume orders. *Footwear News*. p. 16.
3. Time is expressed in days divided by 360.
4. Staff. (February 1991). Ernst & Young 1990 Survey of Distribution Transportation Warehouse Trends in Retail. *Stores*. p. A14.
5. Glusac, E. (March 26, 1996). Floor-ready becoming industry norm. *Women's Wear Daily*. p. 19.
6. Brookman, F. (October 1998). Retailers, Suppliers sort out issue of who pays for source tagging. *Stores*. p. 84.
7. Power, D. (August 5, 1998). Stores stress source-tagging. *Women's Wear Daily*.
8. Ross, J. (December 1997). Office Depot scores major cross-docking gains. *Stores*. pp. 39-40.
9. Reda, S. (April 1994). Floor-ready merchandise. *Stores*. p. 41–44.
10. Moin, D. Markdowns: Designer dilemma. *Women's Wear Daily*.
11. To have an in-stock position of 100 percent, an availability of *every* item *all* the time, would require excessive inventory and result in low turnover.
12. Tosh, M. (April 23, 1996). KSA: Retailers plan to step up EDI. *Women's Wear Daily*. p. 13.
13. Staff. (December 8, 1991). Tracking fashion technology. *Discount Store News*. pp. A20-A21.
14. Ross, J. (September 1996). Are partnerships for real? *Stores*. pp. 24-30.
15. Struensee, C. Dillard's leans on vendors to get with efficiencies. *Women's Wear Daily*.
16. Moin, D. (January 16, 1998). David Farrell: One tough guy. *Women's Wear Daily*. pp. 1, 4-5.

17. Monget, K. (April 13, 1998). No matrix at Kmart. *Women's Wear Daily.* p. 10.

18. Feitelberg, R. (June 21, 1999). Coping with buyer shuffle. Women's Wear Daily. p. 10.

19. Ryan, T. (June 1, 1998). Chargeback debate roars on, a practice that remains a fact of life. Women's Wear Daily. pp. 1, 15-16.

20. Duff, C. (October 27, 1995). Big stores' outlandish demands alienate small suppliers. *The Wall Street Journal.* pp. B1, B5.

21. Staff. (November 30, 1994). Wal-Mart cancel clause "grossly unfair" says court. *Women's Wear Daily.* p. 3.

22. Neumeister, L (November 18, 1997). Suit: Toys "R" Us not playing fair with competitors. *The Boston Globe.* p. C3.

MERCHANDISE CONTROL AND PRESENTATION

- **Merchandising Controls and Report Analysis**

- **Store Layout and Merchandise Presentation**

chapter fifteen

MERCHANDISING CONTROLS AND REPORT ANALYSIS

The word *control* has negative connotations when linked to restrictions of autonomy or creativity. However, controls are critical merchandising tools that provide information about current status and future planning while ascertaining that retailers do not waver from their charted course. Chapter 15 covers some of the ways that controls are used for effective decision making and for reacting to emerging problems.

After you have read this chapter, you will be able to discuss:

The control function in a retail organization.

Control standards.

The analysis of control reports and their use as decision-making tools.

CONTROL STANDARDS

Control involves measuring actual performance against goals or standards and reacting to the causes of any deviations from those goals. Control is a three-step process that includes:

- Establishing goals or standards
- Measuring deviations of actual performance from standards
- Reacting to the deviations

Controls enable decision-makers to react to problems before they become critical.

A **control standard** is a reference point or benchmark used to measure performance. Plans are standards. A *$2.0 million sales goal for August, a $25,000 open-to-buy for March,* and *projected net income of 4 percent of net sales* are all standards. Like plans, standards are often based on comparable prior performance. *Last year's girls department sales during the week prior to school opening* is a standard for measuring *this year's girls department sales during the week prior to school opening.*

The aggregate performance of similar business units is often used as a standard. The percentage sales increase (or decrease) for *all* stores in a chain can be used as a standard to measure the sales performance of *individual* stores. **Penetration** is a measure of the performance of a single business unit as percentage of the aggregate performance of all similar business units. A *4 percent penetration* can refer to the performance of a store that has generated 4 percent of the sales of all stores in a chain or a category of merchandise that has generated 4 percent of the sales of all categories in a department.

Internal standards are derived from data obtained from within an organization. **Industry standards** are derived outside an organization, often by a trade association. The National Retail Federation annually publishes the *Department and Specialty Store Merchandising and Operating Results,* or *MOR,* a listing of industry standards for maintained markup, markdowns, shortage, gross margin, and turnover, compiled by merchandise category and sales volume.

The validity of a comparison to a standard is based on the similarity of the standard to that which is being measured. To quote a trite but apropos cliché, the comparison must be "apples to apples and oranges to oranges." Comparing this year's *July* better sportswear gross margin to last year's *September* gross margin is an invalid comparison in that July gross margins are heavily eroded by end-of-season markdowns.

Comparing the garden-shop sales of a full-line discount store to the sales of *all* garden shops in the chain is not as valid as a comparison to stores in the same geographic region. Regional weather conditions dramatically affect horticulture sales, making a comparison outside the region less valid than a comparison within the region.

A standard is sometimes validated by comparing actual performance to multiple standards. Assume that actual sales for a month are 20 percent under plan and 10 percent over last year. The 30 percent discrepancy between the comparisons to the two standards may be an indication that the plan for this year was unrealistically optimistic.

Multiple standard comparisons sometimes reveal problems veiled by a comparison to a single standard. Assume that a shoe store's actual December sales exceeded plan by 7 percent and last year's sales by 7 percent. The store manager was delighted by this performance until comparing the store's performance to the chain's performance. The manager found that the sales for all stores exceeded plan by 12 percent and last year by 14 percent. The store lagged behind the chain's performance relative to both plan sales and last year's sales by 5 percentage points.

Deviations

A **deviation** is a discrepancy between actual performance and a standard. If planned sales for a week are $2000 and actual sales are $2500, then there is a $500 deviation from planned sales. A deviation's direction is expressed by attributing negative values to deviations less than a standard and positive values to deviations greater than a standard. The direction of a deviation is a performance indicator. A +*$500* deviation from planned sales is favorable while a −*$500* deviation is not. Not all positive deviations are desirable. A +*$500* deviation from planned expenses is not favorable while a −*$500* deviation is.

The degree of a deviation is expressed by dividing the deviation by the standard and multiplying by 100 to convert to a percentage:

$$percent\ of\ deviation = \frac{amount\ of\ deviation}{standard} \times 100$$

The +$500 deviation from plan sales represents a +25 percent increase over plan:

$$percent\ of\ deviation = \frac{+\$500}{\$2000} \times 100$$

MULTIPLE MEASURES

It is often wise to review both dollar and percentage deviations together to determine the significance of the deviations. Consider a comparison of November's plan to actual sales for two outerwear categories in Table A. The +/- *percent* column shows a percentage shortfall in rainwear that is twice the percentage shortfall of wool coats. However, the +/- *$* column indicated that the sales shortfall of wool coats is far more serious in terms of dollars than the sales shortfall of rainwear. Since wool coat sales were planned significantly higher than the rainwear sales, the -10 percent deviation from the wool coat sales plan represents a far greater sales deficit in dollars than the -20 percent deviation from the rainwear sales plan.

The situation is characteristic of a store in a northern climate where November sales projections for wool coats far exceed sales projections for lightweight rainwear. As depicted in Table B, the scenario would reverse itself in April when sales projections for rainwear exceed sales projections for wool coats. In this case, the -20 percent and $10,000 sales shortfall in rainwear would be more distressing than the -40 percent and $2000 sales shortfall in wool coats.

Table A   NOVEMBER

Category	Plan	Actual	+/- $	+/- %
Wool Coats	$100,000	$90,000	-$10,000	-10%
Rainwear	$10,000	$8,000	-$2,000	-20%

Table B   APRIL

Category	Plan	Actual	+/- $	+/- %
Wool Coats	$5,000	$3,000	-$2,000	-40%
Rainwear	$50,000	$40,000	-$10,000	-20%

percent of deviation $= 25\%$

The resulting percentage expresses the degree of the deviation. A $500 increase on a $2500 sales plan (+20%) is more impressive than a $500 increase on a $25,000 sales plan (+2%).

Control Objectivity

Qualitative controls measure performance descriptively: for example, a customer satisfaction survey that asks respondents to rate a store's customer service as *excellent, very good, fair,* or *poor*. Qualitative ratings are subjective in that one person's perception of "good" may differ from another person's. **Quantitative controls** measure performance numerically. Quantitative controls are objective. The calculation of a *5 percent increase over last year's sales* will yield the same figure regardless of who performs the calculation.

Quantitative controls reduce the emotion in the communication between managers. A store manager may complain to a buyer that inventory is *low*. The buyer may argue that the inventory is *not low*. *Low* and *not low* are biased qualitative assessments. The store manager's assessment is biased by a single-store perspective. The buyer's assessment is biased by a multistore perspective. Each party should quantitatively define *low* and *not low* to resolve the dispute objectively. Comparing the store's stock-to-sales ratio to the chain's or comparing the percentage of inventory that the store owns to the percentage of the chain's sales that the store generates is a rational quantitative stance.

Control Intervals

Controls are established at specific time intervals such as hourly, daily, weekly, monthly, quarterly, seasonally, or annually. The frequency of a control is based on the likelihood and/or significance of deviations from standards. Inventory that turns 26 times a year requires more frequent monitoring than an inventory that turns only twice a year. Controls of fast-turning inventories must be established at short intervals to ensure that minimum stock levels are maintained and that replenishment orders are placed before stockouts occur. In general, controls should be established at intervals that will allow a timely reaction to meaningful deviations from standards.

Some controls encompass multiple time intervals. Sales are often controlled by week, month, season and year. Multiple time-interval comparisons broaden the perspective of an assessment. The trauma of a 50 percent deviation from plan sales for a week is diminished by the fact that sales are +20 percent to plan for the month and +15 percent to plan for the season.

Control Levels

Controls are established at the same organizational levels as plans. In most retail organizations sales and inventory are controlled by category, department and division, as well as at store, district, and regional levels. Like plans, controls are used by managers relative to the nature and scope of their responsibility. A store manager may monitor a store's sales by category daily. A district manager may monitor total store sales daily. A regional manager may monitor total store sales weekly. The time constraints of the workday make it impossible for a regional manager of 100 stores to monitor daily the sales of every category in every store. Store managers can perform this task more effectively in that they have a narrower scope of responsibility.

REPORTS

Retail organizations compile various types of management reports that reflect the status of sales, inventory, and profitability by comparing actual performance to standards *(last year, plan)* for defined business units *(store, category of merchandise)* for specified periods *(month, year)*. Some management report titles that are common to many retail organizations include *Best Seller Report*, *Inventory Position Report*, and *Monthly Sales Report*.

Compiling reports was once a labor-intensive, error-prone process that involved tedious paper chasing. Today, computerized inventory management systems compile data into reliable, easily accessible, real-

WHAT ARE BEST-SELLERS?

- Unit sales of 50 or more
- Dollar sales of $1000 or more
- Sell through of 30% or better
- In stock less than 4 weeks
- On hand of at least 10 units

time reports that allow store managers to monitor best-sellers and salespeople's productivity, and to locate merchandise for customers in other stores in the chain. Buyers rely on reports to review sales factors such as location, price, and vendor to make strategic merchandising decisions relative to reordering, transferring, or marking down merchandise. Computerization has facilitated inventory tracking at very precise levels. A men's dress-shirt inventory that was once manually tracked by units and store can be tracked by price, vendor, color, and sleeve and collar size with less effort.

CHECKLIST FOR REVIEWING PROBLEM DEPARTMENTS

Is the percentage of stock appropriate to the percentage of sales? If not, how much stock must be obtained to reach an adequate level? Where will it come from? What is the on-order status?

Analyze the sales by classification. Are poorly performing classes adequately stocked? Is the stock in well-performing classifications depleted?

Are all classes productive? If not, should the nonproductive classes be eliminated so that the productive ones can be further developed through additional floor space and inventory?

Is basic merchandise filled in? *Every* size, color, style?

Are groups broken? Is "piecy" merchandise frustrating customers, inhibiting presentation, tying up inventory dollars, and slowing your turnover?

What are the company's best-sellers? Are they your best-sellers? If not, why? Location? Stock level?

What are your competitors selling?

If stock levels are adequate, can you trade off slow-moving merchandise for more productive merchandise?

Are markdowns being taken in a timely manner? Have you taken a disproportionately large or small amount of markdowns?

Walk the floor. Has prime floor space been dedicated to your most productive classes, resources, and items? Have presentation standards interfered with moving goods quickly?

Figure 15.1

One retailer's checklist for reviewing sales and inventory reports.

Exception Reports

A wealth of readily accessible information has resulted in report proliferation in some retail organizations. To avoid this, some retailers generate **exception reports** that include only major deviations from standards, bypassing minor ones. A sales report may include only deviations that are 10 percent over plan and 10 percent under plan. Filtering out deviations, within a −10 percent to +10 percent range reduces the size of the report and the amount of time needed to review it.

Note that even "good" deviations (+10 percent to planned sales) should be included in an exception report. Since inventory allocations are predicated on planned sales, a store that is running significantly ahead of plan is likely to be underinventoried.

REPORT FORMATS AND ANALYSIS

Though all reports are used to assess performance and as sources of information on which to effect decisions, report formats vary from one organization to another. Though most retailers generate reports of sales, inventory, and profitability, reports differ relative to the level of information, format, frequency, and application. The following are descriptions of actual reports obtained from several retail organizations. The company names have been changed to ensure the confidentiality of the information. The reports represent an infinitesimally small sample of the myriad of report types and formats used by retail organizations.

Turnover Report

Davidson's Department Store generates an annual turnover for more than 500 categories of merchandise at its 12 specialty department stores. Figure 15.2 is a section of the 2001 report for the junior department's knit top category.

Features of the Report   The report includes this year's and last year's sales and average inventory by store and chain, and the percentage change to last year for each. Turnover for this year and last year is calculated by store and chain. Sales and turnover performance can be assessed by comparing a store's performance to the chain's. Turnover issues can be traced to sales and/or average inventory.

DAVIDSON'S DEPARTMENT STORE

2001 TURNOVER REPORT

Department: Junior Sportswear
Category: Knit Tops
Division: Sportswear

	Chain	Westfield	Eastfield	Northfield
Average Inventory LY	$110,338	$ 8,933	$ 7,642	$ 9,651
Average Inventory TY	$118,431	$ 9,324	$ 6,371	$10,497
% Change Inventory	+7.3%	+4.4%	− 16.6%	+8.8%
Sales LY	$548,322	$43,165	$39,063	$47,671
Sales TY	$588,871	$28,160	$46,158	$49,880
% Change Sales	+7.4%	− 34.8%	+18.2%	+4.6%
Turnover LY	5.0	4.8	5.1	4.9
Turnover TY	5.0	3.0	7.2	4.8

Figure 15.2

2001 Turnover Report from Davidson's Department Store for four stores only.

Observations Assume that a 5.0 turnover is acceptable for the category according to industry standards. This year's Northfield sales increased by 4.6 percent, while inventory increased by 8.8 percent. Turnover decreased from 4.9 to 4.8. Though the 4.6 percent sales increase is a desirable result, the proportionately greater amount of inventory required to generate the increase negates the favorable judgment. The objective is to produce a sales increase with an equally proportionate inventory to yield the same turnover (4.9) or to produce a sales increase with a proportionately lower inventory to yield a higher turnover (greater than 4.9). The decrease in turnover is slight, however, and close to the 5.0 standard. Thus, the matter should receive little attention.

An additional 4.4 percent investment in inventory at Westfield resulted in a 34.8 percent decrease in sales, and a dramatic decrease in turnover from 4.8 to 3.0. Westfield's sales performance (−34.8%) is inconsistent with the chain's sales performance (+7.4%), a 42.2 percent deviation (7.3% + 34.8%). The deviations are significant and worthy of investigation. If the sales decline is due to a permanent factor, such as the entry of new competition in the marketplace, then inventory allocations should be adjusted to reflect diminished sales. Assortments should be carefully edited so that only the best-selling resources and items are retained. If the sales decline is due to a temporary factor, such as a store renovation that disrupted business for a period, allocations should remain the same, anticipating that completion of the renovation will alleviate the store's lackluster sales performance.

Eastfield experienced an 18.2 percent sales increase, and a 16.6 percent decrease in inventory, while turnover increased from 5.1 to 7.2. Unlike Westfield, Eastfield's sales and inventory are both headed in the right direction. This year's sales increase was achieved with a proportionately smaller inventory. The only cause for concern is that Eastfield's inventory may be turning too quickly at 2.2 turns greater than the chain's 5.0. Remember that an excessively high turnover may be indicative of stockouts and/or broken assortments. Thus, Eastfield's inventory may need to be fortified by a generous infusion of merchandise to support an optimistically upward sales trend (18.2%) that far exceeds the chain's average (+7.4%).

Note that a $3500 decrease in Westfield's average inventory, and a $3500 increase in Eastfield's average inventory would have yielded turnover figures close to the company's 5.0 standard (4.8 and 4.7 respectively). Balanced inventories among stores can be maintained by regularly monitoring inventory positions and by correcting inequities through the proper allocation of new shipments of merchandise. Some companies resolve inventory inequities among stores by transferring goods from overinventoried stores to underinventoried stores. Many companies avoid interstore transfers, because of high processing and transportation costs and because transferred goods are dormant for the several days that they are in process.

Annual Review of Merchandising Statistics

The Acme Buying Office compiles an annual report of merchandising statistics by department for its member stores. Figure 15.3 is a segment of the 2001 report for men's basics.

Features of the Report   The report includes comparative percentages for this year's and last year's markdowns and gross margin for each member, as well as this year's employee discounts, shortage, and cash dis-

ACME BUYING OFFICE

ANNUAL REVIEW OF MERCHANDISING STATISTICS

Men's Basics

	Mark Downs		Emp. Disc.	Short-age	Cash Disc. to Pur.	Gross Margin		Inventory Data	
	This Year	Last Year				This Year	Last Year	Turn-Over	Age of Inventory
1	4.2	3.5	0.5	0.9	8.0	49.3	49.7	4.6	27
2	8.4	7.7	0.7	2.6	—	45.0	45.4	3.7	05
3	10.7	9.3	0.8	3.4	7.9	43.9	45.3	4.3	26
4	10.0	13.6	0.7	5.6	5.2	43.9	45.3	3.5	33
5	6.2	5.5	0.7	2.1	7.9	47.8	48.5	5.4	—
6	8.6	11.6	1.2	2.4	7.7	46.9	46.8	4.9	07
7	6.4	10.3	2.0	0.7	7.8	48.1	44.7	5.5	17
8	7.5	18.9	1.5	2.1	6.0	43.0	37.2	3.2	23
9	12.8	6.6	1.1	2.8	7.6	45.6	48.5	6.6	11
10	3.9	4.3	0.9	0.5	7.8	49.6	48.4	6.4	01
11	4.6	6.1	0.8	5.5	8.2	45.7	46.3	7.7	04
12	4.5	7.5	0.8	1.7	6.8	46.8	44.1	5.6	—
13	14.1	19.2	0.9	2.5	7.7	44.6	42.5	3.3	04
14	3.9	5.5	0.6	3.6	7.6	48.1	45.9	4.3	20
15	7.5	7.3	0.7	0.6	7.4	47.9	47.7	5.4	23
16	9.5	9.0	1.3	2.4	8.3	45.9	46.5	5.7	07
PAR	4.5	5.5	0.7	0.7	7.9	48.1	48.5	5.7	04
MED	7.5	7.5	0.8	2.4	7.7	46.8	46.3	4.9	11

Figure 15.3

ACME Buying Office's Annual Review of Merchandising Statistics.

count percentages. The report also includes turnover and an aged inventory indicator, the percentage of inventory over six months old, as well the par and median for each group of reported figures. In this case, the *median* is the middle number when the statistics are ranked from worst to best. The *par* is the middle number of the best half of the statistics when ranked from worst to best.

Observations Note that member 8's gross margin improved greatly (37.2% to 43.0%) because of a dramatic decrease in markdowns from the second highest store (18.9%) to the median store (7.5%). Unfortunately, taking fewer markdowns has left member 8 with a high percentage of aged inventory (23%), the fourth highest in the group. Stagnant merchandise has also caused member eight to yield the lowest turnover in the buying office (3.2).

Member 10 is the star of the buying office. At 49.6 percent, member 10's gross margin is the highest in the group because of a low markdown rate (3.9 percent), the lowest for the group. A low markdown rate at member 10 has not resulted in a high percentage of aged inventory or slow turnover, however. Only 1 percent of member 10's inventory is more than six months old. A 6.4 turnover exceeds par, and is the second highest in the buying office.

Stock-to-Sales Ratio Report

Tie One On compiles a monthly stock-to-sales ratio report for each of the five categories of merchandise sold by its ten fashion accessories pushcarts of trendy selections of scarves, hairgoods, sunglasses, and small leather goods. Figure 15.4 is April's report for all categories.

	TIE ONE ON STOCK-TO-SALES RATIO REPORT *April*				
	EOM		**Sales**		**S/S Ratio**
TOTAL CHAIN	$156.7	— %	$24.4	— %	6.4
Midway Plaza	$ 16.3	11.0%	$ 1.3	5.0%	12.5
Hamilton Heights	$ 12.4	8.0%	$ 1.1	5.0%	11.3
Bayshore	$ 15.6	10.0%	$ 2.2	9.0%	7.1
Long Beach	$ 12.4	8.0%	$ 1.4	6.0%	8.9
Town Center	$ 13.1	8.0%	$ 3.2	13.0%	4.1
Canyon Crest	$ 14.7	10.0%	$ 5.6	23.0%	2.6
Riverside	$ 10.3	7.0%	$ 1.3	5.0%	7.9
Eastridge	$ 21.3	14.0%	$ 3.6	15.0%	5.9
Chapel Hill	$ 22.5	15.0%	$ 3.1	13.0%	7.3
Fairfield Commons	$ 16.1	10.0%	$ 1.6	7.0%	10.1

Figure 15.4

Tie One On's April Stock-to-Sales Ratio Report.

Features of the Report The report includes the EOM and sales for each cart and the resulting stock-to-sales ratio. The report also includes each cart's EOM and sales penetrations. Based on the premise that penetrations of inventory should closely match penetrations of sales, the inventory position of each cart can be evaluated by comparing EOM penetrations to sales penetrations.[1]

Observations Note that the greatest discrepancies between EOM and sales penetrations are at Midway Plaza and Canyon Crest: 6 percent and 13 percent respectively. Midway Plaza is overinventoried (high EOM penetrations relative to its sales penetration), while Canyon Crest is underinventoried (a low EOM penetrations relative to its sales penetration). Midway Plaza owns 11 percent of the EOM, but generated only 5 percent of total sales. Canyon Crest owns only 10 percent of the EOM, but generated nearly a quarter of the company's sales (23%). Comparing the problem cart's stock-to-sales ratios to the 6.4 aggregate stock-to-sales ratio further substantiates the inventory inequity. Midway Plaza, with the highest stock-to-sales ratio (12.5), has nearly twice the proportionate amount of inventory to sales for all carts (6.4), while Canyon Crest, with the lowest stock-to-sales ratio (2.6), has less than half of the proportionate amount of inventory to sales for all carts. The inventory should be reallocated to alleviate these inequities.

Inventory Position and Sales

Monkeys and Pumpkins compiles a monthly report of stock-to-sales ratios and sales and inventory penetrations by category of merchandise for ten upscale children's apparel stores. The report also includes month-to-date, season-to-date, and year-to-date sales compared to plan and last year. Figure 15.5 is a segment of the report for May for the infant layette category.

Features of the Report The report lists the BOM, receipts, interstore transfers, markdowns, sales, and EOM for each store and the chain, as well each store's percentage of the chain's BOM, receipts, sales, and EOM. Like the previous report, the report is based on the premise that penetrations of inventory should closely match penetrations of sales. The inclusion of BOM, EOM, receipts, transfers, and markdowns in this report permits a careful analysis of inventory activity within the month. The report also includes plan and actual stock-to-sales ratios for

MONKEYS & PUMPKINS

May

INVENTORY POSITION AND SALES

	Total	%	Broadway %	Crossroads %	Village Square %	South Gate %	Ingleside %	Bel Air %	Buena Vista %
BOM	$227,525		14	14	18	14	9	14	16
Receipts	47,163		11	11	22	11	8	28	10
Sales	54,048		7	—	21	9	10	28	13
EOM Act	198,110		17	14	18	14	8	13	15
EOM Plan	159,100		12	12	23	12	9	16	16
S/S Act	4.2		6.7	4.1	3.0	5.1	3.1	1.6	4.2
S/S Plan	4.6		5.2	4.7	2.8	6.5	5.5	1.9	6.0

SALES TO DATE BY DEPARTMENT AND STORE

	Total	%	Broadway %	Crossroads %	Village Square %	South Gate %	Ingleside %	Bel Air %	Buena Vista %
MTD last yr	$48,902	11	16−		21−	2−	18−	27	—
MTD plan	50,500	7	23−	6	12−	26	71	9	27
MTD this yr	54,048		7	12	21	9	10	28	13
STD last yr	143,151	29	5−	23	12	26	10−	33	—
STD plan	168,200	10	5−	2	8	31	39	12	2
STD this yr	184,854		9	11	25	9	8	28	10
YTD last yr	285,840	26	2−	19	19	6	12−	25	—
YTD plan	341,200	6	4−	9	16	15	2	12	22−
YTD this yr	361,221		9	11	26	6	7	29	10

Figure 15.5

A May Inventory Position and Sales report compiled by Monkeys and Pumpkins.

the month, and month-to-date, season-to-date, and year-to-date sales with percentage comparisons to plan and last year. The format facilitates a concurrent review of both inventory position and sales by store.

Observations Broadway is overinventoried. The store owned 14 percent of the chain's BOM, received 11 percent of the chain's new receipts, but generated only 7 percent of the chain's sales. Broadway's EOM was planned at 12 percent of total, but the actual EOM was 17 percent of total. The store's 6.7 actual stock-to-sales ratio was the highest in the chain, considerably higher than the chain's 4.2 stock-to-sales ratio.

Bel Air is underinventoried. The store generated 28 percent of the chain's sales, with only 14 percent of the chain's BOM. Though new receipts were generously distributed to Bel Air (28%), the allocations sold as rapidly as they arrived, leaving the store with only 13 percent of the chain's EOM. The store's 1.6 stock-to-sales ratio was the lowest in the chain, considerably lower than the chain's 4.2 stock-to-sales ratio.

Note Bel Air's sales growth. Month-to-date, season-to-date, and year-to-date sales are +27 percent, +33 percent, +25 percent to last year, respectively, the highest percentage sales increases of any of the stores. Note also that Bel Air's stock-to-sales ratio was planned at a modest 1.9, while the company's stock-to-sales ratio was planned at 4.6. The meager plan may have been the result of basing the plan on last year's inventory and sales. However, Bel Air's dramatic growth made last year's figures invalid benchmarks.

Sales and Stock-to-Sales Ratios

Allied Specialty Stores generates a monthly report of stock-to-sales ratios for more than 50 categories of merchandise common to most of its 28 women's specialty stores. Figure 15.6 is the sleepwear department report for November.

Features of the Report The report includes monthly sales for the category by store and total chain and percentage comparisons to last year. The report also includes the monthly stock-to-sales ratio for the category by store and last year's comparable ratio. Ranked percentage of sales increases/decreases and stock-to-sales ratios facilitate the assessment of individual store performance. The rankings range from one, the best performer, to 23, the worst performer. Though there are 28 stores in the chain, only 23 have reported figures since the other five stores do not carry the category. Pars and medians for percentage sales increases/decreases and this year's and last year's stock-to-sales ratios appear at the bottom of the report.

Observations Store 15 most typifies the November performance of an Allied store. Last year's 5.1 stock-to-sales ratio defined the median, as did this year's one percent sales decrease, while this year's 5.4 stock-to-sales ratio came very close to the 5.1 median.

Store 28 produced the highest percentage sales increase for the month (28.3%, rank one), but unfortunately, the store's monthly stock-to-sales ratio is one of the highest in the group (7.8%, rank 23). The positive perception of Store 28's sales increase is negated by the excessive amount of inventory that was carried to generate those sales.

ALLIED SPECIALTY STORES

SALES AND STOCK-TO-SALES RATIOS

Department: 3300 Sleepwear
November

| Store | ($00) Sales | % Change | Rank | MONTH STOCK-SALES RATIO | | | |
| | | | | THIS YEAR | | LAST YEAR | |
				Ratio	Rank	Ratio	Rank
1	3,474.9	2.0	11	6.8	22	7.1	22
2	1,616.0	19.2	2	5.8	17	8.9	23
3	710.6	−4.7	14	5.4	13	5.1	12
4	265.3	−11.6	18	4.7	8	4.7	8
5	672.5	−20.3	22	4.7	8	3.3	4
6	180.7	−17.4	20	4.0	3	2.5	1
7	401.3	2.2	10	5.1	12	5.0	11
8	174.7	5.7	6	5.4	13	5.1	12
9	532.8	17.3	3	3.8	2	2.9	2
10	485.3	−8.4	17	—	—	—	—
11	373.4	2.4	9	4.6	6	6.2	18
12	371.4	−7.6	15	4.8	10	5.4	15
13	309.3	−17.7	21	5.6	16	3.2	3
14	157.6	5.6	7	3.2	1	3.4	5
15	221.1	−1.0	12	5.4	13	5.1	12
16	—	—	—	—	—	—	—
17	66.2	−23.8	24	4.9	11	4.2	6
18	99.7	−12.8	19	6.2	19	6.2	18
19	154.5	−4.1	13	4.4	5	4.8	9
20	147.3	4.2	8	4.2	4	4.3	7
21	110.6	12.5	4	4.6	6	4.9	10
22	—	—	—	—	—	—	—
23	49.5	−20.5	23	6.5	20	5.8	17
24	—	—	—	—	—	—	—
25	49.2	6.3	5	5.9	18	6.7	20
26	—	—	—	—	—	—	—
27	29.6	−7.8	16	6.6	21	5.6	16
28	22.2	28.3	1	7.8	23	6.8	21
PAR		5.7		4.4		3.4	
MED	10,675.7	−1.0		5.1		5.1	

Figure 15.6

Allied Specialty Store's November Sales and Stock-to-Sales Ratios report.

Store 9 is a stellar performer. Monthly sales increased by 17.3 percent (rank three), while the stock-to-sales ratio ranked second in the group. Though the stock-to-sales ratio increased from 2.9 to 3.8, the increase is consistent with the par increase from 3.4 to 4.4.

Store 6 is one of the poorest monthly sales performers (17.4%, rank 20), but one of the best stock-to-sales ratio performers (4.0, rank 3). The "better than par" ranking is a dubious distinction, however. The poor sales performance may have resulted from inventories that were too low. A higher stock-to-sales ratio may have generated significantly greater sales.

Vendor Sales Report

Dee Klein's compiles a weekly report of sales by major vendor for each of the 20 departments within its two women's specialty stores. Figure 15.7 is the Vendor Sales Report for the cosmetics department for week ending August 15.

Features of the Report The report includes this year's and last year's sales by vendor, the percentage change from last year's sales to this year' sales, and sales penetration by vendor. The report also includes month-to-date, season-to-date, and year-to-date figures.

DEE KLEIN'S
VENDOR SALES REPORT
Week Ending August 15

	WTD				MTD				STD				YTD			
	TY	LY	%	%	TY	LY	%	%	TY	LY	%	%	TY	LY	%	%
Estée Lauder	4.5	8.3	− 46	32	9.6	8.9	+8	33	25.0	24.2	+3	28	150.1	140.5	+6	31
Clinique	4.5	4.2	+7	32	8.5	8.5	+2	29	28.0	27.1	+3	31	160.2	160.1	0	33
Elizabeth Arden	3.0	3.1	− 3	21	6.2	6.2	+5	21	15.5	14.3	+8	17	90.4	88.8	+2	19
Lancome	20.0	2.5	− 20	14	5.0	5.0	+2	17	20.8	19.8	+5	23	85.3	80.2	+6	18
TOTAL	14.0	18.1	− 23	100	29.3	29.3	+5	100	89.3	85.4	+5	100	486.0	469.6	+3	100

Figure 15.7

The Vendor Sales Report for Dee Klein's cosmetics department.

Observations This week's Estée Lauder sales were 46 percent behind last year's sales for the same week. Though the immediate reaction is one of concern, further exploration reveals that last year's sales were unusually high because of a gift-with-purchase promotion not recurring until next week. Estée Lauder's sales penetration for the week is 32 percent, consistent with the line's month-to-date (33%), season-to-date (28%), and year-to-date (31%) penetrations. Lancome sales are a greater concern to the buyer. The line's sales are 20 percent behind last year with no apparent justification. The line's sales penetration for the week is 14 percent, considerably lower than its month-to-date (17%), season-to-date (23%), and year-to-date (18%) penetrations. Reasons for the sales shortfall, such as low inventory or inadequate staffing, must be investigated.

Sales by Category

Steinert's compiles a monthly report of sales by department, classification, and store for the 50 departments in its ten updated misses apparel stores. Figure 15.8 is the dress department report for March.

Features of the Report The report includes the department's actual and plan sales by store, a corresponding percentage comparison, and a plan and actual penetration of chain total. Departmental sales are broken out by classification for each store. Penetrations are computed for each classification as a percentage of total departmental sales and a percentage of total sales for the classification in all stores.

For instance, career dresses at Willow Station represents 32 percent of the total dress department sales in that store. The category represents 7 percent of the total sales for the category in all stores.

Observation Special-occasion dresses is an important classification at Amity Plaza, generating about half (51%) of Amity Plaza'a total dress business. The category represents only about a quarter (24%) of the total dress department sales in all stores. Though special-occasion dresses is a significant percentage of Amity Plaza's dress business, the category represents only 8 percent of special-occasion dress sales in all stores. The 8 percent penetration ranks at the low end of a range of penetrations that span from 5 percent to 20 percent. The importance of the category is dwarfed by the fact that Amity Plaza is a small

STEINERT'S SALES BY CATEGORY March												
	This Year	Plan			Career		Casual		Special Occasion		Suits		Petites	

	This Year DOL	Plan DOL	PCT	Career		Casual		Special Occasion		Suits		Petites	
Willow Station	10100	12600	20−	3230		1291		3036		1568		965	
	7%	9%		32%	7%	13%	7%	30%	9%	16%	8%	10%	5%
Amity Plaza	5381	5800	7−	1817		269		2760		282		253	
	4%	4%		34%	4%	5%	2%	51%	8%	5%	1%	5%	1%
Village West	4742	2900	64	1955		592		1642		551			
	3%	2%		41%	4%	12%	3%	35%	5%	12%	3%		
Cherry Creek	10553	10600		4549		101		3417		1146		1337	
	7%	7%		43%	9%	1%	1%	32%	10%	11%	3%	13%	7%
Bishop's Corner	22873	24400	6−	7734		3221		5508		4660		1748	
	16%	17%		34%	16%	14%	18%	24%	16%	20%	23%	8%	9%
University Place	18276	16900	8	7072		2855		2668		2036		3643	
	13%	12%		39%	14%	16%	16%	15%	8%	11%	10%	20%	18%
Hickory Hill	12280	13900	12−	3616		1325		3484		2003		1850	
	9%	10%		29%	7%	11%	8%	28%	10%	16%	10%	15%	9%
Lincoln Park	11939	11300	6	2555		1430		2194		1792		3966	
	8%	8%		21%	5%	12%	8%	18%	6%	15%	9%	33%	20%
Westwood Village	31716	33000	4−	11135		4598		6690		3972		5318	
	22%	23%		35%	22%	14%	26%	21%	20%	13%	20%	17%	26%
Chestnut Park	13268	12600	5	5834		1751		2589		1832		1261	
	9%	9%		44%	12%	13%	10%	20%	8%	14%	9%	10%	6%
TOTAL	141135	144000	2−	49503		17438		33994		19848		20312	
				35%	100%	12%	100%	24%	100%	14%	100%	14%	100%

Figure 15.8

Steinert's Sales by Category for March.

store that generates only 4 percent of the company's total dress sales. Thus, special-occasion dresses are significant to the store manager of Amity Plaza, but Amity Plaza's special-occasion dress business is not as significant to the buyer of special-occasion dresses who is likely to favor the two stores that generate over a third of the category's sales: Bishop's Corner (16%) and Westwood Village (20%). The significance of the special-occasion category at Amity Plaza should stimulate a review of the assortment. Perhaps the dress department's total inventory is appropriate for a 4 percent dress store, but does the assortment reflect the fact that 51 percent of the store's dress business is special-occasion dresses, or that casual dresses, petites, and suits each only represent 5 percent of Amity Plaza's dress business? If inventory is allocated based on the total company's penetration of business by class (24% to special occasion, 14% to suits, and 14% to petites), then Amity Plaza may be overinventoried in petites, suits, and casual dresses, and underinventoried in special occasion.

Likewise, the petite category represents a third (33%) of the dress sales at Lincoln Park, but the category only represents 14 percent of total dress sales in all stores. If inventory is allocated based on the total company's penetration of business by class (14% to petites), then Lincoln Park may be underinventoried in this classification.

Sales performance for a single month is too narrow a time frame upon which to base decisions regarding a store's classification structure, or allocation of floor space or fixturing. However, if April's category penetrations by store were to remain relatively stable throughout the year, an analytical merchant might contemplate the following: Five percent of sales in a 4 percent dress store is hardly enough business to warrant carrying casual dresses, suits, and petites at Amity Plaza. If Amity Plaza's assortment is based on the sales, imagine how paltry the selections must be in those categories! Why not discontinue all three categories at Amity Plaza and devote the vacated space to special-occasion dresses? Though a business plateaus at some point, special-occasion dresses seems to have greater potential than casual dresses, suits, or petite dresses, making the expansion of the special-occasion dress category at Amity Plaza a prudent investment of space and inventory.

A similar thought process can be used to analyze Cherry Creek's dress business. If only 1 percent of the chain's casual dress business is generated by Cherry Creek, and if only 1 percent of Cherry Creek's dress sales are generated by the casual-dress category, then why carry casual dresses at Cherry Creek? It seems wiser to devote the casual dress classification's fixtures and inventory dollars to stronger sales-generating classifications, such as career and special-occasion dresses.

	STP	S2W	S4W	S12W	AWS	OH	OO	OP	TWC OW	BAL
BARRY'S BASEMENT STYLE STATUS REPORT *October 8*										
Willow Station	86	145	263	492	41.0	1108		697	27W	411−
Amity Plaza	63	121	220	378	31.5	547		536	17W	11−
Village West	42	76	128	226	18.8	429		320	23W	109−
Cherry Creek	74	129	245	438	36.5	722		621	20W	101−
Bishop's Corner	187	313	600	1157	96.4	1256		1639	13W	383
University Place	53	100	248	578	48.2	819		819	17W	0
Hickory Hill	103	182	338	585	48.8	1074		830	22W	244−
Lincoln Park	67	136	254	568	47.3	846		804	18W	42−
Westwood Village	205	350	602	1206	100.5	1093		1709	11W	616
Chestnut Park	74	119	228	536	44.7	1034		760	23W	274−
TOTAL	954	1671	3131	6164	513.7	8928		0	17W	0

Figure 15.9

A Style Status Report from Barry's Basement.

Style Status Report

Barry's Basement generates a weekly report of the distribution of specific style numbers among its ten off-price men's stores. Figure 15.9 depicts the report for a cotton turtleneck for the week ending October 8.

Features of the Report   The report includes a 12-week sell-through, the number of units sold in the past 12 weeks divided by the number of units received in that period. The report also includes rate-of-sale information by store and chain:

- STP is the number of units sold last week
- S2W is the number of units sold during the prior two weeks
- S4W is the number of units sold during the prior four weeks
- S12W is the number of units sold during the prior twelve weeks
- AWS is the average weekly sales computed by dividing the number of S12W by 12.

- OH is the units on hand
- OO is the units on order
- TWSO is the total weeks supply on hand, computed by dividing AWS by OH.

    The TWSO for the chain is an important reference point for computing OP, or optimum stock, computed by multiplying the chain's TWSO by a store's AWS. OP is the number of units that the store requires to match the chain's TWSO based on the store's AWS.

- BAL is the difference between OH and OP, or the number of units that should be transferred into a store (positive value) or out of a store (negative value) to match the store's TWSO to the chain's TWSO.

Observations   Willow Station, Village West, Cherry Creek, Hickory Hill, and Chestnut Park are overstocked: Bishop's Corner and Westwood Village are understocked. The inventory should be reallocated from the generously inventoried stores.

SUMMARY POINTS

- Control is monitoring or measuring actual performance or status relative to goals or standards.
- A control standard is a reference point, benchmark, or guideline used to measure performance.
- A deviation is the discrepancy between actual performance and a standard.
- Qualitative control measures are subjective. Quantitative control measures are objective.
- Controls are established at specific time intervals such as hourly, daily, weekly, monthly, quarterly, seasonally, or annually.
- Control levels parallel planning levels.
- A report is a compilation of timely information synthesized into a meaningful form.
- Most controls are generated by computerized systems that electronically transmit, process, and store timely information reliably and cost-effectively.
- Exception reports include major deviations from standards, bypassing minor ones.

KEY TERMS AND CONCEPTS

control	exception report	penetration
control standard	industry standard	qualitative control
deviation	internal standard	quantitative control

FOR DISCUSSION

1. Discuss the use of internal versus external control standards. What are the advantages/disadvantages of each?
2. Discuss qualitative and quantitative assessments of a buyer's performance. Discuss the strengths and weaknesses of each.
3. Relate the importance of control systems to the success of EDI.
4. Indentify a factor that should be controlled.
   a. daily
   b. weekly
   c. monthly
   d. seasonally
   e. annually

   Justify the control frequency.

ENDNOTES

1. The percentage of total inventory allocated to a store in a multiunit chain should not exactly match the percentage of the chain's total sales that the store generates. High volume stores should own proportionately less inventory than low volume stores, and thus have higher turnover and lower stock-to-sales ratios. Let us assume that in the case of Tie One On, the match between inventory and sales should be close, though not exact.

chapter sixteen

STORE LAYOUT AND MERCHANDISE PRESENTATION

In large retail organizations, the task of creating attractive shopping environments is the responsibility of professionals with expertise in architectural and interior design, the building trades, and visual arts. Though not directly responsible for store planning, executives and other merchandising buyers play important consultive roles as sources of information on fashion trends, fixture and space requirements, and other merchandise-related topics. To interface with store planners and visual merchandisers, buyers need an understanding of fundamental store-layout and merchandise presentation concepts. Chapter 16 covers some of these topics.

After you have read this chapter, you will be able to discuss:

The value of retail selling space.

Strategies for store layout.

Merchandise presentation.

Fixturing and sinage.

STORE PLANNING AND DESIGN

A store's physical appearance is an image component that conveys a message about offerings, pricing strategy, and market positioning. A **prototype** is a model store that combines elements of decor, lighting, fixturing and signage to create a shopping ambiance consistent with the store's image and target customers. A prototype is a synthesis of standards for operational efficiency, merchandise presentation, and customer service.[1]   Though specialty stores are best known for their distinctive prototypes, model stores are developed within all retailing formats. The development of a prototype facilitates "cookie cutter" expansion whereby a large number of stores are opened in a short time.

Prototypes are often tested in several markets before being implemented, and are periodically reviewed for effectiveness. The cost of constructing a store can range from less than $100 a square foot to several hundred dollars. In conjunction with their *no-frills* strategy, most discounters execute simple store designs of vinyl tile floors, fluorescent lighting, and highly functional fixturing. In contrast, Ralph Lauren's

Figure 16.1

A prototype combines décor, lighting, fixturing, and signage to create a shopping ambiance consistent with a store's image and target customers. *Tourneau Express, Inc.*

museum-like flagship on New York's Madison Avenue is an example of a pricey store design.

Prototype development is a store-planning function. Some retailers operate an internal store-planning department, while others contract professional design firms to develop prototypes. Many retail organizations combine the services of both an internal function and outside firms. The activities of store planning were once limited to allocating floor space, setting construction timetables, and selecting paint colors and wall coverings. Today store planning is a far more comprehensive function that involves market research, merchandising strategies, space management, and interior-graphics and lighting design. Updating and expanding existing facilities is also a store-planning function. Renovations range in scope from replacing carpeting and a few fixtures to gutting and rebuilding entire stores. Store renovations have become more frequent as retailers attempt to keep pace with competition and fast-changing market conditions.

Computer-aided design and drafting (CADD) systems have greatly facilitated store design reducing the time that it takes to design a 200,000-square-foot department store from four months to a week. CADD systems have a database of design shapes, such as wall sections, fixtures, fitting rooms, wrap desks, and even images of folded sweaters that can be called from storage, thus eliminating the need to create unique images for each new project.[2]

Visual Merchandising

Visual merchandising is the retail organizational function responsible for enhancing sales by creating visually appealing shopping environments. Storefront window displays were once the major responsibility of visual merchandising. Historically, windows have played an important role in the notoriety of many retailers. Animated Christmas windows at Lord & Taylor's Fifth Avenue store have become a New York tourist attraction. Under the design direction of Gene Moore, the legendary windows of Tiffany & Co. of New York have featured some of the most exquisite jewels in the world using unusual props such as pasta, dirt, and empty spools of thread.[3] Visual merchandising responsibilities have expanded beyond window displays to include floor layout, the development of standards for merchandise presentation and signage. Visual merchandising is also an influential voice in store design.

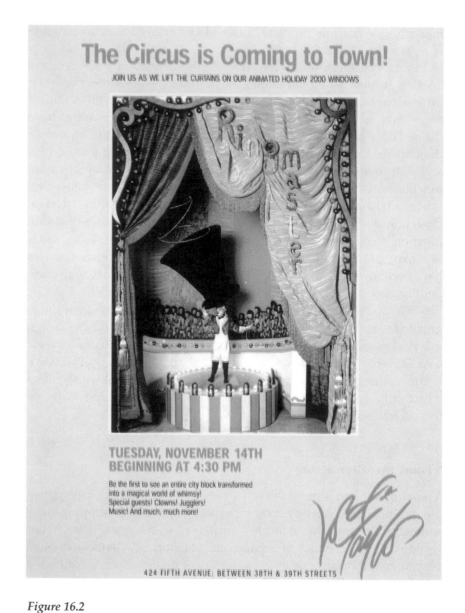

Figure 16.2

Animated Christmas windows at Lord & Taylor's Fifth Avenue store have become a
New York tourist attraction. *Courtesy of Lord & Taylor.*

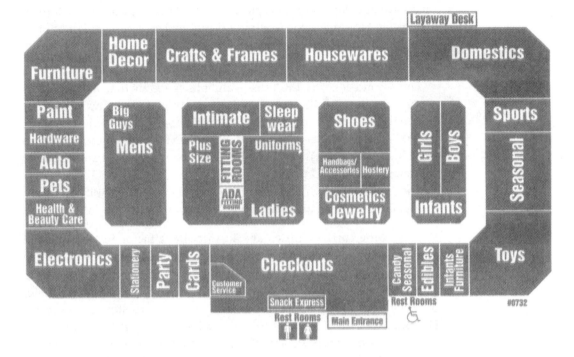

Figure 16.3

Strategically placed merchandise will pull traffic through a store's major aisle to maximize customer exposure to the store's offerings. *Courtesy of Ames Department Stores, Inc.*

Layout

A strategically designed store layout combines the effective use of merchandise and aisles to draw customers through a store maximizing their exposure to the store's offerings. A layout can increase the amount of time and money that customers spend in a store. A layout should be flexible, allowing frequent moves as trends change and as poor-layout decisions surface.

The value of selling-floor space is an important store-layout consideration. Just as the value of a retail site is predicated on customer traffic, the value of space within a store is predicated on the number of customers that pass through or by the space. Consider the following: A four-level department store is connected on the second level to a single-level enclosed shopping center. A mall-level entrance is the only point of entry into the store.[4] Assume that about 4000 customers enter the store on an average day and that typically about 25 percent of the customers are destined for each floor. Centrally positioned escalators are the store's only people movers. Several assumptions can be made relative to the value of each floor as selling space based on the above information:

- The second level is the most valuable space in that all 4000 customers who enter the store must pass through the second level.
- The third level is the next most valuable space in that an average of 2000 customers pass through the third level on a typical day. This includes the 1000 customers destined to the third level and the 1000 customers destined to the fourth level.
- The first and fourth levels are the least valuable space in that only the 1000 customers destined for these floors pass through them.

As traffic carriers, aisles are an important factor in defining the value of selling space. Space that is close to an aisle is more valuable than space remote from an aisle.[5] Aisles are classified according to their size and the amount of customer traffic that they carry. A **major aisle,** or *main aisle*, is a wide aisle that connects a store's extremes. Discounters sometimes refer to main aisles as *power aisles*. Contrasting colors or floor compositions of wood, marble, carpeting, or tile are often used to define major aisles. A **secondary aisle** is a narrow aisle that interconnects major aisles, often carrying traffic through selling areas. Secondary aisles are often not as clearly defined as major aisles. A line of fixtures is sometimes used to define a secondary aisle.

A store's points of entrance affect traffic flow. Assume that the mall in the aforementioned example is expanded with a second level of stores, and that an additional mall entrance is opened to the third level of the four-level store. Assuming that the number of customers who enter the store from each mall entrance is evenly distributed, the value of the second floor will diminish, and the value of the third floor will increase. The redistribution of traffic will effectively equate the value of the two floors. Direct entrances from parking lots and garages also enhance and/or balance store traffic.

Traffic is critical to the sale of certain types of merchandise. Recall from Chapter 6 that fashion goods are often purchased because of their aesthetic appeal. Fashion goods are best placed in heavily trafficked areas to maximize the exposure of their aesthetic qualities. In general, basic goods require less exposure than fashion goods.

Two terms that classify merchandise according to customer purchase habits are important to store planners. Purchases of **destination**

Company Profile 16.1

Sephora—A Makeover in Cosmetics

Sephora has revolutionized the way that prestige cosmetics and fragrances are sold. The French retail chain sells its product line in an easy-to-shop environment that gives customers the freedom to experiment with a vast array of cosmetics and fragrances.

Sephora stores feature a black, white, and red décor that highlights three distinct "worlds": fragrances, beauty, and well-being. Bath and body products are at the store entrance, along with potpourri, scented candles and stylish gift boxes for creating customized gift packages. Further into the store is a color-palette display of Sephora's 200 shades of private label nail lacquers in tiny bottles, and 350 shades of private-label lip-

sticks in sleek cases. Men's and women's fragrances are displayed along the wall in alphabetical order. An extensive assortment of skin-care products is located in a brightly lit, clean, white space in the back of the shop.

Each product in the Sephora shopping environment is available to the customer in an open-sell format encouraging customers to experiment and browse. Trained staff members serve customers by offering advice, product information, and makeovers. The Sephora format sharply contrasts the restrictive and aggressive selling environment in department stores where products are presented from behind a counter by commissioned salespeople assigned to specific lines.[1]

Source:
1 Jinkner-Lloyd, A. (September 1999). *Sephora offers beauty, freedom.* Shopping Center World. *p. 22*

goods are planned. Purchases of **impulse goods** are unplanned. Big-ticket items, such as furniture, are destination goods. Less expensive items, such as candy, are often considered impulse goods. Destination goods are strategically located in remote areas to pull traffic through a store since, as planned purchases, customers will seek them out. Impulse items are located in high-traffic areas to maximize their exposure. Some goods are destination/impulse hybrids. Cosmetics purchases are both planned and unplanned.

The characteristics of basic, fashion, impulse and destination can be cross-linked to define four types of merchandise: fashion/impulse, basic/destination, basic/impulse, and fashion/destination. Note how these four types of goods are strategically located within a store:

- Fashion/impulse goods, such as fashion jewelry, are placed in high-traffic locations for visual prominence. Their aesthetic appeal stimulates unplanned purchases.

- Basic/destination goods, such as mattresses, are placed in remote locations. Because customers seek out basic/destination goods, they serve as magnets that pull customers through a store exposing them to other merchandise. Public restrooms and sales support areas, such as giftwrap, are also customer destinations that pull traffic through stores.
- Basic/impulse goods, such as hosiery, are placed in high-trafficked areas that are secondary to the more heavily trafficked areas in which fashion/impulse goods are placed.
- Fashion/destination goods, such as outerwear, are placed in locations that are less heavily trafficked than the locations of basic/impulse goods, but not as remote as the areas occupied by basic/destination goods. As destination items, customers will seek out fashion/destination goods. However, as fashion goods, they require semiprominent locations.

An **adjacency** is merchandise that is located next to other merchandise for customer convenience and to stimulate the sale of the adjacent goods. Handbags are a good adjacency to shoes, and vice versa. Girls' sizes 4–6x are a good adjacency to girls' sizes 7–14 for the convenience of customers who straddle both size ranges. Private-label goods are often placed adjacent to branded goods, hoping that customers lured to heavily advertised branded products will select the higher margin private labels. Sometimes goods are exposed in more than one location to reap the advantage of multiple adjacencies, a concept called **cross merchandising.**[6] In a department store-table linens can be presented in both the household–textiles area and the china-and-glass area. Store planners are often posed the dilemma of placing goods that cannot be absolutely categorized as basic, fashion, impulse, destination, or any combination thereof. As a destination item, women's innerwear is often placed in secondary locations in department stores. Some stores experimented with moving hosiery from high-traffic main aisles to the less-trafficked innerwear areas feeling that innerwear and hosiery were goods adjacencies. The result was disastrous for many retailers who found that the hosiery sales generated by the innerwear adjacency did not compensate for the loss of impulse sales.

Manny's Men's Shop

To demonstrate these principles of store layout, consider the case of Manny's Men's Shops, a chain of eight men's specialty stores departmentalized as follows:

Manny's Men's Shops

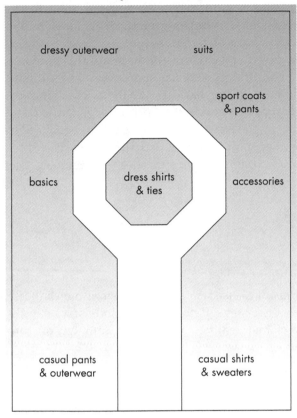

Figure 16.4

The floor plan of Manny's Men's shops.

- Clothing: suits, sport coats, dressy slacks and outerwear.
- Furnishings: dress shirts, ties, accessories (belts, small leather goods, jewelry), and basics (underwear, hosiery, pajamas, and robes).
- Sportswear: casual pants, knit and woven shirts, sweaters, casual outerwear and activewear.

The owner is considering a new location in an enclosed shopping center. The space is rectangular with narrow frontage, necessitating that the departments be aligned in a front/middle/back arrangement. The owner develops the following placement strategy:

- Clothing will be placed in the rear of the store. This is high-ticket destination merchandise that customers will seek. Higher-fashion sport coats will be placed at the front of the department to maximize their exposure.

- Sportswear will be placed in the front of the store. Visually exciting presentations of the store's most fashionable merchandise in this prominent location will lure customers from the mall and stimulate impulse purchases.
- Furnishings will be placed in the middle of the store. This potpourri of categories is a good bridge between sportswear and clothing. Underwear and hosiery are a basic/destination, basic/impulse hybrid. As basic/destination goods they do not warrant a prime location, but as basic/impulse goods, their sales will be enhanced by customer traffic en route to the clothing department. Shirts and ties are a perfect adjacency to suits in that suit sales will stimulate sales of shirts and ties.

FIXTURES

Fixtures are store furnishings used to present or store merchandise. Commonly called *racks* or *counters,* fixtures also include service desks, display props and customer seating. Fixtures fall into several categories based on their use.

- **Floor fixtures** are free-standing units for presenting goods on the selling floor.
- **Top-of-counter fixtures** are units placed on top of counter-height fixtures (38 inches) to display goods such as carded earrings.
- **Display fixtures** are used to show goods not available for customer selection.
- **Storage fixtures** are used to store fill-in or backroom inventory.

Some fixtures are multifunctional. A floor fixture may have drawers for storing fill-in merchandise or understock. The storage function in fixturing has significantly diminished in importance as retailers endeavor to improve turnover by carrying lower inventory and less reserve stock.

Floor fixtures are classified according to customer accessibility. A **closed-sell fixture** restricts customer access to merchandise requiring salesperson assistance for making selections. Easily damaged or highly pilferable big-ticket items, such as fine jewelry, are housed in closed-sell fixtures. An **open-sell fixture** permits customer access to merchandise allowing selection without the salesperson assistance. Open-sell fixtures are far more common than closed-sell fixtures for two reasons:

- Use of open-sell fixtures results in lower selling costs, since fewer salespeople are needed to service customers.
- Customers are more likely to purchase goods that they can readily test, feel, or try on.[7] Federated Department Stores is experimenting with open-sell cosmetics fixtures. The cases open from the front so that both the sales associate and the customer stand on the same side of the case giving customers easy access to the merchandise.[8]

Several types of floor fixtures are designed for hanging goods:

- A **four-way** is a four-armed fixtures often made of chrome. Goods are hung on four-ways so that their most visually appealing side faces the customer.

Figure 16.5

Customers have easy access to the cosmetics in this open-sell fixture. *Courtesy of Jordana Cosmetics.*

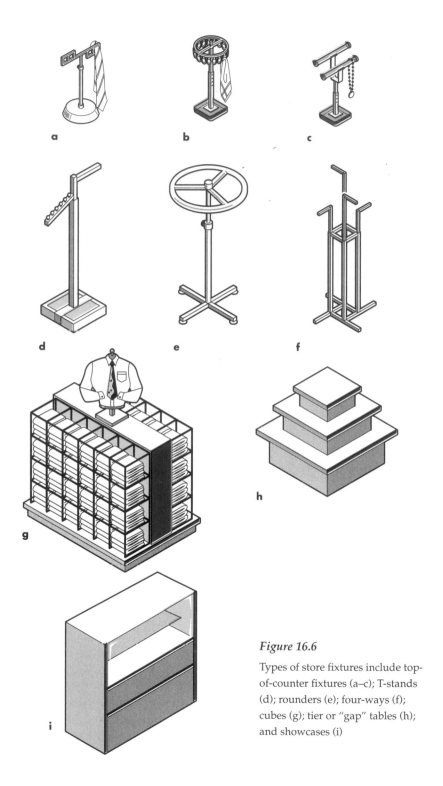

Figure 16.6

Types of store fixtures include top-of-counter fixtures (a–c); T-stands (d); rounders (e); four-ways (f); cubes (g); tier or "gap" tables (h); and showcases (i)

- A **T-stand** is a two-armed version of the four-way.
- A **rounder** is a circular-shape rodded fixture. Rounders have greater capacity than four-ways or T-stands and take up proportionately less selling-floor space. Rounders are used when facing out is not critical to effective merchandise presentation, as in the case of basic goods or clearance merchandise.

Other fixtures are designed for nonhanging goods, such as flat, packaged and folded merchandise:

- A **showcase** is a closed-sell fixture used primarily in department stores for presenting high-ticket or fragile goods, such as jewelry and prestige cosmetics and fragrances.
- A **tier table,** commonly called a "gap" table, is a shelved fixture popularized by the Gap, primarily used to present folded apparel.
- A **platform** is often used to stack goods in large cartons, such as sets of dinnerware and countertop appliances.
- **Cubes** are typically made of glass and used to present folded goods, such as shirts and sweaters.
- **Lip tables,** or *dump tables,* are used for haphazard presentations of clearance goods.

Most floor fixtures are designed to maximize capacity, minimize the use of floor space, and attractively show merchandise. Mobility and flexibility are important fixture characteristics in that fixtures need to be moved and/or adjusted often to accommodate seasonal changes in merchandise assortments.[9] Many department stores annually transform their female outerwear departments into swimwear departments and then back again. Fixtures must also accommodate changes in the merchandise itself, such as changes in the physical dimensions of packaging. **Modular fixturing** has this adaptability in that individual units are designed to be used separately or configured into large groupings. **Slatwall systems** are another type of adaptable fixturing. Slatwall is a series of horizontal "slats" separated by grooves onto which chrome hardware, plexiglass, or glass fixtures can be easily mounted to shelve, peg, or hang goods.

Vendor Fixtures

A **vendor fixture** is a fixture supplied by a vendor to distinguish its brands from the competition and to enhance consistent presentation of their product in all stores. Vendor fixtures run the gamut from corrugated cardboard top-of-counter units to custom-designed fixtures for

H. TRIPLE TOWER (DI 09)
24 Pair Locking Merchandiser

Figure 16.7

Some vendor fixtures are top-of-counter units. *Costa Del Mar*®

in-store shops for upscale brands such as Ralph Lauren, Liz Claiborne, and Nautica. Inexpensive vendor fixtures are often provided without charge with a minimum order. More expensive fixtures are priced to cover the cost of production. Vendor fixtures are especially desirable for products not easily presented on conventional fixturing because of their shape or packaging. Vendor fixtures often include point-of-purchase (POP) signage or graphics that are linked to national advertising campaigns. Though vendor fixturing for hardlines is common, an increasing number of softlines vendors now offer fixture programs. Retailers must be conscious of the compatibility of vendor fixtures with other fixtures and the store's overall design. A selling area with an assortment of vendor fixtures may give a very disjointed visual impression.[10]

MECHANDISE PRESENTATION

Merchandise presentation involves the application of standards or techniques to show merchandise to maximize its attractiveness and to facilitate customer selection. Merchandise presentation involves grouping merchandise together on a fixture or within an area in the

Figure 16.8

Displaying merchandise by category facilitates customer selection. *FRCH Design Worldwide.*

store based on one or more similarities. Goods may be grouped based on common:

Merchandise Category A presentation of a complete selection of a category or item utilizes the breadth and depth of an assortment to create a strong visual impression. Presentations by category facilitate customer selection when the item or category is the primary selection factor. ("Please show me your selection of socks.") Goods that are often presented by category include shorts, sweaters, and microwave ovens.

Color Merchandise of the same color is often presented together to create color impact. Color statements are often associated with a seasonal color trend or a holiday theme, such as red for Valentine's Day. Likewise, goods are often presented by design or print, such as paisley or stripe, to tie in with a seasonal fashion trend. Color presentations facilitate customer selection when color is a primary selection criterion.

("Where are the white blouses?" or "I need a black leather handbag to go with these shoes.")

Colors within a multiple color assortment are arranged in vertical blocks. The visual impact of goods such as bath towels, knit shirts, and socks is maximized when the colors are arranged from left to right, warm to cool, light to dark.

Figure 16.9 is an example of a color spectrum used for color blocking. Note that the spectrum begins with white and ends with black. The warmest color is yellow and the coolest color is blue. Transitional colors (such as peach) bridge the colors from which they are derived (yellow and orange).

Fabrication or Composition Goods are often grouped by fabric as part of a seasonal fashion statement or to create tactile statements, such as "soft dressing." Silk neckties, satin robes, and woven and knit tops are examples of goods presented by fabrication. Nonapparel goods are also presented by the material of which they are made, such as *down* pillows, *silver-plated* hollowware, and *leather* handbags. Color, fabrication, and composition are sometimes linked, as in the case of straw hats, brass hollowware, and sterling-silver jewelry. The presentation of fine jewelry by stone and metal effectively creates a color presentation: red (ruby), green (emerald), black (onyx), sapphire (blue), and sterling (silver).

Style Merchandise is presented by style for customer convenience and visual impact. Goods often grouped by style include men's dress shirts (long sleeve and short sleeve), women's hats, (narrow brim and wide

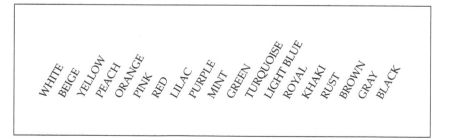

Figure 16.9

Colors within a multiple-color assortment are arranged in vertical blocks from light to dark, warm to cool, left to right.

brim), and silk scarves (square and oblong). Vendor styles are also grouped together, such as Levi's 501, 505, and 550 blue jeans.

Price/Quality Goods are grouped by price and/or quality to facilitate customer selection when an assortment has a wide range of quality or price points. A department store may group handbags as designer (Louis Vuitton, Gucci, and Fendi), bridge (Coach and Dooney & Bourke), better (Liz Claiborne), and moderate (Capezio).

Size Merchandise is sized to facilitate customer selection. Sized merchandise is typically presented from small to large, left to right, top to bottom, front to back. In a sized presentation of denim jeans on a shelved wall, the pant with smallest waist and shortest inseam is at the upper left of the presentation, and the pant with the largest waist and longest inseam is at the lower right of the presentation. Sizing is often used to present broken assortments such as markdowns.

Vendor A brand's complete assortment is often displayed as a unified presentation or "shop." The concept creates impact and strong brand identity and facilitates brand-driven purchases of goods, such as cosmetics and hosiery. Vendor presentations are appropriate for presenting coordinated merchandise such as Liz Claiborne and Alfred Dunner sportswear. Vendors encourage this "shop within a shop" concept by supplying retailers with fixturing, signage, and floor plans.

There are innumerable themes by which goods can be grouped together for presentation, such as end-use presentations that show customers how goods can be coordinated or used together. Examples include table settings of china, crystal, and flatware; room settings of furniture; and layered apparel coordinates of jackets, pants, and tops. Lifestyle presentations are targeted to customers of a specific demographic or psychographic profile. A department store's junior and young men's departments are examples of lifestyle presentations. Music, color, and lighting distinguish these areas from the rest of the store.

The foregoing criteria for grouping merchandise are often combined in a hierarchy to create a standard for presenting merchandise. Men's knit polo shirts may be presented by:

- Vendor (Ralph Lauren)
- Fabrication (interlock and mesh)
- Color (blocked on a wall left to right, warm to cool, light to dark)
- Size within each color (top to bottom, small to extra-large)

PRESENTATION STANDARDS FOR JEWELRY

- Present jewelry in shallow (third vision) showcases. Arrange merchandise from the front to back of the case. Create a balanced symmetrical look with a focal point in the middle of each case. Group sets and coordinating pieces together on ramped pads, encompassing a pair of earrings with a matching necklace. A coordinating bracelet or pin should be presented directly to the side to encourage multiple sales. Do not clutter the cases. Minimize duplication of styles in a case, and store duplicates in drawers directly below the presentation. Sales associates should sell from the drawers, not the case, unless the last piece is in the case.
- Use top-of-counter fixtures for earring presentations. Earrings should relate to the merchandise in the case below. Group earrings by "story," i.e., pierced, clip-ons, vermeil drops, buttons, hoops, stone, and so on. Top-of-counter fixtures are limited to two per five feet of showcase and must be carefully placed to achieve a balanced look. Sparsely filled fixtures should be removed from the counter.
- Tailored goods are presented by vendor and identified with signage. Never mix vendors in a case. This merchandise is produced by story or look and must be presented in that fashion.
- Present fashion and designer jewelry either by vendor or look, with the exception of Dior, which is always presented by vendor.
- Feature fashion looks of sterling presentations. Use interesting pieces as a focal point.
- Display 14K earrings in boxes or within a case; 14K chains should be displayed on ramped pads according to type and size of chain. Do not angle necklaces. Display vertically or horizontally to the front of the case. Group together matching fashion sets and use display ramps, bangle holders, ring holders, and so on to enhance the presentation.
- Always present clearance jewelry on separate fixtures or promotional lip tables.
- Watches are presented by vendor and identified by signage. Swatch should have its own case. Better watches, such as Seiko and Citizen, can be presented together. Fashion watches, such as Guess and Fossil, may be presented together and should be set up by band color. Swatch should be merchandised by color in the suggested patterns. Citizen and Seiko should be presented on their own showcase pads.

Figure 16.10

DKNY and Ralph Lauren have vendor shops with stores. *Courtesy of Fairchild Publications, Inc.*

Though often associated with presentations of softlines, merchandise presentation standards are developed for accessories and hardlines as well. Crate & Barrel uses product color and style to create exciting presentations of housewares and decorative accessories. The Zale Corporation has experimented with a unique, customer-friendly approach for presenting jewelry. Jewelry stores typically present merchandise by metal and stone. Zales presents goods by category, so that rings, watches, necklaces, and other items are grouped together regardless of metal or stone. The approach assumes that customers are more likely to shop by category ("I want to see a selection of rings."), than by stone ("I want to see a selection of jade.").

Retail organizations ensure consistent presentations within their stores by publishing merchandise presentation guidelines by category of merchandise in manuals distributed throughout the organization. Though the standards are based on a combination of objectives such as visual appeal, customer convenience, and ease of maintenance, balancing these objectives is sometimes a struggle. Most department stores present men's dress shirts in a vendor/color/size hierarchy creating brand and color impact. However, some men consider size the primary criterion for selecting a shirt, and they are frustrated that shirt selections are not grouped together by size, regardless of brand or color.

SIGNS

Signs are a store-image component that facilitate shopping by identifying merchandise by characteristics such as category, brand, size, style, and product features. **Permanent signage** is made of durable materials not intended for frequent change, such as exterior lighted signs and in-store signs identifying selling areas. **Temporary signage** is made of disposable material, such as paper or card stock, and is intended for frequent change. The most common forms of temporary signage include in-store signage on fixtures. Temporary in-store signs are important sales-promotion vehicles that reinforce advertising, stimulate impulse purchase, and enhance customer convenience by calling attention to promotional events and prices. Fact tags, banners, and reprints of newspaper advertising are among the various forms of temporary in-store signage.

The most common uses of temporary and in-store signs are for the identification of:

- Brand—*OshKosh B'gosh*
- Category or item—*Men's Crew Neck Sweaters*
- Shop-within-a-shop—from our *Signature Room*
- Characteristics or features of merchandise—*medium* or *100% Cotton*

REDUCED FOR CLEARANCE LOOK HERE FOR GREAT SAVINGS	GOLD KEY Misses Knit Tops **14.90**	**TWO-FOR VALUES** Jantzen V-Neck Sweaters 2/48.00 28.00 each
Goose Down Pillows 19.97 Reg. 40.00 Savings Deducted at Register	TAKE AN EXTRA **20% Off** REDUCED PRICE Savings Deducted at Register	INFANTS 0–9 MOS. **INFANTS 0–9 MONTHS**

Figure 16.11

Examples of temporary in-store signage.

- Price—*25% off ticketed price*
- Promotion—*Anniversary Sale*
- Policy—*All Sales Final*
- Service —*Open a charge and receive 10% off your first purchase*

Temporary in-store signs date back to 1929 when Milton Reynolds developed the concept of "talking price tags" to promote the sale of his Printasign machine. Today, computer signmaking systems transmit sign copy from central locations for printing at multiple store locations.[12]

SUMMARY POINTS

- A prototype is a model store that combines elements of decor, lighting, fixturing, and signage to create a shopping ambiance consistent with the store's image and target customers.
- Visual merchandising is the organizational function responsible for enhancing sales by creating visually appealing shopping environments. The value of retail selling space is a function of customer traffic.

- A strategically designed store layout combines the effective use of merchandise and aisles to draw customers through a store to maximize their exposure to the store's offerings.
- Fixtures are store furnishings used to present or store merchandise.
- Merchandise presentation standards are techniques for displaying goods using the attributes of the merchandise to maximize its attractiveness and convenience of selection.
- Temporary in-store signage reinforces advertising, stimulates impulse purchases, and enhances customer convenience.

KEY TERMS AND CONCEPTS

adjacency	lip table	showcase
closed-sell fixture	major aisle	slatwall systems
cross merchandising	modular fixturing	storage fixture
cube	open-sell fixture	temporary signage
destination goods	permanent signage	tier table
display fixture	platform	T-stand
floor fixture	prototype	top-of-counter fixture
four-way	rounder	vendor fixture
impulse goods	secondary aisle	visual merchandising

FOR DISCUSSION

1. Make a list of several categories of merchandise. Characterize each category as basic/impulse, basic/destination, fashion/impulse or fashion/destination. Examine the various items and vendors within the category. Do the categorizations change for various items and vendors?
2. Visit a local department store or general merchandise discounter. Evaluate the configuration of the store's aisles. Evaluate selling-area adjacencies and adjacencies within several areas.
3. Visit several specialty stores that are targeted to clearly defined groups of customers. What are the elements of store design that appeal to the target customers? Why do they have this appeal?
4. Evaluate a store's temporary in-store signage.
5. Assume the role of a fashion buyer for an apparel department and explain how your merchandise should be presented.

ENDNOTES

1. Burns, C. (October 1997). Retail Design Twists & Turns. *Shopping Center World*. pp. 26–28.

2. Crosby, L. (December 1995). Architects offer clients high-tech view. *Shopping Centers Today*. p. 8.

3. Staff. (November 16, 1999). Stars come out for holiday windows. *Women's Wear Daily*. p. 15.

4. A highly unlikely circumstance but the example serves a point.

5. Staff. (August 1994). Enticing shoppers to follow the yellow brick road. *Chain Store Age Executive*. pp. 60–61.

6. Staff. (October 18, 1993). Tear down the walls. *Home Furnishings Daily*. pp. 14–15.

7. Staff. (October 10, 1994). *Home Furnishings Daily*. pp. 6, 8.

8. Hammond, T. (August 20, 1999). Macy's West unveils open-sell approach on new beauty floor. *Women's Wear Daily*. pp. 1, 8.

9. Martin, K. (August 1994). Mikasa offers upscale look with outlet prices. *Chain Store Age Executive*. pp. 48–49

10. Owens, J. (March 10, 1998). GlobalShop target: Stores seeking to reclaim identities. *Women's Wear Daily*. p. 19.

11. Wilson, M. (January 1995) Merchandise format showcases merchandising strengths. *Chain Store Age Executive*. pp. 120–121.

12. Staff. (Winter 1999). Stopping traffic versus driving traffic. *Ideations*. pp. 1, 4.

APPENDIX

Analysis of Retail Sales for 2000

Retail Chains and
Their Corporate Parents

ANALYSIS OF RETAIL SALES FOR 2000

(in millions)

Company	2000 EARNINGS	1999 year ago	% of change	2000 SALES	1999 year ago	% of change	Comps
Wal-Mart Stores	6,295	5,377	17%	191,329	165,013	16%	5.1
Sears[a]	1,343	1,453	-8%	40,937	39,484	4%	2.4
Target[b]	1,264	1,144	10%	36,362	33,212	9%	2.4
Kmart[c]	(244)	403	vs. profit	37,028	35,925	3%	1.1
J.C. Penney[d]	(409)	336	vs. profit	32,649	32,510	0%	-2.3
Federated[e]	(184)	795	vs. profit	18,407	17,716	4%	2.0
May	858	927	-7%	14,454	13,854	4%	0.5
Gap	877	1,127	-22%	13,673	11,635	18%	-5.0
Limited[f]	428	461	-7%	10,105	9,766	3%	5.0
TJX	538	522	3%	9,579	8,795	9%	2.0
Dillard's	(6)	164	vs. profit	8,567	8,677	-1%	-3.0
Kohl's	372	258	44%	6,152	4,557	35%	9.0
Saks[g]	75	190	-60%	6,581	6,434	2%	0.2
Intimate Brands	432	459	-6%	5,117	4,632	10%	4.0
Nordstrom[h]	102	203	-50%	5,529	5,149	7%	0.3
ShopKo[i]	(16)	102	vs. profit	3,517	3,048	15%	0.7
Spiegel[j]	121	85	42%	3,061	2,916	5%	-8.0
Neiman Marcus	145	117	24%	2,959	2,712	9%	N/A
Ross Stores	152	150	1%	2,709	2,469	10%	1.0
Tiffany & Co.[k]	191	146	31%	1,668	1,472	13%	12.0
Lands' End[l]	35	48	-28%	1,462	1,417	3%	N/A
Talbots	115	58	97%	1,595	1,309	22%	16.3
Abercrombie & Fitch	158	150	6%	1,238	1,031	20%	-7.0
Charming Shoppes[m]	51	45	13%	1,617	1,206	34%	1.0
American Eagle	94	91	3%	1,093	823	33%	5.8
Ann Taylor[n]	52	65	-20%	1,233	1,085	14%	-0.5
Pacific Sunwear	40	35	13%	589	437	35%	3.5
Wet Seals	20	14	38%	580	524	11%	3.9
Gadzooks	13	6	111%	288	240	20%	7.6
Hot Topic	23	14	72%	257	169	52%	16.7
Chico's FAS[o]	28	15	83%	259	155	67%	34.3
Total	12,964	14,960	-13%	460,596	418,372	10%	

a. *Results include a $41 million benefit for all of 1999. Comps are for domestic stores.*

b. *The year-ago included special charges from debt extinguishment of $28 million and $41 million for 2000.*

c. *Fiscal 2000 included a $463 million after-tax charge while fiscal 1999 saw a $230 million after-tax non-recurring non-cash charge for discontinued operations.*

d. *Fiscal 2000 and 1999 included charges of $488 million and $169 million, respectively.*

e. *Assest impairment charges equaled $927 million in fiscal year 2000. Fiscal 2000 also included a $35 million charge related to the Fingerhut division.*

f. *Results include special items, due in part to the spin-off of Too Inc. in the form of $23.5 million benefit for all of 1999.*

g. *After-tax charges primarily related to the sales of nine stores to May Co. totaled $57.5 million in 2000.*

h. *The write-down of an investment in Streamline.com and other non-recurring charges account for a $32.9 million for 2000.*

i. *Comps for ShopKo stores only. Fiscal 2000 included a pre-tax charge of $9.2 million and pre-tax gain of $47.1 million. Fiscal 1999 included a pre-tax charge of $8.1 million, a pre-tax gain of $56.8 million and a pre-tax loss of $6.2 million.*

j. *2000 included a $4.1 million benefit from an accounting change. Comps are for the Eddie Bauer division.*

k. *Comps for domestic stores only.*

l. *Fiscal 2000 included $1.8 million reversal of a special charge.*

m. *Comps for the Fashion Bug only. Fiscal year 2000 included a $6.7 million non-recurring gain, a $3.5 million pre-tax restructuring credit and a $2 million tax provision as well as an after-tax gain of $1.2 million for the repurchase of convertible subordinated notes.*

n. *Fiscal 2000 includes a $962,000 extraordinary charge.*

o. *Comps for company-owned stores only.*

RETAIL CHAINS AND THEIR CORPORATE PARENTS

Retail Chains	Corporate Parents
A Pea in the Pod	Mothers Work
Abercrombie & Fitch	Abercrombie & Fitch Co.
Afterthoughts	Claire's Stores
A.J. Wright	The TJX Companies, Inc.
Ann Taylor	Ann Taylor Stores Corp.
Ann Taylor Factory Stores	Ann Taylor Stores Corp.
Ann Taylor Lofts	Ann Taylor Stores Corp.
Arden B.	The Wet Seal
August Max Woman	Casual Corner
Babbage's Etc	Barnes & Nobles
Babies 'R' Us	Toys 'R' Us
Baby Gap	Gap
Banana Republic	Gap
Banister	Jones Apparel Group Inc.
Barclay Jewelers	Kroger Co.
Barnes & Noble	Barnes & Nobles
Bath & Body Works	The Limited, Inc.
B. Dalton	Barnes & Nobles
Bergdorf Goodman	The Neiman Marcus Group
Bergner's	Saks
Big Kmart	Kmart
Big Lots	Consolidated Stores
Biway	Dylex
BJ's Wholesale Club	BJ Wholesale Club, Inc.
Blockbuster	Blockbuster Inc.
Bloomingdale's	Federated Department Stores
Bon Marche	Federated Department Stores
Books Etc	Borders Group
Borders Books and Music	Borders Group
Boston Store	Saks
Braemar	Dylex
Burdines	Federated Department Stores
Calvin Klein	Jones Apparel Group Inc.
Carson Pirie Scott	Saks
Casual Corner	Casual Corner
Casual Corner Outlet	Casual Corner
Casual Male Big & Tall	J. Baker
Champ Sports	Venator
Claire's Accessories	Claire's Stores
Contempo Casual	The Wet Seal
Costco	Costco Wholesale Corp.
CVS	CVS Corp.
CVS Procare	CVS Corp.
Dockers Outlet by Designs	Designs Inc.

RETAIL CHAINS AND THEIR CORPORATE PARENTS (continued)

Retail Chains	Corporate Parents
Eagle Hardware and Garden	Lowe's Companies Inc.
Easy Spirit	Jones Apparel Group Inc.
Easy Spirit Outlet	Jones Apparel Group Inc.
Eaton's	Sears Roebuck and Co.
Eckerd Drugstores	J.C. Penney Co.
Eddie Bauer	Speigel
Eddie Bauer Home	Speigel
Eddie Bauer Outlet	Speigel
Elder-Beerman	Elder-Beerman Corp.
Elder-Beerman Furniture Super Stores	Elder-Beerman Corp.
Enzo Angiolini	Jones Apparel Group Inc.
Evan-Picone	Jones Apparel Group Inc.
Executive Suites	Jones Apparel Group Inc.
Expo Design Center	Home Depot
Express	The Limited, Inc.
Faconnable	Nordstrom
Factory Finale	Jones Apparel Group Inc.
Fairweather	Dylex
Famous Barr	The May Department Stores
Famous Footwear	Brown Group
Filene's	The May Department Stores
Florsheim Shoe Shops	Florsheim Group
Foley's	The May Department Stores
Foot Locker	Venator
Foot Locker Outlets	Venator
Fred Meyer Jewelers	Kroger Co.
F.X. LaSalle	Brown Group
Galleries of Neiman Marcus	The Neiman Marcus Group
Gap	Gap
Gap Kids	Gap
General Shoe Warehouse	Genesco
Georgia Lighting	Home Depot
Goldsmith's	Federated Department Stores
Hecht's	The May Department Stores
Herberger's	Saks
Hold Everything	Williams-Sonoma, Inc.
Home Depot	Home Depot
Homegoods	The TJX Companies, Inc.
Icing	Claire's Stores
Imaginarium	Toy 'R' Us
Jarman	Genesco
J.C. Penney	J.C. Penney Co.
Jo-Ann Etc	Jo-Ann Stores
Jo-Ann Fabrics and Crafts	Jo-Ann Stores

RETAIL CHAINS AND THEIR CORPORATE PARENTS (continued)

Retail Chains	Corporate Parents
Johnson & Murphy	Genesco
Jones Company Store	Jones Apparel Group Inc.
Jones New York	Jones Apparel Group Inc.
Jones New York Country	Jones Apparel Group Inc.
Jones New York Men's	Jones Apparel Group Inc.
Jones New York Outlet	Jones Apparel Group Inc.
Journeys	Genesco
Kaufmann's	The May Department Stores
KB Toys	Consolidated Stores
KB Toy Outlet	Consolidated Stores
KB Toy Works	Consolidated Stores
Kids Foot Locker	Venator
Kids 'R' Us	Toys 'R' Us
Kmart	Kmart
Labels	Dylex
Lady Foot Locker	Venator
Lane Bryant	The Limited, Inc.
Last Chance	Nordstrom
Lazarus	Federated Department Stores
Lenscrafters	Lenscrafters Inc.
Lerner New York	The Limited, Inc.
Levi's Outlet by Designs	Designs Inc.
Levi's/Dockers Outlets by Designs	Designs Inc.
Limbo Lounge	The Wet Seal
Limited Stores	The Limited, Inc.
Littman Jewelers	Kroger Co.
Lord & Taylor	The May Department Stores
Lowes	Lowe's Companies Inc.
L.S. Ayres	The May Department Stores
MacFrugal's Bargains	Consolidated Stores
Macy's East	Federated Department Stores
Macy's West	Federated Department Stores
Marshall Field's	Target Corp.
Marshalls	The TJX Companies, Inc.
McRae's	Saks
Meier & Frank	The May Department Stores
Mervyn's	Target Group
Mimi Maternity	Mothers Work
Motherhood Maternity	Mothers Work
Motherhood Maternity Outlets	Mothers Work
Mr. Rags	Claire's Stores
Naturalizer	Brown Group
Nautica	Genesco
Neiman Marcus	The Neiman Marcus Group

RETAIL CHAINS AND THEIR CORPORATE PARENTS (continued)

Retail Chains	Corporate Parents
9 & Co	Jones Apparel Group Inc.
Nine West	Jones Apparel Group Inc.
Nine West Outlet	Jones Apparel Group Inc.
Nordstrom	Nordstrom
Nordstrom Shoe	Nordstrom
Nordstrom Rack	Nordstrom
Northern Elements	Venator
Northern Getaway	Venator
Northern Reflections	Venator
Northern Traditions	Venator
Odd Lots	Consolidated Stores
Odd Lots Furniture	Consolidated Stores
Off 5th	Saks
Old Navy	Gap
Outlet Stores	Sears Roebuck and Co.
Outlets	Williams-Sonoma, Inc.
Parade of Shoes	Payless Shoe Source
Parisian	Saks
Paul Harris	Paul Harris Stores
Paul Harris Direct	Paul Harris Stores
Payless Shoesource	Payless Shoe Source
Petite Sophisticate	Casual Corner
Petite Sophisticate Outlet	Casual Corner
Pic 'N' Save	Consolidated Stores
Pied a Terre	Jones Apparel Group Inc.
Pottery Barn	Williams-Sonoma, Inc.
Proffitt's	Saks
Radio Shack	Radio Shack Corp.
Randy River	Venator
Rena Rowan	Jones Apparel Group Inc.
Renner	J.C. Penney Co.
Repp	J. Baker
Rich's	Federated Department Stores
Robinsons-May	The May Department Stores
Saks Fifth Avenue	Saks
Sam's Club	Wal-Mart Stores
San Francisco Music Box Company	Venator
Sears	Sears Roebuck and Co.
Sears Canada	Sears Roebuck and Co.
Sears Furniture	Sears Roebuck and Co.
Sears Hardware	Sears Roebuck and Co.
Shoe Studio	Jones Apparel Group Inc.
Stone & Co.	Genesco
Strawbridge's	The May Department Stores

RETAIL CHAINS AND THEIR CORPORATE PARENTS (continued)

Retail Chains	Corporate Parents
Super Kmart	Kmart
Talbots Accessories & Shoes	Talbots
Talbots Kids	Talbots
Talbots Misses	Talbots
Talbots Outlet	Talbots
Talbots Petites	Talbots
Talbots Woman	Talbots
Target	Target Corp.
The Jones Stores	The May Department Stores
Thrifty's	Dylex
Tip Top	Dylex
T.J. Maxx	The TJX Companies, Inc.
Todd Oldham	Jones Apparel Group Inc.
Toys 'R' Us	Toys 'R' Us
Ultimate Outlet	Spiegel
Underground Station	Genesco
Velvet Pixies	Claire's Stores
Victoria's Secret	The Limited, Inc.
Villager's Hardware	Home Depot
Walden Books	Borders Group
Wal-Mart Discount Stores	Wal-Mart Stores
Wal-Mart International	Wal-Mart Stores
Wal-Mart Supercenters	Wal-Mart Stores
Wet Seal	The Wet Seal
Williams Sonoma	Williams-Sonoma, Inc.
Winners	The TJX Companies, Inc.
Work 'N Gear	J. Baker
Youngers	Saks
ZCMI	The May Department Stores

GLOSSARY

acquisition the purchase of one organization by another, sometimes called a takeover.

additional markdown a percentage off the already marked down price

additional markup a markup added to an existing markup to increase a retail price.

adjacency a product or product category strategically located next to another product or category for customer convenience and to stimulate sales.

advance dating delays the beginning of a payment and/or discount period until a specified future date. Also referred to as post or seasonal dating.

advertising conveys a message to a large group of people through a mass medium.

anchor a major shopping-center tenant.

anticipation an additional discount for paying an invoice prior to the cash-discount date based on the prevailing interest rate.

assets that which is owned by an organization.

average inventory the amount of inventory on hand within a period computed by dividing the sum of the beginning and ending inventories by two.

bait and switch the illegal practice of luring customers with a low-price advertised item with the intent of selling them a higher-price item.

balance sheet a statement of an organization's assets, liabilities, and owners' equity.

bankruptcy occurs when an organization becomes insolvent or incapable of paying its debts.

basic goods goods that remain the same from one season to another.

basic stock method an inventory planning method that asserts that a beginning-of-month inventory should equal planned sales for the month plus a basic inventory.

beginning-of-month (BOM) inventory the inventory on hand at the beginning of a month.

better line an apparel line priced at the upper end of a department store's selection.

bidding war a series of counter-offers by two or more parties interested in acquiring the same organization.

billed cost the cost of merchandise that appears on a supplier's invoice.

blind item an item for which consumers have no price reference.

book inventory a recorded perpetual inventory value.

bottom-up plan plans developed at the lower levels of an organization as building blocks of an organization-wide plan.

branch a microcosm of a large urban flagship store offering the same categories of merchandise but in limited selections.

brand a name and/or symbol associated with certain product characteristics, such as price, quality, fit, styling, and prestige.

brand-driven purchase a customer choice based primarily on brand.

brand extension using an existing brand name on a new product or product line to reap the benefits of the brand's reputation.

breadth the number of unique items, categories, styles, brands, sizes, colors, or prices in a merchandise selection.

broken assortment residual items within a group or set of related or coordinated merchandise.

bridge line an apparel line made with less expensive fabrics and fewer details than a designer's top-of-the-line creations.

budget, or mass-market, line a lower-priced apparel line carried in stores that include full-line discounters.

buyer a person who buys and prices merchandise for resale.

cannibalization results when a retailer spins-off a new merchandising concept too closely related to existing businesses, or when a chain opens new stores too close to existing stores.

case-packed goods prepacked merchandise with a standard assortment of sizes, colors, and styles.

cash dating payment arrangements with no provision for discount or payment periods.

cash discount a reduction in the amount due on an invoice when payment is made on or before a specified date.

cash-discount date the expiration date of a cash discount period.

cash-discount period a payment period that begins on the date that an invoice is issued and ends on the cash discount date.

cash dating cash payment arrangements, often referred to as COD (cash-on-delivery).

cash flow the balance of cash coming into and going out of an organization.

cash on delivery (COD) cash payment is due upon the delivery of the goods.

catalog retailing a form of direct-response marketing.

catalog showroom a nearly defunct type of discounter that sells consumer electronics, home accessories, sporting goods, toys and juvenile products, and jewelry by catalog and in a retail showroom.

category a group of related merchandise, sometimes called a classification.

category killer a discounter that offers a deep selection of branded merchandise in a single merchandise category at discounted prices, thus "killing" the category of business for other retailers.

category management managing a category of merchandise as an independent business unit.

central business district (CBD) an urban hub of commerce and transportation, commonly called downtown.

centralization performing functions for an organization's remote facilities from a single location, usually a corporate office.

chain two or more stores with the same ownership and identity.

classic a long-enduring fashion.

clearance advertising features goods at discounted prices.

clearance markdowns price reductions that induce the sale of various types of residual or slow-selling merchandise.

closed-sell fixture a store fixture that restricts customer access to the merchandise, requiring salesperson assistance for making selections.

closeout store a discount store operated by a retailer to clear slow-selling or end-of-season merchandise from its regular-price stores.

cocooning a lifestyle trend associated with the increasing amount of time that people at home engaged in activities such as entertaining, exercising, or working.

commissionaire an agent who represents retailers that wish to purchase goods in foreign markets.

common carrier a trucker whose rates are based on established tariffs and schedules between designated points.

community center a shopping center with approximately 100,000 to 350,000 square feet of retail space often with a supermarket and full-line discounter as major tenants.

complementary stores stores that sell goods that complement each other.

component percentage a ratio that expresses an income-statement component as a percentage of net sales.

conglomerate an organization that unites the ownership of independently operated subsidiaries.

consignment goods goods not paid for by a retailer until they are sold.

consolidator a transportation intermediary that combines less-than-truckload (ltl) shipments from multiple shippers into truckload (tl) shipments.

consultant an adviser that offers expertise in a certain area on a fee basis.

consumer the ultimate user of a product or service.

consumer publication magazines and newspapers available to the public at newsstands.

contest a sales-promotion activity that requires participating customers to demonstrate a skill.

contract carrier provides services to individual shippers or groups of shippers based on individually negotiated agreements.

control monitoring or measuring actual performance against goals and reacting to the causes of any deviations from goals.

control standard a reference point or benchmark to measure performance.

cooperative advertising involves shared advertising expense between two marketing channel members.

corporate function performed within a company's central organization or corporate office.

cost the wholesale price paid to a supplier.

cost complement the difference between markup and 100 percent.

cost of goods sold includes payments to suppliers for merchandise, plus work-room and shipping costs, less discounts and returns-to-vendors.

cotenancy requirement a retailer's requirement of the presence of compatible tenants in a shopping center.

cross-docking a logistical concept whereby a retail distribution center functions like a trucking terminal at which merchandise arrives from suppliers in one bay and is distributed to stores in another bay without any processing.

cross-merchandising presenting merchandise in two or more locations in a store.

cubes a store fixture used primarily to present folded goods.

cumulative markup an aggregate percentage markup on goods with varying markup percentages.

current ratio the ratio of an organization's current assets to its current debts.

custom broker a licensed independent agent who represents clients in customs matters.

damage markdown a price reduction on goods after delivery from a vendor.

date of invoice the date that an invoice is issued.

dating the period allowed for the payment of an invoice.

days of supply the number of days an inventory will last if sold at a current rate of sale.

decentralization individual stores within a multistore organization are responsible for buying their own merchandise.

demographic segmentation the identification of markets by characteristics such as gender, age, education, and income.

department a group of related merchandise; a functional organizational unit that performs related activities.

department manager a person responsible for the merchandising and operational activities of an area in a store defined by department or division.

department store a retailer that caters to multiple needs of several groups of consumers that is most often an anchor of an enclosed shopping center.

depth the selection within an assortment of goods.

designer brand a designer name used as a brand name, also called a signature brand.

designer line the exclusive creations of a reputed apparel designer.

destination merchandise a consumer purchase that is typically planned.

deviation the discrepancy between actual performance and a standard.

direct competition occurs when stores offer the same merchandise to the same customers.

direct marketing a direct relationship between a retailer and a customer without the use of a retail facility.

direct-response marketing uses a non-personal print or electronic medium to communicate with consumers.

direct sales force a manufacturer's sales staff that sells products directly to retailers.

direct selling selling one-to-one to customers using explanation or demonstration.

discontinued merchandise goods that will not be part of future assortments.

discount special price reduction in the cost of merchandise.

discounter a retailer that sells goods at prices lower than the conventional prices of other retailers.

display fixture a store fixture used to display goods not available for customer selection.

distribution center the location to which suppliers ship goods at which point they are unpacked, prepared for the selling floor, and redistributed to stores.

distributor allocates arriving shipments of merchandise to individual stores based on a store's capacity, current sales trends, and inventory levels.

district manager responsible for a group of stores located within a defined geographic area.

diversification entering a new line of business that differs from present businesses.

diverter third-party wholesalers.

divestiture the sale of an organization's assets.

division a group of related departments; another name for a subsidiary.

divisional merchandise manager a person responsible for a merchandise division in a retail organization.

door-to-door selling the practice of canvassing customers at home.

drawing a sales-promotion activity in which participants register to win a prize.

e-commerce a popular form of electronic retailing in which a retailer operates a Web site that allows customers to shop over the Internet.

economies of scale savings associated with conducting large-scale business.

electronic data interchange (EDI) an information-trading partnership between a retailer and a producer, sometimes extended to include a producer's suppliers.

electronic retailing a form of direct marketing that includes television shopping channels, infomercials, and online computer shopping services.

employee discount a discount on employee purchases typical of the retail industry.

end-of-month (EOM) dating dating in which the payment and discount periods begin at the end of the month in which the invoice is dated, not the date of invoice.

end-of-month (EOM) inventory the inventory on hand at the end of a month.

ethnic segmentation the identification of ethnic groups as targeted markets.

everyday low pricing (EDLP) a value-oriented pricing strategy of offering merchandise at promotional prices on a day-to-day basis without the support of advertised sale events as promotional vehicles.

exception report a report that includes only major deviations from standards, bypassing minor ones.

expenses incur in the day-to-day operation of an organization, including payroll, rent, utilities, advertising, and interest on debt.

external standard a benchmark derived from information external to an organization.

external theft shoplifting by people who are not employees of the organization.

extra dating adds additional days to payment and discount periods of an invoice.

factor a financial intermediary who buys manufacturers' receivables at discounted rates and then collects payment from retailers.

fad a fashion with a very short life cycle.

fair trade insulates small independent retailers from price competition with large chains that paid lower wholesale prices because of quantity discounts.

fall on the 4-5-4 calendar, the season that begins in August and ends in January.

family lifecycle a sequence of family life stages based on marital status and the presence or absence of dependent children.

fashion a mode or expression accepted by a group of people over time.

fashion director a person responsible for providing buyers with information on dominant trends so that buyers can strategically select assortments.

fashion follower a trend-setter emulator.

fashion goods goods that change frequently.

fashion laggard a consumer who is either slow to adopt a fashion or slow to give it up.

fashion leader a trend-setter.

fashion life cycle the evolution, culmination, and decline of a fashion.

festival center a shopping center of specialty stores, pushcart peddlers, and walkaway food merchants that is often a tourist attraction within a city's cultural and entertainment center. Also, called an urban specialty center or festival marketplace.

field function performed in a remote or satellite operation away from the corporate office.

fill-in order an order to replenish sold-out sizes/styles/colors of a basic inventory assortment.

first in, first out (FIFO) an accounting concept that assumes that goods acquired at the beginning of a fiscal period are sold before goods purchased later in the fiscal period.

floor fixture a free-standing store fixture used on the selling floor to present merchandise.

floor-ready merchandise (FRM) merchandise ready for selling-floor presentation upon arrival at a retail distribution center.

forecasting an attempt to predict trends or outcomes.

forecasting service an organization that studies prevailing socioeconomic and market conditions to predict trends as far as two years in advance of a selling season.

4-5-4 calendar an accounting calendar used by most retailers to structure their fiscal year.

four-way a four-armed store fixture used primarily to present apparel.

franchise a contractual agreement giving a franchisee the right to sell a franchisor's product line or service, subject to standards established by the franchisor.

free on board (FOB) a transportation term followed by indications of the point to which a supplier pays transportation charges, and the point at which the title of the goods passes from the supplier to the retailer.

free-standing stores stand-alone facilities with their own parking areas.

friendly suitor an acquiring company buying another company to give it financial assistance and growth.

friendly takeover the acceptance of acquisition of a company by another organization.

full-line discounter a discounter that offers a wide assortment of hardlines and softlines that includes private-label goods and lower-priced brands not offered at department stores. Also called a general merchandise discounter.

general manager a person with the ultimate responsibility for the merchandising and operation of a store.

general merchandise manager a person who manages a group of merchandise divisions.

geodemographic segmentation involves segmenting markets by neighborhoods typified by lifestyle.

geographic segmentation the identification of markets by geographic region of the country.

gift with purchase (GWP) free premium with a purchase of goods.

gross margin return on investment (GMROI) a measure of performance that combines gross margin and turnover.

gross sales net sales plus customer returns.

group buying pooling orders from many retailers to meet minimum order requirements or to take advantage of quantity discounts.

hardlines nontextile products.

high fashion apparel in the early stage of the fashion lifecycle available through designers or exclusive stores.

hostile takeover an acquisition resisted by the organization being acquired.

image the way a store is perceived by the public.

impulse goods unplanned purchases.

income statement a statement of revenue, expenses, and profit for a specific period.

indirect competition when stores offer the same merchandise categories but different prices and brands.

industry standard a benchmark derived outside an organization, often by a trade association.

initial markup the first markup added to the cost of merchandise to determine an original retail price.

initial public offering the first offering of stock on a public exchange.

institutional advertising image-oriented advertising that reinforces a store's position as a leader in value, service, fashion, selections, or prestige.

intermodal transportation combining two or more modes of transportation.

internal buyout the acquisition of an organization by its employees.

internal standard a benchmark derived from information within an organization.

internal theft shoplifting by employees.

inventory reconciliation an attempt to resolve large discrepancies between book and physical inventories.

invoice a vendor's itemized statement of the goods shipped, their unit and extended cost, and any additional charges for transportation and/or insurance.

joint venture a foreign expansion strategy involving a partnership between a retailer and a foreign partner.

junk bonds high-yield, high-risk commodities issued by retailers to finance acquisitions.

knockoff a less-expensive imitation or copy of a successful branded product or product line.

landed cost the actual cost of an import that includes expenses for overseas buying trips, packing, shipping, insurance, storage, duties, and commissionaires' and customs agents fees.

last in, first out (LIFO) an accounting concept that assumes that goods acquired at the end of a fiscal period are sold before goods purchased earlier in the fiscal period.

lease department a retailer that operates as a department within another retail store.

leveraged buyout an acquisition financed through debt.

liabilities debts owed by an organization.

licensing an agreement that involves the use of a merchandising property in the design of a product or product line.

line function an organization's mainstream activities.

lip table a store fixture often used to "dump" clearance goods. Also called a dump table.

liquidity the likelihood of assets being converted to cash.

long-range plan an organizational plan that covers a three-to-five-year period or longer.

loss results when expenses are greater than revenue and net income is negative.

loss leader an item priced below cost to generate store traffic.

loyalty program an individualized mass-marketing strategy of tracking customer purchases to anticipate their future needs.

maintained markup the difference between the cost of merchandise and the actual selling price.

major aisle a main aisle that connects a store's extremes.

major showroom building a building with showrooms for a particular merchandise category or group of related categories.

manufacturer uses labor and machinery to convert raw materials into finished products. Also called a producer.

manufacturer's outlet a discount store operated by a producer to unload overruns, irregulars, and slow-selling goods returned from department and specialty stores.

manufacturers' rep an independent sales agent who sells manufacturers' products within a defined geographic territory.

manufacturer-sponsored specialty store a store owned and operated by a manufacturer to sell its product line.

manufacturer's suggested retail price (MSRP) a retail price established by a producer.

markdown a downward price adjustment.

markdown cancellation a tactical markup.

market a place where buyers and sellers come together; a group of people with the desire and ability to buy.

market center a cluster of merchandise marts.

marketing channel the flow of goods from point of production to point of consumption. Also called the distribution channel or the distribution pipeline.

market segmentation the process of identifying niche markets undersatisfied or dissatisfied with current marketplace offerings.

markup the amount added to a wholesale cost to establish a retail price.

markup cancellation a tactical markdown.

mass fashion mass-produced fashions extensively distributed through multiple retail channels.

mass market a large group of customers with similar characteristics and wants.

matrix a corporately derived list of preferred merchandise resources.

megabrand a brand that encompasses several related merchandise categories.

memorandum goods goods not paid for by a retailer until they are sold, however, the title of the goods passes from the vendor to the retailer when the goods are shipped, and then to the consumer at the point of sale.

merchandising in the apparel industry, planning, developing, and presenting a product line suitable for a business's intended consumers; in a retail organization, all of the activities associated with buying, pricing, presenting, and promoting merchandise.

merchandise mart a building that houses an entire market under one roof to facilitate one-stop shopping for retail buyers.

merchant-wholesale distributor a marketing-channel intermediary who buys goods from manufacturers and then resells them to retailers.

merger the combination of two or more companies to form a single organization.

minimum advertised price (MAP) the lowest advertised price allowed in a cooperative advertising agreement.

minimum order a dollar or unit amount that defines the smallest order that a vendor is willing to accept.

mixed-use center (MXD) a retail, office, parking, and hotel complex that sometimes includes a convention center and/or high-rise condominium or apartment complex in one development.

moderate line an apparel line priced at the low end of a department store's selection.

neighborhood center a shopping center with approximately 30,000 to 150,000 square feet of retail space often with a supermarket or a large drug store as major tenants.

net income the difference between an organization's revenue and expenses.

net payment date the last day of the net payment period.

net payment period the payment period that begins on the cash discount date and ends on the net payment date.

net sales gross sales minus customer returns.

niche market a small group of customers with characteristics that differ from the mass market.

off-pricer a retailer that sells manufacturers' irregulars, seconds, closeouts, cancelled orders, and other retailers' end-of-season merchandise.

open-sell fixture a store fixture that permits customers to make selections without the assistance of a salesperson.

open-to-buy the difference between planned purchases and merchandise on-order.

open-to-ship the number of units needed to meet a store's planned inventory projections.

organizational chart a diagram that depicts a company's corporate structure and lines of reporting and responsibility. Also called a table of organization.

outlet center a strip or enclosed shopping center with a tenant mix of factory outlet stores and off-pricers. Also called a value-oriented center.

out-of-home advertising billboard and transit advertising.

overage a discrepancy between a book and physical inventory where book is less than physical.

owners' equity the difference between an organization's assets and liabilities.

party plan a direct-sales strategy that uses the home of a host/hostess to demonstrate a product line to a group of invited customers.

past-due order an order that has not been received by the purchase order's specified delivery date.

pedestrian mall a shopping center with an open-air walkway between stores that is closed to vehicular traffic.

penetration the measure of a single business unit as a percentage of all similar business units.

percentage-variation method an inventory planning method that asserts that a beginning-of-month inventory should be a percentage of an average inventory.

perishable goods merchandise with a limited shelf life or selling period.

permanent markdown markdown that will not return to a higher price at a later date.

permanent signage signs made of durable materials not intended for frequent change.

perpetual inventory an inventory accounting system whereby the value of an inventory is maintained on a continual basis by adjusting a beginning physical inventory by purchases, sales, and price changes.

personal selling one-to-one interaction with a customer.

physical inventory counting and valuating inventory item by item.

planned purchases the amount of goods needed to ensure that inventory levels are appropriate for planned sales.

plan of reorganization (POR) a plan to reorganize a bankrupt organization so that it can become profitable.

planogram a visual model of product arrangements.

planner a person who projects sales and inventories based on an analysis of sales history, current market trends and an organization's performance objectives.

planning involves establishing an organization's goals or objectives and strategies to achieve them.

platform a store fixture used for stacking large packaged goods.

point-of-sale (POS) system a network of computerized cash registers linked to a central processing point called a back office.

positioning refers to the marketplace position that a product occupies relative to other products within the same category.

power center a shopping center with a tenant mix composed of big box discounters, such as category killers, warehouse clubs, off-pricers, full-line discounters, and supercenters.

predatory pricing a low-price strategy designed to put competitors out of business.

premium a product offered to customers without charge or at a very low retail price tied to a purchase within a product line.

preticketed merchandise goods ticketed by a supplier.

price-agreement plan a type of decentralized buying whereby a central buyer provides stores with a list of preferred merchandise resources from which stores directly order goods.

price lookup (PLU) a system file of stock-keeping units and prices that "looks up" a price at point of sale when a bar code or sku number is entered into a POS terminal.

private buying office a buying office owned and operated by a single retail organization as an extension of its corporate merchandising function.

private carrier refers to an organization's internal fleet of trucks used to transport goods.

private company an organization whose stock is not traded on a public exchange.

private-label merchandise goods that bear the name of a store, or a name used exclusively by a store, that are produced for the store's exclusive distribution.

producer converts materials and/or component parts into products.

product developer a person who establishes specifications for the design, production, and packaging of a retailer's private-label goods and then contacts producers to manufacture the goods according to these specifications.

productivity the number of units of output reduced per unit of imput.

profit results when expenses are less than revenue and net income is positive.

promotional advertising commonly called "sale" advertising, features a retailer's regular offerings at discounted prices.

promotional markdown a price reduction on merchandise featured in promotional events, commonly called sales.

prototype a model store that incorporates an organization's standards for operational efficiency, merchandise presentation, and customer service.

prox dating specifies the day of the following month by which a cash discount must be taken. Also called proximo dating.

psychographic segmentation identifying markets by lifestyles, values, and attitudes.

public company an organization whose stock is available to the general public and is sold or traded on a public stock exchange.

publicity "free advertising" through a mass medium in the form of news coverage.

pull strategy producer-sponsored advertising that stimulates consumer demand for a product.

purchase order a contractual sales agreement between a retailer and a supplier in which items of merchandise, prices, delivery dates, and payment terms are specified.

purchase with purchase (PWP) a paid-for premium with purchase of goods.

qualitative control a descriptive measure of performance.

quantitative control a numeric measure of performance.

quantity discount a reduction in cost based on the amount of merchandise purchased.

quota a restriction placed on the amount of merchandise that may be imported from a country within a time period.

raincheck allows a customer to buy advertised promotional merchandise at a later date at the sale price.

receipt-of-goods (ROG) dating delays the beginning of payment and discount periods until the invoiced goods have been received.

regional center a shopping center with approximately 400,000 to 800,000 square feet of retail space with two or more department stores as major tenants.

regional manager a person who supervises a group of district managers.

regular dating assumes that the date of invoice is the first day of the payment period. Also referred to as ordinary dating.

regular price an original price.

regular price advertising features premier assortments at conventional prices.

reporting service an organization that surveys and analyzes specific industry segments, reporting their findings to service subscribers.

resale price maintenance (RPM) a practice whereby a producer enforces the sale of its product line at manufacturer's suggested retail prices (MSRP).

resident buying office a marketing and research consultant that provides market information, merchandise guidance, and other services to a group of member or client stores.

retail merchandising all of the activities associated with buying, pricing, presenting, and promoting merchandise.

retail price wholesale cost plus markup.

retailer sells products and/or services to final consumers.

return to vendor (RTV) a damaged or slow-selling item returned to a supplier.

rounder a circular store fixture for hanging goods.

salaried buying office a buying office owned and operated independently of its member stores, also called a fee office.

sales-per-square-foot a measure of productivity that reflects the amount of sales generated relative to the amount of retail space dedicated to sale of the goods.

sales promotion activities that induce customer traffic and sales by communicating information pertaining to a store's assortments, prices, services and other sales incentives.

seasonal discount a reduction in the cost of merchandise for orders placed in advance of the normal ordering period.

seasonal markdowns price reductions on goods remaining in stock at the end of a selling season.

seasonal merchandise goods in demand only at certain times of the year.

secondary business district (SBD) a sub-shopping district in an outlying area of a city.

shopping center a commercial complex with on-site parking that is developed, owned, and managed as a unit.

shortage a discrepancy between a book and a physical inventory where book is greater than physical.

shortage fixture a store display fixture used to store fill-in or backroom inventory.

short-term plan an organizational plan that covers a period shorter than a year.

showcase a closed sell fixture used primarily in department stores for presenting high-ticket or fragile goods such as jewelry and prestige cosmetics and fragrances.

showroom a setting where manufacturers, manufacturers' reps, wholesalers, or domestic or foreign importers present their product lines to prospective retail buyers.

softlines textile products.

source-tagging adding antitheft or price tags to goods by the vendor before shipping to stores.

space management the strategic arrangements of products to maximize sales with a minimum investment of space and fixtures.

special events promotional attractions intended to create an exciting shopping atmosphere in a store.

special order an order placed for an individual customer.

specialty store a retailer that caters to the needs of a narrowly defined group of consumers with a single or limited number of product categories.

spring on the 4-5-4 calendar, the season that begins in February and ends in July.

staff function an advisory function that supports an organization's line functions and other staff functions.

stock-keeping unit (sku) a unique item in an assortment distinguished from other items by characteristics such as brand, style, color, or size.

stock-to-sales ratio the proportionate relationship between a BOM and planned sales.

stock-to-sales-ratio method an inventory planning method that uses desired stock-to-sales ratios to plan beginning-of-month inventories.

store image the way that a store is perceived by the public. A store's image positions the store in the marketplace, distinguishing it from its competitors.

store-level merchandise manager a person responsible for the merchandising activities of a store.

store operations the retail organizational function responsible for merchandising and operating stores. Also called store administration or store line.

strip center a linear arrangement of stores connected by an open-air canopy, with off-street parking in front of the stores.

style refers to an item's distinctive characteristics or design features.

subclass a subdivision of a merchandise classification.

subsidiary an operating division within a conglomerate.

supercenter a combined supermarket and full-line discount store, also called a combination store.

superregional center a shopping center with more than 800,000 square feet of retail space and three or more department stores as major tenants.

syndicated buying office a buying office owned and operated by a retail conglomerate.

tactical price change a strategic markup or markdown that falls within a retail price zone defined at one end by a price with a standard markup and at the other end by a price with an inflated markup.

target marketing a response to the wants and needs of a niche market with a marketing strategy that may include a mix of products, services, or advertising.

tariff a duty levied by the U.S. government to restrict foreign competition.

temporary markdown a markdown that will return to a higher retail price at a later date.

temporary signage signs made of disposable materials intended for frequent change.

tiered table a store fixture for stacking nonhanging goods, commonly referred to as a "Gap" table.

time-series comparison a comparison of income statement components of two or more time periods.

top-down plan a plan that originates at the top of an organization.

top management functions that appear at the top of a table of organization.

top-of-counter fixture a store fixture for displaying goods on a countertop.

town centers shopping centers that evolved in towns and suburbs peripheral to cities, important for independently owned specialty stores and service retailers.

trade association an organization that represents the interests of a particular segment of industry supported by dues-paying members.

trade publication a publication for members of a specific segment of industry.

trade show a group of temporary exhibits of vendors' offerings for a single merchandise category or group of related categories.

trend implies the direction or movement of a fashion.

trend setter a person who buys fashion at the beginning of the fashion lifecycle

trickle-across theory proposes the existence of a horizontal adoption process across all socioeconomic groups. Also called the diffusion theory.

trickle-down theory proposes that the origins of fashion can be traced to upper socioeconomic classes and that lower socioeconomic classes imitate the fashions of the wealthy.

trickle-up theory proposes that fashions float up from lower socioeconomic groups to higher socioeconomic groups. Also called the status-float phenomenon.

T-stand a two-armed store fixture primarily used to present apparel.

turnover the number of times an average inventory is sold within a time period. Also called stockturn.

variety store a disappearing retail format commonly called a 5&10 or dime store.

vendor fixture a fixture supplied by a vendor to distinguish its products from the competition and to ensure consistent presentation in stores.

vendor matrix a list of preferred vendors selected at conglomerate level.

vendor partnership a collaboration between a retailer and a supplier that results in greater channel efficiency and better service to consumers.

vertical integration when an organization performs more than one marketing channel function.

visual merchandising a retail organizational function responsible for store decor, signage, display, fixturing, and standards for presenting merchandise.

warehouse club a discounter that sells a limited number of deep-discounted food and general merchandise items in a warehouse setting.

weeks' supply method an inventory planning method that asserts that the amount of inventory required to support planned sales for a week is based on the number of weeks that an inventory will last relative to a desired turnover and planned sales.

wholesaler facilitates the distribution process by buying larger quantities of goods from producers, and reselling smaller quantities to other channel members, a process called breaking bulk.

workroom cost a labor cost associated with altering, assembling, or repairing merchandise to make it ready for sale.

COMPANY INDEX

For company names, see also the "Analysis of Retail Sales for 2000," pp. 434-435 and "Retail Chains and Their Corporate Parents," pp. 436-440

SUBJECT INDEX

In addition to the references below, definitions of specific terms can be found in the glossary, pp. 441-453.